THE MESSI EFFECT

THE MESSI EFFECT

■ ■ ■

HOW THE GLOBAL LEGEND CHANGED THE FUTURE OF AMERICAN SOCCER

PAUL TENORIO

ST. MARTIN'S PRESS
NEW YORK

First published in the United States by St. Martin's Press, an imprint of St. Martin's Publishing Group

EU Representative: Macmillan Publishers Ireland Ltd, 1st Floor, The Liffey Trust Centre, 117–126 Sheriff Street Upper, Dublin 1, D01 YC43

Printed in the United States of America. For information, address St. Martin's Publishing Group, 120 Broadway, New York, NY 10271.

www.stmartins.com

The Library of Congress Cataloging-in-Publication Data is available upon request.

ISBN 978-1-250-36417-3 (hardcover)
ISBN 978-1-250-36418-0 (ebook)

First Edition: 2026

10 9 8 7 6 5 4 3 2 1

For Nikki: The girl with the books on her mirrored dresser, whose love and partnership made this one possible.

And for Jane and Ben. Plus a million.

CONTENTS

THE
MESSI EFFECT

INTRODUCTION

The Messi Effect

As Lionel Messi stood over the ball a few minutes after 10 P.M. on July 21, 2023, all motion in the stands around him stopped.

A sold-out crowd in Fort Lauderdale, Florida, made a pilgrimage to witness Messi make his Inter Miami debut, with many fans paying thousands of dollars for the chance to experience the Argentine soccer legend in person. Just seven months earlier, Messi, at age thirty-five, cemented his legacy as the greatest ever to play the game when he lifted the World Cup trophy for Argentina in Qatar. That he was now somehow here, at a $60 million temporary venue in South Florida, playing for the worst team in Major League Soccer (MLS), against a Mexican side, Cruz Azul, in a tournament that hadn't existed until that night, while the likes of Serena Williams, LeBron James, and Kim Kardashian snapped pictures from on-field suites—it was almost inconceivable.

This was not the first time a generational player landed on these shores. Pelé's 1975 signing to the North American Soccer League's New York Cosmos moved the cultural needle and promised unprecedented growth, but the league folded less than a decade later, in part because of unchecked spending by owners chasing big names. That wasteful, profligate legacy still impacted how MLS did business.

In 2007, David Beckham attracted global attention to MLS when he left Real Madrid to join the LA Galaxy. It had been the most metamorphic moment in the league's history until this night in 2023. As a soccer player, Beckham may not have had the same type of impact as Messi, who had transfixed fans around the world for two decades. To be fair, no one had. But Beckham was England's captain, and his charisma, good looks, and famous Spice Girls wife gave him crossover appeal.

Messi won every trophy of import for club and country, and along the way, he changed what people thought was possible in the game. The way he raced through defenses, the ball seemingly stuck to his left foot as he darted between players hopelessly grasping and kicking out at air; how he invented space that wasn't there; and the ease with which he picked shots and passes no one else could see. Messi's rival, Cristiano Ronaldo, was an Adonis who used speed and power to overwhelm opponents, but Messi, with his five-feet-seven-inch, 159-pound frame, overpowered challengers with his speed of thought as much as his quickness, skill, and genius on the ball.

"Messi is an alien that dedicates himself to playing with humans," legendary Italian goalkeeper Gianluigi Buffon once marveled. "The only hope is that [when we play] he will be from Earth, like the rest of us."

There had always been a hope that Messi would come play in the U.S. at some point, but it all felt a bit aspirational. It was surreal then to see that dream unfolding so soon after his career climaxed in Qatar. Now, though, as the final seconds of the game in Fort Lauderdale ticked away, Messi's debut seemed to be coming to an end without that satisfying Messi Moment.

But then the referee's whistle blew, calling a foul, and everyone in the building knew what it meant. With the game tied 1–1, Messi lined up a free kick from twenty-four yards out, with a chance to win it on essentially the final play of the night. Fans froze, waiting to see whether the GOAT would deliver in this moment.

On the bench, Inter Miami players stood on their seats to watch.

"I wasn't his teammate at that moment," said Inter Miami's teenage midfielder Benjamin Cremaschi, who had become the answer to a trivia question when Messi replaced him forty minutes earlier in the game. "I was another fan cheering for him."

Center back Kamal Miller, who subbed out twenty minutes earlier, looked around at his teammates, some of whom had kicked off their boots. A few weeks earlier, Miller, a twenty-six-year-old from Scarborough, Ontario, had walked into the locker room and saw Messi and Spanish World Cup winner Sergio Busquets sitting at their lockers. Miller's locker was between the former Barcelona teammates. He needed a second to shake off his nerves and remind himself he was now their colleague. It had been a surreal couple of weeks getting used to his new locker mates, but Miller didn't need his new proximity to Messi to have an idea of what was coming.

"Put your shoes on," he told his teammates on the bench. "We're about to run to the corner to celebrate with him."

Messi fixed the collar on his shirt and positioned the ball. He took a few steps back, picked a corner of the goal, and started his run-up. The reaction to what happened next would be illustrative of the potential impact of Messi's arrival in the U.S. As the free kick curled perfectly into the upper left corner of the goal, lifting Inter Miami to its first win in seven games and giving fans exactly what they came to see, the stands erupted. Messi held out his arms and ran toward the end line. In a luxury suite near midfield, Inter Miami's owners were awestruck: Beckham (in his second soccer act, as an executive) hugged his family, and Jorge Mas held his hands to his head. The highlight of this kick would be viewed more than two hundred million times on social media. The Fox Network would cut into its broadcast of the U.S. women's national team's opening game at the World Cup to show the goal. Messi would become the lead of every *SportsCenter* broadcast.

These should have been the first droplets in a Miami hurricane that would touch every corner of the sport and beyond, redefining expectations for the U.S. domestic league, MLS, and boosting already-grandiose ideas about what soccer could one day be in the U.S. Mas, with a front-row seat to it all, could see it as clear as day: There would be a "before and after Messi" in American soccer history. The free kick was the inflection point.

The question wasn't whether Messi would draw attention, but whether the league would be ready for it.

* * *

By most any measure, Messi in MLS has been an overwhelming success.

He sold out stadiums across the continent, setting attendance and single-game revenue records in places like Chicago, New England, Kansas City, and Vancouver. Commercially, MLS and Inter Miami reaped the benefits. Miami turned over $180 million in revenue in 2024, a league record. MLS set new marks in attendance, sponsorship revenue, retail sales, and social media and digital growth.

The Argentine produced on the field, too. Inter Miami won the Leagues Cup trophy in his first season in 2023, helping MLS successfully kick off a new competition. He followed that up by winning the 2024 MLS Most Valuable Player award as Inter Miami set a record for most points in a season and won the Supporters' Shield, awarded to the team that finished atop the table in the regular season. Messi lifted a third consecutive major international trophy with Argentina in the summer of 2024, winning the Copa América at Miami's Hard Rock Stadium. One year later, Messi led Inter Miami to the Round of 16 at the FIFA Club World Cup, the lone MLS team to advance from the group stage of a tournament that featured many of the best teams in the world. Then, in December 2025, Messi's two assists lifted Miami to its first MLS Cup.

The superstar No. 10 was delivering exactly what the league hoped—and more. He was bringing new fans to its product and giving MLS a level of validation globally. He was singular. There was no other person on the planet who could deliver what he did, and there was no telling when or if there would be again. And yet somehow, through his first two years in MLS, the league made no substantial changes to its structure to ensure it capitalized on Messi's presence.

I have covered MLS since 2007, when I started my journalism career at *The Washington Post*, and learned quickly about the purgatory in which the league exists. MLS is fighting for relevance in both the crowded North American sports landscape and a global soccer ecosystem that is encroaching more frequently into its territory. The league isn't fully embraced in either arena.

MLS has evolved dramatically since its early days in the mid-1990s. Beckham's arrival in 2007 helped to push the league forward. Expansion across the country built up infrastructure and permanence. Still, MLS remained mostly an afterthought in the larger sports narrative.

When Messi arrived in July 2023, MLS was thrust into the absolute center of the sports universe. He brought the eyes of the world on them. Hundreds of media members descended on Fort Lauderdale to report on his first practice with the team. "We went from eating hot dogs in Doral [Florida] to eating caviar," joked Inter forward Josef Martínez. Inter Miami's DRV PNK (now Chase) Stadium sold out for an unveiling event amid an epic rainstorm. In the cities Inter Miami visited, ticket prices soared, sometimes more than 1,000 percent above their pre-Messi sale points. Messi's arrival was the top story on *SportsCenter* every day, and across global newsrooms from Argentina to England to Hong Kong. It wasn't just the sports world, though—it crossed over into the celebrity and commercial world, too.

For those of us who grew up in the niche world of American soccer, it felt like a watershed moment. There was a level of excitement centered on the domestic league that never before existed, at least not to these levels. There had long been talk that MLS aspired to be one of the best leagues in the world, but the league was not yet near being part of that conversation. In those first few weeks of Messi in America, it felt like MLS owners had found the "easy button" to get there.

I knew that Messi in America was a story that needed to be told but that it couldn't be a book that was just about a season in the life of Inter Miami. This story was about more than just Messi's exploits on the field, or even what it's like when the most recognizable athlete on the planet stepped into a mostly anonymous MLS locker room. The American soccer ecosystem had changed dramatically since Beckham first brought global attention to these shores, and it was still being reshaped in real time. Once relegated to pay-per-view television in the 1990s, soccer now flooded our devices. American fans had access to leagues across the world at the push of a button—everything from the English Premier League to the Bundesliga, Champions League, and Mexican first division, Liga MX. Women's soccer, long a standard-bearer for the sport because of the U.S. women's national team's success, was exploding at the club level with the National Women's Soccer League. The sport also punctured the pop culture consciousness with shows like *Ted Lasso* and *Welcome to Wrexham*. Now, the greatest player in the sport's history was playing a part.

When Messi arrived in America, the U.S. was bracing for an unprecedented era in the sport's history on these shores. The country would host three consecutive international tournaments in the coming years: 2024 Copa América, 2025 FIFA Club World Cup, and 2026 FIFA World Cup. If there was a time for MLS to make a leap, this was it.

The league, though, seemed stuck. With the World Cup on the horizon, it had made little movement toward substantial change. MLS was insistent that its product and its long-held identity of slow, conservative growth were still effective. The moment was slipping away even as the league insisted everything was going as planned.

Then Messi arrived and seemed to shock MLS into action.

When I first started reporting for this book, I expected the sweeping impact of Messi's arrival to entice league owners to make bold moves to claim a larger piece of a pie that the whole of the sport was chasing. I wasn't alone. Many believed Messi was exactly the leverage MLS needed. "Evolution is inevitable and change is likely," Mas said after the league's board meeting in Washington, DC, three days after Messi was introduced as an Inter Miami player.

But even with all of the fanfare and attention around Messi's arrival, MLS owners couldn't immediately agree on how to take the league forward. Less than a year before the 2026 World Cup kicked off, a moment long billed as "rocket fuel" for the league and sport, they were still debating how they should evolve. Whether they reached consensus in time or not, and if the decisions they made were the right ones, would dictate MLS's future—and its ability to capitalize on the foundation it had spent three decades putting in place.

The Messi Effect therefore could not be a story solely about one man's exploits on the soccer field. It is instead a business story as much as anything else, a tale of how "the sport of the future" has very much arrived, the jostling to maximize the biggest commercial market in the world, and how signing the greatest player in the history of soccer influenced that power struggle.

1

A Lasting Change

Inter Miami owner Jorge Mas looked out the window of his black SUV as the team's caravan eased through traffic behind a police escort on the Atlanta highway.

In the lanes next to him, fans leaned out of moving cars, phones in hand, to snap photos of the passing Inter Miami buses. They wore the Albiceleste shirts of Argentina, the Blaugrana of Barcelona, or the pink No. 10 Inter Miami top that had become, in the last two years, as ubiquitous as those iconic jerseys. As the buses pulled onto the downtown streets of the city, winding toward the angled roof of Mercedes-Benz Stadium, the hordes of fans walking toward the venue stopped and cheered. It was a scene Mas had witnessed for two years now, no matter what city Miami visited.

Lionel Messi was in town.

Nearly two years after the legendary Argentine began his Inter Miami career by curling that stoppage-time free kick into the upper corner of the goal for a win against Cruz Azul, the momentum of his dazzling debut was beginning to fade. A-list celebrities no longer journeyed to Fort Lauderdale to pay their respects, MLS was once again mostly absent from the greater sporting consciousness, and while that pink Inter Miami jersey was everywhere, the foundation-shaking change for MLS and American soccer that felt so inevitable that night in 2023 in South Florida had still not yet happened.

One constant remained, though: Messi was pulling people into stadiums—and dragging MLS into arenas it otherwise would have missed entirely.

It was June 29, 2025, and Inter Miami was set to face Messi's former club, the reigning UEFA Champions League winners Paris Saint-Germain, in the Round of 16 at the FIFA Club World Cup. The knockout game in a major international tournament was exactly the type of global platform Mas dreamed of when Messi signed, and just like on his first night in Miami, the Argentine delivered when the moment demanded it.

Another signature Messi free kick, this time in the group stage against the Portuguese club Porto, lifted Inter Miami to MLS's first win over a European team in official competition. Soccer consulting firm Twenty First Group's predictive model initially gave Inter Miami a 15 percent chance to make the last 16. But no dataset could fully account for Messi's otherworldly ability to change a game with one swing of his left foot. When his free kick against Porto hit the back of the net, that number jumped to 82 percent. Miami won once and drew twice in its three group stage games to advance, but it was Messi's goal that ultimately made the difference.

Inter Miami advancing should have been a celebratory moment for MLS. Instead, the tournament felt more like a missed opportunity.

* * *

Mas, the billionaire chairman and owner of MasTec, a South Florida–based energy infrastructure construction and engineering company, stepped off the elevator and into the lobby of the team hotel earlier that morning in good spirits.

There were no expectations for Miami in this game. Paris Saint-Germain destroyed Inter Milan 5–0 in the Champions League final one month earlier and looked like the best team in the world by far. Messi or not, Miami wasn't supposed to win. They weren't even expected to compete.

"Irrespective of the outcome," he offered, "it's a big day for our club."

On seeing the throngs of Messi fans on his journey into the stadium, though, Mas's mood started to shift. He knew the league's own research showed that fans judged MLS referentially against other leagues. At home, MLS was dismissed by diehard soccer supporters and casual sports fans as being levels below the best leagues in the world. Abroad, MLS was considered a retirement league more than anything else. On both sides of the Atlantic, it was still an afterthought.

Changing those perceptions was essential to the league's future success.

Three MLS teams—the Seattle Sounders, Los Angeles FC, and Inter Miami—qualified for this newly expanded version of the Club World Cup, which featured some of the biggest teams in the world, including Paris Saint-Germain, Real Madrid, and Manchester City, as well as top teams from every continent. It was a rare opportunity for MLS to face opponents from around the world in meaningful competition. Millions of people, both at home and abroad, were watching this tournament. Winning games and putting on strong performances could change minds.

Months earlier, at a committee meeting in Los Angeles, Mas practically stood on the table to implore his fellow owners and league executives to make changes that would let their teams better compete on such a stage.

"We're carrying the league into a global tournament in which, going in, we're significantly overmatched," Mas said at the meeting. "It's not close. Help us. Let us build a team."

If they weren't ready to change the rules for the whole league, Mas argued that the MLS teams in the Club World Cup should be given the green light to spend more. Other owners countered with the obvious: It would taint the league competition.

"So what?" Mas retorted. "So what? Let's put that aside. What you guys should be worried about is the valuation of your teams and the health of the league. Because if we go in there and we perform well, team valuations will go up $200 million—easy. If we fail, every negative narrative about this league will come to the surface and affect our valuations. You want to compete globally? This system is not gonna work."

While clubs from other challenger leagues like Brazil and Saudi Arabia loaded up on talent ahead of the tournament and pulled off impressive wins, MLS gave its teams only an extra $750,000 in salary cap space for the competition, or about one week's pay for Real Madrid star Kylian Mbappé. It was not nearly enough to make a meaningful difference. It was also merely a symptom of the bigger problem: MLS hadn't evolved quickly enough in the previous five years for its teams to compete meaningfully at this level.

Going into the tournament, Twenty First Group rated MLS's trio as three of the six least likely to advance deep in the competition. Unsurprisingly, the MLS teams looked mostly overmatched. The Seattle Sounders and Los Angeles FC combined for five losses and one draw in six games. Without Messi's heroics, MLS likely would have failed to advance one team in a tournament played on its home soil.

The league tried to spin positives. "Our teams had the chance to go head-to-head with some of the best clubs in the world—and they held their own," Garber declared in one of several positive stories the league's official website published.

But barring an Inter Miami miracle against Paris Saint-Germain, the Club World Cup failed to change the perception of the league.

* * *

As Mas strode out onto the field at Mercedes-Benz, he looked around at the stands starting to fill in. It was actually amusing to see the different styles and colors of Messi jerseys scattered around the building. The generational star was once again delivering, opening the hearts and minds of fans who otherwise would have dismissed MLS outright. They were there to watch a player they would tell their kids and grandkids about, but the league had not acted to convince them it was worth staying once he was gone.

"More people around the world will watch this game tonight than we will get for the rest of the Apple deal this season," Mas said, referring to the league's subscription service, MLS Season Pass, on Apple TV.

The missed moments were adding up. Beyond selling tickets, sponsorships, and jerseys, the league had thus far failed to meaningfully capitalize on Messi's presence. Discussions on how to change roster rules to allow teams to sign more talented players were still dragging on and looked unlikely to take effect until 2027 at the earliest. The 2026 World Cup was coming to the U.S., Canada, and Mexico in one year, the first one hosted in North America in thirty-two years, and MLS was not going to debut any major changes immediately off the back of that tournament either.

It was a mystifying approach. For nearly a decade, league stakeholders teased 2026 as a defining moment for the sport. The greatest player of all time was competing in their league. Yet, they were talking about 2027 or 2028, when the boost supplied by both would either be gone or significantly reduced. It only upped the stakes. If MLS got this wrong, it would be a long climb back.

Mas had not signed Messi just for the short-term boost. The commercial spike was nice, of course, but he dreamed of lasting impact—in the same way that Beckham's signing with the LA Galaxy in 2007 and the creation of the designated player (DP) rule altered the league's trajectory. Mas walked across the field to meet up with Beckham, his Inter Miami co-owner, for an interview with DAZN. The broadcasters were streaming the game in seventeen different languages to more than two hundred countries around the globe. With the teams warming up behind them and the fans in the stadium chanting Messi's name for the first of many times that day, Beckham was asked what changes he would like to see for MLS to become more competitive.

"There has to be changes within the league, there has to be changes within the rules, but this league is not that old," he said. "To see where we've come and where we want to go, there is a lot of good work that's been done, but still a lot to be done for the future."

It was a political answer from the former LA Galaxy franchise player, who had long proved to be an exemplary spokesman for MLS. Mas wanted more. And fast. This game, with the eyes of the footballing world on Atlanta, only reinforced the ticking clock on Messi's on-field impact. The legend was in discussions about a contract extension, but he wouldn't be around for the next Club World Cup in 2029. If MLS stakeholders were going to change the perception of the league's place in the sport's hierarchy, and if they were going to convince people that the league was a true up-and-comer in the ecosystem, they were running out of time for Messi to play a part in it.

After the interview ended, Mas headed to an elevator to get to his suite. As he stepped into the lift, he chatted with Xavier Asensi, the club's chief business officer. He asked Mas about DAZN's question and what *he* thought needed to happen for MLS to be truly competitive. Mas was decidedly less political than Beckham.

"Take it down to the studs," Mas said. "Down. To. The. Studs."

* * *

Signing Messi in 2023 was meant to be a wrecking ball to break through the league's structure. But two years later, the MLS board of governors still had its collective hand hovering above the detonation button that could bring it all down to the foundation.

Beckham was right. In a relatively short amount of time, MLS owners built a stable business: a league that filled stadiums around the country. But the product in those stadiums was now lagging, and the league's strategy hadn't evolved fast enough. Mas was hardly the first person to voice an opinion that the league had to change. For a decade, sporting directors within MLS had been sounding the alarm that the league had outgrown the reins placed on it by league headquarters. So, too, did the media covering MLS. The signs were there that the global game was growing at a faster rate.

MLS had to catch up.

Change, however, rarely comes without resistance. In MLS, that pushback came from some of the league's most influential voices. To be fair to those preaching caution, charting the future for MLS was complicated. The then-twenty-nine-year-old league didn't have the media revenue that the most powerful sports organizations depend on to fund growth. The restraints in place had been prudent for most of MLS's existence. Tight spending rules limited costs and allowed owners to focus on building out infrastructure—and they did spend billions of dollars constructing soccer-specific stadiums and training facilities that now dotted the country. They poured hundreds of millions of dollars more into development academies to produce homegrown talent. That part of MLS commissioner Don Garber's legacy was undeniably positive. He first saved the league from bankruptcy in 2001 by convincing owners to quadruple their investment and bet on soccer's commercial market in the U.S. Then he guided MLS through an era of expansion and growth. His leadership gave MLS permanence in the U.S., something once thought impossible in a country where numerous pro leagues had come and gone.

But as MLS built out that security, the globalization of the sport brought more competition to its backyard. Eventually, the bubble that owners and executives built around their league to keep costs down was pierced by a global marketplace they could not control. European teams arrived in the U.S. to poach young talent. MLS was buying more players from around the world. The transfer market grew far more expensive as multi-club models proliferated and the reach of scouting networks extended to every country and league. Still, league stakeholders, buoyed by a more conservative group of owners, held the reins on spending tightly, limiting further growth in the process. The approach now threatened to stymie all the progress MLS had made. What was once prudent now felt more like an anchor weighing down the league's growth.

That reflected on Garber's legacy, too.

It was clear that the league needed a different strategy. Messi accelerated talks around what the next era of MLS should look like. Garber was now leading the board through what he called "one of the biggest decisions the league will have made in its history." But MLS continued to move slowly—or, as they might spin it, "deliberately." For two years they "studied" potential changes. Meanwhile, the markers and milestones of an extraordinary era in American soccer—and of Messi's time in the league—continued to pass by.

As Mas walked toward the team suite ahead of the Paris

Saint-Germain game, kickoff just minutes away, he found his brother Jose, the CEO of MasTec and the team's co-owner, pacing outside on the empty concourse. Jose was the more analytical of the two, a counterbalance to Jorge's dynamic personality. But, like his brother, he was uber competitive—and he was frustrated. He saw this coming months before.

"We're not going to get a lot of chances at this," Jose had said seven months prior in an interview from his office in Coral Gables. "We have the greatest player in the world. We're on a world stage in our home country, and we have an opportunity to really showcase how far MLS has come. And I don't know that this opportunity is going to come again anytime soon. If we don't execute on that—and we have to overperform what the expectations are—I think we failed."

Now, standing on the concourse, he lamented how much bigger this moment might have been. Inter Miami was in the knockouts, sure, but what could the trio of MLS teams have done if the league had been ready to make more aggressive changes? If they had leaned in more after Messi signed in 2023?

"They only gave us $750,000," he said.

Jorge nodded and headed toward the suite, then turned back toward his brother.

"History only remembers winners and people who do shit," he said.

The league's lack of action hadn't given Inter Miami even a puncher's chance at winning this game against Paris Saint-Germain. Even Messi wouldn't be able to single-handedly overcome the staggering gap in talent and investment. The European champions would go on to trounce Miami 4–0, a result that told only a fraction of the French club's dominance.

But as for the latter? Jorge Mas was committed to making sure he didn't lose that battle. He was determined to *do something*. He still believed the legacy of Messi in Inter Miami pink would be one of lasting transformation for MLS—and with it, the future of the entire sport.

It was why, six years prior, he got on a private jet and headed to Barcelona. He knew there was only one player on Earth capable of sparking change on such a grand scale.

2

Courting Messi

Jorge Mas and David Beckham stepped off the private jet in Barcelona in September 2019 for a visit that would last no more than just a few hours but would eventually upend the future of soccer in the U.S.

The group on the plane also included Beckham's best friend, David Gardner, and the then–Inter Miami sporting director, Paul McDonough. After descending onto the tarmac, the group went straight to a van headed for the hotel, where they were whisked through a side door, ascended a private access stairwell, and then to a service elevator to a suite.

A few minutes later, Jorge Messi, Lionel's influential father, entered the room.

From the first days of joining the Inter Miami ownership group in 2017, the Mas brothers shared Beckham's ambition to go after the biggest stars. A congratulatory video when the franchise was announced in 2018 included a message from Messi in which he said jokingly that "maybe in a few years you can give me a call." Inter Miami couldn't wait that long. Less than a year later, the parties sat face-to-face for the first time.

The meeting was conversational and focused on big picture

ideas. It was meant to be a get-to-know-you session more than a business pitch. Mas had often joked to his friends that he was always selling the city of Miami. Around the table in Barcelona, he painted a verbal picture of his hometown. While many imagine the excess of South Beach, Mas saw the city through the lens of his family story. To him, Miami was "a hardworking community, a community of immigrants that come here seeking freedom, a better future. We have the glamour and the glitz, but really, the underlying heartbeat of this community is its diversity. It's a cultural mosaic."

Inter Miami had yet to take the field—they would kick off their 2020 expansion season six months later—but that's what Mas wanted his club to represent: the entire mosaic of the city he loved so much.

"There's a thread that unites all," Mas said. "And I think *fútbol* is a tool to do good and to unite our communities."

Jorge Messi explained that his son had long planned to play in the U.S. Leo saw the impact of Beckham's time in Los Angeles and liked the idea of helping to grow the sport. The door was open.

"We would love your son to play for our team one day," Beckham said. "We know he can't come yet, but one day we would love to have Leo in Miami."

The Inter Miami quartet immediately headed back to their private jet and took off for France. Mas left feeling like he understood what was important to the Messi family.

Over dinner that night at Chez l'Ami Louis, a buzzy bistro in Paris famous for its roasted chicken, the energy from the meeting in Barcelona radiated through the group as they toasted with glasses of red wine. Landing Messi was no longer just some pipe dream or a line to drop with reporters to generate buzz. It might actually be possible.

But signing an icon like Messi was never going to be a straightforward recruitment.

* * *

Three years later, on November 15, 2022, the MLS board of governors meeting broke for lunch at the 1 Hotel in Brooklyn. A group of MLS executives, including commissioner Don Garber, deputy commissioner Mark Abbott, chief financial officer Sean Prendergast, and general counsel Anastasia Danias, sat with the Mas brothers separate from where other MLS team owners mingled over a meal.

There was just one subject to discuss: Messi.

Since that secret hotel suite introduction in 2019, Mas maintained his relationship with Jorge Messi, speaking regularly and flying overseas to meet in person. He shaped a pitch around the ideas exchanged at that initial meeting in Barcelona.

"Your presence at Inter Miami, in MLS, and in the United States of America will change the sport," Mas told the Messis. "And how many times in a lifetime do you get to change a sport?"

The Mas brothers informed the MLS executives at the 1 Hotel that day that they were ready to make a real push to sign the Argentine legend. Inter Miami's owners wanted to go over their initial ideas for a contract proposal. Because of the DP rule—adopted ahead of the 2007 season to allow the LA Galaxy to sign Beckham and allowing teams to sign three players who would otherwise exceed their salary cap—there were no limitations on how much Miami could pay Messi. But Mas knew that it would take more than money to lure Leo to MLS. He would need the full buy-in of the MLS board of governors.

Inter Miami's owners and executives discussed the deal's potential structure over meetings in Mas's office in Coral Gables with his brother, Jose, and Inter Miami chief business officer Xavier Asensi, who joined the team's front office after more than a decade at Barcelona, where he rose from project manager to chief commercial officer. Mas knew the financial part was not going to be easy to figure out. Miami was competing with Barcelona, Paris Saint-Germain, and the Saudi Pro League. Messi already had a formal and controversial agreement with the Saudi Arabian government as a spokesperson. MLS would have to be creative.

In Mas's office, all sorts of ideas were batted around to try to increase Messi's potential compensation. Perhaps Messi could get a cut of all gate revenue for Inter Miami games around the league. Mas thought it made perfect sense. It was, essentially, a promoter's fee. MLS executives didn't love that idea.

When Beckham signed with the LA Galaxy, his contract included a percentage of all increases in team revenue as well as an option to purchase the rights to an expansion team for a set $25 million fee. Garber, though, said that kind of deal would never again be available. When Beckham signed, MLS expansion fees were at $10 million. When Messi arrived, San Diego had just paid $500 million for rights to the thirtieth MLS franchise. Mas felt it was vital, however, for Messi to have actual ownership of the MLS project, just as Beckham did a decade and a half before. Mas proposed the idea that Messi would get an ownership stake in Inter Miami—between 8 and 10 percent—when he signed. Ten percent of the club, valued by *Forbes* in February 2023 at $600 million, was more than just cash value. Mas knew the valuation would jump significantly if Messi signed. And with a $1 billion stadium, Miami Freedom Park, set to open in 2026, the value of the stake would see another massive spike in a few years.

"It is a way to have Lionel come into a situation where he feels vested and all-in," Mas said. "I need Messi all-in."

Few players would demand such a unique structure, but it was one of the strengths of MLS's single-entity business structure. The league's owners were partners. They understood the benefit to the entire enterprise. The MLS board approved the plan.

First, though, Mas had to close the deal.

* * *

A few days after the MLS board meeting ended, Mas flew to Doha, Qatar, for the World Cup. At the final, he sat about ten feet away from Jorge Messi during the most important moment of Lionel Messi's career: a penalty kick triumph over France that ended any argument that he didn't deserve a place alongside—or above—Pelé and Diego Maradona as the greatest to ever play the game. Mas sat next to Atlético Madrid's Argentine coach Diego Simeone during the final, listening to insight from the manager on tactics and the flow of play. However, Mas couldn't help but relate to Jorge Messi as a father.

"Their journey since he was a little boy was being played out in front of them on the world's greatest stage," Mas said. "The World Cup final. Their 'why.' Here it is. To watch the ebbs and flows and to watch the unadulterated joy when they won, as a father, I was looking at it through Jorge's eyes. It was like, 'Wow.'"

Mas tweeted out a congratulations to Argentina for their historic win, but the tweet didn't mention Messi or provide any hint of where Mas sat. The Inter Miami owner is a showman. He wants to entertain. But he felt there was an important element in the chase for Messi's signature that could set Inter Miami apart from other bidders: discretion. He knew the Messi family would be facing pressure from every angle. He wanted Inter Miami to be the exception.

After he returned from Qatar, reports started to emerge that Messi had agreed a deal to extend his contract at Paris Saint-Germain. Mas remained calm and tight-lipped. Even as friends told him that Messi's World Cup triumph ensured the Argentine wasn't coming to MLS, he felt confident as ever. He stayed patient. And quiet.

In January 2023, Mas and Asensi flew to Rosario, Argentina, Leo's hometown, to meet with Jorge Messi. At a meeting in his office, surrounded by memorabilia from Leo's career, they laid out the plan discussed at the MLS board meeting months earlier in Brooklyn, including the equity stake. Mas emphasized that the deal was also about family. They had details on a school for Messi's kids, neighborhoods where they could possibly live, and arrangements to make their life easier in Miami. Negotiations began in earnest.

"I left there feeling very confident that we had something that was super unique," Mas said. "And I knew nobody could match the uniqueness."

On April 4, 2023, the MLS board of governors met again, this time in Northern California. The formal meeting took place in Palo Alto, but owners also toured the headquarters of their new media partner, Apple, in Cupertino. There, they sat for dinner with Apple executives.

Like the Mas brothers, Apple's senior vice president of services, Eddy Cue, is a Cuban American from Miami. Mas and Cue had met at dinner parties in Miami a few times, and the deal with MLS brought the pair back together. When the Apple-MLS arrangement was finalized early in 2022, Mas told Cue he was working to land Messi.

"I'm gonna need your help whenever that day comes," Mas said.

"At the time when he told me that, I said, 'Look, you should connect us with him, and that way we could start building a relationship with him,'" Cue recalled. "And so he connected us with them, and this idea of following him for the World Cup came up.

And so we were like, 'Okay, that's a great idea. It's gonna be awesome.'"

Apple produced a documentary that followed the Argentinian team behind the scenes during its tournament in Qatar. Its cameras were there to capture Messi's legacy-defining win. Now, in Cupertino, Mas told Cue that the day had come. He needed the tech company to help get the Messi deal over the line.

The relationship established through the World Cup documentary paved the way for negotiations concerning Messi's potential signing in Miami. Discussions with Apple included a revenue share with Messi for new international subscribers to Apple's MLS Season Pass service. It spoke to the enormity of Messi's influence and the uniqueness of MLS's partnership with Apple. It wasn't unheard of for television partners to be involved in league business—broadcasters influenced the reshaping of college football conferences, for example—but to be involved in a player's contract was entirely new territory.

"We wanted to get involved in some fashion or another, but we did not want to get involved in a typical way, which is, 'Okay, just pay him around that,'" Cue said. "There was something about that that just didn't feel right. So we came up with a different strategy that definitely gets him paid, but he earns it. It's probably never been done in sports. And I think it worked really well for everybody."

Inter Miami was not directly involved in Apple's discussions with Messi, but the tech giant's involvement undoubtedly added another compelling reason for him to choose MLS.

As the European season came to a close in early May, Mas knew it was time to try to finalize the deal with Messi. In addition to being a majority owner of Inter Miami, he was the president of Real Zaragoza, a club in Spain's second tier. That position provided some insight into the financial hurdles Barcelona would face to bring Messi back. Reports were also emerging that the Messi family had already informed Paris Saint-Germain that Leo would not return to the Ligue 1 side.

Mas flew from Miami to Spain to meet with Jorge Messi for one final pitch. He knew he would never be able to compete with the financial might of the Saudi professional league, which was backed by the Public Investment Fund, the kingdom's sovereign wealth fund. The Saudi offer reportedly exceeded $1 billion. He circled back instead to the themes from that first meeting in Barcelona in 2019. He believed Messi could help shape the sport in the U.S., and he pitched Jorge Messi on the lasting impact for Leo and his family. The proximity to Argentina was important. Miami is a nine-hour flight to Buenos Aires, compared to thirteen and a half hours from Barcelona and more than twenty hours from Riyadh. Miami's deal also provided a chance for Messi to be involved with the team and the sport in the U.S. once he stopped playing. The equity in Inter Miami meant he could benefit from the impact he made on MLS well beyond the life of his contract.

The question was whether the Messi family saw the same value in those opportunities that Mas did.

Inter Miami had come close with many big names before. The club's initial coaching search involved talks with Roberto Martínez, Marcelo Gallardo, and Patrick Vieira. They courted players like Willian, Luis Suárez, Javier Mascherano, and Edinson Cavani, whom the group flew to see in Paris after that first meeting with Jorge Messi. There was no guarantee that Inter Miami would reach a deal.

Messi was compelled by the idea of a return to Barcelona, the club where he built his career and won ten La Liga trophies and four Champions Leagues. But the dire financial situation that forced him to leave Barcelona in 2021 was not much better. There were no assurances that Barça would be able to register him even if he signed, and a return likely would have forced them to sell several other players. It would be a difficult reunion.

The competing offer from Al Hilal, one of Saudi Arabia's top teams, was eye-popping. After Al Nassr signed Cristiano Ronaldo in December for what Saudi state media reported was $210 million per year, including image rights and commercial or ambassadorial deals, the Saudi Pro League was making another push to sign top players. The better contracts coming out of Saudi Arabia shook up the global transfer market and wooed stars like 2022 Ballon d'Or winner Karim Benzema and his France teammate, N'Golo Kanté, who signed with Al-Ittihad; Brazilian forward Roberto Firmino, who signed with Al-Ahli; and Portuguese midfielder Rúben Neves, who signed with Al Hilal. But the ultimate target was Messi, and reports pegged Al Hilal's offer as high as $1.3 billion over three years.

Globally, few people expected Miami to win out. Messi was less than a year removed from winning the Golden Ball as the best player when he won the World Cup with Argentina. He had twenty goals and twenty assists in all competitions for Paris Saint-Germain, ranking him among the most productive players across the top-five leagues in Europe. He could clearly still be one of the world's best players at the very highest levels of the game. What could possibly compel him to decamp off to MLS?

Even internally at Inter Miami, some staffers felt the odds were stacked against them. Mas, though, remained optimistic. Six weeks after that final pitch, he was behind his desk in Coral Gables when his cell phone rang.

He saw Jorge Messi's name.

3

A Shifting Landscape

MLS needed Lionel Messi even more than Inter Miami wanted him.

The league's growth mostly mirrored the trajectory of soccer's popularity in the U.S. Launched in 1996 as a condition of the U.S. hosting the 1994 FIFA World Cup, MLS survived near bankruptcy in 2000 and then the contraction of teams in Tampa and Miami after the 2001 season to establish a permanence that never previously existed at the sport's professional level.

In the decade and a half since Beckham brought global attention to the LA Galaxy, the league executed a strategy focused on expansion and infrastructure. It grew from thirteen teams in 2007 to thirty teams—several of which were owned by some of the wealthiest people in the world—twenty years later. Expansion fees rose from $10 million to $500 million during that time period. The rapid scaling up was fueled by success stories in cities like Toronto, Seattle, Portland, Atlanta, and Los Angeles, each of which told a tale of an enterprise on a sharp rising trajectory.

The monuments to that growth were stadiums and training facilities around the country—seventeen soccer-specific stadiums were built between 2008 and 2022. Club valuations went up alongside those buildings. In 2023, *Forbes*' average valuation of an MLS team was $577 million, up from $37 million in 2008. The league's media rights rose too, from $8 million to $250 million annually. It was a blueprint focused on "building long-term stability and viability," MLS commissioner Don Garber said.

Under the surface, however, the reality was far less shiny.

As MLS's footprint swelled, its domestic impact plateaued and tension built behind the scenes. The expansion era altered the dynamics of the league's boardroom. Garber, in his twenty-fourth season as commissioner in 2023, liked to quote the advice former NFL commissioner Pete Rozelle gave him when he left American football in 1999 to take on the *other* football: "Keep the owners who don't like you away from the ones that haven't made their mind up yet." That was becoming an increasingly difficult task.

Whereas he once sat in a room with the league's three remaining investors—Robert Kraft, Lamar Hunt, and Phil Anschutz—trying to keep MLS afloat, the board now met in vast conference rooms filled with one hundred people representing thirty ownership groups. The legacy investors who launched MLS sat alongside newer owners, many of whom paid hundreds of millions in expansion fees to join the party. Investment levels and investment horizons differed, as did opinions on how to move the product forward. Building consensus was harder than ever. Garber's long-preferred desire for unanimity was practically impossible. With the landscape shifting under its feet, the league's relevance slipping, and the 2026 World Cup just around the corner, Garber understood MLS was facing a critical juncture in its history.

The sixty-five-year-old commissioner assumed office in 1999, just five years after attending his first soccer game: the 1994 World Cup final. The insular American soccer community scoffed at the idea that an NFL executive would know anything about running a soccer league. But the Queens, New York, native was a salesman at his core, and MLS needed someone who could peddle the sport to a country that had not yet embraced it. A quarter century later, Garber was the most influential voice in American soccer.

Messi was the most valuable player MLS could possibly sign, the one individual on the planet who could put the league in a global spotlight, but Garber was the gatekeeper. He had the power to dictate how that partnership would play out.

The commissioner often cautioned that MLS was still very much in start-up mode. Enterprise valuations were up, but most teams were still losing money. When the league launched in the mid-1990s, finding soccer on television was difficult. He saved the venture in 2001 by convincing owners to launch Soccer United Marketing (SUM), the league's commercial arm, purchasing the broadcast and sponsorship rights to the 2002 and 2006 World Cups. The league was right to anticipate a boom in the commercial market for soccer, and they monetized it to great success.

But they soon found competition for those dollars and fans.

* * *

The transformation of soccer in America started on a Friday afternoon, October 26, 2012, when NBC executive Jon Miller took a phone call in his empty office and heard Premier League CEO Richard Scudamore on the line.

In his presentation bidding for the Premier League broadcast rights in 2012, Miller, the president of acquisitions and partnerships at NBC, displayed a photo of Times Square from the early 2000s. Among the throngs swarming that attraction in midtown Manhattan, the visible apparel featured logos of baseball's New York Yankees and Chicago Cubs, the NBA's New York Knicks and Los Angeles Lakers, and the NFL's New York Giants.

Then, Miller put up a photo of the LED-lit tourist trap a dozen years later. This time, visible emblems included Arsenal, Liverpool

F.C., Tottenham, and Manchester United. The difference highlighted what Miller first noticed in his own living room: People were falling in love with a soccer league on the other side of the Atlantic.

The NBC executive recounted the impetus for his interest in bidding on Premier League rights. On his way out the door for an early morning tee time one day, Miller encountered his teenage son cozying on the couch for a predawn kickoff of the North London derby between Tottenham and Arsenal. He knew well enough not to ignore something that could pull a teenager out of bed at such an ungodly hour, and that's how he found himself trying to convince Scudamore that NBC could deliver something more for England's top soccer league than what they were getting from Fox and ESPN.

It was a two-pronged pitch from NBC: First, they would market and promote the Premier League at the same level as other major American sports.

"Which we did and continue to do," Miller said.

The second part would prove more important considering soccer's rapid growth in the U.S. market.

"It's a mantra that we subscribe to and that we live every day, [which] is that we are not the network of soccer, we are the network of the Premier League," Miller said. "Everything that we do is with an eye towards: How do we make the Premier League the dominant brand of the sport in the U.S.?"

Scudamore had regularly visited the U.S. since the age of ten, and he spent several years working for Thomson Corporation running newspaper operations in the southern and eastern U.S. He knew the market. He didn't even mind calling it "soccer." In fact, he liked to point out that he had annual "soccer star" sticker albums growing up in England.

The fifty-four-year-old executive from Bristol returned to the

UK to serve as CEO of the Football League in 1997 and joined the Premier League in 1999. He negotiated numerous media rights deals, both at home and abroad, totaling billions of dollars. Never before had a potential media partner so convinced him they would elevate the product.

"I was wowed by [NBC]," he recalled. "But then, of course, I had the job of convincing the clubs that they were worthy partners—particularly the American [Premier League club] owners, who, without naming names, were absolutely of the view that ESPN was the only place sports in America had to be in order to get the airtime and the promotion."

He didn't see it that way. While Scudamore felt ESPN and Fox did an admirable job with the Premier League, he recognized ESPN's crowded schedule. There was no way they could match the sort of undivided attention NBC was promising. He spent the next few weeks convincing the Premier League's American club owners to get on board.

Once they were, he dialed Miller with the news.

"We would not be where we are without [Scudamore's] vision and understanding of what we could bring," Miller said.

That call in 2012 shaped the sport's growth in the U.S. over the next decade.

NBC's Premier League coverage effectively mainstreamed a sport that for decades lived on obscure cable channels and in corny SOCCER IS A KICK IN THE GRASS t-shirts sold in niche catalogs. If you looked hard enough or played long enough on youth fields across the U.S., you'd find a community of expats and diehards who tuned in to the limited viewing windows for games from the UK and Europe. NBC took that trickle of soccer nerds and turned it into a waterfall.

"In one hundred years' time, they will look back at the history of soccer in America and they will pinpoint 2013, for me, as the time that soccer in this country took a quantum leap," said Rebecca Lowe, the former BBC broadcaster who shipped her life across the Atlantic and became the face of the American network's coverage.

NBC treated the Premier League like a marquee property. That brought more viewers to an increasingly compelling product, which, in turn, made soccer fandom in vogue.

When it took over the Premier League deal in 2013, the combined audience of ESPN and Fox was thirteen million fans over the course of the 2012–13 season. By the end of NBC's third season in 2015–16, those numbers were up to thirty-nine million fans. Millions continue to tune in to the Premier League every weekend. In 2023–24, NBC averaged 546,000 viewers per television match window, the most in its Premier League history.

The popularity of the Premier League, which regularly drew television audiences double and triple that of MLS, sparked a rush of broadcast and streaming deals. By 2023, in millions of living rooms across the country, Americans could wake up, pour a coffee, and turn on NBC to watch the English Premier League. Or, with a few clicks, they could tune in to the German Bundesliga, Italian Serie A, French Ligue 1, and even England's lower divisions. The UEFA Champions League was a part of the American weekday afternoon sports lexicon.

Americans' interest in those competitions created a stark contrast against which fans could judge MLS's on-field quality. The most-watched soccer league in the country was Mexico's Liga MX, and its best teams regularly beat MLS opposition in the Concacaf Champions Cup. The eyes of the footballing world were turning toward North America. So were the hands grasping for a piece of the pie.

"There's no question now that America has become the ATM for the soccer world," Garber quipped.

The commissioner liked to say MLS was a "league of choice," but with everything on offer, Americans were opting to tune in to other soccer leagues at a higher clip. It needed to find a way to tap into those television audiences. While MLS successfully established a strong local business built around a robust commercial operation and an entertaining in-stadium experience (as indicated by strong ticket sales in many markets), that was just two-thirds of the puzzle for a successful league.

The third piece, media rights, was the most vital. But to accomplish that goal, MLS had to grow from a locally driven business model to a national one.

* * *

Media rights revenue is the lifeblood of sports leagues, fueling both growth and quality.

The NFL's media rights were valued at about $10 billion per year when Messi arrived in the U.S. The NBA's latest media deal will pay $76 billion from 2025 to 2036.

The value of the Premier League's NBC deal cascaded well beyond American audiences and into the ecosystem of a global sport. The Premier League stood out from even the biggest American leagues in one way: more than 50 percent of its media revenue came from abroad. Its most recent domestic deal paid north of $8 billion from 2025 to 2029. The agreement with NBC was worth another $2.7 billion over six years. Rights deals in Europe, the Middle East and North Africa (MENA), Asia, Africa, and Latin America brought additional billions.

The Premier League soon outranked every other league in global soccer, dwarfing the other Big Five leagues: Germany's Bundesliga, Italy's Serie A, Spain's La Liga, and France's Ligue 1. According to UEFA's *European Club Finance and Investment Landscape* report released in 2025, the Premier League's aggregate revenue ($7.7

billion) was nearly equal to that of the second- and third-ranked La Liga and Bundesliga combined.

Media revenue was split evenly across the twenty Premier League teams for many years. That model changed, but the difference between the most popular clubs and the lowest payouts was capped, which allowed the league to maintain a relatively comparable level of quality top to bottom.

"That's why the league is very competitive. That's why the bottom teams can beat the top teams. That's why it maintains its global appeal around the world," Scudamore explained. "Because all games are competitively intense, and that's down to international media rights."

Premier League teams also pumped that broadcast revenue directly into the transfer market, further increasing the quality of the competition as its clubs outspent other leagues. It spent nearly $4 billion on players in 2023, according to UEFA's report. No other league spent more than $2.3 billion.

"The sporting competition comes first," Scudamore said. "You don't run a sports league where the commercial starts first." Those words would raise eyebrows for many who work in and around MLS, where it often felt as though the opposite was true.

For years there was a chicken-or-the-egg-first debate in MLS. Without more revenue, owners didn't want to spend more on the product. Without bigger television audiences, MLS couldn't demand a heftier media contract that would bring in more revenue.

Years of ratings that trailed well behind the most popular sports leagues in the U.S. should have offered an obvious answer to the debate. Viewership numbers lagged because the product wasn't as good or compelling as the many other soccer offerings. The owners needed to spend to improve the product if they wanted those larger audiences and, with them, a better television deal. But MLS leaders were confident that the league's steady progress would pay off over time.

When its media deal expired at the end of the 2022 season, the market for MLS's media rights might have forced league stakeholders to confront those issues. Longtime partners ESPN offered similar numbers to the league's previous contract, far below what MLS stakeholders hoped for and subterranean when compared to the $450 million the Premier League earned annually from NBC. Other broadcasters were hesitant to jump in. MLS executives thought they were close to a deal with Amazon, but it fell apart in the late stages.

"That was the two-by-four upside of the owners' heads, when we realized we've been talking about this media deal for years and all of a sudden you get there and the bidders aren't there," said former Atlanta United and AMB Sports CEO Steve Cannon, an alternate governor on the MLS board for several years. "That was a shocking, shocking moment."

Ahead of the 2023 season, MLS unveiled a ten-year, $2.5 billion media deal with Apple. Garber and deputy commissioner Gary Stevenson salvaged what could have been a disastrous negotiation by landing one of the world's biggest companies as a partner. The tech giant was only beginning to dip its toe into live sports, but it saved the league from confronting a potentially embarrassing reality.

"I give Don all the credit in the world for nurturing that Apple deal," Cannon said.

The $2.5 billion agreement was well above what the market had otherwise offered, but it came with drawbacks. Some saw the partnership as a long-term negative because it allowed MLS owners and executives to kick the can down the road to confront the reasons why other offers never materialized from media partners—at least, not in the way they hoped.

The deal's ten-year term was also seen by industry experts as a liability, not a strength. On day one, MLS was still $200 million per season behind the Premier League—and the Premier League would enter another bidding process before the MLS-Apple deal expired. MLS also covered production expenses at a cost of around $60 million per year, decreasing the real value of the deal.

There was also risk in a deal that was an almost fully streaming partnership—MLS did maintain a small sublicensing deal with Fox—because it limited the league's reach and distribution. While many pro sports leagues had significant inventory on streaming services, they were available to all subscribers to those respective services, whether it was Peacock, Paramount+, or Amazon Prime. MLS wasn't on Apple TV but was instead behind a separate paywall on an app called MLS Season Pass. Drawing a larger audience was now more complicated. The product had to be good enough not just to entice people to watch but also to pay an annual $99 subscription fee for the right to do so.

The alternative path, one embraced by the National Women's Soccer League and WNBA, was to do shorter deals across more media outlets, making the product as accessible as possible in hopes that spikes in growth could influence bigger deals on a shorter timeframe.

MLS executives knew Apple was a gamble, but it was the best offer—by far.

The deal was imperfect, but the status quo was not working either. The league was now partnered with one of the world's biggest companies. MLS's research found that 85 percent of soccer fans consumed the game digitally in some way. Apple was an ideal streaming partner, with billions of its devices in people's hands around the world. And there was the potential for an upside via a revenue share once the league achieved certain benchmarks on MLS Season Pass.

The agreement couldn't be evaluated as a like-for-like with the MLS's previous national television deals with ESPN, Fox, and Univision. Apple took on MLS's entire inventory, and it was an enormous upgrade on the league's previous local cable television packages, which aired the vast majority of its games across the thirty league markets. Those local broadcasts typically had poor production quality, low ratings, and cost teams more than $1 million per season to produce. Even the best-performing local deals had ratings that hovered in the same neighborhood as the worst NHL teams. And MLS's national television partnerships often cast them as second-class citizens.

Trying something different made sense.

Now fans could get everything in one place, anywhere in the world—and all at a high level of production. If it worked—if audiences continued to move toward streaming and MLS pulled those eyes to its product—it would be a revolutionary move. But if it didn't work—if being behind a streaming paywall pushed MLS out of sight and out of mind—the problems could compound.

"You can like the Apple deal. You cannot like the Apple deal. But it was a roll of the dice worth making," Los Angeles FC owner Larry Berg said.

Apple gave the league a path forward, but it wouldn't deliver the relevance the league needed. Messi provided a chance to solve that problem and complete that final piece of the puzzle. Who would be better at selling the league than the most popular athlete on the planet?

He wasn't a replicable model—there is only one Messi—but this was a chance to bring viewers to MLS and to convince owners that fans would be drawn to a world-class product—or, in this case, a world-class player.

If Miami's star could bring new fans through the gates, it would buy time for MLS to figure out how to keep them. With the 2026

fanned the flames of hope that Messi might return: "Leo knows this is his home and that our doors are open and that we will be delighted if he decides to come back to Barça," Xavi told the media in April 2023. "But it depends on many factors."

As Messi navigated through the interview with Polo and Masnou that June afternoon, however, the pain of what happened in August 2021 was clearly still there.

"The truth is that I obviously had a lot of desire, a lot of hope to be able to return," he told them. "But on the other hand, after having experienced what I experienced, the exit I had, I did not want to be in the same situation again and wait to see what was going to happen and leave my future in the hands of another, so to speak. I wanted to make my own decision, thinking about my family."

Messi was a thirteen-year-old prodigy when he left Rosario for Barcelona. The Argentine kid with a growth hormone deficiency arrived in Catalonia as a curiosity. Horacio Gaggioli, an Argentine player agent who was sent tape of the wiry kid scoring loads of goals for Newell's Old Boys academy team, was shocked when Messi landed in Spain for his trial. "I thought I had been duped," Gaggioli told *The Athletic*. "I thought to myself: 'This small child can't play football. He's tiny.' His leg looked like a finger. 'They're going to break this kid's legs.'" Messi erased those doubts when he stepped on the field at his trial. Weeks later, Barcelona sporting director Carles Rexach famously finalized the contract on a paper napkin, agreeing to pay for Messi's hormone treatments in addition to a sizable salary.

> *In Barcelona, on December 14, 2000, and in the presence of the gentleman Minguella and Horacio, Carles Rexach, technical secretary of FCB, commits under his responsibility, despite the opinion of others who are against signing Lionel Messi, as long as the agreed fees are maintained.*

Gaggioli sold the napkin at auction in 2024 for nearly $1 million.

Barcelona protected and nurtured Messi. He debuted for the first team at age sixteen and in La Liga as a seventeen-year-old, winning the first of many trophies that season. In two decades with the club, Messi cemented himself as one of the greatest to ever play the game. He scored a record 672 goals across 778 appearances in seventeen seasons for Barcelona, claiming ten league titles, four UEFA Champions Leagues, three Club World Cups, and six Ballon d'Ors, the trophy awarded by *France Football* magazine to the sport's top player.

When his contract expired in the summer of 2021, Messi was determined to stay at his first and only professional club. He agreed to a new deal that would pay him about half his previous wages. Messi went on vacation in Ibiza and returned on August 4 to his home in Castelldefels, a Catalonian suburb about twelve miles south of Barcelona, where he received a call from the U.S. from his father with an update. The tone during conversations with Barcelona executive Rafa Yuste seemed foreboding. Messi messaged Joan Laporta, who had recently been reelected as Barcelona's president. The conversation calmed his nerves. But later that afternoon, Yuste called Jorge Messi with bad news. Laporta decided Messi's deal wasn't happening.

Jorge Messi traveled to Barcelona and met with Laporta. His decision was final. La Liga rules limit team spending based on a club's financial performance in recent seasons. Barcelona was over that cap. Even with Messi agreeing to take a significant pay cut, Barcelona would be unable to register Messi to play.

Days later, on August 8, 2021, Messi tearfully said goodbye to the only club he knew.

"When I heard about it, it was like a cold shower," Messi said at his farewell press conference. "It was hard to hear it. We are still getting used to it in whatever way we can. When I leave here today it will be even harder.

"Today I have to say goodbye to it all. I've spent my whole life here. I arrived when I was thirteen, and I'm leaving with my wife and my three Catalan-Argentine children. I have no doubt that we are going to come back because this is our home. I promised my family."

The rapid change of course meant Messi had to choose a new destination quickly. There was no Plan B. He opted for Paris Saint-Germain in a deal that came together in just a matter of days.

Messi arrived in Paris to much fanfare, but behind the scenes, the adjustment was difficult. His family lived in a hotel for six months. There was little privacy or normalcy. Eventually, they found a house and a school for the boys. Life settled into a rhythm. But things didn't go smoothly over two seasons in the French capital.

Paris Saint-Germain failed to win a Champions League title despite fielding three of the world's best players: Messi, Kylian Mbappé, and Neymar. Some fans booed Messi in his final appearances. The World Cup win in Qatar was the personal saving grace, of course, but Paris Saint-Germain had been an imperfect solution to the hasty exit thrust upon him.

The sting of the way it went down at Barcelona—a deal agreed, then reneged—lingered over Messi's footballing existence. As he considered his next steps in the summer of 2023, his desire to return to Barcelona clashed with memories of his exit and the complex financial uncertainty that still hovered over the club. More importantly, the World Cup win granted Messi a measure of freedom he had long sought. For years he'd been dogged by one question. Could he win a World Cup for Argentina, as Diego Maradona had? As Messi's former Argentina manager Jorge

Sampaoli once put it, that pressure had been like "a revolver put to his head." But now, unburdened, having completed his legacy, there was a level of freedom that Messi hadn't enjoyed in more than a decade. He yearned for something he hadn't experienced in some time: a chance to simply enjoy the game again. Messi had achieved everything possible on the field. He was ready to embrace what that afforded him.

"I'm also in a moment where I want to get out of the focus a little, think more about my family," Messi told Polo and Masnou, as the sound of his kids playing blended with the birds in the background. "As I said, I just had two years which, on a family level, was difficult. I didn't enjoy it. I had a month that was spectacular for me, having won the World Cup, but taking that out, it was a difficult stage for me. I want to rediscover myself with enjoyment, with the enjoyment of my family, my children, the day-to-day."

"Where will you play next?"

Messi looked down to his left. A slight smile crept across his face.

"*Tomé la decisión de que voy a ir a Miami,*" Messi said.

I made the decision to go to Miami.

"I think that the time came for me to analyze it and think about leaving European football, especially after having won the World Cup, which was what I needed to close my career in this way," Messi continued. "And, well, to experience the U.S. league in a different way and enjoy the day-to-day much more. Obviously with the same responsibility and desire as always, to want to win and to want to do things well, always. But with more peace of mind, for sure."

* * *

The interview went live on *Mundo Deportivo*'s site at 3 P.M. Eastern. Inter Miami posted its announcement video twenty minutes later, and over the next ten minutes gained more than one million social media followers. That number would continue to explode over the next few days.

But if the words set off celebrations in the Inter Miami offices, they caused a bit more of a maelstrom at MLS headquarters in New York. The announcement caught everyone off guard. MLS executives scrambled to put out a statement that there was no official deal yet with Messi, but that they were excited to welcome the star to their league.

It was an early indication of just how little control MLS would exert on Messi's time in America. This was Messi's show. Everyone else would try their best to keep up and to maximize the moment—to differing degrees of success.

5

From Beckham to Messi

David Beckham was roused from sleep in his hotel room in Japan by his buzzing cell phone.

"Really? Turn your phone off," Victoria mumbled to her husband as he sat up to read the texts.

Beckham put on his glasses and looked at the messages.

"Leo's coming! It's done. He's announced it," he said.

"What do you mean he's announced it?" Victoria asked.

"He has gone on TV and said he's coming to Inter Miami."

For nearly a decade, Beckham labored and persevered to move his expansion team from concept to reality. More than once, it looked like the project, initially named Miami Beckham United LLC, was dead. Now, the best player in the world was coming to play for Inter Miami. He called Mas and couldn't help but get emotional.

Messi's announcement extended Beckham's legacy as one of the most influential figures in American soccer history. The charismatic superstar helped make MLS relevant when he signed with the LA Galaxy in 2007. His arrival drove interest in the league and spurred an era of significant growth. With Messi on board, his team had the chance to inspire similar changes.

On the most basic level, it was simple: Without Beckham, there would be no Inter Miami; and without Inter Miami, there would be no Messi in MLS.

You could connect the dots directly from Beckham's 2007 arrival in Los Angeles to Messi signing with Miami sixteen years later.

First: The Beckham Rule

Without the creation of the Beckham Rule in MLS, it would have been impossible for a team to sign Messi—or any other star player. The "official" term was "designated player rule," and it provided MLS teams a roster slot to pay players outside of the cap, at the owner's expense.

The rule opened the door for other big-name stars to follow Beckham to the U.S.—and they did. It was an influx of talent that changed MLS forever.

How teams would use the designated player rule, or DP rule, evolved. MLS often turned to younger and in-their-prime difference makers rather than celebrity players. But what the rule consistently did was allow teams to bring stars to MLS, and that drove excitement and interest in the league. When Messi signed, each team had as many as three DP slots to use on highly paid players. For the most part, those star players drove the success of clubs on the biggest stages.

Second: The Creation of Inter Miami

Beckham's deal with MLS included a clause that allowed him to purchase an expansion team for $25 million, one of the most profitable terms ever put in a sports contract. It became a golden ticket to a billion-dollar asset. But the option came with stipulations.

Beckham had to play in the league for the entire five years of his contract, and over the course of that span, MLS had to expand substantially from thirteen clubs to a point where it was at the threshold of twenty.

"I would tell you the likelihood that that would have happened if you were a betting person would be pretty damn close to zero," MLS commissioner Don Garber said, chuckling. "And it happened."

At the time Beckham signed with the LA Galaxy, MLS's latest expansion team, Toronto FC, paid just $10 million to enter the league. By the time he triggered the clause, MLS expansion teams were selling for $150 million. It gave him a dramatically discounted seat on the MLS board of governors.

He eventually launched his club in Miami, a market glamorous and cosmopolitan enough to one day attract a superstar from Argentina.

Third: The Creative Structure of Beckham's MLS Contract

Like Beckham, Messi took a percentage of the Inter Miami shirts and gear sold by Adidas and Fanatics. And just as Beckham's expansion clause offered him an incentive to promote and build MLS, Messi's Apple agreement made him an active partner in the league's development. It also partnered him with one of the world's biggest tech companies.

There was no expansion team clause in Messi's contract—MLS would "never do that again," Garber said with a smirk that acknowledged the hundred million dollars or so the league had forfeited. But Messi instead received an ownership stake in the Miami franchise.

The structure was far different, but the idea was the same: to make Beckham and Messi part of MLS far beyond their playing days.

The benefit of that structure was clear from how Beckham's reach now extended into its third decade with the league. If Miami could create a similar dynamic with Messi, his influence would be felt long after his playing days were done.

Beyond those links from one generational star to another, there was a deeper connection. Beckham understood better than most why Messi's arrival mattered. Beckham, like many others, saw MLS at a critical crossroads—much as it had been when he first landed in America. He believed Messi could boost the league's fortunes in the same way he did: by bringing more attention to the league and inspiring a new generation of fans.

Beckham's multimillion-dollar contract hadn't just spurred rule changes in MLS; it pushed the then-twenty-year-old league to grow from relative infancy into adolescence.

Messi's job now was to take MLS into adulthood.

* * *

Whatever Messi did in Miami, he would be building on what Beckham started.

The former England captain's arrival in America could never be just about soccer. MLS was still a struggling venture in 2007, just a few years removed from near bankruptcy. The Englishman was there to sell: tickets, jerseys, and legitimacy.

"Wayne Gretzky was a transformational figure for the National Hockey League," Garber once said. "Michael Jordan and Magic Johnson were transformational players who took the NBA from what it was to what it is today in many ways. David was today, for us, where we are now, that transformational player. He was our Michael Jordan, our Wayne Gretzky. He was the guy who came here and basically said, 'It's okay. This league is all right. It's not the Premier League, but that's okay.'"

Beckham was keenly aware of his influence. He bought into every part of the job. He arrived in MLS not just as the biggest name the league had ever signed, but also as a willing salesman. He spoke after LA Galaxy games, standing in front of a gaggle of press in markets across the country. He got on the plane, sometimes even when he was injured, just to give fans a glimpse of the star they paid to see, even if it might not be on the pitch. He was also willing to speak out on league issues and become an advocate for MLS growth.

"If I can make a difference and make people more aware and make kids realize that you can actually go into higher levels and make a great living playing soccer, that's what I'm going over there to do," Beckham told *Sports Illustrated* after announcing his move to MLS. "I'm not silly enough to think I'm going to change the whole culture, because it's not going to happen. But I do have a belief that it can go to a different level, and I'd love to be a part of that."

However, he wasn't just a champion for MLS. He also utilized his platform to advocate for change, everything from the quality of team hotels to the fields on which MLS teams played. "My role was bigger than being a soccer player," he once said. "I wanted to elevate the league. I wanted to elevate the sport."

The move to MLS was questioned throughout the footballing world—"David Beckham will be a B-list actor living in Hollywood," frowned then-Real Madrid president Ramón Calderón—but Beckham kept front-of-mind that his playing days were finite. The decision to come to America was a calculated one. It was about the long term as much as it was about the short term.

It hinted at what Garber would learn after the superstar's playing career was over: Beckham was as savvy a businessman as he was a free-kick artist.

"He is a remarkable man who, because of his humble, quiet nature, outside of this unique celebrity quality, is just a run-silent, run-deep guy who just keeps his head down and operates as a businessman the way he did as a player," the MLS commissioner said. "He will outwork and outhustle everybody and has incredible doggedness that I've never really seen in anybody that I've ever worked with before."

Beckham's LA Galaxy move tied his future to a league that Fabio Capello, his manager at Real Madrid and later with England, would later say "has no value." Capello may have been closer to the truth than anyone around MLS's Fifth Avenue headquarters would want to admit. The version of MLS to which Beckham arrived was far different than the one Messi would sign with sixteen years later. The quality of the teams, stadiums, training facilities, travel, and accommodations was lacking in 2007. The league was trying to survive, but it also needed to professionalize.

It's easy now to look back at Beckham's time in MLS and call it a success, but it took years of failure to get there. The challenge to adapt and then thrive was even bigger than Beckham anticipated. Injuries and a loan to AC Milan soured the LA Galaxy fans on Beckham in his first season in Los Angeles. There were GO HOME FRAUD banners and a locker room divide between him and American star Landon Donovan, fueled in part by the late Grant Wahl's best-selling book *The Beckham Experiment* that laid the issues out for the public to see.

Beckham faced valid questions and skepticism concerning his promise to grow soccer in America. Eventually, he "remembered my responsibility to the MLS."

"I had to make it work," he recalled in a Netflix documentary about his career.

The reenergized superstar played a key role in the LA Galaxy's back-to-back MLS Cup triumphs in 2011 and 2012, playing sixty games with nine goals and twenty-seven assists across those title-winning seasons.

"Winning the MLS Cup was probably one of the most rewarding moments of my career," Beckham said. "I think I stood there on the pitch and went, 'It worked.'"

The two trophies weren't important just for Beckham to validate his own decision. They were crucial to the long-term footprint of the deal, said Tim Leiweke, the former AEG executive who recruited the English star to MLS.

"One thing above and beyond the business sense, you've got to find the right person," Leiweke said. "There was economic upside, but you've got to have the personality to put the burden on your shoulders. David stayed with us for five years. It took us a while to win, but then we started winning championships. He knew [winning] was more important than the expansion franchise [clause], the economic opportunities, the sponsorships. We had to win. If we didn't win it was a failure.

"We're not talking about [Messi] today without that. If David wouldn't have won and it was just a publicity stunt, it's different . . . David paved the way and convinced people like Messi that it works here."

* * *

It wasn't clear that Messi wanted to be a Beckham-type spokesperson for MLS.

The Argentine star was unlike the Inter Miami founder. Messi rarely spoke to the media, even skipping the postgame press conference after his legacy-defining World Cup win in Doha. But he also knew he didn't need to use his voice to have an influence. So prodigious was his talent that he managed to be the most famous person in the world while simultaneously remaining one of the least known or understood.

The aura surrounding Messi was generated by his performance—the supernatural skills that commanded the attention of the football-loving world. He shaped the moods of entire countries with the instep of his magic left foot. He understood that his presence alone could grow MLS. Whether it would be enough to change MLS entirely was another question.

Messi was also arriving in a league that had grown beyond many of the issues Beckham had advocated to change. Teams no longer flew on commercial flights to games; charters were greenlit during COVID-19 and remained standard. Hotels were typically top-of-the-line. And while Beckham played on artificial turf with football lines laid for NFL games, most MLS teams now had their own soccer-specific stadium with real grass. (Although five MLS teams still played on artificial surfaces.)

In that way, Messi's impact would mostly be measured by how he propelled the league into its next era.

* * *

It took two years for owners to design and then approve the DP rule that allowed the LA Galaxy to sign Beckham. MLS's early reluctance—and the rule's ultimate success—served as a meaningful precedent to reflect on as Messi arrived and debate picked up about how the league might evolve.

The DP rule pushed past the constraints MLS owners built to protect their league from overspending. Unlike MLS's early days, when players like Jorge Campos and Marco Etcheverry were paid a bit more on the side by the league itself, any overage on the maximum salary under the DP designation would be paid by the club owner. By giving teams the ability to spend beyond the cap, there was a fear that it would potentially upend the competitive balance that owners coveted.

When the DP initiative first came to a vote in 2005, owners voted down the proposal. Even LA Galaxy owner Phil Anschutz disliked the rule. It took a year, but in November 2006, the rule passed. Beckham came out of contract with Real Madrid less than two months later. MLS owners had taken it to the absolute last-minute deadline.

When the vote passed, Anschutz pulled Leiweke aside.

"You're right, this *is* a good idea," he said. "We need to do this for the league because if we're ever going to expand our ratings and our audience and get credibility in our country, we're going to need a star to break through."

Beckham undeniably brought star power. He sold out stadiums around MLS. Even then, not all owners bought in. Two years into Beckham's MLS stint, just five of the fifteen potential DP spots were filled league-wide.

"It tells you that right now the league isn't really going for this, that most of the owners are not interested," Wahl said in an interview with *The New York Times* when his book was published in 2009.

Eventually, that resistance started to fade. Within a few years, MLS offered each team a second DP spot. The LA Galaxy's acquisition of Irishman Robbie Keane, the former Tottenham Hotspur star, would completely alter the narrative around Beckham's time in MLS. Keane, Beckham, and Donovan became a star-studded trio for the LA Galaxy, winning back-to-back MLS Cups in 2011 and 2012.

The DP rule entirely remade what MLS looked like. The

mechanism was used to add big names like Thierry Henry, Kaká, Bastian Schweinsteiger, Zlatan Ibrahimović, and Didier Drogba, as well as up-and-coming stars or lesser-known players who thrived in MLS, like Miguel Almirón, Nicolás Lodeiro, Josef Martínez, and Diego Valeri. The level of the league—and MLS's place in the global transfer market—surged as a result.

But the slow burn before MLS dove all-in on the DP rule proved that no single player, no matter how famous, was a shortcut to growth. Beckham was a catalyst for change, but it was up to the MLS owners to act. It took them some time, but they eventually leveraged the moment.

Messi presented a similar opportunity.

For all the evolution since Beckham arrived—sixteen new teams, seventeen soccer-specific stadiums, billions in expansion fees, and a museum's worth of stars who donned MLS team jerseys—MLS was still looking for a greater share of the American soccer market.

The parallels between Beckham and Messi were hard to ignore. League executives liked to tout their flexibility: MLS changed playoff structures seemingly every other year, and it introduced new rules and roster initiatives to solve what it believed were very specific problems. But many on the board and at MLS headquarters remained resistant to foundation-altering change.

Once again, there would be a hesitancy to adopt the sort of sweeping reform that could redefine MLS's place in the sport.

Messi's arrival and the momentum that came with it would test whether MLS could learn from its own history. If MLS stakeholders took anything away from the Beckham experiment, they would know that while a transcendent player like Messi might present a path to the league's transformation, it was their decisiveness—or lack thereof—that would determine how far and long the Argentine's legacy would reach.

Change would require more than Messi playing in a pink shirt. The owners themselves would have to be the featured players.

Beckham's partners at Inter Miami had no problem with that idea.

6

A Willing Disruptor

Two hours after Messi declared Miami his new home, Jorge Mas finally had a chance to breathe.

The Inter Miami owner stood at his office window in Coral Gables, Florida, and looked east. The markers of his life were laid out in front of him. There was the home in Little Havana where his father first moved after leaving Cuba as an exile in the 1950s. The Caballero Rivero Woodlawn North Cemetery where his father was buried. The skyline of the city his family helped rebuild after Hurricane Andrew. To his left, construction was underway at Miami Freedom Park, the $1 billion stadium project for his MLS team.

A rainbow arched over the scene as Mas took it all in.

The sixty-year-old billionaire reflected on the years of work that went into the seismic surprise received earlier in the afternoon when Messi stunned the world by announcing that his next move would not be returning to Barcelona or signing a $400-million-per-year-contract in Saudi Arabia. He was joining Inter Miami, the South Florida club that had begun play just three and a half years before.

If Beckham's legacy gave the blueprint for how to maximize

Messi in MLS, Mas was the owner charged with seeing it through. He was an odd hero for MLS but might have been the perfect man for the moment. The league needed a disruptor. The bombastic Miami native was more than happy to oblige.

Mas was largely seen as a maverick in league circles. He fancied himself as a dreamer and a fighter, and he saw little distinction between the two. He was raised that way. His father, Jorge Mas Canosa, fled Cuba with nothing to his name. He washed dishes and delivered milk around Little Havana before eventually acquiring the company that became MasTec.

Mas Canosa grew into a powerful, if controversial, leader of the anti–Fidel Castro movement through the Cuban American National Foundation, a lobbying organization modeled after the American Israel Public Affairs Committee (AIPAC). He won influence on both sides of the political aisle, including with U.S. presidents Ronald Reagan and Bill Clinton. Mas Canosa drove a bulletproof Mercedes-Benz 560 SEL and carried a loaded .357 magnum in his briefcase. He once challenged a Miami city commissioner, Joe Carollo, who would eventually become mayor, to a duel on "a field of honor" after Carollo squelched a development deal.

"People perceive me as a strong personality, and I am," Mas Canosa once told the *Miami Herald*. "Everything I do is with intensity."

Mas grew up watching his father accumulate political influence and host heads of state at their family home. Mas Canosa, in turn, made sure his sons Jorge, Jose, and Juan Carlos learned every aspect of the family business. "It was important for my father, coming from where he came from," Jorge said. "It was something he instilled in us." Jorge would often hold out his hands when telling stories about his childhood to show where the calluses formed when working summers on a restoration crew, filling ditches with sod or temporary paving. He learned to drive a Bobcat simply so he could have some shade during those brutal South Florida summer days.

In the 1980s, as the family business grew, he told his father that one day they would ring the bell at the New York Stock Exchange. Mas was named president of the company in 1994. They rang the bell on February 14, 1997, and shortly after became the first Hispanic-owned company in the U.S. to break $1 billion in revenue. On the office desk behind him was a small note on which he scrawled two words: *31 cents*. It was a reminder of how far MasTec's stock fell during the 2000 telecom crash. At the time, Mas told people close to him to buckle up. "It's going to be a hell of a ride," he warned. MasTec grew back into a Fortune 400 company.

Mas, alongside his brother Jose, MasTec's CEO, brought the same determination to their stewardship of Inter Miami.

"We were from immigrant parents who came to this country with nothing but the shirt on their back, not a penny to their name, who had to fight for everything, who had to excel," Jose Mas said. "Failure wasn't an option each and every day. They had to figure out how to get better, how to compete with people that were bigger, stronger, smarter. But yet, here we are. We put ourselves in a position to be able to own a sports franchise. That tenacity, that will to survive, I call it, 'Think like an immigrant.' Which is: There is no option but to succeed. There is no room for failure."

The two brothers counterbalance each other. Jose is quieter, more focused on execution. Under his leadership, MasTec's revenue grew from $930 million in 2007 to $12.3 billion in 2024. "My brother grounds me," Jorge said. "He's very analytical in his thinking."

Jorge is the visionary. One person who worked for him claimed he was the Jerry Jones of MLS, a big personality with equally lofty aspirations. Like the outspoken Dallas Cowboys owner, Jorge is not media shy. Like Jones, he is brash and unafraid to take on the establishment or to push the limits of what it takes to win.

Or even go beyond those constraints. That willingness to overstep boundaries very much informed the state of the team to which Messi would arrive and the challenge Mas faced in effecting change.

* * *

Just two years before Messi's announcement, MLS fined Jorge Mas and Inter Miami half a million dollars for breaking its roster rules when it secretly paid French World Cup winner Blaise Matuidi several million dollars outside the salary cap. Inter Miami listed Matuidi's earnings as $1.33 million, when in reality, it was compensating him via a side agreement. Matuidi's actual salary was more than $5 million. Inter Miami's three DP slots were already filled. The hidden money for Matuidi was an unauthorized workaround. Inter Miami's roster, therefore, was not in compliance. A subsequent league investigation found that Inter Miami also paid multiple agent fees off the books to lower other players' respective cap hits. Inter Miami played its inaugural season not with just four DPs but with five.

Garber dropped the hammer on Inter Miami—and Jorge Mas.

"The integrity of our rules is sacrosanct," the commissioner said when announcing the punishment, which included the fine to Inter Miami and Mas and a $2.2 million reduction in general allocation money (GAM), an MLS roster rule tool that essentially served as salary cap space.

Mas and Inter Miami may have been caught, but cheating the roster rules was more commonplace than Garber wanted to admit. Paying agent fees off the books was hardly an invention of Inter Miami's front office. An anonymous survey of team general managers in *The Athletic* indicated that most clubs skirted the rules. A year and a half after Inter Miami was sanctioned, the LA Galaxy were hit with punishments, including a transfer ban, for similarly hiding payments for DP Cristian Pavón, an Argentinian World Cup winger who had arrived in MLS on a "free loan" in 2019.

In the wake of his punishment following the Matuidi investigation, Jorge didn't shy away from responsibility. Neither did he back down from his beliefs in how the league needed to change. He insisted that he would continue to "push the envelope, but within the envelope," and later took aim at what he saw as an upside-down tendency in MLS circles to limit and punish ownership groups who were looking to spend and invest more in the league's on-field product.

"It's no secret that there are a segment of owners in the league that do not want to spend money, that are okay with the status quo, that are very happy with their financial situation and circumstances because they invested in the league X amount of years ago and it's just a cash cow. They're clipping coupons and life is good," he said then. "That's not why we got into this. We got into this for very different reasons."

The coupons quip obviously did not win over many colleagues in the MLS boardroom. Jorge was in damage control mode on multiple fronts for the next several years. But that was him. He did what he felt he had to do and said what he wanted to say and then dealt with the fallout later.

"Maybe we came in rubbing people the wrong way," Jose said. "Maybe we were a little too brash, a little too aggressive."

Maybe. But it was also likely going to take that level of aggression to jerk MLS out of its status quo. And as cocksure as Jorge was, he was also right. The league had, for almost its entire existence, built an infrastructure that catered more to lower-spending owners. Ambitious owners *were* expected to fall in line. The idea,

MLS executives maintained, was to ensure a high level of competitive balance while simultaneously controlling costs.

In the hours after Messi's announcement, Jorge's cell phone did not stop lighting up with messages of thanks and congratulations from other MLS owners. It brought an enormous level of satisfaction to the Miami owner, who felt his ambition for the league up until now had been stifled and villainized instead of celebrated.

The Mas brothers might have felt like outsiders at times, but they were not alone in their desire to see change.

As the league expanded, new owners joined who were willing to spend more for their on-field product. Most of those new owners were billionaires many times over and entered MLS paying hundreds of millions in expansion fees, as well as infrastructure and start-up costs. Their outlook on MLS's strategy differed drastically from some of the legacy owners who launched the league, or teams that came in paying expansion fees in the range of $30–$40 million.

Despite the growing coalition of more aggressive-minded owners, few offered any sort of public dissent about the league's strategy. Even team sporting directors, many of whom vehemently disagreed with the way the league was structured, were hesitant to go public with those thoughts out of fear of reprisal by league headquarters. Mas stood out because he was happy not to toe the company line.

That didn't always rub people the right way—but it also didn't make him wrong. As one owner later offered: "I agree with what Jorge is saying. I just don't necessarily want to go about things the same way."

A movement was growing within the league that while the philosophy built around competitive balance was important to MLS's foundation, it couldn't be the doctrine if the league was going to grow. The more progressive wing of owners advocated loosening the spending restrictions, which didn't just limit how *much* teams could spend but also *how* they could spend it. MLS wasn't just being outspent by the best leagues in the world, its spending was also far too imbalanced. The system wasn't driving the level of quality commensurate with the cash outlay. MLS executives vehemently disagreed with that assessment. They argued that the system protected MLS from many of the global market's inefficiencies. But that wasn't reflected in how rosters were built—or in how MLS compared to other global leagues.

On the other side of the aisle, a more conservative group of owners held firm. They argued that MLS didn't have the revenue to justify more liberal spending. And, more importantly, how much more money would have to be spent to bring in the revenue that would justify it? For some owners, higher spending likely also meant their teams would not be able to compete against deeper-pocketed rivals. Even worse: it might force them to sell.

"Nobody wants to be in a situation where they're funding massive losses all the time," Jose Mas acknowledged. "So there's this push and pull, right? Money doesn't solve all problems. Just because you spend a lot of money on players doesn't necessarily mean that all of the other things get fixed at the same time. So I get both sides of the argument. Quite frankly, I understand where different people are coming from."

Still, the Mas brothers believed smarter spending was the only way to improve the league's standing.

"We have to provide a better experience for fans, we have to provide them the absolute best quality that we can," Jose said. "The reality is we're going to have to spend money, we're going to have to make investments to improve all the things around the league that will, hopefully, over time, drive more revenue. . . . We have to start creating the narrative that our league is better."

The Mas brothers were determined to get there. Jorge would drag the league to the finish line if he had to. It's why, from his earliest days involved with Inter Miami, he targeted Messi. He realized early that the fight over the league's future might require a bludgeon. Now, he had Thor's hammer.

"Damn," Mas thought to himself as he looked out across the city that June afternoon. "We did it."

In the earthshaking wake of Messi's public pronouncement, Mas knew there was a lot of work to do for Inter Miami to prepare. Messi's contract was not finalized, let alone signed. The club also had to upgrade its facilities, revamp the team's travel process, fill out its roster, and hire a new head coach.

But he also knew Messi's arrival had the potential to tip the scales for owners who wanted greater change. There was important work to do there, too.

He was convinced Messi demanded legacy-altering change. The Argentine's arrival arguably marked the biggest moment in the history of soccer in the U.S. Mas was determined not to let it go to waste.

In delivering Messi, Jorge had done his job as the disruptor. But he needed to find a way to create consensus in the MLS boardroom. That would prove to be even more difficult than wooing the biggest star in the history of the sport.

7

A New Normal

More than one month after Lionel Messi announced his next club, he had yet to show up in South Florida. Despite his absence, the swirl of activity outside of the training facility in anticipation of his arrival had become so commonplace—the fans standing on the corner as players drove in, the security guards required to open the gates to the employee parking lot by hand instead of a passcode on a keypad, the new faces milling around the facility—that Victor Ulloa didn't even notice the team's social media team filming his arrival as he walked into the building early on the morning of July 12.

Ulloa stepped into the locker room, saw goalkeeper Drake Callender, and then turned to his right. Messi was sitting in front of a locker. His three sons—Mateo, Thiago, and Ciro—were playing and climbing in the stall next to him, Ulloa's locker.

"No freaking way," Ulloa thought to himself.

The thirty-one-year-old had spent his entire adulthood in MLS locker rooms. His was a success story of the first generation of domestic players developed out of the league's academies, which launched in 2007, the same year Beckham landed in Los Angeles. Born in Juárez, Mexico, and raised in Wylie, Texas, about forty minutes northeast of Dallas, Ulloa signed with FC Dallas when he was eighteen years old. He played just one game across his first three MLS seasons. But the hardworking midfielder, known more for his willingness to make a tackle than a game-changing pass, forged a decent career over the ensuing decade, starting more than two hundred matches in Dallas, Cincinnati, and Miami.

The locker room makeup had changed dramatically since Beckham's arrival in MLS. Not only had Beckham's example ushered in a steady stream of big-name signings in the following years, but that top-end spending had a trickle-down effect: It raised the floor for everyone else. Whereas Beckham's first LA Galaxy roster had multiple American players making less than $20,000 per year, the minimum salaries in MLS were now a healthier $67,360, reserved mostly for teenagers signed from the academies. The average compensation for a first-team player was $594,390. Ulloa was emblematic of that progress. He played for Dallas's youth teams, signed a pro contract, and earned his way onto the field. He was never a star but became a reliable squad player, and in fourteen MLS seasons, he saw his salary rise from $31,260 in 2010 to $250,000 in 2023.

Ulloa won two trophies in Dallas and helped launch expansion teams in front of sold-out crowds in Cincinnati and an empty COVID-restricted stadium in Fort Lauderdale. His time with Inter Miami had also introduced him to what felt like a uniquely MLS experience: landing on a team with celebrity players that included Argentine striker Gonzalo Higuaín and Blaise Matuidi, the French World Cup winner. Ulloa was a glue guy, the bridge between the young Americans making the minimum salary and the high-end stars, some of whom were earning millions.

None of Ulloa's experiences could have prepared him for what Inter Miami became on that Wednesday morning.

Ulloa and his teammates were at the team hotel in Birmingham,

Alabama, on June 7 when they realized their lives were about to change. Several players rose from pregame naps to find dozens of text messages and missed calls from friends.

"I woke up and thought, 'What happened? Did someone die?'" Inter Miami's left back Franco Negri recalled.

It wasn't a death, but it was life-altering news. The interview had just dropped. Messi was coming to Miami.

"I couldn't believe it," said Negri, an Argentine who realized he was going to play with his hero. "I was shaking. My hair stood on end. It was incredible."

The team was only a few hours from kicking off against the second-division Birmingham Legion in a U.S. Open Cup quarterfinal, but as they walked into the meal room, there was a buzz about what everyone had just learned. The excitement—and the disbelief—was so palpable that interim manager Javier Morales had to address the report.

Morales was part of the early wave of Argentines to sign with MLS in 2007. A midfielder from Buenos Aires, he won the 2009 MLS Cup with Real Salt Lake and earned two all-star nods and one Best XI selection in his MLS career. He, too, was coming to terms with the fact that he might be playing with Messi. His phone was lighting up with messages from agents, media, family, and friends—*really* old friends.

"People from primary school in Argentina were calling me," Morales recalled.

The interim coach leveled with the group.

"This is big news. We're all excited," he said. "But we have a game. We can't be focusing on that [news] right now in this moment."

Inter Miami would go on to squeak out a 1–0 win.

The next few weeks were spent dancing around the obvious amid a sea of change. Messi was coming to Inter Miami, but the players had no idea when he would arrive. In the meantime, they followed the headlines just like everyone else as rumors flew: about when Messi would show up, his famous friends who would follow, and the other players Inter Miami was targeting.

A new coach, Tata Martino, who had coached Messi at Barcelona and Argentina and won an MLS Cup with Atlanta United, was hired, and the team continued to play—and struggle. A 4–1 loss to the Philadelphia Union on June 24 was followed by three consecutive draws, and Inter Miami lingered in last place in the league.

Through it all, Messi still had not been officially announced as an Inter Miami player. Ulloa and his teammates reached a point when they felt it wasn't actually going to happen.

"We were going about our normal days and everything was normal," Ulloa said. "It was really hard to believe, at least for the players. It was like, 'Yeah, there's no way this guy's gonna come. He just won the World Cup.'"

Then one day when he went to work, as he had on so many mornings over the past three and a half years, Ulloa saw his new famous coworker sitting at his locker.

Like many soccer fans, Ulloa idolized Messi. He still had a store-bought Messi Barcelona jersey in his closet. When he saw Messi sitting next to his locker, he thought what almost any fan would think: How the hell do you introduce yourself to Leo Messi?

Trying to play it cool, Ulloa went to greet Callender first. Then he walked over to Messi and stuck out his hand.

"Hey, Leo," Ulloa said in Spanish. "Welcome to the club."

Messi said hello, then told his kids to get out of Ulloa's locker.

"No, no, it's fine," Ulloa replied nervously, grabbing his gear and heading to change elsewhere.

The scene played out similarly for each player who came to training that day, unaware that Messi was in the facility.

On day one, the players held their breath to see how Messi might assert himself around the group. He did not yet have his visa, so he couldn't train, but as the team gathered in the gym before taking the training field, Messi said a few brief words before deferring to the captains.

"He didn't want to come in and make it seem like he was the center of attention," said Kamal Miller, the Canadian center back who joined the team a few months prior. "He gave respect to the captains at the time and didn't want to come and seem like he was completely taking over. So right away, we respected that a lot and appreciated that."

Over the next two days, Ulloa tried to normalize the idea that he could turn his head and talk to Messi. Quickly, the two found commonalities in fatherhood. They talked about their kids. Ulloa heard stories about Messi's humility, but now he was experiencing it in person. He recognized how Messi was trying to integrate himself into the locker room. The superstar was approachable and happy to chat with new teammates.

"We didn't know if he was going to come in and try to change our ways and the culture that we had within the locker room," Ulloa said. "But to be honest, he tried to fit in. We would go and ask him certain things, what he wanted to do, but he was like, 'No, no, what do you guys do?' Then he would be like, 'Yeah, let's do that.' We never saw a side of him that he was like, 'Oh, nope, we're doing this because I say so.' It was the complete opposite. And that was surprising."

Messi was trying to accomplish the impossible: act like everything was normal. He arrived without an entourage. A personal bodyguard, Yassine Cheuko, was there, as was his father, Jorge Messi, on occasion. But in those first days, the retinue was more limited. Messi was accessible to just about everyone on the team.

Accessibility, though, comes with some degree of awkwardness, and Ulloa soon realized he had a dilemma. As one of Inter Miami's veterans, Ulloa had the privilege of being the administrator of the team's WhatsApp group chat, which meant controlling its membership. When new players joined the roster, Ulloa invited them to the group. When they left, he removed them. It was an unremarkable responsibility until he walked into the locker room on that Wednesday morning. Now, Ulloa realized that he probably had to at least offer Inter Miami's new star player entry into the chat. Considering Messi's eagerness to blend quickly into the group, Ulloa figured he would at least want to know about the text chain.

But how exactly do you ask Messi to join the WhatsApp group? Asking for Messi's number so early felt forward, but Ulloa decided he just had to go for it.

"Hey, man, we have a WhatsApp group with the guys. I don't know if you want to be a part of it or not, but I just wanted to let you know," Ulloa said to his locker mate.

"Absolutely," Messi replied quickly. "Here, take my number."

Ulloa entered Messi's number into his phone and then added him to the team chain without a mention to the rest of the group.

Just like everything else changing around the club, this was, somehow, the new normal.

* * *

A new normal was exactly what Messi was seeking.

For many foreign stars who arrived in MLS, life at the top of the sport in Europe had been restrictive. Footballers are under a microscope. Every action on the field is analyzed, every word in an interview dissected. The spotlight follows them to their lives away from the field, too. They often find it difficult to do essential day-to-day things like grocery shopping, eating in restaurants, or catching a movie.

For some, their lives are marked by the moment they surrender those normalities. Brazilian great Kaká remembered the date it all changed: March 8, 2001, the day after his debut for São Paulo in Brazil. He was eighteen years old, and as he walked through the aisles with his mother at a grocery store, people suddenly started approaching for autographs.

"It was the biggest surprise of my life because, literally, my life changed overnight," Kaká told me in 2015, after his first season with Orlando City.

It's why the Ballon d'Or winner found so much joy in the simple things upon his arrival in Florida. Kaká wasn't completely anonymous, of course. But on the day of his first MLS game in March 2015, with his face plastered on billboards around the city and on the front page of the *Orlando Sentinel*, Kaká came down for breakfast in the courtyard of the Alfond Inn in Winter Park, Florida, and dined outside with his family, not one fan approaching for a signature.

It was the type of normalcy nearly every big-name signing found, to some degree, when they came to MLS. French superstar striker Thierry Henry would occasionally ride the Port Authority Trans-Hudson (PATH) train from his home in SoHo to his New York Red Bulls games in Harrison, New Jersey. Italian legend Andrea Pirlo could patronize restaurants in Manhattan. Even Messi's famed former coach, Pep Guardiola, who took a one-year sabbatical in 2013 and lived in New York City, was told off for coaching kids during a game in Central Park by a father who had no idea he was questioning one of the greatest managers in soccer history.

Messi was renowned before he turned eighteen, so he never really knew normalcy as an adult. He had lived under the brightest possible spotlight. Messi was also on a different level of stardom than even Henry, Kaká, or any other MLS acquisition—at least since Beckham. Anonymity was not in the cards. That much was made clear on that first Wednesday evening in Florida. The Messis went to a well-known Italian restaurant in Miami Beach called Cafe Prima Pasta, where Messi had first dined a decade prior. The family entered like any other customers, through the front door, much to the surprise of the packed dining room. They sat at a table in the back and enjoyed the penne ciao, black linguini, and agnolotti rosso, Messi's favorite dish. When they tried to leave through a back door, however, dozens of fans waited, shouting at Messi and taking photos. One fan even planted a kiss on Messi's cheek.

The next day, cameras flashed as Messi and his family shopped at Publix, the local supermarket chain. Newspapers did breakdowns of the brands they could see in Messi's cart, which included Lucky Charms cereal.

Messi wasn't going to be able to sneak out anywhere, but he knew that. It wasn't anonymity he sought. He was simply searching for a degree of balance in his life. As Messi said in his interview with Polo and Masnou, he was "looking for other things . . . a little bit of peace."

"I want to rediscover the enjoyment," Messi said. "Enjoyment with my family, with my kids—the day-to-day."

It became clear to Inter Miami ownership almost immediately how much Messi sought that stability. They researched some of the more exclusive neighborhoods in the area, including many closer to Miami proper. Messi, though, wanted to live as close to the training facility as possible. Getting to work and back home quickly was a priority. The Messis found a house just fifteen minutes away. The kids were enrolled in a high-end private school a few miles from the team headquarters, too. It allowed for what quickly became Messi's daily routine: Eat breakfast at home, arrive for his individual workouts and treatment, train with the group, and then return home for lunch and time with the family.

Coming to MLS removed a level of scrutiny from Messi's life. He still wanted to win. This wasn't retirement. And Messi still had a major role with Argentina's national team, which was set to defend its Copa América crown in 2024. But playing for Inter Miami came with a different set of expectations than those at Barcelona.

It was maybe the most jarring part of MLS life for many who came from abroad to play. Winning or losing could alter the moods of cities across South America or Europe, just as it might in Tuscaloosa after the University of Alabama competes on a college football Saturday. MLS franchises did not have that sort of hold over their markets. Former U.S. men's national team coach Jürgen Klinsmann used to reference that lack of pressure, saying players didn't live the impact of a poor performance when they went to the grocery store or butcher the day after the game. "In the big leagues in Europe and South America, if you miss a shot, you're held accountable for it. Then you don't miss it anymore," Klinsmann said. "This is important." In MLS, players had to find the motivation within because incentivization rarely came from public pressure or media scrutiny. For some, the lack of that pressure was freeing. Too often, it could spill over into their lives away from soccer, impacting their families and friends. For others, though, the lack of external motivation was energy-zapping. Some couldn't find the drive they got from the pressure back home.

"In Argentina, you played poorly and you know that on TV, the journalists, fans who are crazy about soccer are going to be there Monday. Sometimes you miss it, miss people saying, 'Che, you're doing things poorly!' For a player, that's good," said Sebastián Driussi, an Argentinian winger who went from playing for Argentine giants River Plate to starring at the MLS club Austin FC.

For the famously self-motivated Messi, who spent a decade carrying the load of every result for club and country on his shoulders, eliminating the bulk of that outside pressure was a featured trait of MLS.

"Soccer, it became difficult," Messi said on an Apple documentary about his arrival in the U.S. "But I was always happy playing soccer and being able to have fun, like when I was a kid. And I can keep doing it here, which was one of the reasons why I made the decision.

"To enjoy again what I had lost."

* * *

Messi may have been chasing normalcy, but his teammates were hurtling in the opposite direction.

The absurdity of their new reality was hammered home when forward Leonardo Campana innocently dropped a question into the Inter Miami team WhatsApp group chat ahead of the Sunday event at which Messi would be unveiled to fans.

"Hey," the Ecuadorian forward wrote. "Does anybody have any extra tickets?"

Few realized that the number Ulloa added a couple of days earlier was Messi's, so it was a shock when their new teammate replied, asking Campana how many tickets he needed.

"Just from there, I was like, 'Whoa.' They've known each other two days, three days," said Inter Miami defender DeAndre Yedlin, a U.S. national team veteran. "Just to show that generosity, that's a great first example of how he is."

Messi's new teammates all rushed to save his number. Some came up with pseudonyms for their famous colleague, the better to keep it safe should they ever be hacked or lose their phone.

And, yes, Campana got those extra tickets for "The Unveil," where Messi would be introduced as an Inter Miami player to a sold-out DRV PNK Stadium.

That Sunday evening, just after 5 P.M., about an hour before the event was set to start, a tropical swell blew through Fort Lauderdale. The storm hit with near-hurricane level winds, causing fans outside the stadium to climb fences to seek cover inside the building. People ducked into stairwells and bathrooms as gusts blew beer stands over and sideways rain pounded DRV PNK.

Underneath the main stand, Inter Miami players took refuge in the locker room. Fans and players alike bunked for nearly an hour as the worst of the storm blew through until they were finally allowed to their seats around 6:30 P.M. The event was scheduled to begin with concerts, but those were pushed to the end of the program. Instead, the crowd whirred as they focused on the empty stage out on the field.

It was, truly, a surreal scene for anyone who had been around MLS. Since Beckham signed in 2007, the league had experienced blips of relevance, but they were mostly limited to in-market celebrations. Sold-out crowds in Seattle, Portland, Orlando, Atlanta, and elsewhere were signs of MLS's progress. But this was different. Fans were climbing fences in tropical-storm level winds to get inside for a look at Messi. The press box was so full that Inter Miami had to use a section of its stands as an auxiliary press box.

An hour after the weather cleared and fans were brought back into the stadium, Inter Miami's owners—Jorge and Jose Mas and Beckham—emerged to kick off the show. Beckham nearly slipped on the rain-soaked stage, his dress shoes less than suitable for the Florida weather. He took the microphone to welcome the fans.

"Please forgive me for feeling a little bit emotional tonight," Beckham said. "Because it really is a dream come true."

The first player introduced was Sergio Busquets, the Spanish midfielder who helped redefine his position playing as a defensive midfielder at Barcelona with Messi. For most MLS teams,

Busquets would be the biggest signing in its history. On this night, he was just an opening act.

After Busquets left the stage, Mas became the emcee. The right side of his collared shirt was folded awkwardly under the blue Inter Miami sport coat he wore. He was soaked from the rain that still fell. But he pumped his fist at the crowd and spoke, alternating between Spanish and English.

"We're doing this Miami-style in the rain," Mas exclaimed. "This is holy water. *Esto es agua bendita esta noche*."

He worked the microphone like a pro.

"This is our moment," he continued. "Our moment to change the football landscape in this country. . . . I would like to introduce to you, your No. 10, Inter Miami's No. 10, America's No. 10, the best No. 10 in the world, Lionel Andrés Messi!"

Messi emerged in a white shirt with a custom Inter Miami–themed No. 10 on his back. The owners held up a pink No. 10 Messi jersey and posed for photos. Then, the man of the moment took the mic. He didn't speak long, just one minute thirty-six seconds, but the crowd cheered nearly every word—a preview of the adoration that resonated throughout the stadium just a few days later against Cruz Azul.

"I'm so happy to have chosen to come to this city, to this project," Messi told the crowd in Spanish. "I have no doubt that we're going to enjoy it and celebrate great things. . . . I've come with the mentality to keep winning, to keep growing, to help the club keep growing."

That growth was already underway inside the organization. Just about everything within the club—from the hotels it booked, to the security in the building and the food the team ate—had to change to accommodate a star who was levels bigger than anyone before in MLS.

Inter Miami was now Messi's team. But someone had to build

the roster around its new star. And in MLS, with its convoluted and complicated set of roster guidelines meant to put governors on teams to maintain competitive balance, that wouldn't be an easy task.

8

A Fading "North Star"

If Messi was going to change American soccer, he was in for a fight against history.

The day after the new face of the league walked out on that rain-slicked stage, Mas boarded his jet bound for Washington, DC, and an MLS board meeting at the league's All-Star Game. He hoped Messi's arrival would quickly usher in change for MLS. But it wouldn't just be about changing opinions in the boardroom.

The degree of evolution Mas wanted meant redefining what had been one of the core tenets of the league's identity—and the very structure that allowed it to grow over the past thirty years.

The turbulent history of North American soccer influenced MLS's construction when it was founded in 1993 as a condition from FIFA for the U.S. to host the 1994 World Cup. Former MLS deputy commissioner Mark Abbott, then a third-year associate at a law firm in Chicago, crafted a sixty-nine-page plan that laid out U.S. Soccer president Alan Rothenberg's unique take on a single-entity business structure he envisioned for MLS. Team owner/operators would be competitors on the field but partners off it, each owning a percentage of the business (MLS) rather than just their respective franchises. The league office would control player contracts and share costs and revenue.

That concept was a response to the profligate spending by the North American Soccer League in the 1970s and 1980s, when Pelé, Franz Beckenbauer, Johan Cruyff, and George Best graced sold-out stadiums before it all collapsed under the weight of the disparity between rich clubs and poor ones. The North American Soccer League inspired a generation of soccer fans, but its downfall created a lull that wasn't overcome until MLS was founded.

"We thought that was critical, given the fact that soccer had failed before, to be able to have that stability," Abbott said. "When you have an unstable league, even the strong teams go out of business if the weak teams ultimately go out of business. So it's the only business in the world where you don't want your competitor to go out of business, right?"

MLS undoubtedly achieved that stability. Three decades after its founding, the single-entity structure remained one of the league's strengths. The commercial side was stable, and the league was financially solid. On the sporting side, however, the single-entity concept was linked to the league's long-standing mandate to prioritize competitive balance over anything else.

That approach was buckling under modern pressures.

Competitive balance was a flashpoint in the debate about the future of MLS. It was a hallmark of the NFL, one championed by the late AFL founder and Kansas City Chiefs owner Lamar Hunt. The Hunt and the Kraft families, two of the NFL's most influential ownership groups, were also founding owners in MLS. Understandably, they preached the NFL gospel. But MLS operated in a far different environment than the NFL. It competed against soccer leagues around the world, as well as with the American sports market—not just for fans, but also for talent.

In 2014, the owners commissioned a study by the Boston Consulting Group (BCG). The release of the results to league owners in 2016 revealed that fans judged the league referentially against international competition. How MLS fared in regional tournaments against Liga MX, for example, was an important gauge of progress. The NFL had no such competition. While MLS's roster and salary rules fostered internal competitive balance, they also restrained MLS from asserting itself as a top league in Concacaf, the region of North and Central America and the Caribbean, let alone as a challenger on the global stage.

From its 1996 inception through 2014, MLS won just two of twenty-four home-and-home series against Mexican teams in official competition. Those numbers improved slightly beginning in 2015, when MLS introduced targeted allocation money (TAM) as a reaction to that BCG study. The TAM rule allowed teams to spend more to improve the top third of their rosters, beyond just the designated players. It was a Band-Aid. From 2015 through 2023, the league improved in the Concacaf Champions League, but still only won eleven of thirty-five series against Mexican teams—a 32.4 percent win percentage. On just one occasion in the previous twenty years did an MLS club (the Seattle Sounders in 2022) win the regional title.

Those results would get almost any coach fired—and yet the league stayed the course, an indication of how entrenched it was in its competitive balance doctrine. MLS executives liked to say that the fundamental principle of the league was that it could innovate and pivot based on the challenges of the day. The creation of SUM and the DP rule were prominent examples. Yet it was also clear there were certain nonnegotiables.

It was increasingly difficult to watch MLS's consistent failures in Concacaf and its persistent self-imposed restraints and not see competitive balance as enforced mediocrity—or what Jorge Mas aptly called "a race to the bottom."

"Everybody sucks, so everybody bad has a chance to win," he lamented.

Despite those continued poor results, even as American consumers had greater access to the top leagues in the world and were watching those leagues in greater numbers, MLS clung to competitive balance as its North Star. This was in part because many of the people who designed MLS were still leading the business and believed deeply in its founding principles. Abbott, the league's first employee in 1993, stepped down as deputy commissioner at the end of 2022, but remained on as an advisor. Commissioner Don Garber and executive vice president Todd Durbin were at the top of the league's hierarchy. Founding owners Robert Kraft, Phil Anschutz, and Clark Hunt were regarded as some of the most influential people in the league. To overhaul the league's design would be to dismantle the very thing they spent thirty years building and protecting.

Competitive balance also protected a league model built on local revenue. Every team having a chance to win, or at least to make the playoffs, was the best way to keep butts in seats in thirty markets. To really grow, however, MLS needed to move from a turnstile operation into a league that could command a national (and potentially global) audience—and secure the revenue that came with it.

Changing that mindset among the more conservative faction of owners would be a real challenge. There were concerns about what would happen if MLS opened up spending, even in a salary-capped environment. Increasing costs without a guarantee that it would boost revenue could be existential for some clubs—or at least force some owners to sell.

"We have been careful to not get seduced by the idea that the solution is to scrap all roster rules and have unlimited spending on players, because we don't believe that will be justified by new revenues," Garber said. "I imagine that at some point we'll have the luxury of being able to not have to continually look through that lens, but that certainly is the lens that we've had to look through over the last number of decades."

For many, however, it was difficult to see how one could possibly argue *against* change. If the league couldn't draw wider audiences, its pathway to growth got narrower. And so many fans turning to other soccer products like the Premier League, Liga MX, and the UEFA Champions League as their "leagues of choice" was *also* potentially existential for MLS.

* * *

MLS didn't measure up to what fans could get elsewhere: It needed to improve the product on the field. Stakeholders also had to change the wider perception of their league. While MLS was not on the level of the top European leagues, casual fans thought it was worse than it was.

The solutions to those problems were linked, but they were very different.

Improving the product mostly came down to how the league invested in its rosters. The soccer consulting firm Twenty First Group ranked MLS outside the top thirty best leagues in the world in its 2023 World Super League Model, which ranks four thousand teams globally based on match results, margin of victory, strength of opposition, and other data points. MLS sat alongside the Turkish second division and Ukraine's first division in terms of quality. By comparison, Mexico's Liga MX was ranked twenty-fifth, Germany's second division was fourteenth, and Argentina's top division was thirteenth.

Twenty First Group's models also rated MLS as one of the least efficient leagues in terms of how money spent turns into performance. Per the data, even MLS's most effective spending clubs were still materially inefficient when compared to global norms.

League rules funneled spending to a narrow band at the very top of rosters: DPs and u-22 players (star players under the age of twenty-two acquired under a specific roster designation). The middle quadrants of rosters sagged well behind not just because there wasn't *enough* money to spend but more significantly because the rules siloed and restricted exactly *how* its teams spent.

Data show that spending better and smarter, perhaps by allowing high-payroll clubs to more easily spread their money across their entire rosters instead of spending such large chunks of it on three players, would vastly improve the product.

The problem wasn't limited to the top of rosters and the risks associated with focusing a large percentage of spending on one, two, or three players.

League executives rightly posited that growing the domestic player pool was critical to MLS's growth and invested heavily in youth development. After two decades, MLS was producing more pro players, but it still wasn't developing enough high-end talent.

In 2022, MLS announced it was launching a third-division developmental league, MLS Next Pro, and ending its partnership with the second- and third-division USL (United Soccer League). The decision came with huge risk. The upside of Next Pro—control over more markets in the country, access to more "homegrown players," and stronger connections through the entire player development pathway—would, realistically, be borne out over a multi-decade timeline. In the interim, as it tried to build out a competitive environment, it could both stagnate player development and pull funding out of the first-team product at a critical moment when more investment was needed. Owners dumped millions into Next Pro, and while MLS heralded players who had come through the reserve teams, those prospects weren't improving the overall quality of the league.

The investment in youth academies was worthwhile, but it failed to recognize the biggest contributor to what had long been called the black hole of player development in the U.S.: those seventeen to twenty-one years old. Creating pro players good enough for MLS was no longer a problem. Producing world-class players, however, remained decidedly out of reach. Improved first teams were critical to that aim. The youth academies were producing solid prospects at younger age groups, but progress was slowing at the most critical age in development. The level of play in MLS set too low of a ceiling.

German giants Bayern Munich targeted American youth prospects under age nineteen because they believed there was still time for younger players to adapt to the speed of play in Europe. After that age, it was hard for most players to reach the highest levels.

"If you watch an MLS game, or even a youth game, it's technically on a very good level, it's athletically on a very good level, but the ball goes a little slower," Bayern Munich academy campus director Jochen Sauer told me in 2019. "They are playing on the whole pitch and you do not have the pressure like you have in Europe and that, I think, is the main factor that the young players have to learn when they start here. Athletically they are on the same level as our youth players, and they have all the basics that they learned in the youth teams, but if it comes to the speed of play, how the ball circulates, that's always a bit different."

It reinforced a most basic notion for MLS: To improve its standing in the short term and to optimize youth development for long-term viability, MLS had to increase its on-field quality.

* * *

With much of the spending focused on those two extremes of the spectrum—the highest earners, few of which actually moved the commercial needle, and in youth development, where not enough players and not enough *good* players were being produced—MLS rosters were out of balance and lacking in depth. If MLS allowed teams to spread out that spending on the first team roster, putting $20 million into eight or nine players rather than the top two or three, its rosters would be more well-rounded and boast more overall depth.

Most teams in Liga MX were built that way, and the Mexican league's dominance in the Concacaf Champions Cup was proof of the strategy's superiority. There might be short-term pain to the domestic player pool as MLS leaned into the global market toward those aims, but the payoff—both short term in driving quality and long term in raising the developmental ceiling—would be worth it.

Advocates for change insisted that it could be done without completely sacrificing the idea that any team could win in any given year. Spending more and spending better weren't mutually exclusive from competitive balance. And there were added benefits beyond just the level of play. Giving teams more freedom in how to spend would also foster different roster-building strategies, widen the pool of front-office talent, and enhance storylines that would make the league more compelling. It would likely also make MLS a greater player in the global soccer economy, which in turn could help drive more revenue.

It was such an obvious issue, but league decision-makers were so stuck in their ways that they kept adding more buckets to address shortfalls. They couldn't see that the overall structure of the rules was the problem.

The question was less about what a new rule book would look like. There were plenty of alternatives to consider: a cap ceiling and floor with some carve-outs, a luxury tax model, or systems that mirrored those found in other American sports leagues. The question was really why MLS insisted that its model was still the best way forward. The league changed significantly in the previous decade of expansion, yet the roster-building model and all the modifications stacked on top of it mostly avoided scrutiny. It was overdue for an assessment.

Slapping on Band-Aids wouldn't work for a rule book that required reconstructive surgery.

* * *

While MLS peddled the NFL-endorsed idea that competitive balance was the most critical factor in keeping fans engaged, the Premier League believed it was just one element.

England's top league had the quality *and* a relatively balanced competition and saw *both* as vital in driving fan interest. The biggest clubs in England typically battled it out for the title, but league executives believed it had enough balance and quality to make games compelling every week. At least one or two previously unheralded teams usually popped up and surprised traditional powers every season.

Even so, balance wasn't the only way to engage and entertain an audience. When Manchester City and Liverpool F.C. were dominating, the Premier League remained the most popular soccer league in the world.

"Flat Earth competitive balance does not necessarily make for compelling viewing and great competition," said Richard Scudamore, the former executive. He pointed to the fact that professional golf was never as popular as it was during Tiger Woods' years of dominance.

"Brilliant golf transcended competitive balance and a different winner every week," he said.

Scudamore believed history demonstrated that fans wanted dominant winners. They liked having villains to hate and preferred the drama of seeing a powerful team fall from grace, or a dynasty form and then conquer. Sports at their best revolved around those types of stories. A dominant Manchester City side wasn't necessarily bad for the attractiveness or allure of the Premier League.

"You're trying to counter human nature and culture by making people think that the ultimate goal is equalization," Scudamore said. "It's not. There's a degree of distribution that helps, but it's about creating excellence."

It was a point argued inside MLS circles by some of the top team sporting executives for close to a decade. Many felt MLS roster rules didn't just hold the league down in terms of quality, but that it also severely handicapped the league from building any sort of sustained narratives from season to season that fans could latch on to. Teams couldn't sustain success. Storylines died before they had a chance to build an audience.

But narratives and storylines are only a byproduct of what ultimately drives popularity. While MLS called competitive balance its North Star, Scudamore said the Premier League's "true north" was "the excellence of [its] sporting competition."

"The Premier League's success isn't down to clever marketing," Scudamore said. "It is down to the best football competition. So what the Premier League has always done is meticulously maintained that its number one objective is to put on the most competitive and compelling football competition you can put on, played in the best stadia, with the noisiest fans, attracting the world's best talent and managed by the best managers you can find."

That idea won over American fans who were used to that sort of exceptionalism within the domestic sporting landscape.

The formula worked brilliantly for the Premier League, but it was one that couldn't easily be replicated by a younger league without the weight of a century of tradition and the gravitational pull of top global talent. For that reason, with the World Cup coming in 2026, NBC and the Premier League believed they were positioned to win over more American fans simply because they had the best product.

Not even Messi could change that.

"The MLS does a great job locally," NBC executive Jon Miller said. "They've got great operators and owners. I think Don Garber has done a terrific job with the league. But the Premier League has the benefit of having the best players in the world, the best teams in the world, and the most competitive and best product on the pitch. And that helps [NBC] deliver in everything we do."

* * *

In MLS, there was increasing frustration that so many of the league's rules were designed to do exactly the opposite. Rather than push for the best players and teams possible, its structure was built to rein in the most ambitious teams—the ones that helped fuel the league's increased relevance and enhanced reputation—while rivals that spent less could coast and still benefit.

It's why there was growing disagreement at the board level about how to move the league forward.

"In the past, we had one hundred percent unanimity on every vote. We don't anymore. Now, there's lots more debate," Garber said. "And that's okay. It requires us to do a little more work on ensuring everybody understands the decisions they're making and what impact that's going to have on the enterprise.

"That's the reality of a maturing sports league. It happens in every other league. You're going to have big markets and small markets. You're going to have legacy owners and new owners . . . I need to be focused and the league office needs to be focused on enterprise success on behalf of all. That's a very, very, very different job than it was ten years ago."

What it required was a strong hand to guide the consensus one way or another, because as the board sat down for its meeting in Washington, DC, in the days after Messi was introduced, even despite the differing opinions, there was an increased understanding on both sides that the model as it stood was no longer working.

Change had to happen.

What that evolution looked like would be determined by the league's aspirations. If MLS wanted to be one of the best leagues in the world, as Garber liked to say, the current model could not support that. MLS would need to spend more and spend more efficiently. It needed a better and more competitive on-field product that could entice bigger audiences, increase relevance, and eventually earn a bigger media deal.

If the league was happy with its current standing—a strong, entertaining local business that brought fans through the gates in its thirty markets—then it probably had to decrease spending to make it sustainable. For the owners who paid expansion fees north of $250 million—and as high as $500 million in the case of San Diego—that seemed like a nonstarter.

That it felt so up in the air was frustrating in itself. MLS spent years organizing its local, national, and international media rights to be ready to go to market when its deal was up in 2022. Yet despite knowing since 2018 that the World Cup was coming to the U.S. in 2026, the league had done little to ramp up or prepare for sporting change around that massive moment.

Mas believed Messi swung the debate in only one direction. He had not yet kicked a ball in MLS, but the reaction to his arrival had been so enormous and unprecedented, and was already driving so much commercial interest, that it started to recalibrate some of the more conservative thinking in the boardroom. Mas walked out of the meeting that afternoon in Washington, DC, beaming.

"I think that all of us collectively understand the opportunity ahead of us, the opportunity to continue growing the league," he said. "Hopefully this is a catalyst for the hyper growth that that I—and all of us—aspire to. . . . There was a significant amount of focus on how we move forward.

"I do think that evolution is inevitable."

In the moment, with the excitement building around Messi's debut, Mas felt the way we all did: There was no way MLS would fail to embrace this once-in-a-league's-lifetime opportunity.

9

"Tell Me All the Trophies I Can Win . . . "

Chris Henderson's predicament laid bare the fundamental flaws in the league's architecture. Inter Miami had just signed the greatest player of all time. Fans who wouldn't normally watch MLS would be tuning in to see what the league had to offer. Henderson's job as Inter Miami's sporting director was to build the best possible team around Messi. But he would have to do so with one hand tied behind his back.

MLS stakeholders undoubtedly wanted Messi to be successful. They wanted Inter Miami to be good.

Just not *too* good.

The entire design of the league's roster rules was to prevent super teams. It was a radical concept in global soccer, and one that Messi likely wouldn't understand. There were no salary caps in the rest of the world. The sport was dominated by what was increasingly becoming an arms race between the highest-spending super clubs, including his beloved Barcelona.

Three days after Messi was presented as an Inter Miami player, Henderson glanced out of his office just in time to see his team's new No. 10 walking around the corner with Jorge Mas.

Dressed in a light blue suit with a pink tie, a dash of the color he'd be donning for the next several seasons, Messi had just posed for signing ceremony pictures. The actual pen-to-paper moment had, in fact, occurred earlier at the home Inter Miami rented for the Messis and was delayed by a somewhat important detail: nobody brought a pen. A house-wide search eventually yielded the instrument that would make Messi's contract official.

In soccer, however, no signing is truly certified without photos of a smiling player, pen in hand, to prove it. Messi was dressed in his best for the occasion. Inside Henderson's office, Mas introduced Messi to the man who would help assemble the squad of players around him, mentioning that Henderson had actually played against Messi in a 2006 friendly between the New York Red Bulls and Barcelona in the final year of Henderson's MLS career. In fact, Henderson, then thirty-five years old, had marked the then-nineteen-year-old as a rising star. Messi scored, of course.

"I don't remember," Messi said.

Henderson laughed.

"Of course you don't remember playing me," he replied. "But I remember playing you."

Messi was arriving to a last-place team in MLS. Inter Miami's place in the standings only hinted at the full story of how tumultuous the team's first three years in MLS had been.

The club debuted during the COVID-shortened 2020 season. They didn't play in front of a home crowd until October of that year, when 350 supporters were allowed into the building. It took until May 2021 for the stadium to be fully open for fans.

The fifty-two-year-old sporting director arrived at Inter Miami ahead of the club's second year as a winner, having helped build a dynasty in Seattle during his thirteen years as the club's top recruiter. The Sounders' success made him one of the league's most sought-after front-office candidates, but he waited for the right job to come around. His patience landed him in Miami in

2021—a prestigious position with enterprising ownership in a sexy market.

Within months, it would turn into one of the most difficult jobs in MLS.

In May 2021, a few months into Henderson's first season, Inter Miami got crushed with sanctions for breaking roster rules around the 2020 signing of Blaise Matuidi—a $2 million-plus fine on the club's roster-building assets over the next two years. Most of Henderson's plans went out the window. Even the players he already had signed now looked like salary cap weight instead of promising additions. He had to figure out how to dig this ambitious team out of a deep financial hole. Henderson had waited years for the perfect role. Suddenly, the job had been flipped upside down. There was little chance of winning in his first years as a sporting director.

Henderson was blindsided and devastated by the news. He called one of his best friends, Tim Harris, to try to get his mind sorted. A former professional soccer goalkeeper, Harris had been teammates with Henderson at UCLA and now worked in the Los Angeles Lakers front office as the president of business operations. He offered his old teammate simple advice: "Change the story." Flip the narrative. You can be successful by turning the situation around.

The message resonated with Henderson, who had a natural tendency to find the best in bad situations—and in people. Soft-spoken and disarmingly kind, Henderson's unshakeable demeanor made him both a perfect counterweight to Miami's ultra-competitive ownership group and the ideal leader during a tumultuous period at the club. For the staff, some of whom had arrived at the same time as Henderson and confronted the same startling news, his empathetic approach steadied the office.

Henderson got to work. He began crafting a plan to build Inter

Miami's roster despite the limitations. They missed the playoffs in 2021, but entering 2022, he started clearing salary and accumulating assets. Sanctions and all, Inter Miami somehow squeezed into the MLS playoffs in 2022, finishing sixth in the Eastern Conference.

"It was the most challenging thing I've ever done in my life," Henderson recalled of those first two seasons. "There's so many times I'm thinking back to the first eight months here that I'm like, if I lived through that, I can get through anything professionally. Things will seem easy in comparison."

By 2023, Inter Miami was mostly free of the pain from those sanctions. But going into the season, Mas told Henderson to keep two designated player spots—and jersey numbers 5 and 10—open. The reasoning was good: The hope was that Sergio Busquets and Messi would arrive together. But it meant Inter Miami's roster would be in purgatory once again.

In MLS, DPs were the difference makers. Winning without them was possible but challenging. Mas was never anything but optimistic, but Henderson had been around long enough to know that you never know if a deal is done until it's done. At one point, Apple cameras arrived for a behind-the-scenes documentary on Inter Miami that was never green-lit. The producers tried time and again to get Henderson to mention Messi. He wouldn't, so as not to jinx it.

"You do things trying to make it work, knowing we're gonna go for it this summer," Henderson said. "And if everything lands, it's all going to change."

The team's scouting staff produced reports on every big-name player they were considering, including Busquets and Barcelona's left back Jordi Alba, but no data was needed or commissioned for Messi. In one graphic on potential signings, the x-axis showed players' age, and the y-axis displayed goals and assists. The outlier in the upper right corner had no name associated with it. It was just the number 10.

Now, in his office, Henderson was standing across from the data point.

The risk of leaving the roster mostly bare had obvious downfalls. Inter Miami was dead last in the MLS standings, and by a decent margin. They were winless in eleven straight MLS games and fired coach Phil Neville in the weeks before Messi signed. Ultimately, though, the long-term strategy paid off. Messi was here, and Inter Miami could now build around its star.

Beckham joined the group from his suite that connected to Henderson's office. Jose Mas arrived as well. As the ownership group took their seats, the ink on Messi's real and fake contracts now dry, Messi made it clear how committed he was in Miami.

"Okay," he said, matter-of-factly. "Tell me all of the competitions and trophies I can win."

* * *

When Messi landed in Miami, he was thirty-six years old and had, by his own admission, accomplished everything possible in the sport.

Lifting the World Cup trophy in Qatar in December 2022 opened the door to the final phase of his career. In his interview with Masnou and Polo announcing where he would sign next, Messi explained that Argentina's triumph offered the leeway to make a decision based on something other than what it might mean for a legacy that was now secured.

"Thank God I was lucky enough to have achieved everything in football," Messi said that day. "And today I look beyond the sporting aspect, which obviously also interests me a lot, but much more so my family and my well-being."

For some, those words were an admission that he was walking

away from soccer's highest level. Much of the footballing world deemed MLS a "retirement league" during the post-Beckham years because of the stream of players who arrived in America at the tail end of their careers. MLS spent the period ahead of Messi's arrival pushing back against that reputation by recruiting more young and in-prime players. Now, the arrival of the greatest of all time—a player who would have been welcomed at any club in the world—somehow sparked the criticism again.

Barcelona issued a passive-aggressive statement expressing disappointment in Messi's decision to choose MLS over a return to Catalonia.

"President Laporta understood and respected Messi's decision to want to compete in a league with fewer demands," the statement read, in part. "Further away from the spotlight and the pressure he has been subject to in recent years."

The subtext of the statement was clear: Signing in Miami was, for all intents and purposes, going to the beach to kick back. It was the sort of discourse that infuriated MLS commissioner Don Garber. Just a few years earlier, Swedish superstar Zlatan Ibrahimović's decision to sign with the LA Galaxy at age thirty-six was used as evidence that MLS was a retirement league. His subsequent success at his older age—fifty-three goals and eighteen assists in fifty-eight MLS games—was weaponized rather than celebrated, proof that the league still didn't measure up. The retirement discourse faded, though, when Ibrahimović left the LA Galaxy to resign with AC Milan in Italy's Serie A at age thirty-eight. Ibrahimović scored twenty-five goals in his first thirty-seven league matches with AC Milan.

"Interestingly, when Zlatan left Major League Soccer, nobody said that he went to go retire in Italy," Garber scoffed. "And frankly, I was insulted by that. I'm not quite sure why we're viewed differently, but that is what it is."

That Messi, six months after winning the World Cup, was now somehow the face of that debate spotlighted the extent of the bias against MLS. The league was undoubtedly at a lower level than most European leagues, but the *perception* of the league was even worse than the reality. MLS spent years pushing its teams to sign younger prospects. The majority of DPs were under the age of thirty. But there was also value in bringing in veterans and aging stars. It happened in leagues all over the world. And those stars were especially valuable for a league that had to compete in a much more crowded sporting landscape. Name recognition brought headlines and new fans to the product. MLS still needed that boost.

Messi, for his part, recognized that his own words were being used to suggest he might not care to win anymore. A few weeks later, in an extensive sit-down with an Argentinian television show *Llave a la Eternidad*, he insisted he would continue to compete for his country—and at his new club in MLS.

"My mentality and my head will not change," he said. "And I will try to give my best for myself and for my new club and continue to perform at the highest level."

The argument that his arrival in Inter Miami signaled the definitive end to his era of dominance discounted both the mentality of one of the world's most accomplished athletes and the obligation attached to that status. Winning the World Cup relieved him of so many pressures. "*Se sacó de encima la mochila de ganar con Argentina*," Inter Miami coach Tata Martino said. He got rid of the baggage of winning with Argentina.

What Laporta failed to acknowledge was the expectation Messi lived with every day, and every time he stepped on the field. He must always be great.

Messi was held to a different standard, compared not with his peers but rather with the absolute elite in the game's history. Any misstep was a mark against his resume. Players like Steven Gerrard and Andrea Pirlo could fail to impress in MLS, and the performances would be waved off as an understandable anomaly by disinterested superstars at the end of prestigious careers. It wasn't held against their legacies. To be considered the greatest of all time, however, Messi couldn't come to MLS and fail to dominate. He didn't have the luxury not to care.

Those at Inter Miami soon realized he didn't have the capacity, either.

* * *

In a modern world obsessed with image and marketing, Messi's global appeal was unique in that while there was a machine that worked to monetize his fame, his introverted personality left his off-field personality mostly unknown outside of his small inner circle. Messi's team, led by his father, had done a good job of protecting him. Messi rarely gave interviews. When he did, it was with friendly media that his team had developed relationships with over many years, most often outlets in Argentina or Barcelona.

It's part of why Messi stood in stark contrast to the celebrity machine that was Cristiano Ronaldo—or Beckham, for that matter. Beckham's 2007 arrival to the LA Galaxy was defined in part by how his then-representatives, 19 Management, led by American Idol creator Simon Fuller, massaged and crafted Beckham's image. He moved to Los Angeles partly because of the opportunity Hollywood provided, both for him and his wife, Victoria.

Messi's American introduction was distinctly different. With hundreds of media members descending on Miami during the Argentine's first days in South Florida, Messi did not even give an introductory press conference. His aversion to media obligations would eventually become one of the defining features of his time in MLS—and a limitation to what his full impact might have been.

Teammates and those close to him fiercely protected his desire for privacy. The few stories that did filter out beyond the locker room revolved mostly around the internal fire that has defined numerous other greats across sports, from Michael Jordan and Kobe Bryant to Tom Brady, Tiger Woods, and Serena Williams.

"Beyond his quality, it's his mentality, his head," Messi's former coach, Pep Guardiola, once said in an interview. "In four years at Barcelona, we played a lot of games in training, and he didn't lose even one. If he had lost, he would've left. He has that competitive mentality that only four or five players in history have. They have something different."

That inaugural training session would be a preview of how quickly Messi could switch his mood based on the whims of a performance or a result. Inter Miami players immediately learned there was truth to the lore of Messi's drive. From the first session, he demanded excellence—and drove his new teammates, many of whom could never dream of playing on the stages he dominated, to maximize their quality.

"There was all the cameras and all the people and the hype and everything for the first fifteen minutes of practice," Ulloa recalled. "Until they kicked everyone out. And then something just switched.

"I can't describe it with words. The best thing I can say is he has an aura. Everybody's level raised instantly. The trainings were unbelievable. The level of concentration, intensity. Everybody wanted to raise their level, play well. Everybody wanted to perform and to win."

Winger Robert Taylor remembered a warm-up drill where players were divided into two teams with no goalkeepers. Players sprint out into the field, and a teammate throws them a pass to head it. An opposing field player is the "goalkeeper" who can make a save.

"One of our teammates throws in the ball, and it's a bad throw," Taylor remembered. "And you can see his frustration in his demeanor. He was mad at the guy, like, 'You're using your hands! Come on. It needs to be better!' It was one of those moments where you're like, 'Damn.' Whoever coached him has said the same thing: that he's the most competitive guy they've ever seen. And he is. Whatever it is, he'll want to win."

That first practice was an extension of the meeting in Henderson's office. Messi remained as locked in and competitive as ever.

"Everything he's won in his career, you'd expect him to be a bit more relaxed," Beckham would say. "But he's a winner. As simple as that: he's a winner. . . . He's still hungry."

The desire was evident that day with Henderson and the ownership group. They went through the competitions in which Inter Miami would compete, from the most prestigious, the Concacaf Champions Cup and MLS Cup, to the ancillary, the Supporters' Shield and U.S. Open Cup. They even speculated on a potential bid to play in Copa Libertadores, South America's club championship tournament, and mentioned the Club World Cup coming in two years.

And then there was the new Leagues Cup competition in which Messi would make his Inter Miami debut. It was their first chance at a trophy. For that reason, it mattered.

"He was taking note," Henderson said.

As the meeting adjourned, there was a clear mandate: Do everything you can to win. Spelling out the trophies available over the next two and a half years emphasized how little time there was to take full advantage.

10

Inside the Whirlwind

Inter Miami players learned over the course of their first three weeks in Messi's orbit that whatever they dreamed might happen was eclipsed by the reality of their life at the club.

Messi was delivering on the field. He followed up his cinematic debut against Cruz Azul with goals in Inter Miami's next two wins—a pair in a 4–0 decision over Atlanta United and another two in a 3–1 victory over Orlando City. Celebrities continued to grace the field-side suites. Dozens of media members still lined the training field and DRV PNK pitch to capture the moments. And another legend of the game joined the locker room: former Barcelona left back Jordi Alba, fresh off captaining Spain to the 2022–23 UEFA Nations League title.

It was all so much that DeAndre Yedlin, a veteran of two World Cups and the English Premier League, the one guy on the team who could act like the attention was old hat, could only shake his head at what was going on around him.

"[These] are guys I've grown up watching since I was a kid," Yedlin said in the midst of the three-game run. "For me it's more than surreal. It's just an incredible experience, and I'm trying to take it all in and just enjoy it."

To anticipate and adapt to the unexpected became the mission as Inter Miami embarked on its first road trip with Messi.

MLS travel was easier since the COVID-19 pandemic, when precautions forced teams to charter regularly for the first time. The switch from commercial to private flights made such a difference for players' physical recovery from grueling cross-continental travel that owners were willing to incur the cost as the world emerged from the pandemic. While Beckham navigated terminals at LAX filled with adoring fans and Kaká once sat in a middle seat on a team flight, Messi would have no such issue. But the private jet would feel like the only routine part of the trip for Messi's new teammates.

They marveled at the crowd waiting as the team bus pulled up to the Renaissance Hotel in Plano, Texas. And they chuckled as they weaved through the hotel kitchen, dishes clinking around them, to reach a service elevator and then a floor where police officers were positioned throughout.

Of course, this is what it must be like to travel with Messi. It was nearing a point where nothing could surprise them anymore.

Then, as they sat at one long table for a team dinner one floor above the Renaissance lobby, Lionel Andrés Messi stood up and sang.

* * *

The walk from Inter Miami's Fort Lauderdale training complex to the doors of DRV PNK's security gate measured 107 steps—a brisk two-minute stroll door-to-door. Until the summer of 2023, Miami players made the pregame walk between the two facilities. Typically, a few fans would tailgate in the parking lot the players cut through. Players would often stop to sign autographs and have their photo taken with fans.

But on the day Messi declared he was coming to MLS, Inter

Miami employees were surprised when they left team headquarters and encountered dozens of fans gathering outside the gates. Messi was still in Paris and news of his intent to sign with Inter Miami was not more than an hour old, but devotees were already descending on his new team's facilities, hoping to catch a glimpse of their hero. They were there again the next day, peering into the windows of the beat-up sedans driven by the data analysts and equipment managers pulling into the employee parking lot. And the next day, and the next.

The customary team walk on game days was scratched not long after announcing Messi's signing. Inter Miami officials decided a bus was necessary to make the one-tenth of a mile drive in front of its own stadium to the loading dock to get Messi inside safely. Thus, on the evening of Messi's first game for Miami—and for every home game after—a throng instead gathered outside the loading dock gate, hoping to see Messi's silhouette through the tinted window as a bus pulled in.

Inter Miami spent the four weeks between Messi's announcement and his arrival planning for every circumstance they could anticipate. The bus idling in the loading dock on game days was a thirty-thousand-pound reminder that things had to change around the club to accommodate a star like Messi—and just about everything did.

Preparation time for upcoming games went from days or weeks to months. Messi's global celebrity required much higher levels of security. Hotels needed an elevator reserved for players and a lobby space separated from typical hotel common areas so players could leave their room while remaining separate from the fans who would inevitably show up to see Messi.

The team chef traveled for away games a day before the players did, so meals were ready at the hotel when they arrived. The trips from the hotel to the stadiums were carefully coordinated to account for delays caused by crowds waiting for a glimpse of Messi. For example, in Dallas, a visiting team's buses typically stopped outside a gate adjacent to the National Soccer Hall of Fame, a building attached to the back of Toyota Stadium, FC Dallas's home in Frisco, Texas. On the first trip to Dallas with Messi, hundreds of fans waited at those fences to see him disembark and walk through the gates and into the stadium. Instead, a route was crafted to pull the bus into a loading dock on the opposite side of the venue via a tunnel typically used by delivery trucks.

Logistics changed at home as well. It was apparent in the weeks after Messi signed that team employees who normally worked out of Inter Miami's office in Coral Gables were starting to show up to work instead at the training ground in Fort Lauderdale, hoping for proximity to Messi. The team cafeteria was suddenly filled with people hoping for a glimpse of the team's new star or his Barcelona brethren. Chris Henderson, the team's sporting director, laughed about receiving hundreds of text messages from agents who wanted to meet with him, ostensibly about the team signing one of their clients. "Could I swing by the facility?" they asked. Henderson started to offer to meet at a nearby Starbucks. The queries dried up. Eventually, training days were closed for all guests of employees unless cleared directly by Henderson.

Henderson also decided that the team needed to install doors with security keypads to separate the first-team side of the facility from the staff areas. He limited how frequently the technical staff, including him, entered that part of the building.

"You don't want to be a jerk, but you've got to protect those guys," Henderson said. "You've got to let [Inter Miami coach] Tata [Martino] do his job."

The team also augmented its behind-the-scenes staff, hiring additional team fitness trainers, including one who had worked before with Messi and the Argentine national team, and investing heavily in high-performance personnel and in other areas the team felt could provide marginal gains, like food supplements that helped maximize performance.

There were also culture clashes that needed to be addressed. After two weeks of training, Henderson learned that nobody was cleaning Messi, Alba, and Busquets' cleats. In Miami, players usually just hosed off their own boots and hung them on racks to dry after training. At Barcelona, and even other MLS teams, cleats were typically cleaned for the player by equipment staff.

"The joke the first ten days is like 'I gotta clean my own cleats?'" Henderson said. "Like, 'I've never done that since I was a little kid.'"

Henderson went to the equipment manager to make sure he knew that he was to clean the star players' boots. The trio even offered to pay for the accommodation. The equipment manager pushed back. *If I clean their boots, all of the players will want me to clean their boots.* If you want to clean everyone's boots, go ahead, Henderson said. But make sure you clean the boots of our three-star players.

The idea that there couldn't or wouldn't be preferential treatment given to star players was farcical. It was commonplace across sports—at all levels. Sometimes there is a purpose to it. Academy players at European clubs were once given the "honor" of cleaning the boots and dressing rooms of the first team as "apprentices." It was about managing egos in both directions: up and down. At once giving younger players something to aspire toward, but also ensuring your best players are taken care of to the highest possible degree. Academy players didn't clean boots anymore, but teams looked for places to create similar dynamics that could help squeeze every ounce of motivation out of their group. Academy fields, for example, were placed at the far end of training facilities so younger players had to walk by the first-team fields they aspired to play on one day.

It was important, of course, to find a balance. Handing too much power or control to star players could backfire. And there were degrees of influence, too. With a player like Messi, Inter Miami was in uncharted territory. Finding that equilibrium would be a defining part of Messi's tenure in MLS.

For Henderson, it was all about building a club culture.

Some cringed at that world: culture. What did it mean, really? It wasn't something measurable. It felt like a nebulous, clichéd idea that got tossed around in either the best of times or the worst of times. Things were good, so the culture was good. The culture was bad, so change was needed. Henderson was not one of those people. He believed in culture, and he believed it was tangible. You could find some of that belief on his social media pages, where he'd often share "Pass it on" leadership quotes.

No person can be a great leader unless they take genuine joy in the successes of those they lead.
Once you become aware of what you are capable of achieving, you won't settle for mediocrity.
Discipline comes easy when you give yourself no other option.

For Inter Miami's sporting director, culture wasn't about platitudes or banality. It was a strategy aimed toward building a winner. In the midst of this massive transition, Henderson believed that building the right environment around the team—and at times creating a bubble around them—would allow the relationships within it to thrive, and that would lead to on-field success.

"It's so the first-team coaches, first-team players can come in and just feel like: I'm at peace here. I can enjoy it. I can work," Henderson said. "It's just little tiny details. And that's culture for me. What are all the little details that you can get right? It's not just words on a wall or people saying we have this. It's being able to deal with all the little things."

The first road trip showed how willing Messi was to blend into the culture of a team that, as Henderson predicted, was bonding over being on the inside of the Messi whirlwind.

* * *

In the lobby of the Renaissance in Plano, dozens of fans milled about, hoping for a Messi sighting after word spread that he was staying there. Some drove for hours with small kids for the slim chance they might get a shirt signed. One fan received a call from a cousin making an ice cream delivery to the hotel, who had his truck diverted to a different loading dock to accommodate the Inter Miami bus. After receiving the intel, the fan rushed over in time to see the bus arrive. A couple of hours later in the increasingly crowded lobby, he rolled up his sleeve to show off his Messi tattoo, which included the date Argentina won the World Cup.

The Renaissance was doing what it could to handle the commotion. Two police officers guarded the elevators. Security guards went from patron to patron asking for keycards to try to clear the space of anyone who wasn't a guest. One fan in an Argentina shirt smiled and pulled out his card; he purchased a hotel room for his family an hour before to maximize his odds of seeing Messi. Other savvy fans sat at the bar and ordered drinks to avoid the sweep.

One floor above them, Messi and his teammates trickled into the meal room and sat down for dinner.

There is a tradition across many sports that when a new player joins a team, he has to stand in front of the group and sing. It's a custom made famous on shows like HBO's *Hard Knocks*, where images of young NFL players squawking out R&B hits go viral.

Inter Miami instituted the ritual but extended it to all new signings, not just rookies or younger players. Stars who previously crooned in front of the team included Argentine striker Gonzalo Higuaín and French World Cup winner Blaise Matuidi. When Inter Miami arrived in Dallas, veterans Victor Ulloa and Yedlin started to craft a plan to see if they might be able to get Messi to take part. The two Americans decided to ask Busquets and Alba if they would sing.

"If I can get one of them to do it," Ulloa schemed with Yedlin, "I think we can get Leo to do it."

Ulloa approached Busquets, Alba, and Messi, who were sitting together. The superstar trio was initially skeptical, as expected. But Ulloa urged Busquets and Alba, especially. Eventually, Busquets decided he was game to sing.

"I'm going to do it," Busquets told his two former Barcelona teammates. "But you guys have to do it, too."

Alba and Messi doubted that Busquets would actually sing. The midfielder's nickname was "The Silent Conductor" because of his quiet demeanor and subtle brilliance on the pitch. Ulloa stood up and clinked his glass to quiet the group. Then, with the unflinching calm he displayed on the ball while under pressure, Busquets, the legendary No. 6, stood and performed a song.

Alba was next. The room turned into a party as the left back belted out the first two words: *Pobre diabla*! It was the reggaeton classic by Don Omar, and nearly the entire room knew the words and joined in.

By the end of Alba's rendition, the entire team was hollering and cheering and urging Messi to go next.

"We were all just waiting, seeing if it was ever gonna happen," recalled Kamal Miller, the Canadian center back. "He just got up like, 'Okay, screw it. I'm gonna do it.'"

Messi stood up on a chair.

"Hola," he said. "Soy Lionel Messi."

Hi. I'm Lionel Messi.

Then, he started to sing.

Al poco que debutó ¡Maradó, Maradó!
La 12 fue quien coreó ¡Maradó, Maradó!

It was a chorus usually bellowed by Argentina fans about Diego Maradona, the forward whose legacy Messi spent his life chasing.

It took just five seconds before the entire Miami team was on its feet. Players twirled napkins over their heads. The staff, seated at another table, joined the players, banging on their tables and cheering.

"There was so much noise," Ulloa said. "It was just like a huge party for thirty seconds until he stopped. And then we all just celebrated."

Two weeks prior, Ulloa was incredulous when he walked into the locker room and saw Messi sitting there. Players were unsure how to talk to their famous teammate. Now, the player who was once a poster on his wall was embracing the most ridiculous of team initiations.

"Nobody was gonna ever question it or look at him sideways for not doing it," Miller said. "But just how much he just wanted to be treated like one of the guys, and not be treated like Messi, it was just cool to see that side of him and that personality."

For so many reasons, Messi didn't need to do it. He wasn't a rookie or some no-name. He already earned the goodwill of the team. But Ulloa said he could see in Messi's face that he understood what the moment would mean within the locker room.

"It was another sign for the group of respect," Ulloa said. "It showed you the type of person he wanted to be, the type of player, the type of teammate. That he was willing to do it, it helped lower those walls. Like, he was ready to just fight with us. And obviously for us we were like, 'Yo, we're gonna leave it all on the line now for this guy.'

"It helped us. It's crazy for me to say this, but it translated to the field. We were willing to do anything and everything. That was such a small gesture, and it went such a big way within the team, within the locker room. Guys were like, 'Oh, this guy is just cool. He's another guy. He's our teammate.' It helped reduce that big gap where you're starstruck, you're a little bit hesitant on how to interact with him. It just helped build that trust and that brotherhood that we were able to create in such a short time."

The payoff came immediately.

The next day, on a scorching evening in Frisco, Inter Miami found itself trailing FC Dallas in the Leagues Cup Round of 16. It was their first deficit with Messi on the field since that opening night against Cruz Azul. Messi opened the scoring in the sixth minute, but FC Dallas answered with three consecutive goals to take a 3–1 lead with just twenty-five minutes remaining. It looked like Inter Miami's Leagues Cup run was going to end here. When young Benjamin Cremaschi scored in the sixty-fifth, it gave Inter Miami life, but another FC Dallas goal restored the two-goal deficit just three minutes later. Inter Miami pulled one back on a spectacular own goal in the eightieth. FC Dallas defender Marco Farfan headed a Messi free kick into his own net as if he were an Argentine teammate in a World Cup qualifier.

Five minutes later, the whistle sounded on a foul just outside the penalty area. It was on the opposite side of the box from his Cruz Azul free kick, but that meant it was an even better setup for a left-footed curler. Messi fixed the ball about five yards outside the top of the penalty area. FC Dallas put four defenders in the wall and another lying down behind it so that Messi couldn't sneak the ball beneath. He wouldn't need to.

Messi stung his free kick with far more power than he used in his debut. The ball zipped over the wall and past the outstretched arm of goalkeeper Maarten Paes. The ball kissed the underside of the crossbar and hit the back of the net to even the score at 4–4. The fans in Frisco, who previously cheered the home team's goals, erupted for Messi's wonder strike. Multiple Inter Miami players just put their hands on their heads in disbelief. Messi raced back toward midfield, waving his arm to try to rally his teammates before the end of regulation, but even he couldn't suppress his smile at the beauty of the goal he just scored, his seventh in four games.

"When you actually see it happening," Inter Miami goalkeeper Drake Callender said an hour later, "it's kind of surreal."

"It's not explainable, to be honest," Yedlin offered. "That's kind of what we were talking about in the locker room. It's just not human-like."

Inter Miami would win the game in penalties. The fight they displayed to come back in Frisco reinforced a belief within the team that, with Messi on their side, there was no match they couldn't win.

11

A Silent Champion, a Loud First Trophy

Amid the utter strangeness of Messi's first few weeks in MLS, where almost nothing felt normal in the world of American soccer, perhaps the oddest part was that no one heard from Lionel Messi.

On the day David Beckham was introduced to the media in 2007, he ran through a carwash of interviews with major national news networks. Zlatan Ibrahimović did Jimmy Kimmel's show. But other than his ninety-six-second message to fans on the night of his introduction and a three-minute postgame interview on Apple TV after the Cruz Azul goal, Messi did not speak to the press. At all.

There was no introductory press conference or even interviews with local or national outlets. Typically in professional sports, the absence of such media work would have been unthinkable. In this case, it only reinforced Messi's reputation for avoiding standard media obligations. On the one hand, it was hard to argue that Inter Miami needed the public relations boost. There was no avoiding the "Messi in America" story. On the other hand, anything Messi said was amplified around the world.

Beckham and Zlatan sold MLS to a wider audience. A silent superstar had a tangible impact on MLS's reach.

After wins over Charlotte FC and the Philadelphia Union in the quarterfinals and semifinals, respectively, of the Leagues Cup—both of which featured Messi goals—Inter Miami was set to play for a trophy seven games into the legend's U.S. sojourn. That was enough to finally break the silence. On August 16, 2023, an email went out: There would be a press conference with Messi the next day.

The tiny media space at DRV PNK Stadium typically fit seventy-five or so media members and staff, but it was clear there was overflow beyond that number for the press conference. It was still a far cry from the hundreds of journalists who lined up an hour before Messi's press conferences, staged in multitiered auditoriums, during the Qatar World Cup, where some reporters applauded the legendary attacker on arrival.

The stakes in Fort Lauderdale were a bit lower. But while the No. 10's legacy in that sense was secured, he now confronted a new responsibility as he finished his career on a different continent. Pelé came to the U.S. in the 1970s to be an ambassador for the sport. Beckham embraced the challenge to build American soccer into something lasting. Was Messi aware of the role he could play as a catalyst and advocate for the sport in the U.S.? *The Athletic*'s Felipe Cárdenas asked Messi the question at the press conference: Did he now carry a new pressure to make a lasting impact? Was it part of the reason he came to Miami?

Messi leaned forward into the microphone. "Well, my decision came down to a lot of things and a lot of issues, which my wife and I thought about and decided on together," Messi said. "My children were also a part of the decision; the family in general. And the truth is, I don't think about all that, what you're saying.

I simply came here to play, to continue enjoying soccer, which is what I've loved all my life. And I chose this moment, this place, for that reason, above all else."

Messi had been in America for four weeks, played six games, and scored nine times. In that time, he demonstrated the power of his presence. Matches were selling out despite inflated ticket prices. Apple was selling more subscriptions to MLS Season Pass. A team that languished in last place through the opening half of the MLS regular season was now playing for the first trophy in its short history. For Messi, those contributions felt sufficient.

He was not Beckham—nor had he ever been. Growing the sport in a foreign country was, in his eyes, beyond his purview. Messi's move to MLS wasn't about Hollywood or chasing further fame. It was about family and balance. Everything he had done since signing with Miami was indicative of those values.

Messi wasn't doing *Good Morning America*. He was going house shopping. He didn't pop in for postgame press conferences. Instead, he asked the club what local soccer team his kids could join. (Miami created new academy age groups and hired coaches so his sons could play for Inter Miami's youth teams, and soon Messi was photographed on the sidelines with his cup of maté at those games at the team facility.) His viral Marvel goal celebrations—from Thor to Iron Man, from Black Panther to Spiderman—were not for a sponsorship deal, as some suspected. They were for his kids.

"I've said this from the beginning: I chose this city. I wanted to be here," Messi said during the press conference. "It was a decision that I made over time. It wasn't a last-minute decision, which has made it easier on everyone. We are where we want to be. It was our decision. When I left for Paris it was something that I didn't want to do. I didn't want to leave Barcelona. That was a last-minute decision. I had to adapt to something new after living [in

Barcelona] my entire life. It was difficult, both from the sporting side and living in a new city. What's happening to me now is the complete opposite."

Messi had not come to be the agent of change for the sport, even if that was part of Jorge Mas's pitch to lure him to Miami—but it didn't mean he failed to understand the conversation that swirled around him.

The press conference ended after just eighteen and a half minutes. After the formal session, Messi had a few more rounds of sit-down Q&As. In an interview with ESPN, Messi was asked about whether, with the 2026 World Cup on the horizon, MLS might make a leap in soccer's global hierarchy. Even as he denied he was motivated by some sort of larger mission to change American soccer, he used his singular media session to put his shoulder behind one side of the debate within MLS.

"I think it has every opportunity to do so. That growth depends a lot on the league," Messi said. "It's an ideal moment to grow. There are important competitions upcoming that will be played in this country. It's time for the league to make that leap and finish growing, finish looking for what it's been seeking for a while. While it's been growing all this time, it's at a point where it can take another step. You have to take advantage, for the good of soccer in the U.S. and globally. Everything is in place here to witness top-level football because of the country, the structure—a lot of things. Hopefully MLS can continue to grow this way."

Like when he sat in Chris Henderson's office that day in July and asked what trophies he could win, Messi revealed some familiarity with the broader issues the league faced. One could only imagine similar conversations about MLS business probably happened in Mas's office. Messi's response also showed he understood what took MLS owners several years to figure out during the Beckham era: His presence could be a driver for change, but he wasn't the one behind the wheel. It would be up to the owners and Garber to leverage Messi's presence.

Just as he might be silent for eighty-nine minutes only to turn a game on its head with one action in the final seconds, Messi similarly knew how to pick a moment with his words. But what no one in the room that day realized was how discerning he would be in choosing his times to talk. The press conference and subsequent interviews that day would be his only media session with American journalists for the entirety of his first two years in MLS.

His aversion to media would be one of the few limiting factors of Messi's influence in America. It was frustrating for the advocates of change within MLS. His voice had the power to apply pressure on league executives in a way few others could. He understood the stakes and what had to come next for the league. Giving an interview at the right moment might be able to swing the debate or public opinion. And while he might be the face of the league, Messi was not going to be an active spokesman or advocate.

For better or for worse, the rest of his talking would come on the field.

* * *

When Messi took a touch with his left foot in the twenty-third minute of the Leagues Cup final at Geodis Park in Nashville, approximately twenty-eight days, twenty-three hours, and twenty-eight minutes had passed since his free kick beat Cruz Azul in Fort Lauderdale.

He would need just three more touches and three more seconds to score his tenth goal in an Inter Miami jersey.

It was a credit to Nashville SC that Messi had been limited for the previous twenty-two minutes and fifty-five seconds. The Argentine wandered the field, looking for a way to impact the game. He moved from the left wing to the right, then dropped deeper into midfield. When he finally found some space, running on to a ball deflected by a sliding Nashville defender, he needed just four touches to open the scoring in Miami's first tournament final. The first touch controlled the ball, the second pushed him into the space past Nashville defender Walker Zimmerman, a U.S. World Cup starter, and the third somehow allowed Messi to keep clean possession as Zimmerman got his own foot to the ball. The fourth was what Messi did best: a shot powered through the space between converging defenders and into the upper corner.

"There are moments in the game," Nashville coach Gary Smith would say later, "where he's just unplayable."

With Nashville SC minority owners Reese Witherspoon and Giannis Antetokounmpo watching, the home team pulled level in the second half. Eventually, the inaugural tournament title came down to penalties. It took eleven rounds for Inter Miami to emerge as champion—Messi finished his easily—with goalkeeper Drake Callender scoring and then saving the decisive kicks.

Messi sprinted to celebrate when Callender made the winning save. And after his teammates tossed him into the air, when the team crowded on stage to lift the trophy, Messi removed his captain's armband.

The night before, during the pregame press conference, DeAndre Yedlin marveled at Messi's effort to ingratiate himself into the locker room. "He could have come in and said, 'I'm doing stuff my way and this that's how it's gonna be,'" Yedlin said. "But he's come in and completely mixed in with the group, mixed in with the old guys, mixed with the young guys, everything just like a regular player. Obviously I had a ridiculous amount of respect for him as a player before I played with him, but I think more so now is just even more respect for him as a human being. He's an unbelievable human being."

Now, on stage, the Argentine sought out Yedlin and put the

armband on the former Newcastle defender, who served as Inter Miami's captain before Messi's debut, so they could lift the Leagues Cup trophy together. The gesture of respect to the team's veteran leader could have been easily overlooked, but it was a public example of how Messi approached his first weeks in the U.S.

* * *

For the ownership group, the trophy was the culmination of an up-and-down odyssey.

Beckham announced in 2014 that he was triggering his option to bring an expansion team to MLS. It took another four years for him and the Mas brothers to confirm that Inter Miami would happen. When the team finally launched in 2020, COVID-19 delayed its ability to play in front of fans. The 2021 cheating scandal caused further disruption. In the tunnel beneath the stadium, as players made their way into the locker room wearing goggles for the champagne-filled celebration, Beckham and Jorge Mas approached a group of reporters.

"We hope it's the first of many trophies," a beaming Mas said. "It was a spectacular night. . . . I think tonight is a vindication of the work that we've put into this project."

"People keep saying [it's like a movie]," Beckham added. "Every time Leo scores one of these goals, every time [Busquets] makes one of these passes, every time Jordi [Alba] makes one of these runs, people say 'Is it a fix?' And it's the biggest compliment anyone can give these players because it is like a movie. You watch these players play, and it's emotional watching them because everything about their play is beautiful, everything about their mannerisms is beautiful, everything about them as individuals off the pitch is beautiful. So when they play, it's emotional."

Inter Miami and Messi's Leagues Cup triumph felt both like the end of a short story and the beginning of something bigger.

The Argentine's first weeks in the U.S. could be tied perfectly in a bow with Inter Miami's first trophy. It didn't matter that the Leagues Cup, however long it lasted, would be remembered almost entirely for the fact that Messi and Inter Miami won the 2023 crown. Or that in the pecking order of MLS trophies, it came dead last. At that moment, it felt enormous. The games were all sold out. Fans were dishing out hundreds of dollars for tickets. Messi was the story of the summer.

For the first time in a long time, MLS had real cachet in the American sports marketplace. There was a belief this could actually go somewhere.

It was now up to MLS owners and executives to do something with it.

* * *

Messi's first weeks proved he was, without question, a revenue amplifier, capable of filling stadiums from coast to coast. He could sell subscriptions, jerseys, and sponsorships. But if that's all he was, then his time in MLS would fall far short of what it could have been.

The temptation to pursue the easy short-term payoff was enormous. But the danger of chasing those highs was evident within weeks of Miami's trophy celebration in the Music City.

Messi left Inter Miami's regular-season game against Toronto FC on September 20 with an injury and missed the next month, including a U.S. Open Cup final that Inter Miami lost to the Houston Dynamo. In his absence, Inter Miami couldn't claw its way out of the last-place hole they had been in when Messi signed, and they missed the playoffs after finishing fourteenth in the fifteen-team Eastern Conference.

As the campaign came to a close with its biggest star absent from the postseason, MLS faded from national headlines. Reality was setting back in, and questions started to turn toward the future. Messi somehow overdelivered on early expectations that began with Mas's reference to holy water at his fan presentation. More than that, the next three years would bring three major international tournaments to the U.S.: the 2024 Copa América, the 2025 FIFA Club World Cup, and the 2026 World Cup. The planet's attention would be on American shores.

As Messi said, it felt as though it was "time for the league to make that leap."

"That is the pressure that we're under," MLS commissioner Don Garber said in his annual state of the league address before the Columbus Crew defeated Los Angeles FC in the 2023 MLS Cup final in December. "To ensure, as everybody's paying attention to us, what is the product that we can deliver?"

Five days later, league stakeholders met to discuss the way forward.

* * *

MLS owners wheeled their suitcases into a meeting space set off from the wood-and-glass lobby of the 1 Hotel in the shadow of the Brooklyn Bridge on the morning of December 14, 2023. The hotel smelled of eucalyptus, cedar, and oakwood. It exuded luxury.

The league might have still been in start-up mode, as Garber claimed, but the setting was a reminder that it was bankrolled by one of the wealthiest collections of owners in sports.

As the billionaire owners mingled adjacent to the conference room where they'd soon gather, the atmosphere was noticeably more circumspect than at their meeting in Washington, DC, five months earlier, fresh off Messi's arrival. That was due in part to Garber successfully moving the goalposts on any important structural changes during his speech a few days before.

"It's really: What do we want to be by 2027?" he said, setting the horizon beyond the home 2026 World Cup that had long been touted as a springboard moment for the league.

It was also because any decisions about on-field evolution had already been made a month earlier in Dallas, where a small group of owners known as the sporting and competition committee met to discuss new initiatives.

Jorge Mas spent the better part of four years trying to get a seat on that committee, which was considered the most influential in league circles because of its sway over roster rules and regulations. Messi became his golden ticket. The gathering in Dallas was his first meeting. Mas attended but then did what no one expected: he mostly stayed quiet. Other than offering an update on Messi's commercial impact, Mas listened more than he talked. He wanted to see how business was done.

"I observed, I saw, and I read the room," Mas said.

Co-chaired by FC Dallas owner Clark Hunt and Vancouver Whitecaps owner Greg Kerfoot, two of the league's more conservative owners, the committee debated. They analyzed. They discussed. They asked for more studies.

What they didn't do was make decisions.

"We are dealing with the Messi effect, which really didn't kick in until the last forty percent of the season," Hunt said a week prior to the year-end board meeting. "I think that's opened a lot of eyes and created a lot of very good discussion. We need to really understand how that's going to impact the league long term. How it's going to grow not only our fan base in the stadiums each weekend, but also how it's going to grow our media subscriptions through Apple. So those are the kinds of things that we're studying.

"I don't want to signal what kind of timing we might be on, because I honestly don't know. But we are having substantive conversations about ways that we can move the league forward."

Mas walked into breakfast that morning already knowing what the few reporters in the lobby would find out later that afternoon: MLS was making no rule changes in the wake of Messi's debut season. At least, none that would have any sort of noticeable impact on their on-field product.

Despite the league's caution, Mas retained his belief that the winds were shifting. New members were joining the committee. Conversations were changing.

"I think this is going to move in the right direction," he said a few months later, reflecting on the changing conversation. "There has been a shift in the mindset. It will happen."

When the New York meeting ended, owners filed out and headed to their waiting black cars. None of them stopped to comment to the three media members who were in attendance.

Like the players who come from Europe and South America, MLS owners were exempt from the type of scrutiny other leagues get. The NFL's annual owners meeting drew hundreds of media members. Owners spoke in media gaggles. League executives held multiple press conferences to discuss league business and announce changes. The NFL event created a week's worth of news cycles in what should have been the deadest period in the league's offseason.

MLS made decisions—or didn't—with almost no one paying attention.

MLS executive Nelson Rodriguez offered brief remarks on some experimental rule changes, including a ten-second clock on substitutions. Any substantive shift would have to wait. How long of a wait was still to be determined.

It was a surprise to even the most cynical of MLS observers. The pressure Garber talked about just a few days earlier felt absent. The league never moved fast when making changes, but slow-playing Messi's time in Miami carried enormous risk.

The league's decision-makers were betting that the Messi bump would last long enough for them to go through their usual exhaustive process. But that risked missing the moment entirely. And while MLS executives might point to how long it took for Beckham-in-LA to alter the face of the league, it was an imperfect comparison because the league now faced far more competition. To act like it was business as usual required ignoring that it was an unprecedented time for MLS and American soccer.

While league stakeholders decided to take their time and study how to move forward, the rest of the American soccer landscape was continuing to accelerate and innovate without them.

MLS couldn't afford to fall further behind.

12

The Biggest Star, but Bigger Competition

One day after Lionel Messi curled his free kick into the upper corner against Cruz Azul in July 2023, lifting MLS temporarily into the global spotlight, more than sixty-five thousand people filled Lincoln Financial Field in Philadelphia to watch Brighton & Hove Albion, a team from a seaside resort town in Southeast England, take on London giants Chelsea FC in a friendly match.

On the opposite side of the U.S., another seventy thousand packed into the Rose Bowl to watch Spanish titan Real Madrid play Italy's renowned AC Milan. A few days later, over eighty-two thousand were in attendance for an exhibition version of Spain's *El Clásico*, the historic Real Madrid-Barcelona rivalry, at AT&T Stadium in Arlington, Texas.

Even as Messi's first weeks with Inter Miami dominated headlines, more than six hundred thousand fans streamed into stadiums to watch the first edition of the Premier League's Summer Series, a six-team tournament, and the Soccer Champions Tour, which attracted some of the biggest names in European football. Every game was a friendly one with absolutely no stakes. Ticket prices soared as high as $600 each. Still, the stadiums were full.

This is what MLS was up against.

Anyone wondering whether Messi might make soccer popular in the U.S. was missing the point. Soccer was *already* popular in America.

Bars were filled with fans watching Premier League soccer every weekend morning. Liga MX games pulled in millions of viewers, and the Mexican national team sold out stadiums across the country. New soccer fans were pulled into the game by television shows that romanticized the history and traditions of the English game. An American studio show was generating global buzz, but it was focused on the UEFA Champions League.

MLS was a small sliver of a wide-ranging American soccer landscape. Messi was its chance to claim more of its own market.

Sure, in some markets—Portland, Seattle, Orlando, Cincinnati, and St. Louis—one could venture into the right pub or neighborhood on a game day and know an MLS team was playing. But for all their success drawing fans to stadiums, MLS teams retained more of a cult feel: passionate followers, but little mainstream resonance.

The next step in MLS's growth was taking the eleven million people who came through the gates in 2023 and leveling up into a league that was on millions more screens—and minds—across the country. It was more than a dilemma; it was arguably existential. Because just as MLS evolved enormously between Beckham's arrival and Messi's, the soccer landscape in which it operated was unrecognizable from the early 2000s.

Soccer's popularity exploded. So, too, did access to the sport. American fans could watch just about any league around the world with the click of a button—and those other leagues mastered how to attract an audience to their product.

It may have started with the Premier League in 2013, but it was accelerating beyond that now.

* * *

Ten years after NBC began its partnership with the Premier League, one of the English competition's biggest personalities stepped behind a broadcast desk in Istanbul with a Champions League medal hanging from his neck.

There was no manager more closely linked with Lionel Messi than Pep Guardiola. They were two geniuses whose ascension happened together, hand in hand, in Barcelona from 2008 to 2012. Messi had already made his debut for La Blaugrana when Guardiola was promoted to head coach in 2008, and he had already racked up more than thirty La Liga goals and scored his first *El Clásico* hat trick more than a year earlier—the first of forty-four three-goal games in a Barcelona shirt. But it was under Guardiola that the Argentine blossomed into the best player in the world.

Guardiola's *tiki-taka* teams overtook global football with their spellbinding soccer. With Messi, Sergio Busquets, Xavi, and Andrés Iniesta, all masters on the ball, Barcelona danced around teams, hypnotizing opponents and fans alike with their passing and movement. The ball pinged between each player as if it were on a predetermined path—and yet with an unpredictability that beguiled opponents. Guardiola's men executed passes and patterns that no one else saw. Even the best teams in the world were chasing shadows against them.

"They do mesmerize you with their passing," legendary Manchester United manager Alex Ferguson said after Barcelona beat his side in the 2011 Champions League final. "And we never really did control Messi. But many people have said that. In my time as manager, it's the best team I've faced."

Messi himself would say that playing under Guardiola at Barça was "when I grew most as a footballer." The Spaniard was quickly regarded as one of the greatest managers of all time, and undoubtedly one of the most influential on how the game was played.

It was no small feat, then, when an hour or so after winning his latest Champions League in June 2023—a weight off his shoulders after a dominant seven years with Manchester City, which included five Premier League titles—Guardiola approached American network CBS's postgame desk and took a microphone. He shook hands with the cast of characters around him: host Kate Scott, former Manchester City defender Micah Richards, former Liverpool F.C. midfielder Jamie Carragher, and French legend Thierry Henry, as well as longtime Manchester United goalkeeper Peter Schmeichel.

"There is so much respect for you at this desk," Scott told Guardiola. "That's all I've heard all evening long."

"It's the funniest show in the Champions League this season," Guardiola responded, with the relieved grin of a man having just added to his legacy. "On Twitter I follow sometimes, some moments."

Americans had long been the outsiders on global football's biggest stages, striving to secure the respect of the rest of the world—whether it was coaches and players trying to make it in Europe, or MLS fighting to be a more impactful player in the ecosystem. Now, Guardiola was lauding an American soccer broadcast after winning a Champions League final.

In the football world, it might as well have been an endorsement from the pope.

CBS's coverage of the Champions League—anchored by non-Americans, yes, but on a distinctly American-style television show—showed that the popularity of soccer hadn't just spread beyond MLS at home. Now the reputation of American soccer abroad was growing beyond its domestic league, too.

* * *

The clip from March 2023 lasted thirty seconds and contained fewer than fifty words, but it racked up more than ten million views across social networks.

Jules Breach, guest-hosting CBS's postgame *UCL Today* show, asked a seemingly innocuous question about the 2006 Champions League, which was the last time three Italian teams reached the quarterfinals.

"Who knocked Juventus out that year?" Breach offered.

"Hello," Thierry Henry replied, raising his hand with a mock scowl, lifting his hands and wiggling his head as if he were to say, "Who else?"

"Who scored in that game?" asked Micah Richards, quick to play along.

The camera zoomed in on Henry, who sent a side eye toward Richards with eyebrows raised.

"Who assisted in that game?" Richards put forward again, this time leaning back and mimicking Henry's pursed mouth.

Henry raised his eyebrows again as his cohosts laughed.

"Who got man of the match in that game?" Richards asked, the pitch of his voice rising.

Henry leaned back with one more overexaggerated frown.

It was the type of viral moment that has made the show so popular. When Henry joined CBS's Champions League desk in 2021, the inclusion of the French World Cup winner and Arsenal legend added gravitas. One of the great players of his generation, Henry possessed a different level of fame than anyone else on set. But on *UCL Today*, the usually reserved Henry started to show more and more of his personality. His sense of humor, and at times a willingness to open up, added another layer to the network's coverage.

"Thierry just brings a level of star power that is different," Scott said. "You just see it with every single player that comes on for one of the interviews live from the stadium, they're all excited to speak to Thierry, they're all excited to hear Thierry speak to them. And Thierry is very good at creating those very, very human moments."

Henry was the first big star to follow David Beckham to MLS. He signed with the New York Red Bulls in 2010, when Beckham was still playing in Los Angeles. The French forward helped the Red Bulls win the Supporters Shield in 2012, the club's first league trophy, and left as its all-time assist leader. But there is no doubt he has become more recognizable and impactful in growing U.S. soccer as a CBS pundit than he had marauding the left wing position for New York for five seasons—or coaching the Montreal Impact for a year.

"Sometimes people come up and say, 'Thierry, can I take a picture?' And I'm like, 'Yeah,' expecting, 'I love Arsenal, Barcelona, the national team,'" Henry reflected in an interview with *The Football Weekend*. "And it's, 'Oh, I love your show on CBS.'"

That phenomenon was a nod to CBS's impact and its ability to create viral moments. It was also an acknowledgment that MLS's reach was limited in comparison. When people think of Henry, they think Arsenal, Barcelona, France—and now CBS. Despite five years in the league, MLS was relegated to a footnote.

More Americans were growing up with far more access to soccer, and MLS was betting that its product would grow with them. But the league's competition for that next generation of fans was growing, too.

In the early 2000s, soccer fans could tune in to ESPN2 to watch two Champions League games on a Tuesday or Wednesday afternoon. Now, just like NCAA basketball's March Madness, fans on a Champions League game day could pull up CBS's streaming service on their second screens at work, or on their smart TVs at home, and watch every single game from UEFA's top club competition. And they did—in droves.

This was the risk of MLS moving too slowly to adapt. In just a few short years, CBS's Champions League coverage was able to break through in a way MLS hadn't—at least not outside of Messi's undeniable draw.

* * *

When fans found CBS's coverage, it highlighted another issue MLS faced back at home.

The quality of the U.S. men's national team (USMNT) was increasingly being measured by the number of its national team players on Champions League teams. Christian Pulisic's success at Borussia Dortmund from 2016 to 2018 and then his $73 million move to Chelsea FC in January 2019 opened a pathway for young American players to move overseas.

A golden generation of American men's players developed out of that trend, with many of them moving to top clubs in Europe. In 2021–22, a record twelve American players were in the group stage of Champions League. Some developed in MLS academies: Tyler Adams, Weston McKennie, Chris Richards, Tim Weah, and Gio Reyna, among others. Notably, only one of those five—Adams—actually played in MLS.

The growing number of Americans abroad reinforced a long-standing debate within USMNT circles. Former U.S. coach Jürgen Klinsmann butted heads with MLS commissioner Don Garber in 2014 when he publicly encouraged American players to leave MLS and seek a higher level in Europe. For some fans, Klinsmann's public declarations justified their opinion about the American domestic league. Too many MLS players in the national team were bad. Players had to go to Europe for the U.S. men to succeed.

National team performance wasn't correlated to the number of national team players based in MLS, but it didn't matter. It was yet another example of the perception gap that MLS wrestled with.

As the U.S. prepared for the 2026 World Cup, the negativity around MLS remained. U.S. coach Gregg Berhalter, a former national team defender who spent almost his entire playing career in Europe, was bashed by some U.S. fans as an "MLS coach" because the majority of his coaching experience was with the Columbus Crew. When he was fired, Argentine coach Mauricio Pochettino was brought in. The former Tottenham, Chelsea FC, and Paris Saint-Germain coach insisted MLS's quality was better than people believed, pointing to Messi's presence as evidence. If the greatest of all time played in MLS and still changed games for Argentina, surely American players in MLS were good enough, too.

But Messi was Messi. He was different.

Fans still pushed for more European-based players in the U.S. team, and the early on-field results under Pochettino showed that the U.S. still needed to lean on those players.

The debate around the U.S. national team upped the stakes for MLS around the World Cup in 2026. The tournament, and MLS players' participation in it, was critical to resetting the narrative around the league. The World Cup was an opportunity to change the narrative around the league—if MLS could get its ducks lined up to utilize it as such.

Changing that perception was especially important as soccer's place in the streaming battles increased access to the European leagues against which MLS was being compared.

* * *

As streaming became more of the viewing norm, soccer evolved into a hugely important part of the broadcast rights equation because networks realized that soccer fans, long starved of regular coverage, would pay to watch their favorite leagues.

Networks moved quickly to snap up properties. NBC put a majority of Premier League games behind its Peacock paywall and saw viewers follow. ESPN added the German Bundesliga and Spain's La Liga. MLS, of course, bundled all of its local, national, and international rights, but by the time it came to market, many of the networks already had soccer properties. Eventually, MLS found a partner in Apple.

CBS pushed even more chips into the game. It created a twenty-four-hour streaming soccer channel, *Golazo Network*, and acquired rights beyond the Champions League, signing deals with, among others, the English Football League, which included the country's lower professional divisions; Italy's Serie A; Concacaf tournaments, including the Nations League and World Cup qualifiers; Brazilian and Argentine domestic leagues; the National Women's Soccer League (NWSL), the thriving and growing women's soccer league; and USL, which makes up the second and third divisions of American pro soccer. It launched *Morning Footy*, a daily show driven by American talent that gave fans an everyday product focused on soccer.

The network understood that it had to find creative ways to pull viewers behind its streaming paywall. *UCL Today* was the main draw, but the answer involved getting its product where younger people consumed their content. CBS leaned heavily into social media.

Pete Radovich, who launched and executive-produced CBS's Champions League coverage, said that from the very first Champions League show, he asked Rush Sawhney, the director of social media, to sit in the control room so that they could pull and post clips quickly and seamlessly.

"You've got to be where you can see me, eye to eye, because you're going to be a part of what we need to do," Radovich told Sawhney. "You're our press release. You're our promotion. You're our commercial. I need you to put out our best stuff so that people see what's going on and then they come in."

The formula worked.

UCL Today alone pulled in 1.6 billion social media views during the 2022–23 season. That number rose the following year, and the network's full slate of shows racked up more than 4.2 billion views in 2023–24. More importantly, Champions League became a top-five leading driver of subscribers for CBS's streaming service, Paramount+, which launched in 2021.

The virality drove the show's power in the domestic soccer market—and its global resonance. While CBS's Champions League coverage is unavailable outside the U.S., the social media clips made it internationally known. Even Pep Guardiola followed it and watched on Twitter, for goodness sake.

CBS's push into streaming and social media came at a time when every league was chasing younger digital viewers. MLS similarly leveraged Messi to do so, partnering with TikTok in 2024 to broadcast a playoff game with a "Player Spotlight" that focused just on the Inter Miami star, the first live-streamed game on the app. The broadcast peaked with 125,000 concurrent viewers and drew more than 6.4 million viewers total, a record for the largest live audience for a U.S. sports event on TikTok.

MLS saw its TikTok follower count soar past five million, with 65 percent of those followers based outside the U.S. In discussions with MLS stakeholders, it was clear they interpreted the league's higher popularity with younger viewers as a sort of safety net of growth. MLS's relative youth compared to other leagues meant it was in the early phase of a generational process of building a fanbase. In the eyes of those stakeholders, the data backed up that fans now growing up with MLS saw it more favorably than their parents did. They pointed to the league's efforts on TikTok, the Apple deal, and a partnership in which live games were aired on EA Sports FC Mobile, the uber-popular video game, as evidence that it was reaching those fans.

It was a trap MLS consistently fell into: measuring progress against itself.

Attendance up? Quality improved? Fine. But if the league's competition was sprinting ahead, the gap was only getting wider. Growth didn't matter if MLS was still losing ground to England and the Champions League.

MLS could pat itself on the back, but CBS's Champions League coverage wasn't just reaching the next generation of viewers; it was also being endorsed by the next generation of the game's star players.

When it started its coverage in 2020, the American network was last in line for postgame interviews. Five years later, the show's global popularity meant players requested CBS ahead of other international networks. That's how, in spring 2025, the American show landed a postgame interview with one of the game's brightest young talents, Barcelona teenager Lamine Yamal, a player some were starting to speculate could challenge Messi's legacy.

When Richards asked Yamal if he had seen the show, the Spanish star replied quickly.

"Yes, yes," he said, his braces showing as he smiled. "I've seen it on TikTok."

Even with geoblocking, social media delivered the show directly to Yamal's pocket. That was the new ecosystem in which entertainment existed.

MLS's Messi Spotlight Cam might have been pulling in viewers on TikTok, but the league still faced difficult questions about its future. What happened when Messi was gone and CBS's Champions League TikTok page was still serving up Yamal, "the next Messi," for young American fans to watch?

The challenge on television and social media was difficult

enough for MLS to navigate. But the company that brokered UEFA's rights with CBS saw the natural next step in leveraging soccer's globalization as going beyond streaming to phones.

They wanted to bring Yamal into MLS's backyard.

13

A Gulf Too Wide

The lasting impact of the buzz around Lionel Messi in MLS was already being put to the test after the league's three-month offseason.

Going into the 2024 season, Messi's presence in Miami wasn't dominating new cycles as it had the previous summer, but it was still generating lucrative opportunities. Inter Miami was intent on cashing in. It scheduled a three-week preseason tour on which Inter Miami would cover more than twenty thousand miles and circumnavigate the globe—to El Salvador and Dallas, to Saudi Arabia and Hong Kong, and to Japan and back to Fort Lauderdale.

Now, some 7,500 miles away from home, stark realities for MLS, Inter Miami, and Messi were setting in. It was February 1, 2024, and the final whistle had just sounded on Inter Miami's second game in Saudi Arabia, a 6–0 drubbing by Al Nassr.

A shirtless Messi stepped into the middle of a silent postgame locker room at the Kingdom Arena in Riyadh and looked around at his teammates.

"Guys," Messi started, the emotion in his voice rising. "We can't play like that. We can't *not* compete. It's unacceptable."

Six days into the junket's Asian leg, frustrations were boiling over.

One player, a bright young winger named Facundo Farias, was lost for the season with a torn anterior cruciate ligament (ACL) suffered during the opener in El Salvador two weeks prior. Players hardly felt like getting on a plane to travel across the world for meaningless friendly games, even less after the biggest draw of the tour—one final meeting between rivals Cristiano Ronaldo and Messi in an Al Nassr versus Inter Miami showdown, billed as "One Last Dance"—was off the table. Ronaldo was injured and wasn't going to appear in the friendly.

"When Ronaldo got hurt, it was just like, why are we even going now?" Inter Miami defender Noah Allen recalled.

Miami lost its first game to Al Hilal 4–3 in an entertaining if error-filled contest three days earlier in Saudi Arabia. Messi, who played eighty-eight minutes in that loss, approached the second exhibition in Riyadh dealing with muscle fatigue. Inter Miami initially published a team sheet absent its star's name, only for the Argentine to emerge for warm-ups wearing cleats and a jersey, much to the crowd's delight. The club deleted its first post and released a new graphic featuring Messi's name on the list of substitutes.

From the street, the Kingdom Arena looked a bit like a giant Neiman Marcus at an American shopping mall. Built in just 180 days, in part to host these games, the stadium included a high wall of suites looming over one sideline and fans stacked around the other three. The vertical design lent a gladiator-style feel to the arena. A block away, the Riyadh Season festival was in full bloom: A Ferris wheel shined in purple neon, a roller coaster rumbled past every other minute, and a mini-Vegas–like sphere lit up the skyline. It was yet another facet of the show the Saudi league was putting on for the world.

Inter Miami was the first guest at the Kingdom Arena, and it had not gone well for the American side.

For eighty-three minutes, Messi watched as Al Nassr ran through his team. The Saudi side led 3–0 at halftime. The rest of Miami's Big Four spent more time throwing their arms in the air in frustration than creating anything with the ball at their feet. Al Nassr added another three goals in the second half.

After every tally, the stadium's video board cut to a split screen. The eternal rivals weren't sharing the field, but they remained the center of conversation. On one side, Messi leaned back in his seat on the bench; on the other, Ronaldo's Cheshire-cat grin told the whole story. The crowd roared with its approval each time. And each time, Messi seemed to recline farther, making it a bit harder for the cameras to get a good angle.

Miami's star No. 10 played the last seven minutes, fulfilling a contractual obligation. His cameo added additional insult to the lopsided affair. Messi's name was now in the box score of a 6–0 defeat.

When Inter Miami returned to its locker room, a frustrated Messi walked into the center of the space. Then he started to speak. For nearly three minutes, he excoriated the group. His teammates had treated the match too much like the meaningless friendly it actually was. But Messi knew the result would be reported as anything but that.

"We should want to play these games," Messi seethed to the defeated locker room. "If you guys don't wake up, we'll go home now."

As he entered his twentieth season as a professional, Messi had long ago learned that every appearance on the field was an assessment, validation, or challenge to his legacy. That scrutiny extended to the club and league he represented. So, yes, the players' frustrations about the tour were valid. Yes, they were four games into the preseason and playing an opponent in midseason form. Yes, jumping through time zones on a globe-trotting odyssey was far from an ideal way to prepare for the MLS campaign. And yes, the Saudi clubs had a distinct economic and thus quality advantage over Miami, even with its household names. But none of that mattered.

To Messi, the ninety minutes that had just unfolded lacked any sort of understanding by his teammates that Inter Miami represented something bigger now. He was right. Around the world, this wasn't a preseason game. It was taken as an assessment of MLS. Inter Miami didn't have the luxury of an off night or the leeway to shake off its preseason rust. Not if it was going to be Messi's team. There was an obligation to meet a certain standard, to always want to win every game.

Always.

He ended the verbal lashing with a message: "From here on out, we're going to win everything."

There were ten months left in the 2024 season. Winning everything was an impossible mandate, but it was the standard Messi had long imposed—on himself as much as on the teams around him. Anything but striving to be the best was unacceptable, but that didn't fit within the structure of MLS. Messi didn't care.

Inter Miami assistant coach Javier Morales stood next to Messi, tasked with translating his words for the team's English speakers. The forty-four-year-old Argentine and former MLS star felt blessed to be on the staff coaching Messi. He had friends getting their UEFA or U.S. Soccer Pro coaching licenses. None of them was getting near the education he was by working with the greatest to ever play the game.

"What I'm learning from this," Morales said, "is a treasure for me."

He discovered, though, that translating for a legend wasn't an easy task. It wasn't just about finding the right words. There was pressure to accurately capture the emotion.

"But in this case it was easy," Morales recalled. "Because he was talking from his heart.

"From my point of view, he is a person that is insatiable. He is never gonna get full of winning or titles, because that is in the way that he lives his life. He doesn't recognize a difference between a La Liga or MLS title. Of course, he *understands* the difference, right? But he wants to win. It doesn't matter where he is.

"We're talking about a player that has won the World Cup and won more titles than anyone in the world. He wants to win. If he is playing a small-sided game in training and he doesn't win, he's pissed. Or if he loses playing cards, or two-touch or whatever. He always wants to win.

"It's the thing that feeds him. But at the same time he is never going to get full."

While Messi fumed about the performance against Al Nassr—a result Inter Miami's own coach had seen coming—MLS buried the score on its website and moved on. An event that had been given top billing all day and then aired live on Apple TV's MLS Season Pass app suddenly had no meaningful presence beyond a meager 135-word recap on the site.

It betrayed the same lack of understanding that set Messi off in the locker room.

MLS was reverting to habit: showcasing the league's positives while ignoring or burying the flaws. But there could be no putting your head in the sand when the greatest player in the history of the game was involved. The spotlight was simply too big.

"Al-Nassr humiliate Messi's Inter Miami as Cristiano Ronaldo watches from stands," blared *The Guardian*'s headline. The *Miami Herald* called it a "Nightmare in Saudi Arabia."

As Messi's second MLS season started, the losses in Riyadh revealed cracks in a partnership that initially felt like a perfect fit. Messi had won everything. He had nothing left to prove. But he was still prepared to compete and strive to be the best. He knew no other way.

Meanwhile, MLS, a league with so much still to prove, remained noncommittal about how it might match and leverage the ambition that Messi in Miami represented.

* * *

The night before the dismantling by a Ronaldo-less Al Nassr, Inter Miami coach Tata Martino sat at a table in an air-conditioned meeting room in the St. Regis Riyadh.

This was Martino's third stint coaching Messi. The sixty-year-old, who also hailed from Rosario, managed the No. 10 at Barcelona in 2013–14 and for Argentina from 2014 to 2016. Martino was the perfect hire for Inter Miami. Appointed during the period after Messi announced he was signing but before he arrived, the Argentine wasn't just well versed on all that comes with managing Messi; he also won the MLS Cup with Atlanta United in 2018 and was comfortable with the league's growth, its quirks, and crucially, its limitations.

A legend of Messi's childhood club, Newell's Old Boys, Martino, with his perpetually mussed gray hair and sweater-over-the-shoulders look on the sidelines, came across as professorial, a teacher at his best in smaller seminar classes. He was reflective and thoughtful around the media, measured but targeted—and with a disarming smile and quick wit.

Almost immediately upon sitting with reporters in Riyadh, Martino sensed that after the 4–3 loss two nights before to Al Hilal—a club that had also wooed Messi—some reporters from his home country didn't fully grasp the gap in spending and depth between the teams his Inter Miami were playing as a primer for a regular season that was still three weeks away.

The Saudi friendlies were meaningless on paper, but Martino

knew the relentless Messi-Ronaldo narrative would draw the eyes of the footballing world.

The veteran manager was already frustrated that MLS sat on its hands after the 2023 campaign, content merely to reap the benefits of Messi's presence. Messi's and Inter Miami's triumph in the 2023 Leagues Cup tournament proved that the world's greatest player could transform a team that had been the worst in MLS when he arrived. His immediate success was the rising tide that lifted all boats, which reflected how the single-entity league was designed to function. Stadiums sold out wherever Inter Miami went. New sponsors rolled in. And yet nothing had changed.

The Saudi Arabia tour, though, opened MLS to a new type of scrutiny.

While global soccer had long ago pierced the bubble MLS originally built around its league, the opportunities to measure itself against outside opponents were sparse. MLS's struggles in the Concacaf Champions Cup provided the only real measuring stick. Messi was changing that in real time. This preseason tour was now pitting Inter Miami against real global competition. And as much as it might help close the perception gap, it could just as easily expand it.

The exhibitions offered huge commercial benefits, but poor results also might stoke global criticism of MLS's progress by an audience that didn't stay abreast of—or care about—the league's cautious and complex roster rules. Martino understood realities that the league remained reluctant to acknowledge. The talent disparity was just as big as the perception gap. Inter Miami would have to punch well above its weight to win in Saudi Arabia. He wanted to make sure reporters at the St. Regis, most of whom traveled from Argentina, understood what they would be watching.

The Saudi Pro League was two years into its disruption of the global football economy, dumping billions of dollars into the

World Cup around the corner, the signing could reset the league's place in both the global and domestic sports landscape.

After Argentina's World Cup victory in Qatar, however, few believed Messi would want to go to MLS. A return to Barcelona seemed to be his destiny. If he left Europe, there was too much money on the table from Saudi Arabia for him to land anywhere else.

As rumors swirled about where he would sign, Messi decided to tell the world his decision on his own terms.

4

"Tome La Decisión . . . "

It was a little after 4 P.M. on June 7, 2023, when the journalists from two daily Barcelona newspapers, Albert Masnou from *Sport* and Fernando Polo from *Mundo Deportivo*, were led to an interior patio on the ground floor of Messi's Paris home.

The reporters walked through the front door, past the main stairwell and a dining room, and into an indoor-outdoor space where Messi sat on a gray couch, with white- and camel-colored throw pillows just to his right. He wore khaki shorts and a white Louis Vuitton t-shirt with blue snow-capped letters that read DO A KICKFLIP. A microphone was clipped to his shirt as birds chirped loudly in the background.

The interview was ostensibly about where Messi would play next, but the next twenty-five minutes with Masnou and Polo were as much about where he wasn't going as anything else. To understand why Messi was picking his next team, it was important for him to make clear where things stood between him and his former club.

For months, it seemed Messi was set for a return to Camp Nou, the home of FC Barcelona. He spoke with his former teammate, Xavi Hernández, then the coach at the storied club, about a potential return. The legendary Spanish midfielder even publicly transfer market to woo some of the game's biggest names. It began with Al Nassr's deal with Ronaldo, which paid the former Manchester United and Real Madrid legend more than $200 million per season. The Portuguese superstar was one of several high-profile players—some on the back ends of their careers, others entering or in their prime—enticed by Saudi largesse, and the government's aim to generate positive publicity through sports, commonly called *sportswashing*.

The Saudis chased Messi too when his contract with Paris Saint-Germain expired in summer 2023. The Argentine already had a deal with the kingdom that paid him $25 million over three years as a pitchman for Visit Saudi, the government's tourism authority. In the end, he turned down a $1.5 billion offer from Al Hilal and opted for MLS. Messi's presence in Saudi Arabia for the preseason friendlies with Miami, then, became a sort of appraisal of his decision.

But Martino knew it wasn't a fair fight—and he wanted to make sure the reporters (and their audiences in Argentina and the U.S.) knew it, too. The veteran manager was also savvy enough to understand that any message he sent in the media might reach the ears of the decision-makers on Fifth Avenue.

"Which team has the best chance of competing? [Which is] better? One that has three designated players and three young designated players, or one that has eight players under the age of thirty at a very good level competing in the league?" Martino asked, rhetorically.

He rattled off a list of in-prime stars who recently left top European leagues to sign for each of Miami's two Saudi opponents. Al Nassr had seven players valued north of $10 million and a squad valuation of around $147 million.

"MLS does not have that possibility," Martino said.

Inter Miami arrived in Riyadh with a roster built around Messi and a trio of his former Barcelona teammates: Jordi Alba, Sergio Busquets, and the newly arrived Luis Suárez. The Big Four had a combined age of 142. Messi was Inter Miami's lone player valued above $10 million, and his $50 million valuation represented more than half the team's roster value. Chris Henderson, Martino, and the ownership group had done their best to bolster the rest of the squad, but options were limited by MLS's restrictive salary rules.

The Beckham Rule inarguably elevated and transformed MLS's trajectory, but it also set the league clattering down a path of constrictive roster regulations designed to put governors on team spending and to address specific areas that league executives determined needed enhancement. Understanding those regulations provided an important insight into how the pursuit of internal balance conflicted with global competitiveness.

One of the most prominent mechanisms was TAM (targeted allocation money), which was introduced in 2015 as a tool to attract players that would boost the top third of the roster behind the DPs. Initially, TAM worked. The level of the league increased as teams signed more good players. (A novel concept!)

MLS executives loved to point to the rule as a sign of the league's flexibility and ingenuity, but after a decade, it was more of an obstacle than innovation. Over the years, teams got more TAM, but the restrictions on how it could be used were still linked to MLS's internal salary cap rather than the rising cost of players in the global market. It became a microcosm of how MLS failed to fully grasp that it was just one cog in a global ecosystem. As one American soccer executive explained, it would be like the U.S. government acting as if it were setting the price for oil. By 2024, TAM no longer effectively served its purpose and what it was created to address. Instead, it functioned mostly to sign average players at market rates—and even then, only if they could be brought in on a free transfer or very low transfer fee. (Jordi Alba was signed as a TAM player, but he was an exception. He took the lower salary because Barcelona was still paying him millions in deferred salary.)

A newer MLS roster designation launched in 2021, the under-22 initiative, incentivized teams to buy younger players who could potentially be resold later. The rule discounted transfer and loan fees from salary cap hits for up to three players under the age of twenty-two—but still capped those players' maximum salary so as not to throw off competitive balance. Inter Miami went all-in on u-22 players to supplement its squad, spending tens of millions on transfer fees to try to reinforce the team around Messi. But signing younger players at the salary levels dictated by MLS meant navigating greater learning curves, which typically translated to a less immediate on-field impact.

For those in the club sporting departments working on signing players, the limitations of the rules were frustratingly obvious. Now, the team trotting out on the field around Messi in Saudi Arabia was a glowing, blinking arrow pointed at MLS's shortcomings for the entire world to see.

"I like MLS a lot and I think it always works to improve, but there is a part of freeing up the rules a little to be able to go out and compete in the world," Martino said. "If not, it becomes a bit complex when you have aspirations of being competitive in the Concacaf Champions Cup and eventually in a Club World Cup."

The limitations of MLS's spending, both how much teams could invest and the restrictive manner in which they were allowed to build their rosters, were best demonstrated by the league's lack of success in regional competition—just three of twenty-seven Concacaf Champions titles through 2023, and only one in the previous twenty years.

It was obvious, too, in the collective valuation of its players.

Despite having thirty teams—ten to fourteen more than other leagues—and thus several hundred more players, MLS's inventory of players was valued at $1.5 billion by Transfermarkt, a site that estimated global player value. That would rank eighth in Europe, behind Portugal and Holland, but just ahead of Turkey, Belgium, and Russia.

Martino wasn't thinking just about the two preseason friendlies in Saudi Arabia. He was looking around the corner at the 2025 Club World Cup and the continued globalization of the sport.

"I don't know if the moment is now, if it will be based on what is coming, on the number of competitions that there are, but it is clear that for [MLS] to continue evolving [change must come]," Martino said. "I don't know when, but it's going to happen, and it's not like it's going to happen without restrictions. It will be gradual and as the league believes it has to happen, but I have no doubt that to go out and compete in the world—for what the league is today, MLS, in its internal competition, has done enough—but to go out to compete in the world, it obviously takes much more."

* * *

While much of the soccer world had a protectionist outlook on Saudi's aggressive assault on the transfer market—one that threatened to upend the sport's hierarchy and challenge the standing of some European leagues already struggling in a post-COVID environment—MLS's sturdy single-entity business model and formidable ownership group, operating in a commercial market that was the envy of the world, became a selling point for why the American league, despite its failings, also had clear strengths.

It was the reason why, a year before, Garber had shrugged off the Saudis as a threat.

"I've seen it happen with China, and I wasn't concerned about that any more than I'm concerned about what's happening in

Saudi Arabia," Garber said, alluding to a similar push from the Chinese Super League a decade earlier that had flamed out spectacularly. "It's quite the opposite. The fact that we can spread the power and influence of professional football around the world, I think, gives us all in emerging markets an opportunity to think that it's not just about Europe, right?"

MLS's growth strategy was essentially the antithesis of the Saudi League's bombastic build-out. But if the Saudi threat highlighted the strengths of the MLS business model, the preseason contests also spotlighted the weaknesses of MLS's sporting design, which remained slow to react to its standing in the global marketplace. The gulf in quality reflected an inability to adapt and lift the ceiling on its core product.

Inter Miami's top-heavy squad wasn't a flaw in MLS's system. It was very much the design. Martino, like many soccer experts working in the league, knew it left MLS teams woefully short of truly competing on global stages. Al Nassr made that clear.

He hoped these types of results, especially with Messi drawing the attention of worldwide audiences, would force the league to confront its flaws.

But MLS's ethos had to change.

Messi only had so many years left on the field. With the Club World Cup coming next summer, MLS risked missing a vital chance to change minds and enhance its reputation. The results in Saudi Arabia were a warning shot.

MLS had to evolve—and to start telling a story as compelling as the competition.

14

From Richmond to Wrexham: The Power of a Story

A few days after the drubbing in Riyadh, Michelob Ultra unveiled a Super Bowl ad featuring Lionel Messi.

As Messi dribbled on a beach, it wasn't U.S. men's national team star Christian Pulisic or any other global soccer star who made a cameo. Instead, it was a character immediately recognizable to a large chunk of the Super Bowl's 127 million viewers: Ted Lasso. Or, at least the actor who plays him.

"That's Messi," an actress in the ad says.

"What? Do you mean Leo?" Sudeikis replies. "We go way back."

That the two biggest soccer personalities to speak to Super Bowl viewers were Leo Messi and Ted Lasso spoke volumes about the different ways soccer was reaching a wider audience in the U.S.—and how much further the game had to go for American players, and its own domestic league, to resonate similarly.

The creation of a character who would introduce millions to the Premier League—and to the traditions and romanticism of the sport itself—began with a limited budget, a few treatment pages, and a list of potential actors.

NBC wanted to make a splash in the promotion of its new

sports property in 2013, but the broadcast rights cost more than expected, and little money remained for a marketing campaign. With less than $500,000 to work with, NBC's marketing director, Bill Bergofin, was tasked with creating a campaign that could elevate the Premier League while acknowledging that, for many Americans, it was a foreign product (and not just because it was British).

"We said, 'Billy, this is all we have,'" NBC's Jon Miller said. "You weren't going to be able to buy a lot of off-channel media. You weren't going to be able to do a lot of things. So he said, 'Let's get really creative.' And about two months later, right around the holidays, he comes in to see me and he says, 'The guys at [ad agency The] Brooklyn Brothers have this idea.'"

The four-minute-and-forty-second-long YouTube video dropped on August 3, 2013.

A mustachioed Jason Sudeikis sat in an office wearing a white polo shirt and a white Tottenham Hotspur visor. He held a phone to his ear.

"Hey, how ya doin'? This is Ted Lasso," he said. "I'm the new head coach of the Tottenham Hotspurs, and I'd like to talk to the queen, please."

The concept, a clueless American football coach in the Premier League, would grow from one video short into the most-streamed original show on television, a cultural phenomenon that brought soccer into living rooms it otherwise never would have penetrated.

"It is kind of a Trojan horse," said Brendan Hunt, the show's co-creator and writer, who also plays Coach Beard, during an interview from the writers' room where he was working on the fourth season, set to premiere in 2026. "If we make people care about these characters and these characters care about soccer, then we're gonna trick you into caring about soccer."

Ted Lasso almost didn't exist—at least not in the way he's known now.

The first idea centered on a British expat in the U.S., and the first call went to John Oliver, then a snarky football-loving correspondent on *The Daily Show*. He wasn't available. Bergofin and the ad agency flipped the idea on its head. Why not depict an American out of his depth in the UK? It wasn't until the fifth try that they landed on Jason Sudeikis, who was wrapping up a ten-year run on *Saturday Night Live*. He said yes.

"Dumb luck that those people weren't available," Bergofin told the *Snap Decisions* podcast in 2023. "Otherwise we never would've gotten to Jason Sudeikis."

But, as Ted Lasso would later quip on the show: "As the man once said, 'The harder you work, the luckier you get.'"

Sudeikis, Hunt, and Joe Kelly, who performed together years earlier in the improv group Boom Chicago, an American troupe based in Holland, convened at Sudeikis's house in the Hollywood Hills. One afternoon around Sudeikis's pool, the trio did bits and workshopped jokes until they had outlined their idea for the shoot.

"We went over there and we shot the commercial," Hunt said. "There were no scripts, really. We kind of had a vague idea of what we're going to do. We knew the setup. It was really slapdash."

Not long after shooting about fifteen minutes' worth of scenes, NBC posted the first video on YouTube.

"We just lobbed it out there—no money behind it, nothing," Bergofin recalled. "Went to sleep and when we woke up there were already one million hits on it—and in 2013, one million hits in less than twenty-four hours on YouTube was not a common occurrence."

The concept took off, and NBC brought the campaign back the following year. This time Lasso was on set with Rebecca Lowe and worked as a color commentator with NBC's top play-by-play voice, Arlo White. It again attracted a huge audience.

Almost immediately, Bergofin and others realized they had a potential sitcom on their hands. In early 2015, Sudeikis, Kelly, and Hunt gathered in Sudeikis's Brooklyn apartment and wrote a pilot, then mapped out multiple seasons. NBC green-lit the show, but it eventually died on the vine.

Then, in 2017, Bill Lawrence, the producer who created *Scrubs*, got involved. NBC signed a co-production deal with Warner Brothers, and Apple TV picked up the series. On August 14, 2020, almost seven years exactly after the character debuted on YouTube, *Ted Lasso* aired for the first time on Apple TV.

This version of Lasso was far different from that of the NBC commercials. The original version was "a sketch character" who "was not supposed to survive any further," Hunt said. The Apple TV Lasso was earnest and likeable—goofy, but genuine.

Amid the pandemic, Lasso's upbeat optimism resonated with viewers. The 2020 season received twenty Primetime Emmy nominations and claimed seven awards, including outstanding comedy series and three acting wins, including one for Sudeikis.

Ted Lasso became soccer's pop culture crossover vehicle. Somehow, a fictional coach had more pull than MLS.

A gourmet food company sold *Ted Lasso* biscuits. People bought AFC Richmond jerseys (the fictional club Lasso coached). Fans traveled from around the world to visit the London pub featured in the show.

The show was so popular that when an American coach named Jesse Marsch was hired to coach Premier League side Leeds United in 2022, the Wisconsin native answered a question about the stigma against American coaches by referencing the fictional coach.

"I think there probably is a stigma [for Americans in England]," Marsch said. "I'm not sure *Ted Lasso* helped. I haven't watched the show, but I get it. People hate hearing the word 'soccer.' I've used the word 'football' since I was a professional football player. I think more and more in the States we're adapting to what the game here is in England and our connection with what this league is and what the culture of the sport is in this country. . . .

"All I can say is the only way I know how to do things is to go all-in, give everything I have to believe in who I am, to believe in the people I work with, and to try to maximize what we are every day."

Then Marsch paused: "So, that sounds like Ted Lasso, I think. From what I have heard."

Ted Lasso set multiple streaming records on Apple TV and was consistently the service's most-watched show. The spring 2023 season, its third, had more viewership than any other original streaming series that year, per *Variety*, despite Apple TV's smaller subscription base compared to rival services. From the show's debut in August 2020 to its season three finale in 2023, *Ted Lasso* generated almost 25 billion viewing minutes, per Nielsen.

Lasso introduced soccer to a wider audience—or at least to more fans outside the typical American soccer bubble—in a way that even Messi might not be able to match.

"I think the *FIFA* video game has done far more. I think the success of our women's national team in the United States has done far more. But if we have added to that conversation, then so be it," Sudeikis told *USA Today*. "I know when we were pitching the show, I would say this show is as much about soccer as *Rocky* is about boxing. And yet it has, in a sneaky way, made people care about this fictional team in this very real story. As someone who knew very little about the game before doing the commercials, much less the television show, you can't help but fall in love with [soccer]."

It was prescient that Sudeikis mentioned the enormous

popularity of the standard-bearing women's national team. When it was announced *Ted Lasso* was returning for a fourth season, set for 2026, the actor confirmed the coach would take charge of a women's team.

It was fitting that a character created to highlight Americans' *lack of* interest in soccer was returning in an area where American dominance lifted the sport's popularity at home. When people thought of American soccer, the four-time World Cup–winning U.S. women's national team was often the first thing that came to mind.

That narrative pivot came at a time in which women's sports were finally being elevated within the wider sports landscape—a movement set in motion due in part to the U.S. women's national team's success and equal pay fight. Unlike on the men's side, the NWSL was being built on the strength of being a world leader in the sport. Its challenges were different. The NWSL was trying to hold off global competition, rather than play catch-up. In the midst of that fight to stay on top, the NWSL was in a similar growth phase to what MLS had undergone from 2009 to 2024. It was expanding rapidly, and its valuations were shooting up. An expansion team in Denver paid a $110 million fee to join the league in 2026.

In the context of its own growth, MLS looked at the NWSL's health as complementary. The primary audiences for the two leagues were different. (For example, the overlap between ticket purchasers of the Seattle Reign and Seattle Sounders, owned by the same group, was less than 10 percent.) Many MLS owners had already invested in the NWSL, and amid discussions around its own future, the league was studying how it might become more involved in women's soccer. The growth of the NWSL was seen as raising the overall American domestic soccer consumer market. Realistically, though, the league was another viable and attractive product for fans to watch at home—and they were choosing to do so in increasingly big numbers in MLS markets like Kansas City, Washington, DC, and in 2026, Denver, which sold fifteen thousand season ticket deposits and already has a waitlist for more.

Now, *Lasso* would give women's soccer global growth an even bigger spotlight.

But the Apple TV show wasn't the only place pop culture's impact was being felt in the real world.

While the show sparked support for a fictional team, there was another program on a parallel path that created new soccer fans, too. It was a reality TV show with a heavy dose of celebrity juice that turned Wrexham AFC, a small, historic Welsh club playing in the dregs of the English pyramid, into one of the most popular teams in the U.S.

* * *

To borrow another quote from *Ted Lasso*, "There is a story in every game, and the story is not always the score."

It is here that MLS struggled the most to match its competition. Many of its clubs were still building their traditions, and in the single-entity structure, team identities often came second to the league brand. But the history and traditions of soccer are where its competitors, and shows like *Ted Lasso* and *Welcome to Wrexham*, found the opening to win new fans.

Sudeikis and the creators of *Ted Lasso* liked to say that the show wasn't a soccer show, but rather an ensemble comedy. Ultimately, though, it was the drama of the sport that formed the spine of the storylines. (Spoiler alerts ahead.) Richmond was relegated from the Premier League in season one. It won promotion in season two. The most romantic parts of the sport, and the jeopardy of promotion and relegation, created the drama around which every other plotline could exist and evolve.

Actor Rob McElhenney recognized those same dramatic

overtones when, during the pandemic, he found himself pulled into a soccer documentary called *Sunderland 'Til I Die*, which is an all-access look inside one of England's historic clubs and its downfall amid mismanagement. McElhenney recognized an opportunity. He bought into Wrexham, which was founded in 1864 and considered to be the third-oldest football club in the world. Wrexham once played in the European Cup Winners' Cup, but it had dropped into the National League, the fifth tier of the English pyramid. McElhenney recruited Hollywood star Ryan Reynolds for financial heft, and they set out to get Wrexham promoted up the English football ladder. And they were going to document it all.

McElhenney did it not because he loved the sport—that part would come later. It was because he understood that sports is storytelling. It is the greatest unscripted drama on television, which is why leagues and properties command such enormous media rights fees.

McElhenney, the creator of the comedy series *It's Always Sunny in Philadelphia*, saw that European football connected that on-field drama to real off-field stakes. He could put faces—and really a whole town—to the live-and-die feeling that many global soccer fans understand. The coal and mining city in northeast Wales, whose hard times were symbolized by the failures of its historic soccer club, had all the ingredients. It was an underdog tale. The chance at promotion and the risk of further demotion—a sports construct popular throughout the world, but a drama that was foreign to closed and static American leagues—offered an extremely sellable narrative arc.

Welcome to Wrexham's first season focused less on the club than on the characters in the city. It pulled viewers into the story. It made them care about a soccer team on the other side of the Atlantic they had never heard of before.

"Sports are kind of meaningless to me unless I know what is at stake for someone," Reynolds told *The New York Times* in 2022. "What a player overcame to be there. What a club means to a community. If I think about the movies that made an impression on me, is *Field of Dreams* a movie about baseball? Not really. It's a movie about a father and son trying to connect. That context is what pulls you in."

McElhenney said he learned about *Ted Lasso* before it aired during a 2020 conversation with Sudeikis and thought he had to rush to get his show out first. In fact, they complemented each other. The fiction of *Ted Lasso* soft-launched the idea of promotion and relegation to an American audience. *Wrexham* introduced the real-world stakes.

Never mind that McElhenney and Reynolds put their thumb on the scale and turned Wrexham from a down-on-its-luck underdog into the heavy-spending favorites of lower-division football. By then, the audience felt committed to the people in the show.

It's why Wrexham could stage its own U.S. summer tour and play friendlies against true global brands like Chelsea FC and Manchester United, and why twenty-five thousand people showed up to exhibitions against MLS reserve teams.

"I know there are a lot of people that are very cynical about this because it's on TV and why should people care about this small team, but Wrexham and that TV show and its rise up the ranks is doing as much for soccer in America as probably MLS is doing right now," American soccer commentator Alexis Guerreros said on CBS's *Morning Footy* show.

That might be a bit hyperbolic, but what *Wrexham* did was similar to *Ted Lasso* in that it brought soccer into living rooms where it might not have existed otherwise. As of 2025, *Welcome to Wrexham* continued to be FX's most-watched unscripted series ever.

It was reaching the new fans MLS was hoping to attract, which illustrated just how many entry points American fans had now to the game. Yes, MLS was the best domestic option if you wanted to consume men's professional soccer live. But you could flip on matches from better leagues around the world throughout the weekend. And now soccer was crossing over into the entertainment space.

"Inarguably, because of more soccer entertainment media—not just us, but *Wrexham* in a huge way—Messi's arrival is in a different context of time than Pelé's," Brendan Hunt said. "Whether that bears fruit, we'll see."

There were no signs, at least not yet, that it provided a lift to MLS. But the popularity of *Ted Lasso* and *Welcome to Wrexham* would inspire the path forward for another American league.

* * *

The Wrexham story resonated in part because it gave viewers real stakes. It was something MLS struggled to deliver.

There was perhaps no question with more lasting power around MLS than when or if the league would ever adopt promotion and relegation. For years, MLS commissioner Don Garber had a go-to answer for the query that was some variation of: "It is not happening in MLS any time soon."

It didn't make business sense for MLS. Owners paid expansion fees in hundreds of millions of dollars. Local governments committed funds to help build stadiums. That money, public and private, wouldn't be there without the guarantee that it was for a first division team.

Furthermore, the idea that those owners, who had committed

far more money to the sport, could potentially drop to a lower division, where the money was smaller and the landscape far less stable, was a nonstarter.

"I think we have been very, very clear in our views on our structure, and the fact that our structure has worked very well in helping to develop our league, and the sport in the U.S. and in Canada," Garber said in 2016.

But no matter how vociferously MLS rejected the idea, hope for pro-rel (promotion and relegation) in American soccer continued to linger around the sport. The push started on the fringes of American soccer's most niche supporters, buoyed by an internet hashtag, #ProRelForUSA. The frequent users were so fervent and unrelenting in their views that the entire movement became regarded as an unserious annoyance as much as anything else. But as the popularity of the Premier League boomed, and with shows like *Ted Lasso* and *Welcome to Wrexham* baptizing new fans into the underdog stories of promotion and relegation, the support for pro-rel in America was mainstreamed.

It highlighted another major challenge MLS faced in how to update and upgrade its on-field product.

The jeopardy created by pro-rel was undeniably enthralling. Every game counted. Moving up or down, as documented brilliantly by *Wrexham*, could shape the fortunes not just of teams but of entire towns. MLS lacked that sort of consequence in its games.

MLS playoff games were by far the most entertaining part of the product because those games were win or go home. But that drama didn't translate to the regular season. Without fear of relegation, there was no significant consequence for losing. Qualifying for the playoffs was the measuring stick for success, but MLS's structure currently had eighteen of its thirty teams reaching the postseason. It sucked the life out of the league's regular season, which was the bulk of its inventory. In Messi's first season in MLS,

Sporting Kansas City opened the season with no wins in its first ten games . . . and then made the playoffs! It was a tough sell for MLS that every game mattered when early-season losses could be so inconsequential.

MLS leaders insisted that competitive balance made the league better because every team had a chance to win on any given day, but it had not yet found a way to reproduce the stakes of promotion and relegation.

It wasn't the only American soccer league trying to crack the problem.

* * *

The USL, which operated second- and third-division leagues in the U.S. but ran independently from MLS, began considering the possibility of promotion and relegation as it looked to add more games of consequence to keep fans engaged—and as a way to differentiate itself in the market.

USL leadership didn't think of the league as MLS's competition. They knew they couldn't compete with MLS's billionaire owners. But MLS clearly felt differently. It took aim at USL when it launched MLS Next Pro, a third-division developmental league. USL leaders believed they had to do something substantive to protect their standing as the established league for smaller American soccer markets.

Paul McDonough, the former Inter Miami sporting director, who was at that first meeting with Jorge Messi in Barcelona in 2018, was handed a multi-season ban by MLS for his role in the Blaise Matuidi cheating scandal. After more than a year out of pro soccer, he landed at the USL and galvanized support for the organization's push toward adopting pro-rel.

"With everything going on in the country and the opportunities for growth with the World Cup, it just doesn't make sense to stay the status quo," McDonough said. "[Pro-rel] was the best idea. This is what people talk about, what people want. It's kind of always been talked about. For our fans, the narrative has always been this is something MLS can't do and we can do—and we can align with the rest of the world."

It was not an easy path to convince USL owners that pro-rel was the right answer.

McDonough pulled a vote off the table at a board meeting in the summer of 2023, just ten days before Messi made his historic debut. The league borrowed MLS's tried-and-true line: It continued to "study" the possibility. Less than two years later, McDonough announced that USL would launch a league that met U.S. Soccer's standards for Division 1. That would give USL leagues with Division 1, 2, and 3 sanctioning. It set the stage for another vote on adopting pro-rel.

In March 2025, during a pair of four-and-a-half-hour drives to and from a college visit to Florida State with his seventeen-year-old son Cameron, McDonough lobbied owners who were on the fence. A few days later, USL owners held a vote via email. Only three of thirty-eight owners voted against pro-rel. One abstained.

For years, #ProRelForUSA was a fringe idea. Now, USL was making the leap MLS leaders long said they never would.

Among the loudest celebrants was Rhode Island FC owner Brett Johnson, who owned Ipswich Town FC and helped steer it from England's third division back into the Premier League in 2024–25. Johnson spent years advocating for pro-rel to be adopted in the U.S.

"The journey with Ipswich Town and seeing what [promotion] does to revitalize a club and, by extension, a community. I truly believe there's nothing like this construct in sport," Johnson said.

The work to get there, however, was far from over for the

USL. It would likely take a change in U.S. Soccer Professional League Standards to allow teams to move up and down between divisions; for example, first division standards require a fifteen-thousand-seat stadium. There are multiple recent Premier League teams that would be unable to meet that requirement.

"There is a ton of work that needs to be done," McDonough said. "And you know the big bad wolf [MLS] is lingering out there that is going to try to stop you, no matter what they say."

But McDonough said the decision to embrace pro-rel has significantly changed the level of interest in USL, both at home and abroad. Teams were inundated with calls from sponsors and partners upon news of the vote, he said. Several markets, buoyed by the potential boost from pro-rel, announced new stadium projects.

Perhaps most intriguing, however, was that USL began hearing from multiple teams in Europe, as well as in the Premier League, about interest in launching or buying teams to be a part of the new venture.

If that happened, "I think it changes the look of everything," McDonough said.

That a lower-division American league was suddenly a potential player in altering the domestic soccer market spoke to just how rapidly the landscape was shifting.

The European teams saw value in USL as a pathway to get their hooks further into the American marketplace at a much cheaper rate than buying into MLS, where the most recent expansion fee was $500 million. It could give them access to young American players and also provide another touchpoint for fans. And, if pro-rel took off and USL's popularity grew, there was significant upside.

The USL wasn't the only emerging pathway for European teams

to increase their touchpoints with American fans. It was the reason why more owners were starting to believe MLS had to go on the offensive to better defend its place in the market. If the league acted decisively enough, it had the power of a commercial and sporting icon to aid its efforts.

15

The Booming Business of Messi

Hong Kong Stadium lies in a valley, the curved roofs drawing your eye to a tropical forest that rises three hundred feet above the south stand.

Throughout the previous two days, any image of David Beckham that flashed on the outdated screen in the picturesque arena prompted a huge ovation. Beckham had filled this stadium before—when he played with the LA Galaxy in 2008. Now, he was back with the team he co-owned to put on another show.

Inter Miami flew to Hong Kong the morning after the embarrassing loss in Riyadh. The team hoped for some sort of positive momentum with the regular season just around the corner.

On the night before the scheduled friendly between Inter Miami and a Hong Kong all-star team, forty thousand fans packed into the stadium for a glimpse of Messi during an open training session. The walk from the closest train station to the stadium felt like a game day—people spilling off the sidewalks into the street, traffic blocked, police officers directing traffic. Once inside the venue, the hordes of supporters screamed and cheered Beckham and his star player when Inter Miami emerged from its locker room. Messi jogged lightly with his teammates at the start of the practice but otherwise did not participate. He did, however, take part in a clinic with kids after the team's short training.

Another forty thousand people returned for the next day's friendly. During pregame ceremonies, the crowd cheered when Beckham hugged Hong Kong singer G.E.M., and then again when he playfully tousled the hair of a small child who approached for an autograph.

Some two hours later, when substitutes rose to warm up and the legend who thousands of fans had come to see wasn't among them, the crowd that had been so adoring of Beckham and the Inter Miami contingent began to turn on its guests.

Messi didn't emerge for warm-ups despite being announced as a substitute. Instead, he exited the tunnel next to Luis Suárez a few minutes before kickoff wearing a pink hoodie, black pants, and white sneakers. It was clear the Argentine forward wasn't going to play. Pitchside and in the suite level, panic was setting in. About fifteen minutes before the opening whistle, the game's organizer, Tatler Asia, was notified that Messi was unavailable due to injury.

"The rest of the first half was spent trying to find solutions for Messi to play, talking, and moving around the pitch," Tatler Asia chairman and CEO Michel Lamuniere later recounted to *The Athletic.*

Even more than a year later, there was no topic that got people at Inter Miami to shut down more quickly than asking what went wrong in Hong Kong. Jorge Mas insisted it was simply "bad communication." Messi was feeling the same discomfort that nearly kept him out of the Al Nassr game a few days earlier in Riyadh. A scan indicated some swelling in his adductor. Some sources within the club said the frustration around a tour that prioritized commercial benefits over the sporting side came to a head. The decision was made to shut down Messi to ensure his health for the regular season. Who ultimately made that call was unclear, but it wasn't communicated to the organizer, which led to the announcement to the crowd that Messi was available.

After a lackluster start to the game featuring many of Inter Miami's reserves, Messi and Suárez stayed glued to the bench as reserves loosened up along the sideline during the second half. The unrest started to build. While Busquets and Alba took the field with a half hour left to play, Messi remained a spectator. By the seventieth minute, fans began to chant the Argentine's name. As the last few minutes played out, the crowd chanted for a refund. Boos rained down at the final whistle.

The jeering continued during an awkward trophy ceremony following Inter Miami's 4–1 win. On the field, framed by the lush green topography to his left, Beckham took the microphone to try to calm the crowd. It may as well have been the sword he was falling on.

"I would like to say thank you very much. I hope one day we can be back to entertain you," Beckham offered.

The crowd booed lustily.

In another attempt at extending an olive branch to fans who were so adoring of their longtime idol a couple of hours earlier, Beckham, dressed impeccably in his Inter Miami–branded suit jacket, took a lap around the field while waving at supporters. Several stood and raised middle fingers.

Before Beckham could reach the safety of the stadium tunnel, G.E.M., the pop star with more than eight million Instagram followers, stepped to the microphone wearing Inter Miami's pink jersey. Out of respect, Beckham stopped to watch the performance. As he locked his hands behind his back, the singer started into a dramatic, somber rendition of "Amazing Grace."

Beckham tried to stand stoically, but his face betrayed his indignation.

The embarrassment of the moment was only the beginning of

the Hong Kong headache. What was supposed to be a celebratory promotional trip had become a global public relations nightmare. After Inter Miami coach Tata Martino apologized in a press conference for Messi's absence, explaining that Inter Miami's medical team deemed playing Messi too risky due to the adductor issue, the Hong Kong government issued a statement.

"Regarding Messi not playing the match today, the Government, as well as all football fans, are extremely disappointed about the organiser's arrangement," the statement read. "The organiser owes all football fans an explanation. The [Major Sports Events Committee] will take follow-up actions with the organiser according to the terms and conditions, which includes reducing the amount of funding as a result of Messi not playing the match."

What could have been a localized public relations disaster escalated three days later when Messi was deemed fit and played for thirty minutes in a friendly in Tokyo.

Chinese newspapers declared Messi's absence in Hong Kong a direct insult and a political move, even tying it to Jorge Mas Canosa's history of lobbying against Fidel Castro's Cuban government. A few weeks later, despite social media posts from Messi meant to calm the backlash, friendlies that Argentina's national team had scheduled to play in China were canceled due to what was perceived as Messi's direct snub.

That his absence from a preseason friendly could spark a global incident reinforced the extremes of his popularity.

From a purely sporting perspective, the preseason tour was an abject failure. And yet, despite the losses in Saudi Arabia and the tremendous controversy during the tour's Hong Kong leg, the globe-trotting itinerary was, like all things Messi touched, a massive commercial success for Inter Miami. The games netted \$25–\$30 million in revenue, putting the MLS club in the same stratosphere as some of the biggest global soccer brands in terms of preseason payouts.

"That's mind-blowing to me," said Inter Miami chief business officer Xavier Asensi, who started his career working for Barcelona. "Because that's an MLS team that did that."

The revenue represented just a small fraction of Messi's commercial impact on Inter Miami and MLS. Evidence of his vast appeal could be found just a couple of miles from where fans booed him in Hong Kong.

* * *

The main display on the ground floor of the Adidas store a few blocks away from famed Victoria Harbour did not feature Real Madrid, soccer's most historic brand, or Manchester United, a commercial colossus. Instead, customers were greeted with the pink shirts of Inter Miami as they entered the store.

It indicated that an MLS team had achieved a measure of global renown not seen since Beckham joined the LA Galaxy.

Within twenty-four hours of Messi's pink jersey going on sale, it became the highest-selling of any player who had changed teams in the history of Fanatics, the sports merchandising company. It surpassed rival Cristiano Ronaldo when he rejoined Manchester United in 2021, Tom Brady when he signed with the Tampa Bay Buccaneers in 2020, and LeBron James when he switched to the Los Angeles Lakers in 2018.

Messi's shirt sold out everywhere, and within minutes.

Online retailer soccer.com told CNN that it sold half a year's worth of Inter Miami jerseys in just one day. Within twenty-four hours of Messi's interview announcing his intention to sign with Inter Miami, Adidas received half a million requests from suppliers for their jerseys.

It set off a race to produce the jerseys.

"It's not like it was white and we had inventory we could repurpose," Adidas executive Tor Southard told *The New York Times*.

One MLS team owner was told that Adidas directed three factories to produce nothing but Inter Miami jerseys to satisfy the demand.

A Social Science Research Solutions sports poll found that Messi was the first soccer player to rank as Americans' favorite athlete for a quarter of a year in the thirty-year history of the survey, coming in first in the fourth quarter of 2023. Inter Miami, meanwhile, ranked as the fourth-favorite soccer club behind the Big 3 of Real Madrid, Barcelona, and Manchester United. Inter Miami owner Jorge Mas called it proof of concept: MLS could break through if it had the ambition to do so.

When people talked about the global reach Messi provided, this was what they meant. For an MLS team to resonate to this extreme was unprecedented. The Argentine immediately turned a five-year-old club into one of the most popular brands in the world. It was a phenomenon no one was ready for—except Inter Miami itself.

* * *

Asensi, a forty-two-year-old executive born and raised in Barcelona, joined Inter Miami in 2021 after a decade with the Catalan club. It obviously wasn't a coincidence. Mas anticipated that his efforts to land Messi would be successful, so much so that, upon arrival, Asensi began to structure all of Inter Miami's commercial deals with escalator clauses and bonuses linked to the possibility that the team might sign a player who won five or more Ballon d'Or awards. Only Messi and Ronaldo have that many.

"If it doesn't come, nothing happens, right? But if it comes, you can benefit from it. You don't have to renegotiate," Asensi said in an interview at Chase Stadium a few weeks after Inter Miami returned from Asia. "What people say is that luck is when opportunity meets preparation. When the opportunity of your lifetime comes, you have to be ready and try to capitalize on it. So this is what we've been trying to do."

Asensi was enormously ambitious, so much so that he alienated people from MLS headquarters in New York all the way to the employees closest to him at Inter Miami's office. But his intense approach yielded huge returns. It was aided by the fact that Messi's impact was, of course, a sensation—both on the field and in his global appeal.

Several sponsorship contracts were timed to expire ahead of the 2024 season so Inter Miami could maximize the commercial impact. That would eventually include stadium naming rights and a new shirt-front sponsor. In 2021, Miami was one of just two MLS teams without a jersey partner. Three years later, Jorge Mas said the club's new deal ranked in the top five in the world, which would put it north of $60 million per year.

Within two months of Messi signing with Inter Miami, the club saw its Instagram following jump from one million to fifteen million. Inter Miami was the most googled team in the world in 2023, ahead of the Lakers, Ronaldo's Al Nassr, and Manchester City. *Forbes* made Inter Miami its second MLS club to reach the billion-dollar valuation threshold ($1.03 billion) in 2024, a 72 percent bump from 2023. Asensi projected the club would make north of $200 million in revenue, far beyond its 2022 income of $50–$60 million.

"We are talking about the greatest of all time in the world's biggest sport, in a moment that the world is more interconnected than ever, and that we have more technology than ever," Asensi said. "So put all this together and you have the atomic bomb. It's massive."

Messi saw a boost, too. He appeared in that Super Bowl

commercial for Michelob Ultra in February 2024 and launched several brands, including a hydration drink called Mas+. The Messi Experience, an interactive tour through Messi's career, launched in Miami, Chicago, Los Angeles, and Mexico City.

MLS also reaped the benefits. The league more than doubled its subscriber count on its MLS Season Pass app on Apple TV. It also saw a 13 percent bump in sponsorship revenue in 2024 to $665 million, according to research firm SponsorUnited. Team valuations rose to $690 million in 2024, a 121 percent increase from 2019.

Nowhere was the impact more evident than in MLS markets when Inter Miami went on the road.

* * *

Most of the sixty-thousand-plus fans who packed into Soldier Field in Chicago in October 2023 knew it was unlikely they were going to see Messi play. The Argentine had already missed three games with an injury and, indeed, he did not make the trip to the Windy City.

But the Chicago Fire was among many MLS teams to take quick advantage of a home game against Messi and Inter Miami. Ticket prices soared. Face value in Chicago exceeded $280 per ticket. Some sold on the secondary market were priced as high as $6,000. Still, the Fire sold twelve thousand tickets for the October match within the first forty-eight hours of Messi's Inter Miami announcement. In the end, it sold out Soldier Field, with more than sixty-two thousand fans streaming in. The game would drive more than $9.5 million in revenue, an MLS record for a single contest and about 55 percent of the Fire's 2023 turnover.

Without Messi on the field, the Fire sensed a competitive opportunity. Chicago trounced Miami 4–1. "I don't think that all the people in pink were from Miami today," Fire captain Rafa Czichos said. "So I hope they're going to be there on Saturday or next season with a different color."

Chicago made sure to do what it could to turn Czichos' words into reality. The Fire offered any fans who signed up for 2024 season tickets a free seat to the 2023 Inter Miami game. And once it was clear Messi was not going to play at Soldier Field, Chicago offered fans a $250 credit toward a season ticket package or a $50 credit for any single game in 2024.

The marketing ploy worked. Chicago saw its attendance jump 25 percent from 2023 to 2024 and sold out the inventory for stadium suites. The club's sponsorship numbers tripled. It was a lesson for other MLS teams on how to create a Messi effect in their own markets.

Multiple MLS teams took note in the ensuing seasons and moved games to nearby NFL venues to amplify Messi's impact. As Messi was filling stadiums and breaking attendance records on the field, MLS leadership studied what, if anything, from his influence could inform the league's next steps.

* * *

It was quintessentially MLS to commission a study on what players, if any, could have the same sort of impact as Messi. It was an easy question to answer: None, of course.

Outside of Messi's longtime rival, Cristiano Ronaldo, who was in Saudi Arabia being paid in levels above what any MLS team could manage, no player came close.

"Messi is a unicorn," said MLS executive JoAnn Neale, who ran the study. "None of the other players are going to compare to what he's driven both from an awareness and engagement from a commercial opportunity. . . . What we have determined is that there are very few players that are going to even come close to fifty percent of what Messi could do."

MLS seemed to be looking for data that might help them determine whether going back down that path of celebrity signings was worth considering. Or, perhaps to back up beliefs at MLS headquarters that it was the wrong path. A study the league commissioned in 2016 encouraged MLS teams to move away from big-name stars and avoid the "retirement league" moniker. Those players, the study said, didn't deliver enough on-field value or commercial boost to justify the price tags. That study significantly dictated league strategy—until Messi's arrival.

Neale explained that MLS wanted "to make sure that when we're investing in [players], they're actually going to drive the product quality on the field." Todd Durbin, another longtime MLS executive, said the study was done in part to determine what "drove affinity" for the most popular players. Messi and Ronaldo lived on a tier to themselves. Below were players like Kylian Mbappé, Erling Haaland, and Lamine Yamal, none of whom were a realistic target for MLS. There might be some players at the next tier who made sense in specific markets, but would they really add enough value to MLS to justify the inflated price tags?

The questions the league was asking missed the most important point of the study.

If Messi was such an extreme outlier, a player whose impact could not be replicated—or at least, not anytime soon—the only takeaway was that MLS needed to do everything in its power to take advantage of his presence in the league.

It was an idea that some of the most influential voices in the sport seemed to understand and tried to impress on MLS decision-makers.

* * *

Four days before 72,610 people packed into Arrowhead Stadium in Kansas City to watch Messi play, FIFA president Gianni

Infantino stood at the dais in a conference room at the Ritz Carlton in downtown Los Angeles to address owners and executives from all thirty MLS teams.

There was plenty about Messi's impact to celebrate, of course, but the league was hesitant to jump feet-first into change, even as Mas and others implored colleagues to move quickly. It was the first time a FIFA president had ever spoken at an MLS board meeting, a nod to the central role the U.S. was now playing in the soccer ecosystem.

That summer, Messi and Argentina would be vying for a third straight international trophy when the 2024 Copa América was played on U.S. soil. The Club World Cup, a personal project of Infantino, was set to be staged across the country in 2025. And, of course, the 2026 World Cup was just more than two years away.

The short-term impacts—the sold-out stadiums and jersey sales and even record-setting sponsorships—were notable. But they would fade with time. Infantino felt it was crucial to send a message to the American league concerning its long-term vision.

"Be bold," he said, as he sat on the stage next to MLS commissioner Don Garber.

MLS could be one of the best leagues in the world, Infantino argued—one of the few with a real chance to compete with the likes of the Premier League—due to the wealth in the room and the appeal of the American commercial market. But to reach those goals, MLS would have to increase its investment, both in the development of domestic players and on its first-team rosters.

Infantino said he was impressed with the owners' passion and commitment to build the game, and the growth of fan bases, stadiums, and infrastructure around MLS. He emphasized that FIFA was not picking up and moving on after the 2026 tournament but rather that it wanted to be partners to elevate soccer in the U.S. But he urged MLS owners to "think big" to take full advantage of the opportunities presented by the Club World Cup and World Cup coming to U.S. shores—and of Messi's time in the league.

Infantino was pushing so hard because the U.S. market was vital to the sport's growth. Soccer didn't need MLS to be popular in America but to truly thrive here—the sport needed MLS to matter. Until the league lifted its own ceiling, however, MLS wouldn't truly resonate at home.

"I think he has very strong views that this is just the beginning of a journey where MLS can continue to evolve and grow with the right level of investment and the right level of support to reach really tremendous new heights," Garber said after the meeting.

As important as anything Infantino said in the meeting, however, was what he declined to comment on as he departed the hotel. Earlier in the day, FIFA settled a lawsuit with Relevent Sports Group, a decision that would add yet another key element to the future of the sport in the U.S.—and add another layer to the decision MLS owners were weighing.

16

Fighting Relevent and Relevance

Less than three minutes into the game, Sergio Busquets sprung Lionel Messi into space.

The fans in Miami rose to their feet as the world's greatest No. 10 took two touches at full sprint, cut across a helpless defender with his right foot, and then released a quick shot with his left as two more opponents converged. The ball clipped off the toe of a chasing center back and caromed over the committed goalkeeper, who could only throw his hands up as the deflected shot rippled the net behind him.

The sold-out crowd bellowed in delight.

It was July 30, 2017, still six months before confetti fell on Jorge Mas and David Beckham at an event announcing their Inter Miami MLS expansion team. On this night, Messi still wore the Blaugrana of Barcelona, facing Real Madrid in the first *El Clásico* staged in the U.S.—and only the second contested outside Spain in the rivalry's 115-year history.

The thought of Messi doing this every weekend in South Florida remained a fantasy, but it was one already being conjured by Mas and Beckham.

El Clásico in Miami was the crown jewel of the International

Champions Cup (ICC), an annual U.S. summer exhibition event featuring some of soccer's biggest clubs on tour. More than sixty-six thousand people converged on Hard Rock Stadium to see the Spanish giants clash. The match anchored a weekend-long celebration that included a free fan festival called Casa Clásico, a youth tournament, a legends and celebrities game, an MMA fight, South Beach parties, and a Marc Anthony halftime show.

ESPN's U.S. broadcast delivered 1.7 million viewers. Ticket sales generated $36.6 million. By most measures, it was a wildly successful event. The hope was that spectacles like this would help the ICC evolve into something bigger, an X-Games–style soccer property that could be packaged and sold as an international tournament.

Within a year, however, Daniel Sillman, the new CEO of Relevent Sports Group, started to see that the ICC model, a tournament built around summer friendlies, was broken. The twenty-eight-year-old Sillman, who had launched his first business as a University of Michigan junior, had cold-emailed the billionaire, Stephen M. Ross, whose name was on Michigan's business school and was now running that billionaire's sports promotion company.

"The economics didn't make sense," Sillman said.

He began to consider how the games might serve a bigger purpose—for both his company and the European leagues trying to crack the American market.

What followed would potentially change the competitive landscape of the sport forever.

* * *

European teams going on summer tours in the U.S. became big business in American soccer's modern era in the early 2000s, when Charlie Stillitano, a bombastic Italian American and the first general manager of the New York/New Jersey Metrostars (now New

York Red Bulls), organized the Champions World Series featuring clubs like Manchester United, Juventus, and AC Milan.

The first series in 2003 rocked American soccer, drawing more than 420,000 fans across eight games. Manchester United averaged 67,884 in its four matches. The exhibitions confirmed the demand for top-tier soccer in the U.S.

MLS, of course, had to reckon with what it meant. In typical fashion, the league brushed it off.

"No, we haven't taken any heat at all on the Manchester United thing," Garber told reporters on the eve of the 2003 MLS Cup. "We had games from April to November. That was a two-week experience. It was a rock concert. It was not something that our board was concerned about."

In the short term, Garber was right. The summer tour buzz didn't upend MLS's business. Despite two years of successful exhibitions, Champions World folded after its 2004 series. Stillitano later sued U.S. Soccer, claiming that the excessive fees paid to the federation for permission to host games contributed to the collapse. The parties settled years later.

The summer tours were revived in 2009 as the World Football Challenge, backed by Creative Artists Agency (CAA), this time in conjunction with MLS and SUM. Stillitano and CAA were still inviting some of Europe's biggest clubs, but MLS teams participated, too.

"In the past, the superclubs came to the U.S. just to build their brands and expand their global footprints, and in many ways exploit their soccer opportunities in the U.S.," Garber told *The New York Times* in 2011. "Now that [MLS] has become better connected to the world, the clubs are coming not only to build their brands, but they are contributing to building the sport in the U.S. Things we have done have given MLS a bounce in its step and resonated with the international football community."

MLS saw it as a net positive. Sold-out stadiums for soccer meant there was demand and potential for growth. And, of course, now MLS and SUM, the commercial arm of MLS, had their hands in the pot.

Relevent bought the event in 2013 and rebranded it as the ICC. While MLS teams occasionally still played summer friendlies against visiting European sides, Relevent pushed to grow the ICC as a standalone brand.

As the Premier League's U.S. popularity surged, demand for the friendlies increased. By 2018, however, Sillman was reassessing the future of the summer tours. Relevent paid clubs to participate in the ICC, but competition in the marketplace was driving up prices. The larger problem, though, was that the games were exhibitions. There were no real stakes involved, and fans were finally catching on.

In 2018, average ICC attendance dropped 18 percent from the previous year. Some stadiums still sold out, but Bayern Munich and Manchester City, champions of Germany and England respectively, sold fewer than thirty thousand tickets in Miami. It boiled down to a simple problem, one organizers acknowledged a year before when promoting the Miami version of *El Clásico*: If the result didn't matter, the tournament wouldn't resonate.

"We know it's not the Champions League," Stillitano told reporters in 2017. "I don't think we'll ever be able to get rid of the moniker of 'a friendly tournament.' It's hard. We were not able to commercialize and sell the media and sponsorship at full value because it was friendly."

Relevent changed its course. In August 2018, the company and La Liga announced a fifteen-year partnership to promote the Spanish league in the U.S. and Canada. As part of that deal, La Liga would stage one regular-season game per year in the U.S.

"This extraordinary joint venture is the next giant leap in growing soccer's popularity in North America," Ross, Relevent's chairman and cofounder, claimed in a statement.

The first game, Girona versus Barcelona, was set for January 26, 2019, in Miami. But when plans went public, there was immediate backlash. The Spanish soccer federation and players union both opposed a league match being played outside the country. FIFA president Gianni Infantino warned the governing body would block it.

La Liga and Relevent pressed ahead. A formal application to stage the game was made to the Spanish federation in November 2018. It was denied.

In April 2019, Relevent applied for sanctioning to stage an Ecuadorian league match in Miami. U.S. Soccer rejected the application, saying it had no choice but to uphold FIFA's position that "official league matches must be played within the territory of the respective member association."

Relevent sued U.S. Soccer on antitrust grounds, eventually adding FIFA as a co-defendant, alleging that U.S. Soccer and FIFA conspired to withhold approval for a game in deference to SUM, Relevent's direct competitor. The lawsuit was about further prying open the door to the U.S. market for the rest of global soccer. The knock-on effect was potentially enormous.

By the time the case was settled in 2025, Messi had traded Blaugrana for Miami pink.

* * *

For more than a decade, MLS was consistent in its response to the dalliances of European clubs in the U.S.

From that first Champions World tournament in 2003, when crowds flooding to Manchester United games sparked questions about why MLS couldn't attract similar interest, all the way to the 2017 *El Clásico* in Miami, MLS's public position was essentially a shrug.

Expansion during the 2010s created enough demand that MLS was not worried about the impact of summer friendlies on attendance. The league was building top-class stadiums and creating enjoyable game-day experiences. It did live soccer well. The European visitors had little impact.

But the league risked underestimating the long-term effects.

MLS had always prioritized the long game. Almost every major decision was made with that extended horizon in mind. It was a philosophy that could be traced back to the investors who stepped up to save MLS in the early aughts.

"One thing that we've learned through being in the sports business for many, many decades is it's a very long-term investment," Clark Hunt said a few months after Messi's arrival. "It's not like a lot of businesses that maybe have a five- to ten-year investment horizon. The sports business is really about generations, and it's about building fans over a very long period of time. My personal view is that it's important to be gaining new fans and growing your brand at all times, but you never are going to arrive at the destination. That's just the nature of it."

It was an outlook that made a lot of sense, especially in the context of Hunt's NFL team, the Kansas City Chiefs. The NFL essentially had a monopoly over professional football. It could afford to operate conservatively and still expect the fan base to grow in size and passion over time. Within the context of MLS, however, Hunt's outlook ignored the fact that the league existed in a globally competitive environment. Other leagues were vying for the same fans—and they were winning them over at a faster clip than MLS.

For three decades, MLS built infrastructure and nurtured its product with a targeted strategy it felt would ensure survival. But that same approach left the door open for ambitious, more proactive rivals. As access to the game grew—through NBC's Premier League deal, CBS's streaming push, summer tours, and even Messi's arrival—the opportunity expanded for competing leagues to take a piece. Fans watching the Premier League on weekend mornings were building loyalties and generational connections to teams an ocean away.

MLS hadn't evolved quickly enough to stave off the competition—and that competition kept advancing further into its territory. Now, MLS was playing catch-up to win over fans in their own backyard.

"It isn't that they're going to come into the sport and they're going to be a Tottenham fan and not an MLS fan [just] because they're a Tottenham fan [already]," Garber said. "It's because we've not connected with them. We've got to do the work to connect with them and have a league that they can believe in."

* * *

Whereas MLS once saw summer tours as good for the sport and therefore good for the league, the idea of regular-season games was not as appealing.

"I don't think it's the best thing for the sport," Garber said in February 2020. "I think regular-season games should be played in home markets."

Five years later, with the inevitability of global games on the doorstep, Garber was insistent that MLS still held the advantage.

"I have always believed that we have the one thing that no other league can really have, which is boots on the ground and now thirty markets with community connection, with great stadiums, with great training grounds, and an opportunity to be part of a shared experience that a family can have with each other by attending and hopefully watching an MLS game," he said. "And everything else—exhibitions and maybe a game here and a game there and tournaments—will never deliver [what] a local sports team can deliver for a fan. Now the job is on us to turn them into a lifelong fan and give them a team that they believe in and want to believe in for the rest of their lives."

Relevent might not have publicly acknowledged it, but the court battle over regular-season games was just one small battle in a much larger fight. The company's pivot to brokering media rights indicated that strategic shift. Regular-season games, of course, were more attractive than friendlies. Real consequences would drive interest back into the live properties that were otherwise losing their appeal. But the games were essentially a marketing tool.

La Liga didn't want to stage regular-season matches in the U.S. for the ticket sales. The revenue wouldn't be worth the effort. The games were an entry point for fans.

"Americans want to see the best, and they want to see the best when it's real and when it matters," Sillman said. "That's the demand for regular-season matches. What you need to do in terms of developing new football fans, or new soccer fans in the U.S. or any international territory, is ultimately bring them closer to the stars, to the biggest clubs and to the stories of those clubs. . . . You have to bring content to the territory where you want to build a fan base. And part of one prong of that content plan is matches."

In the same way the NFL was expanding its slate of international games, MLB was playing its season-opening series in Japan, or the NHL and NBA were exploring international opportunities, European soccer leagues saw an opening to drive value back into their leagues via international media rights. Regular-season games in the U.S. were a tool to accomplish that goal.

The Relevent case reached the U.S. Supreme Court in 2024, but the company settled—first with FIFA in 2024, and then with

U.S. Soccer in 2025. As part of the settlement, FIFA "agreed to a consideration of changes to existing FIFA policies with respect to playing official season games outside of a league's home territory." Within months of the U.S. Soccer settlement, Spain's La Liga moved to approve a game in the U.S. The pushback from players and fans remained strong, but games played outside of home countries felt inevitable. MLS's competition for fans was now primed to move beyond TV screens and into the stadiums in their markets.

"When we started the whole process in the late 1990s, we wanted to raise the overall 'value' of soccer in America," Garber said. "We knew we'd have a lot of boats on that rising tide. Well now that tide has risen really high and there's a lot more boats."

The implications were enormous, and they went beyond just European leagues.

* * *

MLS's partnership with Liga MX, most notably the Leagues Cup tournament Messi introduced to the world with his electric 2023 performance, was built largely on the appeal of Mexican teams playing competitive games on U.S. soil.

If FIFA changed its rules, Liga MX wouldn't need MLS to stage meaningful matches in the U.S.

MLS's southern neighbors were weighing big changes to their structure, including the centralization of their commercial and media rights. Teams in Mexico had long been able to negotiate their own deals. That gave vast advantages to their bigger clubs like Club América and Chivas de Guadalajara, two of the most popular teams in North America, but it also limited the league's revenue—and thus its potential for growth.

Liga MX, playing during prime time in the U.S., regularly pulled more than one million viewers for its games on Univision.

It was the most-watched league in the country. If the Premier League made $450 million per year from NBC, the value of a centralized deal could be enormous for Liga MX.

"I don't think there's a bigger opportunity for growth of a football league in the world than Liga MX has," Sillman said.

As such, Liga MX was fielding interest from potential investment partners. A multibillion-dollar deal between Liga MX, investment firm Apollo Global Management, and NFL owners fell through in 2024 when Liga MX failed to institute governance reforms. But that near-partnership spoke to the league's value in the U.S. market. American groups were also starting to purchase teams in Mexico: Wrexham's owners were among the investors in Club Necaxa, while other U.S.-based groups invested in Querétaro F.C. and second-division club Cancún FC.

"Apollo is now on hold," Liga MX president Mikel Arriola told me ahead of the MLS All-Star Game in July 2025. "[But] we have the offer. We have the evaluation. And we have the interest. So what we have to do before that, is to generate a corporate governance reform in the league in order to [set] the conditions to centralize the TV rights. And then decide if we want a nineteenth partner."

It isn't an easy road to that reform. Multi-club ownership in the league would have to end, and teams likely would have to open their books to potential investors. But if Liga MX can get there, and if it centralizes the rights, it could be an absolute game changer for the league—and for soccer in the region. Liga MX was a sleeping giant that could threaten MLS as the dominant North American soccer league.

"I don't think it's a sleeping giant—I think it's a giant," Arriola said. "But without centralized TV rights—it's an inertial giant, not sleeping. If we don't do what we have to, what the best leagues do, we're giving away too much of a handicap. We're giving away advantages."

What was being left on the table—both by Liga MX's divided commercial policy and MLS's conservative approach—was limiting the ceiling of North American soccer. And it was leaving the window open for other leagues to swoop in.

Arriola believed change was inevitable. He insisted that the partnership between Liga MX and MLS was critical to reaching that full potential. And he professed an aggressive mindset for both leagues.

"There's a direct correlation in soccer between investment and titles, investment and roster quality," Arriola said. "If you look at it in GDP per capita terms, in multiples for team valuations, in capital capacity of a market—the volume of capital in the American market is unmatched anywhere in the world. It's the richest country not just in GDP volume, but in the ability of companies to carry out huge transactions. On the consumption side, you see growth in live entertainment, live sports, and soccer. So it's not a matter of guessing—it's going to happen. North America will be the most powerful soccer market in the world."

It was an ambitious outlook, for sure, and it spoke to how Mexico viewed the market. It was also a natural evolution for what had long been an undervalued but enormous part of the story of soccer's popularity in the U.S.: the Spanish-speaking audience.

17

“Are We Already Retiring Him?”

Even as Lionel Messi opened the 2024 season with the casual dominance that had long defined his career, racking up fourteen goals and fourteen assists in his first fourteen MLS games, one question hovered around his every move.

How long would this last?

Messi was thirty-six, and while he continued to prove he could still do it at a high level—in one 6–2 Inter Miami win over the New York Red Bulls, he set an MLS single-game record for goal contributions with five assists and a goal—it was always colored by the feeling that there was a countdown clock hovering over the sport’s greatest performer.

Nowhere did the fear of a post-Messi existence resonate more than in his home country.

At Argentina’s media day ahead of the 2024 Copa América, photographers snapped photos of Messi and winger Ángel Di María in their blue-and-white shirts. No teammate played more games with Messi in an Argentina jersey, according to Transfermarkt. As the cameras flashed, video picked up a joke from midfielder Rodrigo De Paul.

“Get your shots in now, because this is it,” he said. “They won’t be at the next Copa América [in 2028]. Let's go, because this is the last one."

It was an open secret that Di María, the legendary Rosario-born winger, planned to retire from international soccer after the Copa. But the impending end for one legend inevitably sparked speculation about the other.

The topic hovered over every Argentine camp since Qatar.

Messi was noncommittal when asked in several interviews whether he would play in the 2026 World Cup. He pointed to down moments he suffered with the national team and insisted he was enjoying the afterglow of 2022 and the camaraderie of the group.

"Logically, given my age, it'll probably be soon," Messi said on the Argentine show *Llave a la Eternidad* in 2023. "But I don't know exactly when that moment is going to be. I just think about taking it one day at a time, enjoying all of this wonderful thing that we are experiencing."

Before a pair of World Cup qualifiers in October 2023, a journalist asked Argentina coach Lionel Scaloni whether Argentina was prepared for life without Messi.

"Let's keep in mind that he's still here," Scaloni admonished. "What kind of thinking is, 'When he is gone'? The truth is [Messi] is still active. Let's leave him alone. Are we already retiring him?"

The questions didn't stop. Asked again by ESPN before the start of the Copa América about retirement creeping closer, Messi said he tried not to peek that far down the road.

"I don't think I am [prepared to leave football], either," Messi said. "I've done this all my life. I love playing and I enjoy training, the day-to-day, the games. I am a bit scared of it all ending. That's always there. . . . But I try not to think about it. I try to enjoy it. I do that more now, because I'm aware there's not a lot of time left. . . . I enjoy those small details that I know I'll miss when I stop playing."

Messi was hardly the first sports icon to grapple with what comes after a career so tethered to their identity. It drove Tom Brady to win a record seventh Super Bowl at a record age of forty-three before finally retiring at age forty-five. It pushed LeBron James into his forties with the Los Angeles Lakers, and Diana Taurasi to continue in the WNBA until she was forty-two. It was a reason, perhaps, that James and Serena Williams were at Messi's Inter Miami debut. They identified with that level of sustained greatness and commitment, not to mention the stress caused by the unknown that waited around the corner.

Brady articulated that feeling to *60 Minutes* in 2005, eighteen years before he stepped away. Asked if he had any fears, Brady was quick to reply.

"The end of my playing career, big time," the legendary quarterback said. "Because I guess I've done this for so long and I already know what I feel like in the offseason—that I'm always trying to figure out ways to have a day that's filled with things I like to do. . . . When [football is] done, you don't have eighty thousand people screaming your name. What's it going to be? I don't know. I've heard about astronauts that go to the moon and then come back and they're so depressed because there's nothing they can do in their lives that can ever fulfill them the way that that does."

Messi was coping with the same idea.

"I know these are my last years," he told Apple TV for a documentary about his first months in the U.S. "And I know when I don't have this, I'm going to miss it dearly. Because no matter how many things I find to do, nothing is going to be like this, which I did my whole life."

Fans and media confronted the prospect of soccer without Messi by speculating about it. Argentina was beginning, in its own ways, to brace for the loss.

The national team no longer asked Messi to carry the team

the way he currently did with Inter Miami. Under Scaloni, Argentina embraced a system that complemented Messi when he was in his late thirties. They surrounded their No. 10 with a generation of players that grew up idolizing him, and those younger men gladly sacrificed to open things up for their hero. Alexis Mac Allister, Enzo Fernández, and De Paul became integral midfield workhorses. Messi played underneath the striker, typically Julián Alvarez or Lautaro Martínez, who pressed relentlessly. Messi was still the orchestrator, but Argentina worked to make it easier for him to dictate games.

A day without Messi was coming, yes. But not yet. For now, they would find ways to get the best out of their talisman.

"It's going to happen someday. The longer it takes, the better," Scaloni said in an interview with famed Argentine American broadcaster Andrés Cantor and former Argentina winger Maxi Rodríguez ahead of the 2024 Copa América, shrugging his shoulders up near his ears as he acceded to reality. "We're going to miss [Messi] at some point. It is what it is. [Diego] Maradona left the national team, and someday Leo will, too. The coach won't always be the same person. Things change. But in the meantime, we have to enjoy this."

For now, like Inter Miami and MLS, Argentina was living the Messi effect.

Thanks to their World Cup triumph, La Albiceleste earned the idolatry of a nation (and many outside it). For over a month, Argentina bounced up and down the East Coast, from Atlanta to New Jersey to Miami, then back to New Jersey and then Miami again. They filled stadiums with their fans, continuing the celebration from their epic victory in Qatar.

The party followed them everywhere, into their hotel lobbies and outside of elevator doors, onto streets shut down by fans surrounding the team bus, and even into media mixed zones, where content creators showed off their World Cup tattoos and reached out to players for high fives.

CONMEBOL, South America's governing body and the Copa América organizer, embraced the carnival, blasting Argentine anthems throughout pregame warm-ups, after goals, and following every Argentina win. It was clear that in the U.S., Messi's new stomping ground, Argentina was a home team—and MLS wasn't the only entity intent on cashing in on the Messi effect.

The audience filling Copa América stadiums across the country had long been a force in soccer's U.S. growth.

* * *

The festive atmospheres across the country for the Copa América—filled with the yellow shirts of Colombian fans, sky blue of Uruguay, or blue-and-white Argentines—were a showcase for the reason why the U.S. was seen as such a unique and powerful market for soccer.

The story of soccer's Spanish-speaking audience in the U.S. extended decades before MLS was founded, and it remained an enormous driver of the sport's popularity.

Cantor likes to say he was fortunate to be "the jewel of the crown" when Univision hired him to call soccer games in 1987. No other U.S. network broadcast live soccer, and Cantor, an Argentine American who moved to California as a teenager and graduated from the University of Southern California, sat "on the throne as the only play-by-play announcer in the country," he said.

Cantor, along with broadcast partner Norberto Longo, called every game of the 1990 World Cup for Univision. Cantor then became a household name—or rather, voice—during the U.S.-hosted 1994 World Cup for his "Gooooooollllll!" calls. The long-winded exclamation, adapted from the Argentine radio broadcasters he grew up listening to, earned Cantor a regular invite to the *Late Show with David Letterman*. The 1994 World Cup thrust Cantor—and soccer—into the general consciousness of a wider American audience.

"It gave the sport a lot of visibility," Cantor recalled. "It put a stamp in the landscape saying, 'Okay, soccer is here to stay.'"

For the English-speaking audience, Cantor provided a window into a sport that still felt foreign. For an increasing number of U.S. Latinos, Cantor was the voice of the game that flowed through their veins. In those households, Cantor and Chilean TV host Don Francisco held far more weight than former NFLer Pat Summerall and Letterman.

Soccer's growth following the 1994 World Cup may have been the first real indicator of the Spanish-language audience's influence in the U.S.

While MLS commissioner Don Garber convinced owners to create SUM in 2001 and snap up the English-language rights to the 2002 and 2006 World Cups—paying $40–$60 million and covering production costs for games airing on ESPN and ABC—no such opening existed for Spanish-language coverage. Univision paid $125 million for the same rights. The network, which had been broadcasting the World Cup since 1978, knew the audience would be there. And they continued to set the standard over the next four World Cups.

Former Univision Sports president Juan Carlos Rodriguez pointed to the World Cup successes as reinforcing a commercial blueprint he created when he took command at the network.

Univision initially hired Rodriguez to try to create "a CNN of sports for Hispanics," he recalled. After two months, he told his bosses it was impossible, but that "there was a way to create the ultimate home of soccer in America." Because Liga MX games were played in prime time, and because soccer was the preferred sport for most Hispanics, Rodriguez felt he could build a dominant network around the Mexican league, as well as in partnership with MLS.

"We said, there are two countries within this country: the Spanish-speaking country and the English-speaking country," Rodriguez explained. "And we were able to make as big a splash as we could in Spanish."

Years before Messi signed with Inter Miami, it was an audience MLS saw as vital to its growth. The arrival of the Copa América to the U.S. was indicative of just how much value was there.

Coming out of record-setting 2014 World Cup audiences, Rodriguez wanted to further leverage the strength of the Spanish-speaking audience. He pitched a hundredth anniversary Copa América tournament, a Centenario, in the United States in 2016. On the day before the network's upfronts in New York City in May 2015, Rodriguez sat with twenty figures from the Concacaf and CONMEBOL halls of power at a Greek restaurant called Estiatorio Milos, in part to discuss the tournament. Within weeks, several of those in attendance were arrested as part of the FBI's investigation into FIFA and the bidding process for the World Cup and media and marketing rights around the tournament.

The arrests nearly ended the Centenario before it started, but the tournament got the green light when U.S. Soccer and SUM took on hosting responsibilities. Put together in just seven months, the 2016 Copa América averaged more than forty-six thousand fans per game, the highest in the history of the competition.

Messi and Argentina lost the 2016 Copa América final to Chile in penalties, the same result they suffered a year prior. In the tunnel under MetLife Stadium in East Rutherford, New Jersey, a frustrated Messi announced his retirement from international soccer. The "retirement," of course, didn't last.

Sitting on a table in Rodriguez's office is evidence of the Copa

América Centenario's success: a replica trophy gifted by CONMEBOL.

"It is the most successful event in the history of the U.S. at the ticket office," Rodriguez said.

U.S. Soccer made more than $75 million on the tournament. SUM took in millions more in profit. The Centenario revealed the American appetite for high-level soccer—and the strength of the Spanish-speaking audience. It also meant CONMEBOL left plenty of money on the table.

Eight years later, the South American confederation came back to capture more of the market—and this time they handled the commercial side, marketing, and ticketing themselves. More than 1.6 million people attended games, besting the 2016 figures with an average of 49,121 per game. CONMEBOL later reported $319 million in revenue generated from national team competitions in 2024, including the U.S.-based Copa América, with the federation clearing $112 million in net profit for the year.

It spoke to the power and appeal of the American soccer market—and hinted at just how enormous the 2026 World Cup would be.

* * *

The 2024 Copa América added to Messi and Argentina's dominant legacy. It also felt like a moment of transition into what a future without Messi might look like.

Argentina's star was nursing a muscle issue early in the Copa, which meant that throughout most of the tournament, La Albiceleste had to find ways to get results without No. 10 at his best. Messi scored just once, but he remained an important part of what made the world champions effective. No Argentina player was involved in more sequences leading to shots than Messi, and he had the third-most chances created per ninety minutes during the tournament.

A quarterfinal win over Ecuador exemplified his summer. La Tricolor held Messi to just thirty-two touches in the first half, his fewest in a competitive game for Argentina in which he played a full ninety minutes since 2011. And yet, one of those thirty-two touches led to a golden chance. Another touch set up an Argentina goal. Messi missed a Panenka-style penalty kick in the shootout triumph, but goalkeeper Emi Martínez's heroics kept Argentina alive.

Messi no longer needed to be the hero every time. Argentina learned to win in other ways. The group's unity was evident on and off the field.

After the semifinal win over Canada, a beaming Messi stopped several times in the MetLife Stadium tunnel to speak with reporters. He referred to the tournament—the final national team appearances for Di María and Nicolás Otamendi—as "our last battles."

Messi soaked it all in: the stadium atmospheres, the party in every city—even the adoration of Argentine journalists and content creators who stuck out their microphones hunting for viral moments in the mixed zone. One creator asked Messi to sign his forearm, then returned with the autograph tattooed permanently on his skin.

It hadn't always been like this. Eight years before, in that very same MetLife tunnel, a distraught Messi shocked everyone when he announced his Argentina retirement after another agonizing loss in a final.

"The national team is over for me," Messi told TyC Sports that June night in 2016. "It's been four finals. It's not meant for me. I tried. It was the thing I wanted the most, but I couldn't get it, so I think it's over."

Now, Messi and Argentina were headed to a third consecutive tournament final as a team that always believed it would win. A third straight major international title, following the 2021 Copa América and 2022 World Cup, would be the ultimate payoff after decades of suffering in the biggest moments.

"Argentines are crazy about this national team and crazy about football," Messi said. "This group has been fostering that relationship for a long time now. We've won important things, and these players continue to compete game after game. We don't always play well, but our willingness to compete is spectacular.

"Let's enjoy this moment, but also appreciate what began eight years ago."

* * *

As much as the tournament was a commercial success, undoubtedly boosted by Messi's undeniable draw, the 2024 Copa América final will be remembered as much for the near disaster outside Hard Rock Stadium as anything that happened on the field.

Fans rushed entrances to get in, many without tickets. Security and police responded by shutting the gates, and fans were crushed against fences in the overwhelming heat. Several fainted and were pulled through the barriers unconscious.

The game was delayed until, eventually, mercifully, the gates were opened. People rushed inside. Tickets weren't checked. Fans sat in aisles and concourses to see if Messi and Argentina could win a third consecutive major international trophy.

In the sixty-fourth minute, however, with the game tied 0–0, Messi sat on the field and signaled for a substitution. He tried to play through pain after a first-half tackle but couldn't continue. The enduring image of the tournament was Messi sobbing on the bench, his swollen ankle extended out in front of him, unable to help his team.

"Leo has something that everyone should have: He's the best in history and, even with an ankle like that, he doesn't want to go off," Scaloni said in the postgame press conference. "It's not because he's selfish, but because he doesn't want to let his teammates down. He was born to be on a pitch."

When Lautaro Martínez scored the game-winner for Argentina in the 112th minute, it felt like a torch was being passed. For years, Argentina depended on Messi to lift them in the most important moments. Now, they'd proved they could do it without him.

Still, no one was ready for that final moment to come. Messi meant too much. The coronation and celebration around him deserved a longer run.

"He knows that we won't be the ones to close the door on him," Scaloni said. "He can be with us whenever he wants, even after he retires. . . . Let him decide what he wants."

Whenever Messi decided to walk away, it would alter everything around him, from Argentina to Inter Miami and MLS. Planning for his departure had to start by maximizing his impact while he remained on the field.

18

Messi Fatigue

An interesting trend emerged in the final weeks of the 2024 MLS regular season: Messi fatigue.

It wasn't noticeable among more casual fans, who still packed into away stadiums to see the Argentine play. But it percolated within MLS circles and inside factions of the more hardcore fans of opposing teams. MLS's homepage and that of Apple's MLS Season Pass were practically painted in Inter Miami pink. Messi's bearded face was unavoidable. Messi and Inter Miami understandably dominated national media coverage, too.

As Inter Miami rampaged through the regular season and Messi continued to dominate—over their final seven games, he tallied eight goals and three assists, giving him twenty goals and sixteen assists in just nineteen MLS games in 2024—the bitterness seemed to build. The general dislike aimed toward Inter Miami ultimately was good for MLS, which typically lacked a "Galactic Empire" franchise everyone could hate. One year of Messi turned Inter Miami into the Dallas Cowboys, Los Angeles Lakers, and New York Yankees—the team fans loved to hate.

MLS fans, for some reason, also had a hard time accepting that the reason Messi was covered so exhaustingly was because people were interested. The general sporting public read stories about Messi in numbers that dwarfed other MLS coverage. MLS diehard fans might not have loved it, but reaching those new fans was ultimately a good thing for the league.

The growing disdain toward Inter Miami within the MLS's ecosystem also enhanced the debate surrounding Inter Miami's overall strategy. While MLS stakeholders unanimously believed that signing Messi was good for the league, an anonymous survey of soccer executives by *The Athletic* before the 2024 season revealed split opinions about whether Inter Miami's overall approach was helpful or harmful to MLS's reputation.

Across its entire history, the league welcomed big-name players at the end of their careers. It started prior to David Beckham's 2007 arrival—for example, Lothar Matthäus and Hristo Stoichkov came before the turn of the millennium—and continued after Beckham as well. Thierry Henry in 2010, Kaká in 2015, and Zlatan Ibrahimović in 2019 were among the many idols who moved to MLS when in their late thirties. Messi and friends were not an anomaly.

But since the success of Atlanta United's expansion season in 2017, when MLS's twenty-second team signed little-known attacking players Miguel Almirón and Josef Martínez and fielded one of the most entertaining squads in league history, MLS encouraged members to go in a different direction when filling designated player spots. The new trend was to find the next Almirón.

Miami went in the complete opposite direction.

Signing Messi, of course, was a no-brainer. But Mas bucked the trend by not looking for an in-their-prime partner for the Argentine legend. Instead, he signed a trio of Messi's former Barcelona teammates. Jordi Alba, who turned thirty-five in March 2024, was the youngest of the bunch.

Some team GMs believed Inter Miami winning the MLS Cup

would be a bad look for the league. It might suggest that over-the-hill stars were good enough to dominate MLS—even with Messi being Messi. Others, though, saw Inter Miami's strategy as great for the league. Forget the players' age, they said. Inter Miami had signed several promising young players, too. Instead, look at the money spent. Inter Miami boasted the highest guaranteed salary outlay in MLS—$41.7 million, which was $10.3 million more than second-place Toronto FC—and spent more than $25 million on transfer fees for u-22 players. It did that while also squeezing a huge amount of value out of Alba and Suárez, each of whom was on an annual salary under $1.75 million.

That aggressive strategy might convince other owners to spend more. Miami *should* win, and it would be good for the league if it did.

"They are really moving the needle. They're pushing the envelope, and I greatly respect that," one GM said.

The truth probably existed somewhere in the middle. Pairing Messi with a younger star probably would have better supported him in the long term. But the success of past aging stars showed that it was critical to locker room balance to have players who could relate to playing at the highest levels of the game. Finding players that could relate to Messi was a different challenge—and one Miami clearly embraced.

For all the criticism about Inter Miami's roster, the reality was that it was the MLS rules, not Inter Miami's strategy, that limited the depth of the team around Messi.

* * *

Despite its roster limitations, Inter Miami sat comfortably in first place when Messi returned from injury after his 2024 Copa América triumph. In his star's absence, Inter Miami coach Tata Martino rotated players and pushed the right buttons. Miami grinded out wins and was on pace not just to win the Supporters' Shield, awarded to the top regular-season finisher, but also to set the MLS points record.

With the Shield in reach, however, Miami suddenly hit a rut. And after three consecutive draws, Messi couldn't contain his frustration.

Messi's left-footed shot rescued a point in a 1–1 tie with Charlotte FC on September 28, 2024, but the result prevented Miami from clinching the Supporters' Shield. When the whistle blew, the league's most famous player went after the officials. Whatever Messi voiced, it wasn't complimentary. The referee issued a yellow card to warn the Argentine away. Messi headed for the tunnel, but his anger hadn't faded. Inter Miami trainers were told to stay in the hallway. Inside the locker room, the captain made it clear to teammates that a draw wasn't good enough.

Winger Julian Gressel hinted at Messi's message a few weeks later on a podcast.

"You're talking about the player with the most [team trophies] in the history of the game," Gressel said. "They're coming in and they're expecting the same, and you as a teammate, you kind of have to get accustomed to that and get used to that with Messi, [Luis] Suárez, [Sergio] Busquets, and [Jordi] Alba. It's unacceptable to tie a game, as simple as that. We tied a game earlier in the year, and I remember him being really, really upset in the locker room. He's like, 'We shouldn't tie. We can't tie.'"

As Inter Miami players departed Chase Stadium to head home later in the evening, Miami winger Robert Taylor said he saw a look in Messi's eye. The star said nothing, but he didn't need it. His face said everything. It was almost as if he "had a little moment where he said to himself, 'Well, fine. I'll do it myself,'" Taylor recalled with a chuckle.

Four days later in Columbus, Messi stood before his teammates again, this time for a pregame speech.

"This is about taking a step now and proving that we can win against the best teams," Messi told the group. "They're the defending champions. They're the best team this year. They won the [2024] Leagues Cup. We need to show that we can win this—that we can beat the best teams."

In the first few minutes against the Crew, Messi roamed the pitch, looking to put his stamp on the match. Just before halftime, he broke through. A long ball found No. 10 on a vertical run into space, and he kept possession despite being sandwiched between two defenders. As the goalkeeper converged, Messi calmly touched the ball past him for a 1–0 lead. Less than four minutes later, he curled a free kick around the outside of the Columbus wall and inside the near post. A camera cut to coach Martino, who chuckled and shrugged.

Messi's heroics would be just enough to get the win. Columbus battled back in the second half to cut Inter Miami's lead to 3–2, but Miami goalkeeper Drake Callender saved an eighty-fourth-minute penalty to preserve the victory and clinch the Supporters Shield. Messi pumped his fist at the whistle. A few minutes later, he gave one of his only interviews to American media since becoming an Inter Miami player.

"Happy for this group," Messi said in Spanish on Apple TV. "We knew it was a group [capable] to fight for this, and we took charge from the start because we have the players to do it. I'm happy to achieve the first objective and now think about what's next."

In the locker room, Inter Miami and Mas celebrated winning the Shield with champagne showers.

Realistically, though, the fan-awarded regular-season trophy was considered a secondary prize. The Shield was an imperfect award considering MLS teams played unbalanced schedules. Even the points record Miami chased felt cheapened because teams set the mark four times over the previous seven seasons.

Most MLS observers believed there would be only one true gauge of on-field success.

"[It's] MLS Cup or bust for them to become the best team ever," ESPN analyst Herculez Gomez said. "Because that's what [Messi] was brought here to do.

"Do not forget you do not hand the keys to the kingdom, you don't say, 'Here are your Apple shares to MLS Season Pass. Here are your shares to Inter Miami. Here is the merchandising. Here are all the things we're going to give you,' . . . for you to be ordinary, for you just to be record breaking in the regular season. No. [It's about] legacy. You came here to change Inter Miami and Major League Soccer."

Even Messi agreed. In an interview with Italian news breaker Fabrizio Romano just before the 2024 playoffs began, the playmaker laid out his expectations.

"We were happy and we celebrated the [Supporters' Shield] achievement because it was something difficult and important," Messi said. "But we are aware that [the next one is] the real title we want: the MLS Cup. And we are going to fight for that."

* * *

What unfolded over the next two weeks was exactly the result MLS's design embraced. Competitive balance was the league's ultimate goal, outranking anything else. MLS's top seed, with its biggest and most marketable player, crashing out of the postseason? And doing so against a team that made the playoffs despite finishing twentieth out of twenty-nine teams? It perfectly encapsulated the league's ideals.

"The fact that Miami didn't run all the way through the playoffs is a testament to the competitiveness of Major League Soccer," commissioner Don Garber declared at his state of the league speech at the MLS Cup. "We think every game needs to matter."

That was their story, and they were sticking to it.

Inter Miami and Atlanta United's trajectories could not have been more opposite.

Miami set the record for most points in a regular season. It boasted two twenty-goal scorers—Messi and Suárez—both world-class players who won important trophies at huge clubs. An MLS Cup–winning coach, Martino, paced the sideline.

Atlanta United, meanwhile, was no longer the powerhouse of Martino's era in 2017–18. The club sold its best players in the 2024 summer window and focused on a postseason rebuild. Atlanta tasked interim manager Rob Valentino with finishing out the year.

During the final weeks of the 2024 season, models showed Atlanta with a 4 percent chance of qualifying for the playoffs. On the final day of the campaign, those odds were up to 10 percent. Somehow, it snuck in as the Eastern Conference's ninth (and bottom) seed. Two seasons prior, before MLS introduced an expanded playoff format, Atlanta would have been eliminated. Instead, it had a chance to win a preliminary round match against eighth-seeded Montreal. Atlanta advanced on penalties.

No one expected the playoff run to go beyond that, especially after losing at Inter Miami in the opener of their best-of-three conference quarterfinal series. But Atlanta pulled off the Game 2 upset in front of a deafening home crowd of 68,455. Messi and Inter Miami's stars were surprisingly quiet in the loss, and if there were pink shirts in the stands supporting Messi, no one could tell.

Valentino, a journeyman American center back, spent the majority of his playing career in the lower divisions of U.S. soccer. The closest he came to MLS minutes was making it to the midfield stripe to substitute into a game for the Colorado Rapids during his third professional season, only for the whistle to sound before he could accomplish his dream. He eventually chased his dream to the sidelines as an assistant coach with Atlanta.

Now, he had just beaten Lionel Messi in the MLS Cup playoffs.

Valentino returned to the Mercedes-Benz Stadium field after the postgame press conference to soak in the moment with family. As he left, he shook his bald head in disbelief.

"I don't want this to end," he exhaled.

A week later, he got his wish.

Bolstered by an outrageous performance from forty-year-old former U.S. men's national team goalkeeper Brad Guzan, Atlanta held on for a 3–2 Game 3 win and eliminated Inter Miami in Fort Lauderdale. Messi set up Miami's first goal and scored their second, but it wasn't enough.

Inter Miami was out after just one round of the playoffs. When the final whistle sounded, Messi walked straight off the field and into the locker room.

The result was so perfectly MLS.

Atlanta United, a team that finished thirty-four points behind Miami, abruptly snuffed out Messi's MLS Cup hopes. For all the maneuvering the league did to ensure competitive balance in its roster rules, playoffs were the built-in equalizer.

The first round exit represented a stunning and deflating finish to Messi's first full season in the league. A few weeks later, Messi was named the league's MVP (and, notably, did not give the traditional MVP press conference), but the playoff loss outstripped that award. And it piled pressure onto 2025, the final year of his contract.

Failing to win the MLS Cup also put significantly more weight on Jorge Mas's efforts to secure the other part of his generational signing's MLS legacy.

19

A Race to Reinvent MLS

Twelve days after Lionel Messi made a beeline for the home locker room following Inter Miami's stunning elimination in the MLS Cup playoffs, Jorge Mas and other MLS owners on the sporting and competition committee sat around a conference table in the Great Room at the W Hotel in West Hollywood, California.

They were joined by Garber, a handful of MLS executives, and Apple TV's Eddy Cue.

At stake was the future of the league.

The spike in interest Messi delivered to MLS emphasized the league's strengths: its ability to draw crowds and leverage commercial partnerships. MLS set an attendance record in 2024, drawing more than eleven million fans for the first time. The league claimed that its total attendance ranked third in the world behind the Premier League and Bundesliga, but the figure obviously was goosed by the fact that MLS had nine to eleven more teams than those leagues and, therefore, many more games.

Off Messi's back, MLS set new highs on social media, in merchandise retail sales, and in league and club sponsorship sales. Its social presence grew at a higher rate than any other major men's North American sports league on TikTok, Instagram, and

YouTube. That was led by Inter Miami, of course, which was the most followed North American sports team on TikTok with 9.4 million followers and third-most on Instagram with 17.2 million followers. Messi's Inter Miami jersey continued to rank first in Adidas's player jersey sales across all sports.

Those numbers were great. None of them helped solve the bigger problems MLS faced.

The league still lacked national appeal. People still weren't tuning into games on Apple TV in high numbers, which limited that all-important media revenue. MLS had to find a way to attract more fans.

There were two fundamental issues facing the league: closing the gap in on-field quality between it and other top global leagues, and shrinking the perception gap that existed between what MLS was and what many American sports fans thought it was. MLS was still considered a low-level or minor league. Its stubborn insistence on forced competitive balance enabled a bland product lacking the jeopardy that drove storylines and interest in most other leagues.

MLS had to find a way to evolve—and to change minds.

The question at the committee meeting at the W Hotel was whether the league could alter its path in time to utilize the 2026 World Cup, or if it was too late.

The fact that it felt like a race to the World Cup was itself a failure.

The league's slow-burn build and training-wheels salary cap strategy might have supported the business and kept it stable through those volatile early years, but survival was no longer the goal. Something more drastic was necessary if MLS was going to break out with broader appeal.

MLS had done well to prepare for the end of its previous media deal in 2022. It aligned local, national, and international media agreements to expire at the same time. MLS went to the market with 100 percent of its inventory, looking for a novel type of partnership. The deal with Apple TV had not delivered the kind of interest and windfall that was promised, but whether it succeeded or failed, MLS did the work to land a strong partner and take a big swing.

A similar level of planning clearly had not taken place about how to evolve the sporting product to fully leverage the World Cup. In fact, MLS actually twice extended its collective bargaining agreement (CBA) coming out of the global pandemic, reducing salary growth from 13.9 percent in 2014–19 to 6.6 percent in 2019–24—this at a time when it should have been accelerating. Garber called the slower growth "necessary to ensure the survivability of the league" coming out of the COVID-affected season. But without Messi's 2023 arrival, it's unlikely MLS owners would be weighing the changes for its future with the same sort of urgency.

"The business decisions you make are the result of careful planning, detailed analysis, and relatively known truths," Garber said in defense of the league's continued cautious approach to change. "You know that your media rights are up. When you're dealing with the sporting side, there are so many unknowns, particularly in a league like ours, where we're becoming a bigger player in the global soccer marketplace. But still, we're trying to find our way to what ultimately is the end game. What is the true North Star that we could point to and put a pin in it and say: 'By this time, this is what we want MLS to look like.'

"Because how are you measuring that? Are you measuring it by your revenues? That's what the NFL does. Are you measuring it by your quality of play? Are you measuring it by your position in the global marketplace? There's so many things that go into determining how you can define what your product will look like on the field, because there are factors that are so far out of your control."

Garber said the league had to be careful how it invested in its on-field product because it had little idea of what the return would be on that investment.

"We're trying to ensure that the league goes down a path of sustained growth that will allow us to be ready when we have the financial resources to be able to go out and take more and more risk," he said.

There were some owners who believed that moment would never come without a more proactive approach. The enormous and immediate success in Inter Miami reset the conversation.

Landing the greatest player of all time was a symptom of a league bursting with owners trying to run bigger businesses, with higher aspirations for what their clubs could be. In previous years, a few MLS teams declared they wanted to be "global brands" by tacking an "FC" for "Football Club" onto the back of their name. Inter Miami signed Messi. It was a different universe of ambition.

Whereas MLS always had a few agitators, none more so than Mas, more stakeholders now realized the league was due for a course correction.

A few months before the committee meeting, as Atlanta prepared to host a sold-out crowd for Messi and Argentina at the Copa América, Steve Cannon, an executive who served as Atlanta United's alternate governor at MLS board meetings, noted that the time for debate had largely passed.

"This pulling back and forth, left and right between the progressive wing of the party and the less progressive wing, we don't have time for that," Cannon said in an interview at Atlanta's training facility. "We've got a three-year window to maximize this. If at the end of this window we have not grown our audience base, then things do start to crumble, right? Because at the end of the day, these media companies want eyeballs. And if your audience is only this big, you're not going to get money. Period.

"In a lot of ways there's a burning platform."

MLS leaders were masters at creating change that didn't overhaul anyone's core business, operating instead on the margins. What they were discussing in West Hollywood wasn't a tweak. It was reengineering some of the core aspects of the enterprise.

Messi had been in MLS for seventeen months. The World Cup was nineteen months away. This was the chance to leverage both Messi's popularity and the biggest event in the sport playing out in their backyards. The league spent decades building up a foundation. What they decided now might represent MLS's last big swing. No one could predict when—or if—there would be another chance like it.

It was also a moment in time that MLS leaders always knew was coming.

* * *

Standing at a dais in front of an enormous blue screen in Moscow, FIFA president Gianni Infantino looked out at the hall of global soccer dignitaries.

It was June 13, 2018. The Russian World Cup would kick off a day later, absent a U.S. men's team that missed the tournament for the first time since 1986. The American fiasco forced the country's soccer establishment into overdue self-evaluation and, under enormous pressure from a raging fanbase, a complete overhaul. The failure to qualify for Russia also placed even higher stakes on the announcement Infantino was about to make.

"So, we have a winner for the 2026 World Cup," started the bald-headed FIFA czar, who wore a blue suit jacket with FIFA's logo sewn into the front left pocket.

Eight years prior, the U.S. delegation, including former president

Bill Clinton, sat dejected when then-FIFA president Sepp Blatter announced the Qatari bid had upset the U.S. to host the 2022 tournament. *The Telegraph* reported that Clinton, upon returning to his suite at the Savoy Baur en Ville hotel in Zurich, Switzerland, grabbed an ornament off a table and threw it at a wall mirror, shattering the glass.

The hotel mirrors were safe this time.

"The member associations of Canada, Mexico, and USA have been selected by FIFA Congress to host the 2026 FIFA World Cup," Infantino revealed.

Officials from the three countries raised their arms and pumped their fists, then stood for a group hug. The men's World Cup was returning to North America for the first time since 1994. The implications were massive. The 1994 tournament launched MLS. The 1999 Women's World Cup elevated women's soccer to a historically influential perch. Three decades later, the hope was that the return of the sport's biggest event could be similarly impactful.

"There is no doubt that World Cup 2026 will elevate the sport of soccer to entirely new levels," MLS commissioner Don Garber said in a statement that day.

It would be easy to assume Garber was just a stuffy suit. His history at the NFL and then MLS put him in circles mingling with billionaire owners, Ivy Leaguers, and B-school corporate strategists. But Garber still saw himself as an outsider who shouldered his way into the C-suite with the savvy he picked up as a kid growing up in Bayside, Queens.

Garber attended State University of New York at Oneonta and started his career in public relations at a vocational school near LaGuardia Airport in New York City. Rising to the NFL was a dream. He felt he had to give everything he could to prove himself in an office where his resume didn't stack up—on paper, at least.

"I knew I was smarter and I would work harder," Garber

reflected. "They all had MBAs from Ivy League schools and were members of fancy golf clubs. They had nothing on me. And I knew it."

At the NFL, Garber proved adept at selling and marketing and finding new ways to engage fans. He impressed New England Patriots owner Robert Kraft and Kansas City Chiefs then-owner Lamar Hunt, who recruited him to take over their fledgling soccer league.

Journalists panned the decision to hire an NFL executive with no soccer background to run the league. But Garber was an incredible salesman for a league that needed it. Under his stewardship, MLS first survived and then thrived. It navigated contraction and near bankruptcy in 2001. It grew from thirteen markets in 2007 to twenty-three in 2018, bringing in billions in expansion fees. Franchise valuations continued to rise at inexplicable rates.

"I can confidently say we wouldn't be where we are today, in fact, the league may not still be in business, without Don's leadership," said FC Dallas owner Clark Hunt, son of Lamar Hunt and CEO and chairman of the NFL's Kansas City Chiefs.

* * *

Garber took success stories like the Seattle Sounders and Atlanta United and held them up as proof of concept for MLS's role in shaping American soccer. He found pots of gold at the end of the rainbow—the chance to negotiate a new media rights deal in 2022 was a big one—to justify the investment-phase losses that MLS teams and owners were still taking on. Those milestones buttressed the narrative of a thriving league. MLS franchise valuations soared.

Now Garber had the 2026 World Cup as the ultimate El Dorado, a moment that would validate and reward the league's outlook on growth and investment.

"Imagine any business having a defined moment of truth

eight years from now," Garber teased in an interview with *Forbes SportsMoney* in fall 2018.

Six years into that eight-year runway, however, MLS still didn't have a clear vision for exactly how it would leverage the World Cup. Garber saved MLS once, but survival this time would look different.

Garber had to show he could lead the league from stability to success.

* * *

In the room at the W Hotel, league owners and executives weighed a three-pronged approach that would effectively reinvent the league.

The changes were so substantial that Ferran Soriano, the CEO of City Football Group, which owned New York City FC, floated the idea of rebranding MLS as the "North American Premier League."

That idea didn't gain as much momentum as the resolve to address three core parts of the MLS business: the schedule, the competition structure, and the roster rules. The problems had been there for years. Now, they were all on the table at once.

The primary ideas were as follows.

1. Flip the Calendar

For its entire history, the MLS schedule mirrored the annual calendar. In 2024, the season started in late February and ran through the MLS Cup in early December. The format accommodated a league that stretched across an entire continent with a gamut of different climates. It also allowed a large proportion of MLS's games to be played during the summer, when the American sports schedule is lighter and many top European leagues are off.

From a purely sporting perspective, if MLS truly aspired to be a power player in global soccer, it could not do so without flipping its calendar.

As MLS evolved into a bigger player in the transfer market as both a buyer and a seller, it encountered difficulty during soccer's biannual transfer windows. MLS was not optimized to take full advantage of the sport's economy. Most European leagues operated on a summer-to-spring format, starting in early August and finishing in late May. The bulk of global soccer business was done during the summer window, which fell right in the middle of the MLS season.

If MLS teams wanted to get top dollar for their players, they had to sell them midseason, disrupting locker rooms and altering their competitive aspirations. Similarly, MLS clubs were often trying to buy players over the winter, in the middle of the European season, when foreign teams were less willing to sell (or would put a premium on available players). Newcomers who were signed over the summer had little time to impact an MLS team's season. On top of that, many players came out of contract in the summer, but MLS wasn't optimizing its chances to sign that inventory of free transfers, something that should have been a priority for a salary-capped league.

Flipping the calendar to the summer-spring format would allow MLS teams to become bigger participants in that global market and further grease player sales, a key revenue lever in the soccer business. The proposed schedule change had near-unanimous support from the league's chief soccer officers, who believed it would have a meaningful positive impact on roster quality and the overall level of the league.

The calendar flip, however, wasn't just a boon to the sporting side of the business. The change would optimize what MLS viewed as its most attractive television product: the MLS Cup playoffs.

In its current format, MLS's playoffs not only competed directly against the NFL and college football, but they were also interrupted by a two-week FIFA international break. Any momentum built up at the start of the postseason paused while players left to compete for their national teams.

A move to spring playoffs would pit the tournament against the NBA and NHL, but that was seen as more forgiving than the pressure produced by enormous American football audiences. Crucially, it would allow the MLS postseason to play out from start to finish without a break. There was no FIFA window in May.

"It would be a seismic move," said Portland Timbers owner Merritt Paulson, a longtime member of the sporting and competition committee.

However, there were real challenges to the calendar flip. Due to the geographic realities of the league, MLS would have to take a winter break similar to the ones in Germany, Austria, and Scandinavian leagues.

Even with a pause, though, cold-weather markets like Montreal, Toronto, Minnesota, Chicago, and New England, among others, would likely have more home games in February and November. Those markets would also lose out on their most attractive slate of summer matches. Many teams would have to upgrade their training facilities. Some would have to alter spaces in their stadiums. All of that came at a cost.

Conversely, a summer break wasn't seen as a negative in southern markets like Dallas, Miami, Orlando, Houston, and Austin. Soaring temperatures were becoming more of an issue for those teams, impacting the entertainment value both on the field and in the stands.

MLS studied a change to the summer-spring format twice before, and both times the impact on cold-weather markets squashed the talks. With expansion, however, MLS had more warm-weather markets to accommodate games in February, November, and December. And the benefits from a soccer and media standpoint were generating real momentum.

2. Reformat the Competition

To put it simply, MLS needed to find a way to make more people care more about its games—and for more of the season. Of the three prongs, the competition makeover had a chance to make a meaningful impact on the product's appeal in a short amount of time. And, unlike the other two prongs, it did not cost the owners more money.

The fundamental problem was this: MLS had around 50 percent more teams than the average global soccer league, but it didn't have relegation. Thus, the league had more games, but a smaller proportion of total games with consequence. They further diluted the consequences by qualifying eighteen of thirty teams into the playoffs.

Competitions like the Premier League were able to manufacture a highly entertaining product in part because teams were always either chasing a title or European qualification, or running away from relegation. It was fighting the Wrexham Effect. Could MLS engineer enough jeopardy without promotion and relegation?

MLS decided to study changes to its format that would make more games matter for a longer period of time during the season. In theory, that would create more compelling long-term narratives and lead to increased fan engagement and ticket sales.

The committee considered a proposal designed by Twenty First Group, the soccer consulting firm, that would eliminate MLS's two-conference structure in favor of a single-table league-wide format. Within that single table, teams would also compete in five six-team divisions for division crowns. Divisional winners would be guaranteed a playoff berth.

In this new format, teams would play all their nondivisional opponents either home or away (twenty-four total games), and then each divisional opponent home and away (ten games). That reduced some of the conference imbalance that influenced MLS's current regular-season competition. In addition, by placing the second set of five divisional games at the end of the season, MLS believed it could add more games of consequence for the final stretch of the campaign.

The proposal also included significant changes to MLS's playoff format. The idea was modeled after the Australian Football League, which gave top teams the chance to advance in the postseason while winning fewer games and also giving some higher seeds a "second chance" elimination game against a lower seed.

The proposal was meant to give a more meaningful advantage to higher seeds, which added value to more games during the regular season. It would also create more high-stakes, single-elimination games without losing playoff inventory.

The idea was that the changes would create more "tentpole moments" across the season; limit dead rubber games; improve the regular-season stretch run by creating more playoff uncertainty and increasing the value of seeding position; and create more meaningful matches overall.

3. Revamp the Roster Rules

This was the most important change on the docket at the November meeting in Los Angeles.

As one executive put it: As transformational as the first two prongs might be to the league's structure, they were treating symptoms rather than the disease.

MLS's roster guidelines were overly complicated and far too inefficient. More money was spent outside the cap limitations than inside them. The mechanisms put in place to limit costs and preserve competitive balance made it nearly impossible to maximize quality based on spend. If decades of failures in Concacaf Champions play weren't enough evidence, Inter Miami's failures in Saudi Arabia underlined the issues.

MLS rosters were top-heavy, with enormous disparities in the quality of players. Getting one or two decisions wrong could tank a season—or set back a roster build by years. While every other league in the world had some sort of correlation between spending and quality, MLS did not.

"I see zero empirical evidence that spending money leads to success in MLS at this point in time," said Seattle Sounders owner Adrian Hanauer, a longtime member of the sporting and competition committee.

That was not a flaw. It was by design. Messi's presence in the league had helped place more attention on the issue. Even he couldn't overcome the deficiencies in how MLS teams were built.

How could owners feel any sort of pressure or incentive to spend if it didn't correlate to winning?

Changing the rules was an antidote against the "race to mediocrity" Mas decried.

MLS had been far too slow in reacting to the evolution of the global transfer market. Teams had little wiggle room to add impactful players in their prime. Because acquisition costs factored into salary cap figures, and because MLS teams had just three uncapped spots for players, there were entire categories of players that teams couldn't consider unless they were coming on a free transfer. It was just too costly.

On top of that, MLS was living in an unsustainable spending zone. Teams were putting enough money into rosters that game-day revenue could no longer cover costs. With expansion fees drying up, that became an existential problem. Meanwhile, the product wasn't good enough to attract bigger television audiences and thus more media revenue.

If the aim was to be one of the top leagues in the world, as Garber often said, and if it wanted to truly become a "league of choice," then MLS had to spend more and spend better.

The goal in changing the roster rules was complicated, but it boiled down to two core ideas: MLS had to increase its spending on players, and it had to ease restrictions on *how* teams invested that money.

But there was one big question: How much more money was needed to actually create enough interest that it would eventually drive more revenue?

"The core challenge we have right now is not that owners don't want to spend another $50 million each, because they will do it," MLS executive Todd Durbin said. "What they are wrestling with is: How do I get comfortable with that increase in expenditure actually making a difference, as opposed to just piling onto the losses? That's the heart of it."

There was another issue to consider: If competitive balance wasn't going to be the league's North Star anymore, how far were fans and owners willing to move away from that concept? Durbin pointed to other leagues around the world—for example, Mexico, Holland, and Portugal—where super clubs defined leagues' brands and popularity.

"Is the optimal approach to, rather than requiring all of our teams to spend $50 million, which would be a big roll of the dice, would we be prepared to let those teams that want to run away from the pack do so?" he asked. "And then have the halo effect for everybody else? In other words, would we be prepared to have a league of super teams?"

If not, then what limitations could MLS impose without avoiding some of the same "inefficiencies" people wanted to eliminate from the system? Or, as some owners argued, did MLS have to start from scratch precisely so it could find better solutions to these problems?

* * *

There were several challenges MLS had to solve to green-light the changes.

Northern-market teams sought mitigation for the hit their business would take after the calendar switch and the cost of updating facilities, but some operators were opposed to any sort of mitigation. Both the roster rule changes and the calendar flip would require Major League Soccer Players Association (MLSPA) approval and likely a new CBA, a substantial hurdle amid an increasingly tense relationship between the MLSPA and the league.

MLS also felt these shifts—many of which came at an increased cost to the league but delivered more value to Apple TV—required adjustments to the media partnership.

Before any of this could happen, however, the overhaul required the endorsement of the sporting and competition committee at its meeting in Los Angeles. These changes would then face the larger task of the full board. MLS had long operated with a goal of unanimity. That no longer felt like a realistic path.

"It is really hard to function with thirty owners and thirty teams all with disparity issues, all with different challenges," Jorge Mas said. "You're not going to get thirty teams to agree to everything. So what we need to do is do what is best for the overall. What is best that can push us, right? And if there's four or five that disagree, the majority needs to prevail."

The next steps required a degree of courage and risk-taking that Garber endorsed in 2001, when he was two years into his tenure and pitched the creation of SUM to owners who were bleeding cash. At that moment, Garber asked owners to quadruple down, put more money in, and bet on the commercial market.

Now, for MLS to grow, Garber once again needed to ask owners to take on more losses. The question wasn't just how much more money would be required, but also whether this bet would work. Would the additional spending drive enough audience over the final years of the Apple TV deal to bring in more revenue in the next media contract?

"We've got to really make the right decision and base it on facts and data and thoughtful analysis," Garber cautioned.

What worried some owners was whether Garber, now twenty-five years in and nearing the end of his run, would pound his fist on the table for an idea the same way he did for SUM.

It was complicated. Garber knew he wouldn't be at the helm to implement the bulk of whatever changes were to come—or to navigate the economic fallout. MLS also hadn't prepared for who might come after Garber. There was no succession plan in place, and there was a power vacuum under Garber because Gary Stevenson, his top deputy, was expected to leave around the same time. But Garber's legacy would be tied to whatever course the league took—or didn't take—in the coming months ahead of the 2026 World Cup.

A quarter century into the job, the commissioner was a polished executive, but he very much retained the skills forged in those Queens schoolyards. He wasn't afraid of a fight and was still a savvy political operator. It was clear he was trying to get a read of the room. What wasn't obvious was whether Garber had made up his mind on the right path forward.

The commissioner sensed that business as usual wouldn't be enough to spark the seismic change that was needed. Rather than lean on his deputies in the league office or depend on a committee, Garber crafted a plan for league-wide small groups to discuss and debate change.

"There are a lot of really sophisticated people who understand the game now, including our owners," Garber explained. "So how we engage with them on sporting decisions has changed dramatically because they have a point of view that's learned, that's experienced. They're being advised by very, very knowledgeable technical people, and the league is no longer sitting at the top making decisions for them."

The "pods," as MLS executives called them, were made up of different teams and included owners, chief business officers, and chief soccer officers. It was a good way to manage and involve all constituents, but the pods were also a bottom-up approach to the type of strategic change that typically required a strong hand to guide the organization through the risk.

This strategy would also take longer to get to a solution.

The pods were warmly received by most decision-makers around MLS, who too often felt that they weren't heard when debates occurred over league-wide changes.

"This has been one of the best processes we've ever had. The league's done as good work on this as anything I've seen," Los Angeles FC co-owner Larry Berg said. " I think the owners have been, as a whole, more involved than anything I've seen. It's a higher-stakes decision, and I actually accept the fact that the timing we're on has actually been pretty quick."

Others saw it differently.

As one owner said: "They boiled the ocean with those pods."

The conversations revealed that stakeholders were open to change. Messi and the revenue he generated opened eyes around the league. What was happening with Messi in Miami wasn't going to be exactly replicable, but the Argentine's impact proved a concept: MLS teams could resonate outside of their normal bubble if the audience was given a reason to tune in.

Mas pushed the league to embrace that reality.

"Every single dollar that we spend on roster and players, that's what the fans want," Mas said during conversations about how he wanted to see MLS change. "The fans want to see better players. They want to see better teams. They want to see better quality. I'm fixated on that. I am fixated on that because I have proved out a model that if you invest in players and you invest in winners, you invest in the product that people want to see, your revenue responds."

* * *

At the November 2024 meeting in Los Angeles, Mas argued his support of one area he felt would reduce the perception issues. Inter Miami was one of two MLS teams scheduled to play in FIFA's expanded Club World Cup in the U.S. in the summer of 2025. The Seattle Sounders had qualified by winning the 2022 Concacaf Champions League, while FIFA handed Inter Miami the host's berth as soon as they won the Supporters' Shield—a decision that rankled fans who felt the governing body was shoehorning Messi into the competition. (In June 2025, Los Angeles FC would qualify as a third MLS team in the competition.)

Mas argued that MLS should aim to change its roster rules in 2025 so Inter Miami and Seattle could properly strengthen their squads ahead of the tournament, where they would play teams like Atlético Madrid, Paris Saint-Germain, and Palmeiras. The lessons of the 2024 preseason in Saudi Arabia were still fresh enough in Mas's mind to appreciate the implications that came with the Club World Cup results.

The Club World Cup imposed the same problems MLS faced

in the Concacaf Champions Cup, where its lack of quality depth was exposed by Mexican sides that not only outspent many of their northern rivals but also spread that money up and down the entire roster. Now, MLS's weakness would be displayed on an even bigger stage.

A global competition like this could be a game changer for the league—but it could also reinforce every negative perception. Mas pleaded for rule changes that would allow teams to spend more aggressively ahead of the tournament.

His ask would lead to the typical compromise that came out of the sporting and competition committee: a deal that made neither side happy. MLS teams participating in the Club World Cup were given an extra $750,000 to build their rosters.

Mas was frustrated, but he knew the odds of getting the change he wanted were slim. Historically, it wasn't an easy room to convince.

The longtime co-chair of the committee was Hunt, the FC Dallas owner better known around the country as the owner who built a dynasty around Kansas City Chiefs quarterback Patrick Mahomes and coach Andy Reid.

The Hunts' history in American soccer ran deeper than anyone else's in the MLS boardroom. Clark's father, Lamar Hunt, was a key figure in the league's creation, and, along with Phil Anschutz and Robert Kraft, had kept MLS afloat when prospects looked dour in the early aughts. Lamar Hunt had a similarly outsized impact on the sport itself as a North American Soccer League investor in the 1970s and 1980s. The Lamar Hunt U.S. Open Cup trophy, awarded to the winner of the most historic tournament in American soccer, bears his name.

The Hunt family at one point owned three MLS teams: Sporting Kansas City, the Columbus Crew, and FC Dallas. They sold the first two and kept the latter, which was located in the family's home market. Now Clark, who played soccer at Southern Methodist University, and Dan, the youngest son, ran the team.

Clark Hunt had, over two decades, earned a reputation within MLS circles of being a fierce advocate for that NFL-influenced governing tenet of the league: competitive balance. He wielded heavy influence over the sporting and competition committee, which for many years was known as "product strategy," before a rebrand in 2023. The group weighed changes to the rules and regulations governing the on-field product. Often, the group leaned toward Hunt's conservative instinct, building guardrails into MLS rules that protected against upsetting the balance he felt was sacrosanct.

On more than a few occasions, Hunt's skeptical eye toward change led to confrontations.

In one in-person meeting in Cabo San Lucas in 2019, Berg, then a newer committee member, explained that his team was aiming to sign young DPs who could thrive in MLS and then be sold. As long as a player could be moved for a transfer fee, Los Angeles FC's owners saw young DPs as working capital.

Berg, a Harvard Business School alum who built his fortune in private equity with Apollo Global Management, believed MLS should craft a rule that would allow teams to invest even more heavily in top young players. He pointed to his newest young DP, nineteen-year-old Uruguayan national team prospect Brian Rodríguez, and argued that the winger's MLS success could help grow the league's standing in the global marketplace.

That type of signing is good for everyone in the league, Berg declared. Every team should be happy that Los Angeles FC had landed a player like Rodríguez.

"Well, I'm not necessarily happy about that," Clark Hunt retorted.

Berg fired back at Hunt.

The back-and-forth escalated before eventually petering out. For the most part, the committees were cordial. Debate was almost academic. But there was an inevitability to such arguments in a room filled with billionaires accustomed to getting their way. Berg's advocacy, and that argument, eventually yielded the under-22 Initiative.

Since Messi's signing, however, there was a different level of tension in the discussions. For months now, the league-run pods spitballed the changes. The ideas were big ones.

Flipping the calendar would maximize transfer windows and boost the sporting product. But it would also have a costly impact on cold-weather markets. Overhauling the regular-season and playoff formats would add more games of consequence but would drastically alter what core fans were used to. Scrapping and then rebuilding the roster rules—adding spending, simplifying the salary cap to make it less restrictive, but also maintaining DPs and u-22s to give teams wiggle room to add special players—had been the biggest boardroom flashpoint for years.

A presentation from Twenty First Group's AJ Swoboda endorsed the changes. Passionate debate ensued in the room. There were moments, again, when things grew emotional.

Then, the room quieted.

"I want to share my thoughts," Hunt said in his Texas twang.

While Hunt was typically seen as the bulwark against sweeping reform, and while his family history gave him enormous leverage in the league's power circles, he was also considered by owners as one of the smartest operators in the room.

The proposed three-tiered revamp would essentially flip MLS completely on its head and alter decades of strategy. If there was anyone on the committee who was going to stand against the changes, it would likely be Hunt, and he could often sway the room.

But this time, what he said surprised his colleagues.

"When I first looked at this, I was like: 'I don't like this. I don't understand it,'" Hunt said. "As a result, I was against it. But once I actually sat down and started really thinking about it and tried to understand what it is that this thing's doing, the more I kind of let it sit, I actually came around to really liking it."

Hunt's endorsement was consequential. The owners on the committee left the room believing change could actually happen—and maybe even in time for the 2026 World Cup.

The recommendations would be discussed in front of the whole board in Brooklyn the following month, December 2024.

Mas, though, couldn't make it back to the East Coast before confronting more immediate concerns. Inter Miami coach Tata Martino informed Mas he was stepping down for personal reasons.

The search for a replacement was underway. It would reveal for the first time just how much influence Messi held in Miami. And it would spark an even more ambitious approach from Inter Miami, which was intent to capitalize on Messi, whether or not the league was ready to keep up.

20

The Balance of Power

Lionel Messi was never going to be considered a "normal" player in Miami.

How could he be?

The Argentine was perhaps the most recognized person in the world. His accomplishments in the game were unparalleled. He won more trophies than any player in history. And if that wasn't enough, a clause in his contract defined him as more than just a player—the 10 percent stake of Inter Miami he would acquire when he retired made him a partner in the club.

"It's Messi's team," said Inter Miami winger Julian Gressel, who won MLS Cups with Atlanta and the Columbus Crew before rejoining Martino in Miami in 2024. "It's nobody else's team. It's weird, because you always say, in every team I've been on, nobody's bigger than the crest. Nobody's bigger than the club. Well, Messi is fucking bigger than everybody else, and he's definitely bigger than Inter Miami."

That was Inter Miami's biggest advantage, but it could potentially be its biggest downfall.

There was risk in ceding too much power to a player. From day one, Inter Miami tried to thread that needle.

In MLS, designated players are the quarterbacks and ace pitchers. A good one can win you a title. A bad one can sink multiple seasons. DPs were treated—and paid—accordingly. Due to MLS regulations, the franchise players arguably influenced team success more than even a Patrick Mahomes–level quarterback and shifted most of a club's discretionary spending toward the top three roster spots. Getting a DP signing wrong could cripple a team for years.

There was legitimate value in having the right personalities in those spots. A few weeks into his time with the Chicago Fire in 2017, German legend Bastian Schweinsteiger stopped by a birthday party for American midfielder Dax McCarty being held in a basement bar in the Lincoln Park neighborhood of Chicago. Schweinsteiger's teammates, some of whom had just finished playing college soccer, taught the overdressed World Cup winner how to play flip cup, a beer-chugging drinking game typically seen at fraternity parties.

Schweinsteiger leveraged his celebrity to be a leader and unifier in the locker room and to help build confidence in younger players. In his first year in Chicago, the Fire enjoyed its best season in half a decade.

But a celebrity signing could wreck a team, too.

Misjudging a DP's motivation could often lead to major headaches. Inter Miami experienced that with Messi's former Argentina teammate, Gonzalo Higuaín. "I thought I would come here and play with a cigarette in my mouth," Higuaín spouted in an interview. "And, instead, it is difficult."

How much does intrinsic motivation influence performance? Higuaín had fifteen goals in his first fifty-two MLS games in 2020–22. The striker took the figurative cigarette out of his mouth and really started trying around the time he decided he was going to retire toward the end of the 2022 season. The result? He scored fourteen times in his last seventeen matches, Inter Miami won four of its final five, and the team snuck into the playoffs.

That type of significant impact meant teams often coddled their highly paid players to try to coax on-field production. Messi was that—but amplified. His comfort mattered not just for on-field success, but off the field, too. And not just for Inter Miami, but for all of MLS.

Inter Miami made decisions with Messi in mind before the World Cup winner even signed. Xavier Asensi, the team's chief business officer, wasn't hired from Barcelona randomly. His connection with Messi's longtime club was seen as an asset in No. 10's recruitment. Inter Miami even hired Tuli Arellano, the longtime boyfriend of Messi's sister, María Sol, as an assistant academy coach in January 2023, a full seven months before Messi arrived.

Then, of course, Miami inked his decorated former teammates. The club insisted those players weren't signed at Messi's behest. Henderson and Inter Miami's front office felt that putting those players around Messi held real on-field benefits. In the past, big-name stars integrated more easily into MLS locker rooms when they had at least one teammate who played at a similar level: David Beckham and Robbie Keane in Los Angeles, Thierry Henry and Tim Cahill with the New York Red Bulls. The disconnect between players who had been in the top leagues and those who hadn't could create on-field issues, but it also could be isolating in the locker room. Frustrations could spill out onto the field. One famous example in MLS lore was Zlatan Ibrahimović, who could be ruthless to his LA Galaxy teammates, calling veteran midfielder Perry Kitchen by the name "Kevin" for an entire season.

It was necessary to have at least some world-class players on the roster with Messi, both to combine with him on the field and to relate to him off it. Inter Miami wanted to ensure they did everything they could to optimize his chance of success.

As for Messi's motivation, Miami had zero concerns. His initial 2023 meeting in sporting director Chris Henderson's office ("Tell me what trophies I can win") showed his commitment. He was the first to arrive at the facility nearly every day. And despite his off-field responsibilities, the league's biggest star made one thing clear: soccer comes first. That mentality rubbed off on those around him. A mantra soon permeated the front office: "Every single decision that gets made has to be soccer first."

That Messi had high demands wasn't a surprise. It certainly was felt within the team itself.

It was rare for the star to publicly show up younger or less talented teammates by waving his hands in disgust, like some big-name MLS headliners did. But that didn't mean he didn't push them. Messi spent his entire career at the very highest levels of the sport. He expected perfect touches and consistent performances. MLS was more than a few tiers down from Barcelona, Paris Saint-Germain, and Argentina, but he held every player to a high standard—and he could be biting in his criticisms at times, whether in training or in the locker room.

It hits differently to be dressed down by the greatest player of all time. Not every player coped well with the pressure.

"In this year and a half, I have seen a lot of [players] around that say, 'But it's too much because we cannot even miss a pass.' Or, 'We have to do everything right.' Or, 'If we do something wrong, it's hard,'" Inter Miami assistant Javier Morales said. "You have players with that mentality, and then you have players with another mentality. They say, 'Okay, I have to do better. I want to be at the same level. I want to improve.'

"There is no right or wrong, but I guarantee to you that the players with better mentality have more chances to play the top level, and players who have the other mentality, that they say, 'Oh, but listen, I don't want to play every game at the same level.' Or, 'I don't want to train every day at the same level.' Okay. I know that those players are not going to make it. . . . When you are at the top level, this is how you have to be wired. The strongest survive because the pressure is so high."

For Morales, the more difficult adjustment was actually on Messi's side. The eight-time Ballon d'Or winner had to accept that after spending his entire career at the very highest levels, not every touch from every teammate was going to be perfect. Not every pass will arrive exactly at the right time. Not every run will be rewarded.

"For the top players, it's hard to adapt," Morales said. "This is like if you don't have money and you have to adapt to having a lot of money, it's going to be easier, right? But then if you have a lot of money and you have to be poor, you're going to struggle, right? Because you've already seen what happened in the other place."

It was easy to point to the assembling of Messi and friends and say Messi ran the club, and executives at other teams around the league, many of whom had never worked with a figure even close to his level, lampooned and criticized Inter Miami for exactly that. The better way to say it was probably that the club was centered around the idea of keeping Messi happy. Every decision was filtered through that lens first.

Messi's influence had a grip on the organization, even though it wasn't always the player himself wielding the power.

There were times, however, when it very much was the case.

* * *

Tata Martino appeared at ease in the racing-style chair inside Inter Miami's media room.

The veteran coach had a quiet, kind sensibility that endeared him to just about everyone at the team facility, media included, and that personality was on full display as the press conference started. Martino flashed his trademark smirk as he glanced at a reporter with a penchant for sneaking two questions into what was supposed to be a one-question-only format.

"*Dos preguntas*," Martino said, finally revealing his full grin. "The last [time]."

He laughed.

The mood in the room that day—November 22, 2024—was far different from one month earlier, when Inter Miami was knocked out of the MLS Cup playoffs by his former team, Atlanta United. On that night at DRV PNK Stadium, Martino sat, arms crossed, a slight frown on his face.

Martino had endured immense pressure in numerous other jobs. This wasn't even his highest-stress partnership with Messi, having managed his countryman at both Barcelona and Argentina's national team. But it was clear that the 2024 season had worn on him—and that perhaps his experience told him more adversity, some beyond his control, was ahead.

"*Bueno*," he started. *Well.*

"I'm going to tell you all something everyone already knows," Martino said in Spanish. "But to tone down the rumors and these issues a bit, for strictly personal reasons, I have to leave Atlanta."

He shook his head. Atlanta? No, not Atlanta, Martino chuckled. He noted he had just been talking about Atlanta with somebody before the press conference started.

"I need to leave Inter," he clarified. "We can't return next year. I need to be in Rosario for personal reasons."

The decision surprised everyone at the club. Martino was home in Argentina when he called Messi, then Mas, with the news the prior weekend. The manager offered no further information other than his need to stay in Rosario for at least the next four or five months.

"I called Leo and told him I had a personal need to be in

Rosario, that the first half of the year was going to be complicated for me," Martino explained later to *The Athletic*. "Once I explained that it wasn't a health issue, that it was just a very difficult personal matter behind my decision, he felt more at ease—with the necessary discretion. It wasn't something to discuss in detail, just to communicate a decision. After that, I went through it with the club's leadership and then with the players."

Messi called Mas, who was in Zaragoza, Spain, for meetings with the Segunda Liga club he co-owned. He asked who the owner had in mind to replace Martino.

"I'm putting a list together," Mas said. "Let me think about it."

Inter Miami's front office narrowed the pool of potential replacements to four, but Mas had his own top two: Javier Mascherano and Gabriel Milito. Both Argentines were Messi's former teammates, but Mas also had connections with both of them.

Mas had recruited Mascherano in 2019 as Inter Miami's first major player signing, ordering from Graziano's, a well-known Argentinian steakhouse in Miami, to MasTec's Coral Gables offices during a meeting that stretched for eight hours. They discussed a deal that would've seen Mascherano retire as a player in Miami before joining the academy staff.

"I loved him," Mas recalled of those early conversations.

Milito and his brother, Diego, once played for Real Zaragoza, where Mas was also president as well as part of the ownership group.

Mas called Messi to let him know his top two. He felt it was important to make sure his star player was on the same page about the hire. Messi made clear he wasn't going to try to direct the search.

"Leo was super respectful," Mas reflected. "He said, 'I'm not calling anyone. I'm not talking to anyone with you. This is you. You guys hire the coach.' He's very conscious of 'It's not my gig to put a coach here.'"

Messi was understandably sensitive to how his involvement might look. At both Barcelona and Argentina, he was accused of using his status to influence decisions. At Barcelona in 2020, sporting director Eric Abidal, a former teammate, explained his decision to fire coach Ernesto Valverde in an interview with Catalan newspaper *Sport* by saying that, as an ex-player, he could "smell" when players had an issue with a manager.

Blaming players didn't sit well with Messi, who first went to Instagram and then sat for an interview with another Barcelona publication, *Mundo Deportivo*, to push back on the narrative.

"I don't know what went through his head to make him say that, but I responded because I felt attacked," Messi said. "I felt like he was attacking the players. And too many things are said about the locker room, like [players] control everything, they appoint and remove coaches, bring in players—and especially about me. It's like I have a lot of power and make decisions. And it bothered me that someone from the club, a technical director, would say that . . . putting the players in the middle of a dismissal like the manager's seemed crazy to me. It's the technical director who makes the decisions and has to take responsibility. He's the one who makes the decisions. That's why I came out to clarify things. I knew I couldn't let the sporting director attacking me like that go unpunished."

Mas was unconcerned with the appearance of influence or the power dynamics. He was drawn to the celebrity of professional athletes. He liked handling contracts with big stars and wanted Messi to feel like he had a direct line to the owner. He also knew how critical his star was to the business—both in the present and future.

"I'm not going to hire a coach here without talking to him," Mas said.

Milito was under contract with Brazilian club Atlético Mineiro, making a deal more difficult. Mascherano worked with the Argentine federation as a youth coach, heading up both the under-20 national team and then, later, the Olympic side. He received mixed reviews in both jobs. His u-20s failed to qualify for their World Cup and later were awarded a bid as host. At the Olympics, Argentina's u-23s fell to host France 1–0 in a quarterfinal.

Those results didn't deter Mas. He knew Mascherano's lack of experience was a weakness but still felt he was a strong fit and was willing to bet that Inter Miami could navigate Mascherano's learning curve and keep winning. Hiring a coach who could manage the big stars was as important as anything else.

"For me Masche's biggest thing was working with the young guys," Mas recalled a few months after the hire. "Obviously because he played with the four [big-name players] at Barça, it was an easier transition. But Masche is tough. He's not going to let them walk all over him, and Messi respects him big-time. He was Messi's captain. So the guy has authority. He has a good personal relationship with them. He's got an ability to put the friendship aside. He's managed young kids."

When Mas called the former Argentina captain, Mascherano said he would love the opportunity to work in Miami as long as the Argentine federation signed off. The former midfielder and center back, nicknamed "El Jefecito" or "the little chief," also wanted to speak with Messi.

Mascherano drove to meet with his former teammate, who was still in Argentina, and within forty-eight hours, the deal was done. Four days after Martino's final press conference, Inter Miami named Mascherano head coach.

Around the league, eyes rolled. Of course it was a former teammate of Messi taking charge. The legend must have orchestrated it himself. The optics were enough to declare it as official: Messi ran Inter Miami.

"He's going to have more friends now at Inter Miami. It seems that's the bottom line: What's going to make Leo Messi feel at home?" *ESPN Deportes* host Mauricio Pedroza said on air. "What's going to [make him] comfortable at Inter Miami, and that's probably just being surrounded by the people he trusts, the people he knows, not necessarily the people who are going to be the best for the team. . . . Javier Mascherano, there is no managerial excuse for him to be there. It's all about what makes Leo happy."

Keeping their star comfortable *was* the most important factor in Miami's short- and long-term success. The ability to manage the locker room, to understand the star players, was a close second. But that's why they believed Mascherano was uniquely qualified to coach this Inter Miami team. The team was trading Mascherano's inexperience for what they deemed more crucial to success: managing the stars and everything that came with them.

Mas got out in front of the gossip when he introduced Mascherano as coach. There would be no cloak and dagger about Messi's role. He admitted what most owners didn't: Messi had influence—with Mas's blessing.

"I had a specific conversation with him. Leo gave me what I asked him, which was input," Mas said. "That was Leo's involvement and engagement with me, which [happens] frankly all the time."

It was the first public acknowledgment of Messi's influence on soccer decisions.

Mas had no regrets about keeping his most valuable player in the loop, nor did he think it was abnormal. MLS teams usually keep their biggest assets in mind when hiring a coach or making a major decision. They just don't typically consult with them on coaching hires. No team had employed a player of Messi's prominence, though, let alone one who would become an owner of that team after retiring.

Athlete influence on coaching hires happened in other sports and leagues. In the NBA, franchise players like LeBron James, Giannis Antetokounmpo, Kyrie Irving, and Kevin Durant reportedly were consulted during coaching searches. Even Messi had, in the past, been accused of influencing hires at Barcelona. Coincidentally, Tata Martino's appointment was said to have been recommended by Messi, something No. 10 denied.

The most prominent example in American soccer was David Beckham's management directing the late 2007 hiring of Ruud Gullit at the LA Galaxy. Gullit's tenure did not go well, and Bruce Arena replaced him in summer 2008. That move reversed Beckham's fortunes in Los Angeles; the Inter Miami co-owner won his two MLS Cups under Arena.

"The mistake we made here was not being smart enough—and that's my fault—to see inevitably the conflict that was going to come of this," then-AEG executive Tim Leiweke said of the Gullit hire in Grant Wahl's book, *The Beckham Experiment*. "And it's too bad. The mistake we made is not getting everybody on the same page."

To a lot of people, the parallel was obvious. When Beckham held too much influence on sporting decisions in Los Angeles, the team faltered. When an MLS-experienced manager was hired, they won the MLS Cup.

But Mas felt the club *was* on the same page. Messi wasn't Beckham, and the Inter Miami job was not the same as the LA Galaxy job in 2008. The locker room Mascherano would manage was far different than what Arena built in Los Angeles. The LA Galaxy was filled with MLS journeymen. Inter Miami was mostly South American imports and homegrown players. It wasn't the same job.

The whirlwind around the coaching hire was just the beginning of Messi's growing sway leaking into public view.

* * *

Inter Miami added more than a dozen employees to work with Messi, everything from a trainer to a new equipment manager, dietician, and podiatrist. And while Messi didn't ask for it, few players had the gravitas to prompt their club to create youth teams from scratch just so their best player's kids could have a convenient place to play.

The December 2023 arrival of one of Messi's former Barcelona academy coaches, Guillermo Hoyos, whom Messi once called "my footballing godfather," had the biggest impact.

After coaching Messi and spending five years with Barcelona B, Hoyos had what can charitably be called an itinerant career, working for sixteen teams in seventeen years before reuniting with his former pupil in Fort Lauderdale.

Hoyos arrived at the end of the 2023 season with a staff of four that called themselves "La Structura," or "The Structure." He spent most of his time with the academy and the club's professional reserve team, but for many, it was clear he had designs on something bigger—and that he knew he had Messi's backing if he sought it. As the hierarchy started to change in the front office, that backing suddenly became a central storyline.

Halfway through the 2024 season, Inter Miami hired former Barcelona and Arsenal executive Raul Sanllehi as director of football to oversee all of soccer personnel, including Henderson.

When Henderson was hired in 2021, Mas told him another executive eventually would be hired to run the department, which would allow Henderson to focus on the first team roster and operations. After the sanctions hit in 2021, the plans changed. Three years later, it was jarring when Sanllehi arrived. Henderson successfully navigated the salary cap challenges related to both the sanctions and Messi's arrival, but the club unceremoniously booted Henderson from his office so Sanllehi could move in.

The writing was on the wall.

By the end of the 2024 season, wheels were in motion for more change. The team fired Mark Prizant, a former Manchester United scout and Inter Miami's director of scouting. Niki Budalić, essentially the team's technical director, was moved into a peripheral role. That pair was replaced by Bernardo Loustalot, a lawyer and Hoyos's right-hand man.

Martino's departure was the most visible piece of the upheaval. Some in the club believed the veteran coach saw the turf wars behind the scenes and decided to leave before they got worse. Martino was very strategic and did not want to be put in a position to fail. The coach later insisted it was only for personal reasons that he left. "The thing is, I actually saw the change coming, but I didn't really suffer through it, so to speak," Martino said.

Henderson met multiple times with Mascherano upon his arrival, and the new coach pushed for the MLS-experienced sporting director to stay. But Henderson had an offer to become the sporting director at Atlanta United, where he reunited with Garth Lagerwey, the executive with whom he won multiple MLS Cups in Seattle. He decided to go.

"I had a lot of similar feelings to when I left Seattle in the fact that the team, I felt, couldn't have been in a better spot," he reflected. "We won the Supporters' Shield, set the points record. I felt like I was leaving on a really good note. The owners, Jorge and Jose, were great. David [Beckham] was great. Messi was great. I felt comfortable with it and appreciative of it, no matter the highs and lows of those four years. It was an incredible four years that I don't think anyone in MLS could experience."

Henderson's departure only upped the stakes of the power struggle. For two months, a vacuum existed atop the sporting department. It was unclear who was in charge and making decisions. Sanllehi didn't typically pick players, so Hoyos took on some of those responsibilities. Mascherano was involved. Ownership, of course, played a role.

Somehow, Inter Miami landed all of its top targets. But tension built.

One month after Atlanta hired Henderson away from Miami, Sanllehi boarded the team bus in Las Vegas after a January 2025 preseason game. There, in front of the players, Messi confronted him. The Messi-Sanllehi bust-up leaked in a report by MLS reporter Tom Bogert. The disagreement was ostensibly about Hoyos being on the wrong bus, but multiple people within the team said that it didn't pass the smell test. Henderson and Budalić had almost always rode on the player bus, along with the coaching staff, in 2023 and 2024. It wasn't about the bus; it was about the front-office power dynamics.

After the incident, Sanllehi moved to Inter Miami's Coral Gables office, where nonsporting staff was based. The club claimed this had been the plan all along. Within days of the bus incident, the club promoted Hoyos, Messi's "soccer godfather," and named him sporting director.

Claims that this was Messi seeking power over player decisions missed the mark. There was a difference between getting his guy into the room and making a power play. Messi didn't need Hoyos in the room to have influence. Mas already told the world that Messi had a direct line to the owners. And they were happy to hear from him.

"He has his opinions on the things that we need to do to help him win, and he's vocal about them," Inter Miami co-owner Jose Mas told me in a phone interview four days before the Las Vegas bus confrontation. "And I appreciate that, because I think that he is a very, very interested party. He's decisive. I really believe that he gives great insight into things that he thinks we need to do better as a club. And I think that's great."

Mas laughed when I asked how Messi "was vocal" with suggestions.

"Very professionally," he said. "How's that?"

Mas continued. "He's not intrusive. You read all these articles from these other leagues about stars and the pressure that, at times, they feel they're putting on teams to do things. And he's not like that, right? With the amount of fame and power that he has relative to the influence that he could have on the team, he's really cognizant about the fact that he doesn't want to unjustly influence anything. He wants to be treated like one of the guys. He doesn't want any special treatment, which is quite shocking. But obviously he's pretty well versed in what he's doing. So we appreciate any feedback that he gives us, and I think he does it in a really professional way."

Hoyos's promotion required a generous interpretation of "not wanting special treatment." Ownership, though, felt the drama surrounding the front-office shuffling amounted more to gossip than anything substantive. Shortly after the Sanllehi bust-up, Miami hired Alberto Marrero as chief soccer officer, replacing Henderson. That Hoyos wasn't at the top of the sporting hierarchy, and didn't need to be, was proof that claims of a power struggle were overblown, they said.

But owners couldn't—and didn't—deny that the front-office shuffling went back to the idea of keeping Messi happy.

"Guillermo has input now, where he didn't have input before," Jorge Mas admitted. "So Leo is happy that Guillermo has some input. Leo is a very loyal guy and Leo feels comfortable with him. And that's okay."

There was, of course, risk to the way the club tried to stay pliable to Messi's needs. Inter Miami surrounded Messi with his friends and former Barcelona teammates in part to make him comfortable, as well as to put proven quality around him. But the trade-off was an older and slower team that had to overcome the defensive deficiencies of its name players. It hired a coach in Mascherano who could manage the personalities of the ex-Barcelona quartet, but he had little experience in charge of pros and no familiarity with the unique challenges MLS presented, like continental travel and drastically different climates. Inter Miami accommodated Hoyos' desire for input, but with Henderson and Martino gone, no decision-makers in the front office had experience crafting MLS rosters.

But ownership felt those trade-offs were worth it. It was all good as long as Messi stayed happy—and as long as Inter Miami kept winning. In February 2025, Jorge Mas went to the team facility to meet with Messi and make sure he could ensure both for the coming years.

21

Formulating the Future

Jorge Mas and Lionel Messi met in the same office lounge where, eighteen months earlier, Messi asked which trophies he could win.

After a year and a half in Miami, Messi had two trophies but had fallen short of MLS Cup and Concacaf glory. Mas wanted to ensure that Messi was around to elevate that legacy and add a few more championships. He needed Messi in Miami longer than 2025. But the stakes were bigger than on-field results.

The Argentine icon's arrival injected hope into the MLS and American soccer ecosystems. His first month—the free kick, the goal-filled wins, the Leagues Cup triumph—lifted an entire league to a new level of relevance in unprecedented fashion. He changed the conversation about MLS's potential.

In many ways, he continued to deliver on that initial hype.

He won the 2024 MLS MVP award and was still selling out stadiums, but the energy that once hummed above Messi in Miami—that this was something metamorphic for MLS—wasn't there anymore. As time passed without broader, more lasting change, optimism about what the league might look like once Messi left was waning.

If he walked away after the 2025 season and MLS could point

only to the tickets and shirts it sold and a few more big checks cashed, it would be a historic missed opportunity.

Mas understood better than anyone the short- and long-term consequences of failing to extend Messi's contract. Keeping the icon in Miami beyond 2025 bought time for MLS to map its future, but it also held massive local implications. Inter Miami's sponsorship deals depended on Messi in Inter Miami pink. More importantly, the team was scheduled to open its new billion-dollar stadium in 2026.

A few months prior, Miami Freedom Park started going vertical. Mas could see the progress outside from his office window. The construction site constantly reminded him of the stakes. Before he delivered Messi to Inter Miami, Mas supplied the political capital to get a stadium deal done in South Florida. Now, the venue was twelve months away from opening. Messi was the biggest draw in the sport. He could baptize the new building like no other player on the planet could.

After a preseason training session, Messi met Mas in the office. No. 10 was dressed casually in Inter Miami gear. Mas and Messi started with small talk. They discussed family and the offseason, changes to the team, the new roster, and expectations for 2025. Then the conversation shifted to the future. Mas knew Inter Miami needed Messi in the lineup for the 2026 home opener.

"We've got to talk about the contract," he told Messi. "We've got a year left."

Messi tried to lighten the mood as the serious business started.

"No, I see you've been giving interviews saying that I'm going to be here next year," Messi said, eyebrows raised.

Messi understood Inter Miami needed him to stay. He also wanted to make sure it was clear who would make that decision.

"No, no!" Mas replied in faux shock. "I said I *hope* you come next year! I only say it's my hope, my wish, my heart."

Messi laughed and nodded. *Sure, sure.*

"I want this to be your last contract," Mas said. "Three years."

Messi shrugged.

"*Año por año*," he retorted. "Let's see."

Year by year, my ass, Mas thought to himself.

"Three years," the owner replied.

The two went back and forth, trading ideas for what might come next.

Messi didn't love looking too far into the future. The unknown waiting there for him was daunting. Messi preferred to think only about the here and now. In that way, it was fitting that some of the lasting images of Messi's first two years in Miami revolved around fatherhood. Looking too far into the future as a parent means missing the surprise each day can bring—the little moments that are too ephemeral to risk overlooking. His constant presence at his sons' academy games, relaxing under a pink or black tent with friends and family, was a nod to the overwhelming appeal of life in the U.S. and of enjoying the day-to-day, as Messi liked to say.

When Messi first arrived, people talked about the normalcy he sought, citing examples such as his trips to the grocery store. In reality, normalcy was found in those moments on the sidelines of a youth soccer game, just being a dad.

"The three of them are with the ball all day long," Messi said in an extensive interview on the *Simplemente Fútbol* program. "I'm in a place where I'm lucky to be able to enjoy it, too, to be able to accompany them. They come here every day to the club to train all week after school. Then they compete in matches. Being able to be there, being able to come and having that opportunity to be there with them, for me it's spectacular. Being able to do it as a family."

Messi admitted he wasn't sure what would come after his playing days. His life had for so long revolved around having a ball at his feet that he could hardly fathom a day might come when that wouldn't be the case. Nor did he want to. The fear of trying to fill that gigantic void pushed him—not just to keep playing, but to find joy in the everyday of it.

He was happy at Inter Miami because it didn't force him to move on. He could embrace being in the moment, keep playing the sport he loved, but also begin to live a life outside the game, too. Perhaps his next steps would also allow him to blend the sport and his family.

As they sat in the office that February day, Messi told Mas he and his family were happy in Miami. This is where he would end his career. But Messi also wanted to win. And he wanted to make sure Mas and the club put the right pieces around him. Messi wanted to know if MLS was ready to push its business forward.

"He's sitting there going, 'I'm filling every stadium.' And in his mind, it's like, we're killing it, we're helping the league, and they can't move fast," Mas recalled. "It's almost embarrassing."

Eventually, Messi relented on the three-year proposal—or at least to having a conversation about those terms.

Mas set a meeting for early March with Jorge Messi. Over a Graziano's lunch brought in to Inter Miami's Coral Gables office, Mas and Jorge Messi hammered out the framework of a new deal. It would be a multi-year deal. A few clauses were included that would impact points added to his 10 percent ownership stake, increasing his future influence in the club.

They reached an agreement.

With the paperwork now in the lawyers' hands, Mas shifted his focus to apply pressure on the league-wide issues Messi kept asking about. He texted Los Angeles FC owner Larry Berg.

Along with Portland Timbers owner Merritt Paulson, Berg had taken over as co-chair of the sporting and competition committee in February 2025. One of the more ambitious owners in

MLS, Berg was also a superior political operator. While many saw Mas as being unable to take off his Inter Miami hat, Berg could pick up the phone and negotiate.

As the MLS board of governors prepared for an April meeting in Chicago, Berg whipped votes and gauged owners' positions. The meeting would determine how much support there was for significant change. No one had any idea how it would go.

"Messi keeps asking," Mas texted Berg.

"I'm doing my part," Berg replied.

It remained up in the air whether a vote would happen in April, but Berg sensed momentum building toward evolution.

* * *

Two months after Mas and Messi sat down to hash out his future in Miami, Berg relaxed in the elegant seventh-floor lobby of the Four Seasons Hotel in Chicago. The next morning, April 10, 2025, the MLS board would gather to discuss the three-tiered changes they had spent the previous eighteen months studying and debating: flipping the calendar, updating the competition structure, and revamping the roster rules.

It was shaping up to be one of the most important meetings in league history.

The realities of MLS's bottom line and the increased competition across the American soccer landscape meant standing still wasn't really an option.

"The status quo isn't good enough, so that always helps, right?" Berg asked. "We're not in one of those situations where anyone is satisfied with the status quo."

Upon beginning play as an expansion team in 2019, Los Angeles FC's ownership group—which included Berg, Bennett Rosenthal, and Brandon Beck as co-managing owners, as well as a host of celebrity investors such as actor Will Ferrell, U.S. women's national team great Mia Hamm, and NBA legend Magic Johnson—developed a reputation for its progressive outlook on shaping the league.

It also quickly established itself as one of MLS's most successful clubs, winning three trophies in its first six seasons and twice reaching the Concacaf final. Los Angeles FC's success gave its ownership group credibility. This credibility helped elevate Berg to his position as co-chair, where he was uniquely positioned to push the league forward.

In his first presentation to the sporting and competition committee in February 2025, Berg prioritized efficiency. The powerful group of owners debated, analyzed, argued, and discussed, but rarely acted decisively. The Los Angeles FC owner focused on improving the process and breaking that penchant for paralysis by analysis.

In the months before the April meeting, Berg and Paulson worked the phones to gauge support and identify holdouts. They were surprised at how quickly a groundswell of support built behind flipping the calendar. There were a lot of "yes" votes, although many were tied to contingencies or conditions. Some of those contingencies conflicted with each other.

A handful of teams in colder climates would pay the freight for the change, but Berg saw the compensation or quid pro quo those owners sought as manageable.

"The dollars are small enough that they shouldn't drive a major strategic decision," Berg said. "But those dollars are really important to some people—really important. I feel like if we can get consensus on the major strategic decision, we can go back to our working groups to figure those things out."

Paulson, the son of former U.S. Secretary of the Treasury Hank Paulson, believed owners' sudden openness to change was driven by one factor in particular: Messi.

"He was an eye-opener," Paulson said. "The extent of the

impact he had in Miami and for the league was just next level. The discussion was then: Do we need to put a firmer foot down on the accelerator here? He was very much a catalyst for those discussions."

If change was going to come, Berg and Paulson were charged with getting other league owners to step on it. The World Cup was approaching. Messi's contract was winding down. Time was running out to maximize change.

"It has created a sense of urgency that I have found very helpful," Berg said.

The near-perfect in-person attendance at the Chicago meeting revealed its importance. The board wouldn't vote, but there would be a straw poll. The league office, led by MLS executive Nelson Rodriguez, spent months canvassing stakeholders during the pod sessions. Every owner had a full understanding of the stakes. Now, each would get a chance to speak. Viewpoints would then be tallied. The results would dictate the future of the league.

"I don't think anyone believes that not changing is a potential outcome," Berg said. "People have different views on what should be changed, and I respect that, but I don't know that anybody's coming up and saying, 'You know what? We got a really good thing going. We don't need to change a thing. We're gonna risk it all.' No one is in that mode. We all understand we're a challenger league. We're growing and we have to keep doing things. What those things are—people differ."

Berg believed change was inevitable. He was less optimistic that the sense of urgency would match the moment.

"I usually find we get to the right place," he said. "It always takes longer than I want it to."

It did not take long for Berg's suspicions to be confirmed.

A few minutes past 8 A.M. on April 10, in a long conference room on the eighth floor of the Chicago Four Seasons, MLS commissioner Don Garber opened the board meeting. Owners sat at tables around the room, each with a microphone. Club presidents and chief business officers were stationed along a back wall.

"Today we are going to be discussing the future of our league," Garber said.

The agenda included some of the most monumental proposals the league had considered in its relatively short history. With that in mind, Garber believed it was important to put at least one part of the debate to rest immediately.

"Any changes we decide on," he said, "will not be implemented until 2027."

With one sentence, Garber sucked the urgency out of the meeting. His proclamation that no changes would be implemented in 2026, before owners even weighed in, was shocking to some in attendance. As one owner later scoffed, "Did I miss the board meeting where we debated that?"

Others, though, saw it as a prudent move by Garber. The commissioner took any debate about the timeline off the table and put the focus on the proposals.

The decision to aim toward 2027 meant conceding at least some, and possibly a lot, of the enormous bounce the World Cup offered. It was the result of an evolution that MLS waited too long to begin. Garber spoke in 2018 about that "defined moment of truth eight years from now." The league had not acted toward that change until Messi arrived in the summer of 2023. Now, Garber was declaring the big changes MLS was weighing wouldn't come until at least a full year *after* that defined moment of truth.

MLS executives excelled at moving the goalposts, but it was a hard sell to see the delay as anything but a missed opportunity. In December 2024, MLS vice president Nelson Rodriguez, dispatched to the media as the sacrificial spokesperson, claimed tying reform to the World Cup was a "romantic and somewhat artificial timeline." Now, four months later, Garber declared after the April board meeting that he wasn't "remotely concerned" about MLS missing its World Cup opportunity. It was PR spin—and it was not an opinion shared around the league.

Launching a revamped league in 2027 would produce less impact than unveiling the "new MLS" in the immediate wake of the World Cup's closing whistle. It was a question of how much the league would lose—and what the long-term impact would be of ceding that ground.

League decision-makers tried to soften the delay by pointing out that MLS launched a year late after the 1994 World Cup. It was supposed to debut in 1995 but ultimately started in 1996. Better to get it right than rush, they said. But it was flawed framing. For one, the extra year didn't ensure success. MLS nearly folded in 2001. For another, it wasn't 1996 anymore. The internet rewired everything in the ensuing thirty years, including sports fandom. Attention spans shrunk.

MLS had an eight-year runway. Now they were shrugging off an urgency precipitated by their own lack of action.

Adding to the frustration was that MLS hadn't just missed its first chance by moving too slowly in the years after the World Cup announcement. It squandered its second chance, too. Messi's 2023 arrival in Miami ignited discussions around much-needed structural change. His enormous commercial impact reframed how owners thought about spending on stars and reset conversations about how the league could increase relevance with a wider audience.

"All of a sudden you see things happening that you never thought could happen," Garber told reporters the night of the Leagues Cup final in August 2023. "Maybe there are ways that we should be thinking about our business perhaps a little bit differently."

In other words, if not for Messi's influence, MLS might be even further behind in its need to evolve. And still, they couldn't get reforms over the line in time for the World Cup in 2026.

The league remained frustratingly constrained by its own bureaucracy. April's straw poll at the Chicago board meeting sketched out a potential path forward. Getting there would require political finesse and logistical gymnastics. Garber's decision to target 2027 wasn't a strategy. He knew MLS needed more time.

The sport's global spotlight barreled toward MLS at a moment of institutional uncertainty: A boom-or-bust media deal with Apple TV, a CBA that expired in January 2028, and a leadership transition.

To flip the schedule to a summer-to-spring calendar, MLS would need approval from the MLSPA. Complicating matters, with the CBA set to expire right in the heart of what would be the first full season under a revamped schedule, early renegotiation would almost certainly be required. League executives also intended to discuss the proposed reforms with Apple—both to assess the implications and, ideally, to extract additional value from the deal.

MLS still had to vote, but a mountain of work remained on both sides of that official tally.

22

Taken to the Limit

The tug-of-war between MLS's past and its future began to spill out from the boardroom and onto the field and transfer market during the 2025 MLS regular season. Inter Miami and Lionel Messi were central to both conflicts.

On a late April morning, the day before what was then the biggest game in Inter Miami's history, a dozen reporters stood along one sideline in Fort Lauderdale as the team worked through a one-touch rondo, soccer's version of keep-away. For most MLS teams, twelve journalists at a training session would be considered a crowd. But two years earlier, as Messi jogged out for his first Inter Miami practice, hundreds of media members packed together on the far side of the same practice field, dripping sweat and jockeying for position as a news helicopter circled overhead.

Life at Inter Miami had since settled into a decidedly more MLS existence.

Inter Miami was preparing to host the second leg of a Concacaf Champions Cup semifinal against the Vancouver Whitecaps. The continental competition was one of only two truly significant legacy-making titles available to MLS clubs. Only one MLS club, the Seattle Sounders in 2022, lifted the Champions Cup in its modern, home-and-away format. The previous year, Liga MX giant Monterrey unceremoniously dumped Inter Miami in the quarterfinals. For Messi and his decorated colleagues, the Vancouver match offered a perfect shot at redemption—for that loss, and for the 2024 MLS playoff failure.

Miami trailed the series 2–0 after losing the opener on the road against the mostly anonymous, low-budget Whitecaps. With the away goals rule in effect, Inter Miami faced a steep climb in Fort Lauderdale. Around the club, however, belief lingered. There was a steady confidence Inter Miami would find a way to fight back at home. Inter Miami had needed to come from behind in the quarterfinal against Los Angeles FC, and No. 10 had delivered. The Argentine scored twice during a furious three-goal rally. There was little doubt Messi would deliver again in the semis.

The atmosphere at DRV PNK Stadium on April 30, 2025, matched the moment.

A sold-out crowd waved pink flags. Bad Bunny blared from the speakers. A hype video played on the big screen. Inter Miami, a last-place team before Messi's arrival, was now hosting a continental semifinal.

On paper, the Whitecaps had no business winning this series. Their best player was injured. Their roster was a mix of MLS journeymen and budget signings. Vancouver was typically one of the league's lowest spenders, and at the end of the 2024 season, its owners put the team up for sale. Yet in the spring of 2025, the modest Whitecaps were having a moment.

The club's new coach, a Dane named Jesper Sørensen, demanded an aggressive, attacking style of play. Led by American forward Brian White and midfielder Sebastian Berhalter, the son of former U.S. men's national team coach Gregg Berhalter, Vancouver was atop the MLS standings. The Whitecaps also navigated a minefield of storied Concacaf rivals to reach the final four, taking down Costa Rican giant Saprissa, then Liga MX powerhouses Monterrey and Pumas UNAM to earn a shot at Messi.

Vancouver controlled the first leg against Inter Miami at home. But nine minutes into the second, Messi looked ready to deliver on his promise to Mas. Inter Miami took the lead on a goal crafted entirely by its Barcelona quartet. Sergio Busquets found Messi, who then connected with Luis Suárez. The Uruguayan striker promptly fed an overlapping Jordi Alba, who drilled a shot past the keeper.

The host's 1–0 lead held through halftime, but Vancouver's young squad came out flying in the second stanza. The Whitecaps scored three times in the second half to emphatically extinguish Miami's Champions Cup dream.

"It hurts because we were hoping to reach the final," Inter Miami coach Javier Mascherano said. "Yes, we won the (2023) Leagues Cup, but we know the most prestigious tournament in the Concacaf region is the Champions Cup. We wanted to establish ourselves among the best. But sometimes, you have to admit when the opponent has quality and outplayed you. Tonight, they outplayed us."

The loss made clear that, in the biggest moments, Messi's impact would depend as much on those around him as on anything he did. Inter Miami had a strong team, but MLS's constraints meant a roster like Vancouver's, built much differently under the same limitations, could still be better. Inter Miami poured millions into its stars, but the rules limited what it could do outside of those six top spots. If Miami's form dipped and a team like Vancouver surged, the margins were thin enough that the underdog wasn't truly overmatched.

But those restrictions still created the same limitations outside of MLS.

One month after overwhelming Messi and Inter Miami in Fort

Lauderdale, Vancouver went to Mexico City for the Champions Cup final and got absolutely battered, 5–0, by Liga MX titans Cruz Azul. The Whitecaps arrived on a fifteen-game unbeaten streak. But, as in so many past editions of this tournament, Liga MX's quality and depth overwhelmed the best MLS had to offer. Cruz Azul scored on their first five shots on goal and outshot the Whitecaps 18–0. For the twenty-third time in twenty-four editions of the competition's modern version, a Mexican team wore the crown as the region's best team.

MLS executives could keep banging the drum about competitive balance, but the league on the whole continued to fall behind its rivals. Those truths were evident across multiple competitions. Two weeks after Vancouver was embarrassed in Mexico City, MLS's limitations were on display again as teams started play in the FIFA Club World Cup. Seattle played three and lost three. Los Angeles FC lost two of three, including a defeat to Tunisian side Espérance. Miami advanced but was dominated by Paris Saint-Germain in the knockout stage.

Garber called it "one of the defining moments for our league." That was true, but not in the way he intended. MLS's performance did what Mas predicted at that committee meeting in November 2024: It reinforced negative perceptions of the league—both globally and domestically. MLS teams may not have completely embarrassed themselves, but in a tournament where teams from Brazil and Saudi Arabia made convincing impressions on viewers, MLS teams underwhelmed. If the aim was to change minds and entice people to give MLS a chance, that didn't happen—no matter what Garber said or what league advocates tried to spin.

The promise of the Messi effect hovered tantalizingly close. And yet, two years in, it wasn't clear whether any part of this era—beyond the profit-and-loss sheet—would reach its full potential.

Messi's story in Miami wasn't finished, of course. The "Beckham experiment" looked like a failure until it wasn't. The LA Galaxy missed the playoffs in Beckham's first two MLS seasons, but Los Angeles reshaped the team around him in later years. Ownership hired Bruce Arena, an MLS champion coach, and signed Robbie Keane, who became a transformational player. Two championships later, Beckham's on-field legacy was secured.

The first two years of Messi in Miami were more successful than Beckham's opening act in Los Angeles. Inter Miami won the first trophies in its history: the 2023 Leagues Cup and the 2024 Supporters' Shield. Messi was the reigning league MVP. But it still felt like that wasn't enough.

Inter Miami's ownership group was emboldened by the failures in the Champions Cup and the league's struggles at the Club World Cup. MLS might still be deciding next steps, but Inter Miami didn't have the luxury to wait around forever. Messi, too, was inspired by the Club World Cup. It changed how he thought about his role in shaping the sport in the U.S.

23

MLS 3.0

The story of the 2025 MLS All-Star Game was the star who wasn't in Austin, Texas, rather than those who were.

Lionel Messi was a no-show for the late July festivities, although the league didn't confirm his absence until the day of the game. It was yet another example of Messi's unwillingness to conform to his duties as an ambassador for MLS.

Debate erupted around his snubbing of the league's marquee midseason event. His backers pointed out that Messi played ninety minutes of every game for Inter Miami leading into the exhibition, and how that was far more important than the All-Star friendly. Detractors noted that other big stars were playing heavy minutes but still showed up to the game.

Messi faced a one-game suspension for skipping the event—the consequence of a league rule that was put into place without MLS executives fully thinking through the silliness of forcing its best players to miss games of consequence in favor of an exhibition.

Despite his absence, Messi's presence was heavy in Austin if you knew where to look—and not just because of the headlines his no-show generated. On the day of the game, with security guards protecting the escalators up to the third floor of the hotel, where the league was meeting, MLS owners discussed the changes to the league structure, a conversation first put on the table when the Argentine legend arrived two years prior.

Board members grew increasingly frustrated in the three months after April's meeting in Chicago. The debate over flipping the calendar, and especially whether to compensate owners in northern markets for any mitigation needed on stadiums and training facilities to accommodate colder months, grew more polarized. Some owners were "no" votes if they had to pay for mitigation. Others were "no" votes if they didn't receive it.

MLS commissioner Don Garber liked to say that the greatest power of the league was its owners. He had long advocated harmony on the board. But consensus was an increasingly scarce commodity with thirty teams and thirty owners, and at the Fairmont Austin, the commissioner stood in front of a divided room.

A few months earlier, Garber supported mitigation. He even formed a committee to study it. The group projected costs for the cold-weather markets and drew up a register of dollar values. As the July meeting approached, however, the owners against mitigation started to get more vocal.

With the growing divide threatening to stall the change Garber knew MLS needed, the commissioner put his shoulder behind one side of the debate more forcefully than he had in the previous two years.

In Austin, Garber let owners have their say first. Then he recommended the calendar change and gave the room a history lesson. He pointed to multiple occasions where owners had voted or acted against their own self-interests in order to do right by the league. Phil Anschutz and the LA Galaxy had a strong local television deal on which they turned a profit, one of only a handful of teams with such an arrangement, Garber noted. They gave up that agreement so that the league could negotiate all local rights as part of its media deal, which was eventually signed with Apple. The LA Galaxy also did not block Los Angeles FC's stadium deal, despite its proximity in the market. It was good for the league to have two teams in Los Angeles, including one with a fantastic downtown stadium location, even if it made the business more difficult for the LA Galaxy to split the market.

Garber rattled through other examples from the league's history with a clear message to the owners: This isn't about just one decision. The commissioner contextualized flipping the calendar against three decades of sacrifices owners made over the years. It went back to the design of the single-entity model: Owners were partners, acting for the better of the greater venture.

By the end of the meeting, the board reached an overwhelming consensus to move forward with the changes—with no mitigation for colder markets. Not every owner was happy; there were still two or three that preferred not to change the calendar and a few others that wanted to be paid for the trouble, but there was a better understanding of why the league needed to act.

It was a critical step toward the next evolution of the league, pending talks with the MLSPA and Apple.

"Don got the support he needed," Los Angeles FC co-owner Larry Berg said. "And frankly, it was pretty overwhelming. It was very well done, because everybody left feeling good about it."

That night, ahead of the All-Star Game festivities, Garber got up in front of the press and, for the first time publicly, soft-launched the changes the owners had hashed out earlier that day. He said aligning the calendar was "seismic."

"It's not something we should do lightly. We obviously have teams across multiple climate zones, multiple time zones, unlike any other league in the world, and if we do make the change, we're not going to go back on that decision."

Overhauling the competition format would “make the regular season more meaningful,” he said. “It’ll be more aligned with the rest of the world in terms of how they play their competition. And I think our playoff format will be really cool, really unique, very different from anything that happens in North America.”

The last piece was “a review of our entire roster strategy,” he said. The league had more work to do there. It was the most important piece of the puzzle, and it would likely require the most work—both internally and with the MLSPA.

Garber unveiled the changes as “MLS 3.0,” a nod to the league’s thirtieth anniversary in 2026 and to its next thirty years of growth.

“It is about moving forward, as we always do, with energy and with purpose and with ambition,” Garber said. “It is about the next era of growth for our league.”

The conversations that Messi’s arrival kick-started two summers before were yielding real fruit. There was still lots of work to do to get the changes across the line, but Garber going public with the league’s intention was significant.

There was no more hiding from what was coming.

* * *

As MLS took real steps toward its evolution, the Apple partnership played an important role. The league needed its media partner to sell its next iteration, and to help it reach a wider audience.

Apple was willing. The television partner wouldn’t be a speed bump on MLS’s road to transformation.

In 2025, the third season of Apple TV’s MLS Season Pass, the deal remained far from perfect. Subscription numbers weren’t where MLS wanted or expected them to be. The product wasn’t reaching new fans. Some team owners said they were experiencing a downturn in local relevance, both in discussions about their teams on local media and, in some cases, in attendance.

But both sides felt it was far too soon to panic.

"I think people forget we're only two years into this thing," Portland Timbers owner Merritt Paulson said.

As MLS weighed the changes, the league and Apple TV had plenty to discuss. The television product would benefit from a calendar flip by putting the playoffs in a far more favorable spring window, but that would come at a cost to MLS owners. They wanted Apple TV to ease those costs—whether it was financially or with concessions around the MLS Season Pass product. MLS leadership felt it needed better marketing and promotion of its product. It also needed to solve problems with access and distribution.

Apple TV, meanwhile, advocated both behind the scenes and publicly for MLS to spend more and acquire more top players. MLS Season Pass wasn't perfect, but fans were tuning in at a higher clip to watch Messi or Liga MX teams during the Leagues Cup. It was yet another indicator that the product needed updating.

The partners came to a solution. Apple agreed to bring the league out from behind the MLS Season Pass paywall in 2026. Sunday Night Soccer on Apple TV performed significantly better than other MLS games. Now, the MLS inventory would move to the service and be available for all Apple TV subscribers—alongside Formula 1, which signed a deal with Apple in October 2025. Apple didn't publicly share the number of subscribers, and estimates varied widely, but *Variety* pegged the number at forty-five million in spring 2025. Apple executive Eddy Cue said the number was actually "significantly more" than those estimates. It was a huge change. MLS would now be exposed to a far greater base of potential viewers than just the hardcore fans willing to pay a hefty subscription.

Apple was also motivated to discuss alterations to MLS's sub-licensing deal with Fox. MLS and Fox were entering the final year of a deal to air thirty-four regular-season games and eight playoff matches, including the MLS Cup, but there was little promotion around those games. The 2024 MLS Cup ratings were historically bad, even accounting for the fact that the game was also aired on MLS Season Pass, where most diehard fans would have tuned in. Fox was also broadcasting the 2026 World Cup, so it was critical that the network was motivated to give MLS a more aggressive marketing lift before, during, and after the tournament.

Apple had shown itself to be flexible and accommodating. The harder negotiation would come with the players' union.

* * *

MLSPA leadership had been expecting the league's call since Messi first arrived.

The union knew that MLS owners were weighing major changes and also believed the league was ready to move into a new stage of growth. But the relationship between the league and its players was historically fraught.

Through two decades of contentious negotiation, the MLSPA had won increased rights and compensation for its players. In each CBA negotiation, beginning with the first in 2005 through the most recent in 2020, the union seemed to target a specific area beyond overall spending increases. They bargained for free agency. They increased minimum salaries. They pushed for better bonuses and health and retirement benefits. The strategy was simple: The MLSPA felt the league was always going to increase its spending to grow the business. Prioritizing other areas seemed like a smarter play.

In 2020, what had long been an antagonistic relationship progressed into more amicable territory. The two sides agreed to a new CBA in February 2020, three weeks before the deadline. Both sides expressed satisfaction with the deal. But COVID-19 shut sports leagues down a few weeks later. In the pandemic's wake,

MLS twice renegotiated the CBA, leveraging the losses incurred from a season of empty stadiums to extend the agreement by three years and temporarily pause previously bargained salary growth.

MLSPA executive director Bob Foose began to question the union's previous strategy. Maybe MLS owners weren't so keen on growing after all. In the course of the renegotiations, and up until Messi's arrival, Foose saw MLS as suddenly happy to limit spending as much as possible.

The knockdown effect of that postpandemic negotiation was coming back to bite MLS in 2025. Instead of the CBA ending as initially negotiated—at the end of the 2025 season and ahead of the 2026 World Cup, which would have allowed the league to address important reforms before the tournament—it now expired on February 1, 2028.

Even though both sides felt motivated to move MLS forward, neither one wanted to be the first to request an early round of CBA talks. Both were concerned it might cost them leverage in negotiations. But they were missing the forest for the trees.

In June 2025, discussions about FIFA Club World Cup bonuses potentially opened the door to wider talks about the CBA. Those negotiations, however, didn't seem to ease the path to a new CBA. Seattle Sounders players warmed up for an MLS game with shirts that read "Club World Cup Ca$h Grab" as they sought more bonus money. Sounders owner Adrian Hanauer lambasted the team after the game for the stunt.

The two sides finally struck an agreement on the bonuses the day before Inter Miami lost to Paris Saint-Germain, but it came at a cost.

"While we were ultimately able to reach an agreement, players were deeply disappointed with the league's approach to the negotiation," the union said in a statement. "Stonewalling, threats, and retaliation will not be effective strategies as we move into the major negotiations ahead of us."

Garber's decision to push the league's changes into 2027 bought time for MLS to negotiate, but the increased tensions between the sides at a time when the league needed a willing partner were ominous.

On the surface it seemed like a simple solution. MLS wanted to flip the calendar. Players were on board with the changes. The league also wanted to add money to the system and allow teams to spend it more freely. The players should have been extra motivated to get that done—and as quickly as possible.

Instead, it felt like things were moving backward rather than getting closer to a deal.

* * *

Still, it was beginning to feel that Messi's impact would not just be a short blip but rather would result in lasting change. He wasn't the only reason for the momentum. There was an inevitability to MLS's advancement: Evolve or die.

Messi's arrival undoubtedly put MLS on the path to this point, as did the reality of a fast-approaching future without him in Miami pink. The league studied what happened to Barcelona and Paris Saint-Germain after Messi left. The new fans he brought mostly went away. Messi's commercial sway faded. No one could replace the greatest player of all time. His popularity was essentially unrivaled. Taking advantage of the amplification while he was here was one thing, but the more important mission was ensuring the reverberations of Messi in MLS lasted beyond his time playing in the league.

"We can't make decisions about where the market is today," Garber said. "We've got to make decisions about where we see the market going, and bypass tomorrow and be thinking about many, many days after tomorrow. . . . We need to grow a global media product, and that is going to take time, and it's going to take a lot of thoughtfulness, and it's going to take a lot of investment."

Garber's legacy as MLS commissioner was built on learning to catch that next big wave, like the founding of SUM, David Beckham's signing in Los Angeles, Seattle and Toronto's success, the ensuing era of expansion, billions in infrastructure investment, and skyrocketing valuations. The final chapter was now being written.

Garber's contract was up at the end of 2027, a month before the CBA was set to expire. The next two years would test the ambition Garber had long claimed—that MLS wanted to be one of the best leagues in the world. How he navigated the league through change—whether MLS could build something lasting from Messi's presence, or whether it would let the moment pass—had the potential to determine as much about how he was remembered as any other accomplishment.

* * *

Inter Miami was determined not to miss its opportunity.

Its needs were more immediate. Inter Miami needed to win trophies right away.

When the summer transfer window opened, the club aimed big. It chased Messi's Argentina teammate, Rodrigo De Paul, as its top target.

The deal was complicated. Inter Miami already had three designated players. By the letter of MLS rules, De Paul was an impossible addition. The thirty-one-year-old midfielder was making around $7 million per year for Atlético Madrid, one of the biggest clubs in Europe. He still had one more year left on his contract, and the Spanish side wanted a transfer fee for the World Cup winner.

With the help and blessing of MLS, Inter Miami negotiated a short-term loan that included an option to buy reportedly north of $15 million. De Paul, intent on playing with Messi, agreed to defer all but $800,000 of his salary with Atlético Madrid. Miami had every intention to pick up the option in January once Sergio Busquets' deal expired and they had an open DP spot, but if it was an "obligation" rather than an option to buy De Paul, it would classify him as a DP, and Inter Miami would not be roster compliant.

Sporting directors around MLS cried foul. The team and league had done gymnastics to make the deal fit within the letter of the law, but in reality, it was a barely disguised fourth DP. De Paul deferred his salary, but knowing he'd get paid on the back end—he had already agreed to a four-and-a-half-year deal with Inter Miami. The transfer fee might have been an "option," but the idea that Atlético Madrid would accept the move without a guarantee was fantasy. The frustration wasn't just the obvious workaround, it's that Miami did it with the league's blessing.

MLS decided it was not going to stand in the way of its most prominent team, which was in the midst of negotiations with its most famous player, from securing the services of a high-end talent like De Paul. It would make Messi happy. It would make Inter Miami better. And while it was yet another "friend of Messi," this one was still a starter for Argentina with several good years left in his legs.

This is how MLS worked.

The flexibility touted by league officials wasn't just on a macro level; it was on a micro level, too. The league rules were actually called "roster guidelines" expressly because they could be manipulated at the whim of league officials. Atop the long-form handed out to teams, MLS spelled it out: "The League reserves the right at any time to modify these Guidelines, create exceptions to these

Guidelines, and/or rescind these Guidelines, in the League's sole and absolute discretion." The ability to work around roadblocks in the name of what was "best for the league" was a necessary peccadillo that kept the league agile in its early years. Now it felt more like arrested development.

The league couldn't grow if the rules weren't really rules, and the rules would never be forced to modernize if league officials always felt like they could conjure workarounds whenever they deemed it necessary.

With De Paul on the roster, Inter Miami eased its way through the 2025 Leagues Cup, downing Mexican sides Club Necaxa, Atlas F.C., Pumas UNAM, and Tigres UNAL before bouncing in-state rivals Orlando City in the semifinal behind two Messi goals. Inter Miami faced the Seattle Sounders in the final on August 31 in front of more than sixty-nine thousand fans at Lumen Field in the Pacific Northwest.

Seattle, like Vancouver, built its roster far differently than Inter Miami. It was crafted mostly around domestic players brought through the academy and the second team. Its coach, local legend Brian Schmetzer, had the perfect tongue-in-cheek joke ready to go ahead of the game. "Messi is arguably the greatest player the world has ever seen," he said. "But we have Paul Rothrock."

Rothrock, twenty-six years old, came through Seattle's academy, played college soccer, and spent several seasons in the lower divisions before breaking into the Sounders starting XI in 2024. It was the perfect illustration of the vast spectrum of players within MLS, from global icons to local grinders.

Two years after Messi opened his MLS career with a Leagues Cup crown, Rothrock scored the final goal to put an exclamation point on a 3–0 Sounders win over Inter Miami. It was yet another disappointing tournament result for Inter Miami. The team had won two trophies in two years, but the failures were starting to stack up: two Concacaf Champions Cups, two Leagues Cups, and one MLS Cup without more hardware.

The loss was also further evidence of how MLS's system limited the effectiveness of even the highest spenders in the league. Inter Miami was spending $48.97 million on player salaries in the spring of 2025, the most in the league at that juncture. More than $35 million of that outlay went to Messi, Sergio Busquets, and Jordi Alba. The brilliance and magnetism of Messi, who, in addition to his on-field genius, also helped Miami recruit his talented friends Luis Suárez and De Paul to sign with the club for below-market salaries, still couldn't overcome a roster that had clear holes due to a budget allocated on a handful of his former teammates.

One could argue that Inter Miami might have headed off the issues by using its DP spots on other players, but they were far from the only example of high-spending MLS teams that allocated such a high percentage of their payroll to just three players and saw wildly inefficient results.

Despite Inter Miami's loss in the final, De Paul's signing felt like a transition point for a league that was finally embracing the change that was coming. A few weeks after the Argentine was announced in Miami, Vancouver signed German national team and Bayern Munich legend Thomas Müller in a short-term deal that had a similar end-of-season trigger. Shortly after that, Los Angeles FC broke the MLS transfer record in acquiring South Korean star Son Heung-min for around $26 million.

The former Tottenham star was an idol in his native South Korea, and, like Messi, brought with him an enormous commercial boost for Los Angeles FC. Son was more willing to be a vocal advocate for MLS. He did interviews with *Good Morning America* and *ABC News*, among other outlets, in his first month in MLS. He also acknowledged that Messi in Inter Miami influenced his decision to sign in Los Angeles.

"I come here not [just] because of him, obviously, but it also influenced me because he was the first one who joined MLS and made the league even bigger," Son said. "So I wanted to be like him. [I am not] hiding this."

Los Angeles FC co-owner Larry Berg admitted Messi in Miami influenced ownership's thinking, too.

"I don't know if we would have had the guts to do Son if [Jorge Mas] hadn't done Messi and if we didn't see how successful that turned out to be," Berg said. "That was a proof of concept. It was like, 'Wow, that's aggressive.' And then it paid off in spades."

Son had a similar, if diminished, commercial return to Messi. He was selling tickets across MLS. His jersey was the highest selling in the world for Adidas in his first week after signing with Los Angeles FC. MLS eventually signed an expanded broadcast deal in South Korea.

Garber saw it as a sort of test case as to what might come next in MLS. It was clear that what Messi did in Miami was not replicable. The Argentine was the most iconic athlete in the world's most popular sport, a generational player so great that he inspired a following that elevated above the sport itself. But on a smaller scale, MLS wanted to understand how much star power—real star power—could lift the league to a strong position in the greater sports consciousness, and whether doing so could change the dynamics of the teams' respective business models.

"It's going to be very interesting to see the impact that Son has on LAFC, on its fan base, both here and in Asia, but also on their commercial business," Garber said during an extensive interview from his office in September 2025. "And if that proves to be an extension in its own way of this concept of signing big-name players when they're really still performing at the top of their game [and are] still enormously popular, not viewing MLS as a place to go to leave, but a place to go to further their journey, then who knows who's next."

The summer of 2025 wasn't the first time multiple MLS teams made splash signings. A decade earlier, a run of established big-name players signed with teams across the league, including Frank Lampard, Andrea Pirlo, Kaká, and Steven Gerrard. Ten years later the difference was that MLS was spending beyond just the biggest names. De Paul, Müller, and Son represented a fraction of a significantly more aggressive approach from MLS teams in the transfer market. Combined, MLS teams spent more than $330 million in transfer fees in 2025 across their winter and summer windows, nearly double what was spent in 2024 ($188 million).

The transfer activity was proof of the financial heft of a league that, despite limiting how much teams could spend, was clearly capable of competing more aggressively in the marketplace. But there was still so much room to continue to grow, and to better support the star signings.

MLS was still well behind the top leagues in transfer outlay. The Premier League spent more than $4 billion in the 2025 summer window alone. Spain, Germany, and France each spent north of $600 million in the same months, while Italy exceeded $1 billion.

That was the danger of MLS measuring progress against itself. Progress only truly counted if it was making gains on its competition. If MLS 3.0 was going to work—if signings like Messi, Son, and De Paul were going to be different from Thierry Henry, Kaká, David Villa, and the many other stars who had come before—it needed to let teams actually compete.

24

A Lasting Legacy in Miami

Before the *agua bendita*, the cinematic free kick, the whirlwind first month, and the club's first trophy, before the sold-out stadiums, record-setting performances, playoff and Champions Cup heartbreak, and MVP honors, Inter Miami owner Jorge Mas sat in his Coral Gables office and pondered the potential legacy of a journey that hadn't yet begun.

Mas believed unrelentingly in the seismic impact Messi would have on MLS. For three minutes, he preached. He called it "endless" and "transformational."

"We have an unprecedented opportunity ahead of us, myself and my partners in the league, all the other owners," he proclaimed. "We are going to seize the moment."

Two years later, Mas and his partners in the league were still fighting to live up to that initial optimism. Separate from MLS, however, Mas had a vision for Messi's long-term influence in Miami. That blueprint went beyond the years covered in his still-unsigned contract extension.

"When you think of Lionel Messi—I'm thinking ten or fifteen years from now—the greatest that ever played, no doubt, what's the first thing that comes to your mind?" Mas asked in a sit-down interview in his office in 2025. "It's probably one of two images: Argentina lifting the World Cup and Barça. How do I get Inter Miami and the pink into that mix?

"Ultimately, it's going to be defined by the amount of these that we lift."

Mas raised his arms skyward, hoisting an imaginary trophy.

"When it's over, [the hope] is that it's going to be discussed as not the end of his career, but part of his career," Mas continued. "My goal is that the Messi legacy, the Messi image, is tied to Inter Miami, and that Inter Miami is tied to Messi. . . . He's going to be an integral part of everything that we're building."

MLS accomplished something similar with David Beckham, whose influence on American soccer was now as much about Inter Miami as it was his LA Galaxy days. Nearly two decades after he signed with the Galaxy, and thirteen years after he played his last game with them, Beckham's brand was still closely linked to MLS.

To secure that sort of association, the end of Messi's playing days couldn't be the end of his time in Miami.

* * *

Messi still wasn't certain what would come next after he retired.

"I honestly don't know," he said in the interview at the end of the 2024 season with Fabrizio Romano. "I know that I wouldn't like to be a coach. But I'm not sure about what I can become in the future."

Inter Miami goalkeeper Óscar Ustari, who played with Messi in Argentina's youth national teams and now closed out his career with him in MLS, told an Argentine radio station he saw Messi very involved in the club's academy and "on top of everything" there. Perhaps that's where his future lay.

Mas hoped the connections being forged on the youth fields, with Messi's sons wearing the same Inter Miami pink, would bond the player to the club—and to Miami as home. The ownership stake also carved out a permanent place for him with Inter Miami, and Mas insisted the legendary No. 10 would be as involved as he, Jose Mas, and Beckham.

"I see Messi having a significant impact on the sporting side," Mas said. "I think having him as part of this project will continue to keep Inter Miami at the forefront of people's minds. . . . If you look at what we're building economically and everything we're doing commercially, we're a big team. If we're allowed to take the shackles off, we'll be bigger. And that'll come."

Mas believed players would want to come play *for* Messi's team as much as they currently wanted to come play *on* Messi's team. And he was convinced Messi would still seek the thrill of chasing results.

"He's a competitive beast. All he wants to do is win," Mas said. "I one hundred percent guarantee you that once his boots are hung up and he's in a different role, his competitiveness isn't going to want to leave."

For now, though, Mas was satisfied because Messi wasn't ready to stop playing. And he was still changing games. In September, Messi flew to Argentina for the last World Cup qualifier he would ever play in his home country. With his family there watching, Messi was visibly moved by the crowd chanting his name during warm-ups. Then, he scored twice to lead Argentina to a 3–0 win.

It was a reminder that Messi's on-field dominance extended beyond just what he continued to do in MLS. His desire to keep playing—and keep winning—with Argentina was still pushing him forward.

That drive to win is what tied Mas's vision for Messi and Inter Miami to his broader optimism around MLS's future.

* * *

Messi changed how MLS stakeholders thought about the league's potential.

Five years after Inter Miami played the first game in its history, "everyone knows who we are," Mas said. "Think about that." Inter Miami was a globally recognized club. It was Messi's team, so people wore the team's pink shirts. They tuned in for the games. They bought tickets when the team was in town.

This was the Messi effect Mas also wanted for the league—and for American soccer.

When the Argentine first arrived two years prior, Mas could gaze out of his office to the east and see the empty plot of land where Inter Miami's new home would be built. Now, he pointed to the bones of the stadium sprouting from the ground. It would be sold out in 2026, he declared. He based that prediction on the team he fielded in 2025. Imagine what it might look like if he were allowed to do more.

"I want to [continue to] have great players here, top players in the world here," he said. "I want to win Champions Cup. I want to compete worldwide. I want to win the next Club World Cup. I want to freaking win."

Mas's bombastic nature made it difficult for some owners to believe he could understand their realities. Not every market was Miami. There were MLS owners who argued they would never attract a big-name star. But Inter Miami's owners weren't naive to that truth. Growing the league wasn't just about spending more money. It was also about strategy and ambition.

"*Fútbol* is a global sport. It's not an American sport. It's a global sport. And we need to compete on a global stage and a global level, because we have a global audience," Mas said. "As we continue to take our team profile up, we're dragging the league up with us."

No one was pushing for chaos—just evolution.

"His impact has got to last forever, and if it doesn't, then we failed," Inter Miami co-owner Jose Mas said. "If we can't take what this moment brings to the sport, the U.S., our team, and make it perpetual, then I think we all lost an incredible opportunity."

On the day Messi officially signed his three-year contract extension in October 2025, Inter Miami's owners went down to the stadium construction site to shoot a video. Messi, on the cusp of being the first player in MLS history to win back-to-back Most Valuable Player awards after leading the league in both goals (twenty-nine) and assists (nineteen), brought his wife and kids. David Beckham brought his parents. The four owners—Jorge and Jose Mas, Beckham, and Messi—walked around the stadium together.

Messi liked the idea of being an owner, a partner in a project he could see being shaped right in front of his eyes. And he wanted to pull American soccer closer to the rest of the world. He was pleased with how Miami performed at the Club World Cup and decided to launch a new youth tournament, the Messi Cup, in part to give MLS academies more global competition. He felt it would encourage the league to grow.

Messi also decided to be a bit more vocal with his views on the league's future.

"I think that growing soccer in the United States is possible," Messi told NBC News in an interview released a few days after his contract extension was announced. "I think there are still big changes to be made so that teams can continue to grow, but I think there is a very important foundation in place where teams are prepared and want that growth, and I think it's time to do it. . . . For starters, every team should have the opportunity to bring in players and sign whoever each team wants, without limitations or rules for players to bring them in. I don't think that today all teams in the United States, all clubs, have the power to do that, and I think that if they were given the freedom, many more important players would come and help the growth of the United States."

That Messi was finally using the power of his voice to encourage MLS to evolve was significant. Signing Messi was always about creating a movement that tapped into the aspirational ethos of the sport itself. Now, he was a more active ally in promoting the more aggressive approach.

It went back to the pitch that came out of the hotel meeting in Barcelona all those years ago. Signing Messi was about changing the sport forever.

That aim remained.

25

The Messi Effect

When the ball curled off Lionel Messi's left foot in the dying moments of his debut in Inter Miami pink in July 2023, as it unbelievably and yet somehow entirely predictably settled into the upper corner of the net, as the crowd roared and the Argentine legend ran toward the end line in celebration, one couldn't help but wonder just how far it might all go.

The greatest player of all time had pulled MLS with him into the center of the sports universe. For a league that desperately needed something to lift it into relevance, Messi was delivering a pathway there.

Two and a half years later, Inter Miami was a global phenomenon. Behind the Argentine's typical on-field brilliance, the club successfully climbed out of the MLS basement and won its first two trophies. Away from the field, Messi's pink jersey was one of the most iconic and recognizable shirts in sports: Stadiums sold out every week across the league, with fans trekking to watch him play, and Inter Miami more than tripled its revenue from the season before Messi arrived.

The question was, What did any of that mean for MLS? This

was the crux of the existential problem the league faced as it debated the next phase in its evolution.

There was no individual on the planet who could have delivered what Messi did, and no telling when another player like him would exist again. Yet even he had not solved those problems just by showing up.

MLS was a strong local business. Its teams regularly filled stadiums. The league's commercial operation was more than adequate. But MLS still didn't resonate nationally. Its television audiences lagged behind both other American and global soccer leagues. It was falling further behind the competition in the quality of the product it put on the field, too.

"There is no magic bullet," MLS commissioner Don Garber conceded.

Messi, though, opened the possibility for something bigger. He flipped the market on its head so drastically, and amplified Inter Miami's reach so dramatically, that it forced the typically cautious, glacial MLS to accelerate toward league-altering reform. Those changes would ultimately stand as a permanent testament to the Messi effect.

His legacy, though, would be defined not simply by the way his presence compelled MLS to evolve, but by the lasting impact that evolution had on the league.

* * *

Decades of investing in and building a foundation set MLS up to make a leap forward.

There was a reason why so many voices—from those on its own board, to FIFA president Gianni Infantino, Apple executives, and Messi himself—urged the league to take action. MLS exists in the most desirable commercial market in the world, with millions of untapped potential fans. It boasts world-class facilities and has one of the wealthiest ownership groups in professional sports.

The possibilities were enormous.

Reflecting on Messi's influence in MLS during an interview from the league's headquarters in midtown Manhattan in September 2025, Garber called him "the capstone on the growth over the last generation" and declared that Messi "set the stage for our next chapter of what MLS ultimately can be."

Messi's overwhelming success in Miami gave MLS owners enough confidence that there was a path toward national relevance—and the corresponding revenues—to warrant a more proactive approach.

But the league was still determining exactly what its future would look like.

"The true impact of the Messi effect is it proved the basic premise of MLS, which was that North America can support a top-level men's division one soccer league and be a player in the global marketplace," Garber said. "[Take] everything we believe—that this is a great market, that we have exploding demographics, that people are growing up with the sport and now are participating as fans or as influencers [and] are helping to grow the game on a wide variety of levels—and then Messi comes and explodes the deliverable of what it can be.

"And now you start taking a step back and saying: We have a team that's profitable. We have a team that's one of the most popular teams in the world. That is selling more merchandise than almost any other team in the world. That's attracted audiences, attendances, and commercial revenue on par with many of the other top clubs in the world.

"Can that be replicated in other markets with similar decisions?"

The uncomfortable truth was that the league didn't know the answer to that and many other questions.

If MLS better competed for players—not just two or three stars on each team, but also in-prime starters from top leagues—its place in the global ecosystem could change dramatically. But the relationship between on-field quality, fan affinity, and viewing audience was unproven.

If MLS doubled its spending and leveled investment out across the roster, potentially decreasing some star power, would fans recognize the overall jump in quality and watch a better product? Or did Messi prove that MLS needed star players to convince fans to tune in?

"If we believed that player spending directly correlated with media revenue, and ultimately on audience, then our owners are smart and they're brave. They would make those commitments," the commissioner said. "The challenge is that we have not seen that evidence consistently enough to force us to totally change the way we've been going about our business."

There was also a chance that the domestic market would reject anything short of the absolute highest levels of the sport, the Champions League and Premier League, which were now so readily accessible for fans.

In other words, the changes MLS was weighing might not materially alter its place in the sporting landscape or drive the media revenue to justify the increased costs. But Inter Miami's success convinced league owners a more aggressive strategy was at least worth a try.

Messi's legacy would hinge in part on how confidently MLS approached the next steps.

* * *

Garber's launch of MLS 3.0 moved the league toward change, but executives hadn't yet set a timeline for when those alterations would come, other than that it wouldn't be in time to capitalize immediately off the back of the 2026 World Cup.

No one could project the magnitude of the cost MLS would pay for missing the World Cup moment, but it was clear the league would pay a cost. Garber defended delaying changes until at least a year after the tournament.

"We need to make the changes that we're going to make because they're the right decisions at the right time for history, not because we need to make them by August of 2026," he said. "Because that's just not the way the world works. We're not going to have a whole bunch of people that have just watched the World Cup say, 'Oh, I like MLS more now, because they changed their roster rules.'"

League data showed that there was a massive bounce for domestic leagues coming out of a home World Cup. Considering that the 1994 World Cup was still the most successful in the history of the sport, and that the 2026 tournament would be playing a new expanded format that included forty-eight teams instead of thirty-two, it promised to be the biggest sporting event in history.

Garber was adamant that the league could still get plenty out of the enormous platform created by the World Cup by using it to unveil and sell the changes that were coming to MLS in 2027.

"There's no doubt that the World Cup will be an enormous driver of interest, awareness, and energy around the sport," he said. "But we're not building this league for seminal moments; we're building this league for the future. Those seminal moments have to be properly managed to ensure that you have a productive future, but to put all of our energy into 'You've got to get this done by 2026' almost defies how we're thinking about the World Cup.

"I'm not thinking of it as a Taylor Swift concert. I'm thinking of it as a key moment in the history of the game here in North America, and how do we make some decisions in and around that to ensure that we're capturing the opportunity. But that doesn't mean you tear up the playbook and start again.

"You might evolve your playbook, but the basic plan of smart, strategic and thoughtful, collaborative investment is what got MLS to where it is today. And nobody believed we'd be here."

Garber was nearing the end of his reign atop MLS. His contract expired at the end of 2027. With the battle over what change would come to MLS mostly settled, the most important power struggle pivoted to who would lead the league into its next era.

The next commissioner would have a strong foundation on which to build. But what traits MLS owners prioritized would speak volumes about the board's priorities. Would they look for someone with global soccer experience, or prioritize an executive with knowledge of the American sports landscape? Much of the league's corporate leadership had been entrenched at the top of American soccer for decades. There was a belief new voices were needed.

For now, though, the ship was still Garber's to steer.

His ability to push MLS toward the calendar change was vital, but it was less clear whether he was convinced the league needed the type of roster-building reform many owners were seeking—a change that was essential for real growth.

The commissioner insisted MLS's roster rules were efficient. "You're just wrong there," he said when asked about the system's inefficiency in producing quality. The league's argument focused on how MLS teams spent relative to revenue and in producing competitive balance.

"We've had twelve winners in twenty years," Garber argued. "The Bundesliga has had two."

What it didn't account for enough was whether that money

was building the best possible rosters, which in turn would produce the best possible competition.

Considering how much was riding on MLS getting it right, it was worrying that the league leadership might not be ready to completely let go of the strategies that had steered them to this point. (Perhaps it wasn't a surprise considering that, more than two years into Messi's time in Miami, the league had barely touched a rule to maximize his impact.)

But even while the commissioner didn't yet seem on board with a total overhaul of roster construction, he did acknowledge that some sort of change had to happen as MLS pushed into its future.

There was no avoiding that truth.

"It's all related to money," Garber said. "Fans and others spend a lot of time on how the money is spent. The real issue is, how much money are we spending, right? There are those that believe the way to do that is to change the way you spend the same amount of money, [but] we need to generate more revenue so that we can spend more money on all the things that will drive [the] popularity of our league.

"Every day I come to work . . . [and think about] how do we manage what we have, and how do we become courageous about allocating resources to capture what we don't have. That's been my role every day for the last twenty-six years. . . .

"We have to sit down and decide, how are we going to divide up every dollar, and how are we going to prioritize our investment? Whether that be an investment in players, investment in stadiums, investment in people, on and off the field, investment in marketing, investment in technology and data. All of that is part of the ask, and it all comes together to try to make the league more valuable or popular.

"And that's the end game: Drive audience. Have more fans. Make more money."

* * *

Messi accomplished all three of those things in Miami, but it was clear he alone wasn't the answer for MLS.

The solution could be found by looking back to that first month of Messi in the U.S., or in the global soccer competitions MLS was now trying to catch.

Americans were ready to embrace the best soccer they could find.

It was why millions watched the clip of that first free kick in Fort Lauderdale, and why they paid 1,000 percent mark-ups to see Messi play in their home markets. It's why they showed up at soccer pubs at 7 A.M. on Saturday mornings to cheer on clubs an ocean away, why they filled stadiums for summer exhibitions, and why they would turn out in record numbers for the World Cup in 2026.

The path forward was the same one Messi declared when he arrived in MLS.

"It's an ideal moment to grow," he said in those thrilling first weeks. "You have to take advantage, for the good of soccer in the U.S. and globally. Everything is in place here to witness top-level football because of the country, the structure—a lot of things."

"Hopefully MLS can continue to grow this way."

Somehow, it still wasn't certain which way the league would go. But there was only one right answer. For the Messi effect to be the start of a new era for the sport in the U.S., MLS needed to truly chase the goal it had long extolled: to become one of the best leagues in the world.

EPILOGUE

For all the trophies that he has won, there was Lionel Messi in the Inter Miami locker room, bouncing up and down and singing as his gray MLS Cup championship T-shirt was soaked with the champagne and beer being sprayed around the room.

The Argentine legend had set up all three goals in Miami's 3–1 win over the Vancouver Whitecaps on December 6, 2025, including a highlight-reel assist to seal the result, taking the ball off his chest and sending teammate Tadeo Allende through before the ball touched the ground.

It wasn't the bright lights of the UEFA Champions League or World Cup. But for Messi, who had once sat in Chris Henderson's office and declared, "Tell me all the trophies I can win," it was important.

So much so that, half an hour later, just after 6:30 P.M. when Messi emerged from the locker room and headed to his black Cadillac Escalade in the loading dock at Chase Stadium, he was still wearing his pink cleats. A smile remained plastered on his face.

With his driver's side door open, Messi stopped for an interview with Marcelo Benedetto, one of the most esteemed soccer reporters in Argentina.

"This was the goal: to be MLS champions so that the club continues to grow," Messi said. "Positioning [Miami] at the top was a great challenge when I came here, and that's why I'm happy."

When the last question was answered, nearly two hours after the final whistle sounded, Messi finally slipped the boots off the preternatural feet that had delivered the forty-eighth team trophy of his career, more than any other player in history. Then he got into the car, fired up the engine, and drove out of the stadium.

The MLS Cup championship sealed Messi's immediate-term legacy in the U.S. In two and a half years with Miami, he delivered the type of unequivocal success that followed him throughout his career. Messi's arrival in 2023 took a brand-new organization still searching for a way to successfully marry its ambition to reality and turned it into a global brand.

On the sporting side, he had now won three of the five trophies on offer for an American MLS team: the Leagues Cup, Supporters' Shield, and now MLS Cup. He set an MLS record with fifteen goal contributions in the postseason and delivered the largest viewership for an MLS Cup final in league history: more than 4.6 million people tuned in to see Messi lift the Cup. He also collected back-to-back MLS Most Valuable Player awards, the first in league history to do so.

But what mattered most—a legacy that would spread outside of Inter Miami and across MLS, and would last beyond when Messi stopped playing—was still up in the air. As substantial as it all was, if Messi's legacy was just trophies and ticket sales, MVP awards and pink jerseys, it would fall well short of what it could have been.

For Messi in MLS to matter beyond the surface level, bigger change still had to come. Messi had done everything he could do. He had sold jerseys and tickets, scored goals, won trophies, and pulled in new fans. There was nothing more he could do directly, on the field or off, to make it happen. His legacy rested in the hands of MLS's owners and commissioner Don Garber.

That was why, an hour before Messi drove away, with celebrations still ongoing in front of the supporters' section and confetti glittering under his black Oxford shoes in the penalty box, Inter Miami owner Jorge Mas was already starting to think of what had to come next.

"The story continues," he said, shouting above the fans' singing. "It's the culmination of everything we've worked for. It's been super hard to get here. But finally we're showing the world what's possible.

"It ain't over."

* * *

One month earlier, MLS owners had taken a step toward securing Messi's longer-term legacy.

During the final board of governors meeting of the year, on November 13, 2025, at the Four Seasons in Palm Beach, Florida, following two years of studies and debates, the board finally voted on and passed two key elements of the MLS 3.0 plan: to redesign the regular season and postseason format; and, crucially, to flip the calendar to a summer-to-spring schedule.

Beginning in 2027, the MLS season would start in mid-July and run through late May.

"Today, our owners made a decision that I think is one of the most important decisions in our league's history," Garber told reporters.

Garber wasn't wrong. There was a reason why it had taken the first two and a half years of Messi's time in MLS to get to a place where league stakeholders felt comfortable calling a vote. It was a process that involved nearly every important decision-maker at the team and league level. That the league hadn't started working on evolution sooner or reached a decision faster was still frustrating for many who had long seen reform as necessary, but Garber and league executives were stubbornly set on not accelerating decisions that would fundamentally alter how MLS operated in the global soccer business.

Even still, the Palm Beach vote alone wouldn't be enough to secure Messi's legacy. More was needed if these changes were going to be as impactful as Garber sold them.

Without significant updates to the roster investment model, the league wasn't addressing its biggest issue: improving the on-field product in a way that might attract wider audiences, increase relevance, and drive more revenue.

It went back to the battle over what the league's North Star needed to be: top-end quality, even if that meant more focus on bigger markets or competitive balance. Whereas that competitive balance once helped the league grow, it was now limiting MLS's chance to compete.

"Soccer has always been a global game and a global business," said AJ Swoboda, founder of Formation Partners, an advisory and investment firm working across global professional sport, who advised MLS on its competition and calendar changes. "MLS's roster rules, while technically balanced and designed to avoid waste, began dragging everyone down the economic drain when compared against the global sport. Even the best teams and the most forward-thinking owners can't build competitive squads efficiently.

"The league's 'North Star' on sporting spend should have been updated over a decade ago, to be competitively balanced within the league, while simultaneously boasting above average financial efficiency in the global landscape. And at the bare minimum, the league's owners should expect to be average. To be regularly one of the most inefficient leagues in the world at turning spend into performance is a crisis."

Messi's extension gave the league more time to overhaul that investment model in time for the audience the Argentine brought with him to still be around when it made those changes, but there was a new incentive to push the league forward quicker: The league renegotiated terms on its media deal with Apple. Its content was moving outside of the MLS Season Pass paywall, which would open up the league to a much wider audience. The deal now was set to end in summer 2029, three and a half years earlier than initially planned.

That gave the league a deadline to not only improve the product but also compel more people to watch in time to maximize the offers when it came to market again.

But, as Messi proved a few weeks later, change could come quickly—and ferociously—if executed right.

* * *

David Beckham came sprinting out of the Inter Miami locker room ninety minutes after the final whistle sounded on Miami's MLS Cup win, the red bottoms of his Christian Louboutin dress shoes flashing as he made a beeline out onto the confetti-covered field and toward the stage where Messi had lifted up the trophy an hour before.

Six and a half years earlier, in March 2019, on this exact site, Beckham stood on a much smaller stage with Jorge Mas. The platform overlooked a field of weeds, trees, and waist-high grass that had overtaken the shell of old Lockhart Stadium, a relic of American soccer's past triumphs and failures. Beckham and Mas announced they would build a new stadium on the site as Inter Miami's first home while they finalized plans for a more permanent solution.

That Messi's overwhelming influence turned Inter Miami into a global brand over the previous three seasons made it easy to forget just how far the club had come in such a short amount of time.

Beckham hadn't forgotten. He had lived and suffered it.

The England superstar spent years trying to start the team in Miami. Stadium issues and the lack of the right local partner had threatened those dreams. At one point, MLS offered him $50 million to buy back the rights to a team that he had written into his contract when he came to the league in 2007. Beckham turned down the buyback, such was his faith that an MLS club in Miami would be a success.

Messi validated that decision in a big way.

It's why Beckham was running out himself to find the MLS Cup trophy, which somehow had been left behind when the team made its way inside the locker room to continue its celebrations. The newly appointed officer of the Order of the British Empire wanted to fetch it himself, overjoyed at becoming the first to win the title as both player and owner. He snagged the twenty-one-pound, two-foot-tall silver cup in his right hand and sprinted back inside to rejoin the festivities.

Fourteen years earlier, it was Beckham's sporting legacy in America that shifted when he won his first MLS Cup with the LA Galaxy. He understood how important a championship was to validating a project; that Messi in Miami would have been regarded differently in history without a title. It's why he burst into tears and grabbed his son at the final whistle.

But Beckham also understood that his role on this night in Miami meant more than those championships in LA in 2010 and 2011.

"When I first came here, almost twenty years ago, I knew that there was going to be a challenge, but in all honesty, I knew the potential of what America had for this sport," Beckham said in an interview on the field. "I always promised the commissioner that my commitment wasn't just to the Galaxy, it was to improving and making this sport stronger in this country. . . . Tonight is just one of those nights that I'll never forget. It has to be one of the greatest moments of my career."

Nearly twenty years after he first arrived in MLS, Beckham's brand was still attached to the league. The designated player rule—designed to bring Beckham in—changed the makeup of the on-field product forever. His Miami team had brought the greatest player of all time and just lifted a trophy.

If the Messi effect was to be considered anything near as impactful as Beckham's influence, it needed that sort of lasting change.

On the other side of midfield from where Beckham snagged the trophy, MLS commissioner Don Garber stopped to soak in the celebration unfolding around him. Garber typically tried to avoid reflecting too much on how the league had grown over the previous quarter century.

"If you take a look back, you'll never be able to look forward," he said.

But on this night, he was granting himself an exception.

"I'm really moved," he said.

Garber's instincts, though, were right.

It would be a mistake to look at Messi and Miami's triumph as an end rather than a beginning. If the league was going to capitalize on this moment, the MLS Cup win couldn't be seen as an exclamation point on Messi's time in the league.

It had to be leveraged as a step toward something bigger. To reshape American soccer forever.

ACKNOWLEDGMENTS

Putting together this book would not have been possible without the help of so many people. Thank you first to Pete Wolverton, my editor at St. Martin's Press, whose belief, patience, and understanding guided this book to a better place. I'd also like to thank my agent, Susan Canavan, and WLA Books for having the faith in me to take on this project, and Adam Duerson, whose guidance in the early days made the book happen.

I owe an enormous debt of gratitude to my friend Brian Straus, who stepped up to help me through the most difficult portions of writing this book. Without his time, honesty, and edits, I'm not sure this book would've gotten done. He is one of the very best American soccer journalists, and I'm so thankful for his help.

Thank you to Sam Stejskal, whose partnership over many years together at *The Athletic* gave me the confidence to take this on, and who became one of my best friends and confidantes. Thanks for always lending an ear and talking me through structure, but most importantly for making me laugh and keeping me sane and focused on the things that matter most.

A huge thank-you to my editors at *The Athletic* for their graciousness as I took on this project and balanced it with my day-to-day work: Laura Williamson, Martin Rogers, Avi Creditor, Emily Olsen, Alex Abnos, Brooks Peck, Steven Ginsberg, and David

Jordan. A huge thank-you to my colleagues who lived through those early days of Messi with me at the Courtyard Fort Lauderdale Downtown, Felipe Cárdenas and Pablo Maurer. Felipe, I so appreciate your hard work, camaraderie, and friendship from the summer of Messi in 2023 through the 2024 Copa América and everything in between and since. Thanks to Tom Bogert, Josh Kloke, David Ornstein, Henry Bushnell, Meg Linehan, Jeff Rueter, Melanie Anzidei, and others who encouraged and helped me along the way. A huge thank-you, also, to my good friend Doug McIntyre for reading a draft, providing edits, and giving me an important mental boost. To Seth Wickersham, George Quraishi and Robert Andrew Powell for their guidance. And to the late Grant Wahl, whose book, *The Beckham Experiment*, blazed a path for soccer books like this to exist.

This book was based on hundreds of interviews across multiple years, specifically for this book but also while reporting for *The Athletic*. Most of those interviews were on the record, but many were on background, and I am grateful to everyone who spoke with me to give me a better understanding of Messi's impact and the American soccer landscape. That includes several people who won't be named here but who were critical to my reporting.

Messi in Miami would not have happened without Jorge Mas's vision, and this book would have looked far different if not for his understanding of my vision for the project. He was generous in both his time and honesty. A thank-you, as well, to Jose Mas, whose insight was always sharp and perceptive. And to Cristina Canales, without whom none of it would have been possible.

The book was also possible because of those who tolerated me at Inter Miami, especially the communications crew of Molly Dreska, Rafa Cabrera, Michael Franca, and Paola Garcia, but also the players, coaches, and execs who sat for interviews in different settings, from hotel conference rooms in Riyadh to Chicago, especially Chris Henderson, Xavi Asensi, Javier Morales, Victor Ulloa, Julian Gressel, Noah Allen, Franco Negri and Kamal Miller.

I spent a lot of time lingering outside of hotel ballrooms to track down MLS owners and executives. The communications staff at MLS, especially Lauren Hayes and Dan Courtemanche, always kept me company and worked to make my life easier. Don Garber, Gary Stevenson, and Todd Durbin were gracious and understanding of my reporting over the last several years, even when they didn't always agree.

Thank you to the many MLS owners I spoke with while working on this book, much of which was on background. I appreciated the willingness of Larry Berg and Merritt Paulson to speak on record as important topics went in front of the board. Thank you also to Steve Cannon, who sat with me on his final day before retirement, and Adrian Hanauer. They provided important insight into the growth of Atlanta United and Seattle Sounders, respectively, and the role those teams played in the MLS story, and their perspectives on the league remained critical to the book even as the structure of the story changed.

To those who gave me a better understanding of the influence of the Premier League, NBC, the Champions League, and CBS: Jon Miller, Rebecca Lowe, Richard Scudamore, Pete Radovich, and Kate Scott, and to Paul-Michael Ochoa and Dan Masonson. To Brendan Hunt for using one of his lunch breaks while writing the newest season of *Ted Lasso*; Eddy Cue, Sam Citron, and others at Apple; Danny Sillman at Relevent; Paul McDonough and Valerie Panou at USL; and Andrés Cantor, Juan Carlos Rodriguez, and Mikel Arriola.

Thank you to JT Batson and Lindsay Horan, who took the time to lend their expertise about American soccer and the U.S. women's national team, and to AJ Swoboda for his insight into global and American soccer.

Last, I'd like to thank a few people who shaped my path to his book. First, my coach Clyde Watson, who ingrained in me the beautiful, tiki-taka style of soccer I love so much and who molded how I think about the game today. And to all my TAP teammates, whose brotherhood reinforced my love of the sport.

To my siblings, Sarah, Sam, and John Thomas—thank you for your support. To my Uncle Paul, for his constant faith in me. And thank you, Jane and Carmen, for always being there for me and for us.

Mom: Your consistent belief and love boosted me through my early days of playing soccer and my pursuit of a journalism career. You were always willing to fly to Chicago to help when I had to jet somewhere for this book, and you've always been there to lift me up as a son, father, and now, author. I hope you understand how much it has all meant to me.

Nikki, you took on so much more while I was hopping on a plane and chasing Inter Miami around the world or hiding away in my office at home to report and write this book. Your strength, patience, and support steered me through this process. I could not have done this book without you. Jane and Ben, you give me purpose every day.

And last, to my dad. You emigrated from Costa Rica and passed your love of soccer on to me, worked seven days a week parking cars and cutting lawns so that I could have more—so that I could play the sport and chase my dreams. This book is part of your legacy. I miss and love you.

INDEX

ABOUT THE AUTHOR

John Dorton

Paul Tenorio is a senior writer for *The Athletic* who has covered American and global soccer since 2007. His work has also appeared in *The Washington Post*, in the *Orlando Sentinel*, in *FourFourTwo*, and on ESPN. A proud Costa Rican American, Paul grew up in Mount Vernon, Virginia, and graduated from Northwestern University's Medill School of Journalism. He lives with his wife and two kids in Chicago.

LAST TIME IN LAKE GENEVA

Officer Ryan Brandt responds to a 911 call at the Mailboat and finds Captain Tommy bleeding from a gunshot wound and his mail jumper Bailey crying over him. This is the first time she's shown emotion for anyone, and Ryan quickly realizes that Tommy alone holds the key to Bailey's heart, closed after years of abuse in foster care. If Tommy lives, maybe there's hope of saving Bailey, too.

Tommy is airlifted to Froedtert Hospital in Milwaukee and Ryan drives Bailey to see him. Bailey feels like she's intruding; she isn't as close to Tommy as the other people in the waiting room. Besides, everyone she cares about either leaves her or dies. The universe couldn't be any clearer that she doesn't belong. But Ryan seems determined that she and the captain ought to be together.

Detective Monica Steele is furious that Chief Wade Erickson thought the murders of the last members of the Markham Ring were solved and the violence was over. Now Wade's best friend is fighting for his life. Shaken, she almost accepts the temptation of comfort from Ryan, her ex. But he has no idea the devastation he caused when he cheated on her ten years ago. He never knew that Monica had finally gotten pregnant. In the aftermath of his betrayal, she kicked him out and had an abortion—without ever telling him.

After days of drifting in and out of consciousness, Tommy comes to and finds Bailey at his bedside. He has no memory of what happened and Bailey has to inform him. Realizing how close he came to death, Tommy finally screws up the nerve to tell Bailey the secret he alone knows: His fugitive son was her unknown father.

Bailey slips away to a hospital bathroom, where she comes unglued. The thing she's literally dreamed of is true: Tommy is her grandfather. Far from bringing her joy, it fills her with terror. In her experience, family are those people you never get to keep, and losing Tommy is her worst nightmare. Terrified, she cuts off her visits with Tommy, much to Ryan's dismay.

Meanwhile, Bailey's foster dad Bud Weber is pleased with his handiwork; he taught Tommy a swift lesson, and he's confident the captain won't dare report Bailey's mysterious bruises again. But Bud's boss, The Man Upstairs, is furious. By working his own side gig, Bud has risked ruining The Man's own murderous plan. The Man lets Bud know that his services are no longer needed. He's fired.

Jimmy Beacon, the young dishwasher at Bud's restaurant, finally finds his courage to express his feelings to Bailey—only to discover her holding hands with Noah Cadigan, the boy who coached him on how to approach a girl in the first place. He storms off in a rage. Jimmy's elderly friend Roland Markham tries to comfort him. But when conversation turns to Jimmy's younger sister Amelia, who was kidnapped, raped, and murdered, Jimmy's fury overflows. Roland points out that Jimmy might, in fact, be closer to the killer than he knows; it's said his boss, Bud Weber, has a taste for little girls. Jimmy searches Bud's office and finds the bow Amelia was wearing the day she was killed.

At his wit's end with both Bailey and Monica, Ryan talks with Bill Gallagher, the police chaplain and a foster father many times over. He advises Ryan to let Monica share her side of the story—when she's ready—and to love Bailey relentlessly to overcome her years of abuse. Considering his own unreliable track record, Ryan isn't convinced he could be the pillar of strength Monica and Bailey need.

Jimmy confronts Bud Weber with his evidence, as well as his means of revenge—a homemade bomb. They chase each other through the crowded tourist town with the cops on their heels. When Jimmy closes in and pulls the cord, Bill Gallagher runs from the crowd and throws himself over Jimmy and the bomb, absorbing the blast with his own body. When the dust settles, he and Jimmy are dead, as well as a Lake Geneva police officer. Bud gets away barely scathed.

While Monica and Ryan spring to bring order to the chaos, Monica's phone rings. A mysterious voice asks if she's figured out yet that everything's connected, from the murders of the members of the Markham Ring to this apparently unrelated bombing by a troubled youth. The voice claims to know the town's deepest secrets and how to exploit them—including Monica's. He implies that he knows about her aborted child.

When Monica demands to know his name, he replies: "I'm The Man Upstairs."

MAILBOAT

FRIDAY, JULY 11, 2014

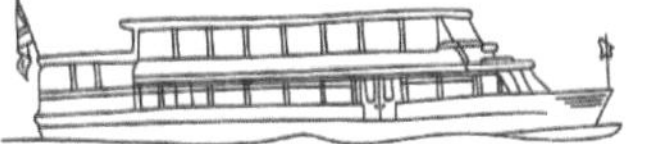

Chapter One
RYAN

Rain trickled along the black visor of my service hat in two glistening streams that pooled in the center, grew, thought about falling, then fell. One by one, the droplets struck my hands, clasped in front of me, and soaked into my white gloves. I ran my fingers along the brim, stopping the never-ending flow for a moment, and focused my attention on the young woman under the black canopy singing "Amazing Grace" in crystal tones while strumming a worn guitar.

The casket—closed—was white with gilded scrollwork. It dazzled even in the rain, as if the angels had ripped down the pearly gates and torn up the streets of gold to build it. As if nothing less would do for their beloved, fallen saint. Bill Gallagher. Our chaplain. The man who had saved hundreds of lives by throwing himself over a boy and his bomb. I'd never be able to erase the image of carnage. I still couldn't believe what Bill had done. In the microcosm of time between his spotting the bomber and his flinging himself over the boy, he'd made up his mind. Thrown aside life and everything it had to offer. Sacrificed himself for his town and the people he loved.

I hoped the angels had lined his casket with their own feathers to cradle his broken body. I hoped they greeted him with harps and a crown of glory.

He deserved it.

I flicked my head to shake off another droplet and turned my eyes to Bill's family, standing under the black canopy. His wife Peggy. His three children by birth. His four children by adoption. The seven of them grown with partners and kids of their own, an army of grandchildren.

Two kids stood center front, Peggy's hands on their shoulders. A boy and a girl, maybe six or seven. Their position with the family was uncemented. They were Bill and Peggy's last two foster children. With the tragedy that had struck her life, Peggy could have easily picked up the phone and asked social services to re-home them. No sooner asked than done, the kids would have been out of her house within twenty-four hours. To re-home them so quickly, the kids probably would have been split up. Given the unpredictable path of foster care, they might never have seen each other again.

But clearly Peggy hadn't called. There they stood with the family as if they were blood-born and not someone else's forgotten children. Bill wouldn't have had it any other way. Once a child entered under his roof, that child was forever a Gallagher, in spirit if not in name.

The young woman with the guitar strummed the final chord. Her voice trailed to silence. Rain thrummed on the canopy and the coffin. Chief Wade Erickson stepped up to a microphone and raised it several inches to match his height. His navy blue uniform sported five gold stars, signifying him as the highest ranking official in the Lake Geneva Police Department. His eyes traversed the crowd—friends and family in black, police officers in navy blue.

"We are gathered here to lay to rest our brother, Bill Gallagher, a beloved pastor, chaplain, friend..." His eyes traveled to the family. "...father, grandfather, and husband."

Peggy smiled with soulful gratitude and hugged the children closer.

Wade turned again to the crowd, his jaw working emptily for a moment. "But beyond that, Bill was... the bravest man I have ever had the honor of knowing." His eyes went hollow, haunted. As if the shock of Bill's sacrifice hit him as hard as it did all of us. Wade soldiered past the look of emptiness, found his words again. "He was a man so full of love for his fellow creatures, whoever they may be, that he willingly laid down his life for them, with no regard for his own."

The chief's open vulnerability triggered my own. A lump rose in my throat, choking off my windpipe. My memory flashed back to one of my last conversations with Bill. *Relentless love.* That's what we'd talked about, this insane concept he'd introduced me to. A love so resolute, nothing could force it to back down. Not fear, not rejection, not even a boy with a bomb.

"Am I capable of relentless love?" I'd asked that night.

"We all are," Bill had replied. *"If we want to be."*

And the very next day, I'd gone and decided I wasn't. Like a coward, I'd started filling out apps for other departments. Other jobs I could work when my temp patrolman's job in Lake Geneva ended. Places far away from Bailey Johnson, the foster girl I cared about beyond explanation. From Monica Steele, my ex, whom I still loved with all my heart.

But not with relentless love.

That had been before the bomb. Before the fear of losing Bailey and Monica had become horrifyingly real. Bill's selfless act of love for complete strangers shamed me from beyond the grave. Was I too weak and afraid to love Bailey and Monica as relentlessly as he had loved this town?

Bill had also challenged me to quit dwelling on myself, on my lead-weighted feelings of worthlessness and shame. In a nutshell, he told me to focus on getting shit done. Being there for Bailey despite my fears and probable incompetence. Figuring out what it really was Monica needed, then either providing it for her or getting the hell out of her way so she could get it done herself.

I fixed my eyes on the casket and drew a shaky breath. Bill had had a way of shedding a spotlight on things that made them so simple, the path laser clear. Was there any hope I could hang onto that light, even without him around to make sure the battery was fully charged?

I heard his voice in my head. *Yes, you can, Ryan. If you want to.*

"Let's pray," Wade Erickson said. "Heavenly Father..."

I tipped my chin toward my clasped hands—but not before glancing down the military-straight row of my brothers and sisters in blue. Monica Steele stood at the far end next to her partner, Detective Sergeant Stan Lehman. She looked amazing in her tailored, navy blue dress uniform, her gold insignia and badge shining, her glossy mahogany hair twisted in a tight bun at the base of her neck, below her service cap. She was a solid wall of poise and determination—but also feminine elegance—a lethal combination of elements a man would be crazy to mess with.

That's what I'd always loved about her. Her strength. Her will. This woman could take care of herself. And yet, once upon a time, she had permitted me into her life. To love her. To stand beside her. To see her vulnerable side. To be her husband. Her lover. She set me on fire like no one else ever had or ever would.

"...in Jesus' name," Wade concluded, "Amen." And I realized I'd forgotten to pray to anyone but the goddess at the end of the row.

"Amen," the crowd muttered.

"Amen," I joined in.

Feet stirred, but for a moment, no one spoke, no one moved. Finally, Peggy Gallagher stepped toward the casket. Laid a single red rose on the lid. Laid her arm across her entombed husband. Whispered. Wept. Then walked away.

Her children and grandchildren were next, laying their roses on top of Peggy's until they'd built a pyramid of red and green. Brothers and sisters hugged each other. Cried.

Last of all, Bill's final two foster children stepped forward. With down-turned faces, they hesitated. But Peggy smiled and encouraged them forward. Standing on tiptoe, the boy nestled something orange, red, and fuzzy amidst the flowers. When he stepped away, I saw what it was. The knitted lion hat Bill had worn while playing with the children. Perhaps the one item these kids most associated with him. With his love. His relentless love.

Don't let me down, Ryan, his voice whispered through my head again. *You can do this.*

As the crowd began to break up, rearrange itself, converse in hushed tones, I looked toward Monica. Lehman had left. She was talking with Steph Buchanan, one of the telecommunicators. Without me really telling them to, my feet carried me toward Monica—as if they'd known all along what to do and had just been waiting for my head and my fears to get out of the way.

Chapter Two
MONICA

He was looking at me. Ryan. Just standing in the rain, staring like a sad puppy. I took a deep, shaky breath and tried to focus my attention on my conversation with Steph. If Ryan had noticed me tremble, hopefully he would attribute it to the funerals—Bill's today, Mike Schultz's yesterday. Losing both our chaplain and a fellow officer, and burying them one after the other, had left me shattered. But no one needed to know that.

I'd barely spoken to Ryan since the day the bomb went off downtown. He'd thrown himself on top of me to protect me from the shrapnel. And now I could barely look at him, much less speak to him. His nearness sent shivers through my body like it used to lifetimes ago, and I couldn't begin to explain it. He still loved me. It was obvious in his every move, his every look.

The terrifying question was... what if I still loved him?

By the time I saw him coming towards me, the drowned puppy now hopeful, it was too late to run. Oh, God, why? My mind scrambled to maintain the threads of my conversation with Steph. If I looked occupied, if Ryan could feel the ice rolling off my shoulders, maybe he would leave me alone.

But just as I thought of something to add to the conversation, Steph squeezed my hand. "I'm going to talk to Angie."

"Yeah, sure." My mouth betrayed me with a smile. What I really wanted to say was, *No, Steph, cover my six here.* Didn't she see Ryan coming? But maybe she did, and maybe that was why she was walking away—to give us space to be alone.

Great.

Ryan cocked his head, eyes searching for clues as to my demeanor today. He approached me cautiously as he always did. But his spine remained straight. That's just what a dress uniform does to your psyche; it's impossible to slouch, to disrespect yourself or this sign of your office. It brings out the best in you.

And it brought out the best in Ryan. The straight lines of his jacket underscored his calm, his command. Meanwhile, his compassion shone out from a pair of coffee-brown eyes under his rain-speckled visor. His well-toned biceps filled out his sleeves. He was gorgeous. I'd always been a sucker for a guy in uniform.

No, that wasn't true. I'd always been a sucker for Ryan in uniform. There had never been any other guy. Not even after I dumped him.

He stopped in front of me. Dipped his head and scratched the back of his neck. "A bunch of us are going to Foley's," he said. It was a bar on the north side of the lake. "You know. After the reception."

No surprise. As cops, we swallowed as much heartache as we did coffee and liked to wash them both down with something stronger at the end of the day. Especially a day like this.

Ryan glanced in different directions and then at me. "You, ah... you want to come?"

I furrowed my brow. He was... inviting me to drinks? In what way? Was I just joining the group? Or was I *going out* with him?

"Uh..." I hesitated.

He lifted a palm. "You know, whatever you want to do."

His rush to offer an escape implied he'd hoped for the latter—that I would go out with him. My stomach twisted into knots. The same place it always did, right beneath my solar plexus. The empty place. The place where I'd briefly carried our child. Ryan still knew nothing. Never had a chance to. I'd seen him with another woman, then ended the pregnancy without telling him a word. Even though I tried to convince myself that I was okay with my decision, my psyche was a wreck.

I forced sounds through my lips. "I was just going to go back to the office."

He huffed a laugh through his nose. "Oh. Of course." The smile on his mouth implied humor, fondness, and familiarity.

He knew I didn't have a life away from my desk in the detective bureau—and apparently he found that endearing. Of course, he and I had always lived life in the fast lane. He understood my need to be busy. Especially now. Three weeks ago, we had found a man from California tied to the end of a pier on the lake. His ID said his name was Will Read. Our records knew him better as Fritz Geissler, the boy who had grown up in Lake Geneva, the young man who had made millions breaking into banks as part of a ring, the fugitive we'd been seeking for seventeen years.

Things had only gotten worse when his last living partner in crime, Jason Thomlin, had turned up dead as well. Then Jason's father Tommy had been shot. Then a bomb had gone off in the middle of downtown.

And then someone we still hadn't identified had called my personal cell phone. Claimed to be the one behind it all. Called himself The Man Upstairs. And he suggested he knew about my unborn child.

I really didn't have time for things like Foley's.

"You won't take one night off?" Ryan asked with a hopeful smile I remembered well. "For Bill? For Mike?"

I glanced away over the gathering of mourners. "I'll see how I feel. After the reception." At the moment, I felt sick to my stomach. Thinking about The Man Upstairs did that to me. So did thinking about the secret I was hiding from Ryan.

He nodded. "Fair enough. Need a ride back to the church?"

"No." I'd brought my own car.

"Okay." He toed the grass but made no move to leave. For several seconds, we both stood awkwardly. He finally cleared his throat and gestured toward the black canopy and the line of people waiting to extend their condolences to the family. "I'm gonna give my regrets to Peggy."

I nodded. Good. I needed him to go. Now. But he lingered as if hopeful I'd come with him. When I didn't, he nodded, then strode away through the sprinkling rain. The water had darkened the shoulders of his jacket and the top of his hat.

He was gone. Finally. Great. I supposed I should go mingle, if nothing else than to confirm my verbal cues with a physical one and show Ryan I wasn't even thinking about him anymore. But I hated the thought of making small talk. There was no one here I wanted to spend time with.

Except Ryan.

Eventually, I forced myself to join my partners from the detective bureau, Stan Lehman and Mark Neumiller. We talked about the rain, and when was the last time any of the patrol units had a wax? Maybe they were due. But my eyes kept drifting to Ryan.

When he finally got to the head of the line under the canopy, he gave Peggy Gallagher a hug. She wrapped him in a tight embrace, a ferocious mama bear whose felt duty was to comfort all those around her. A woman who wouldn't shed her own tears until she was home, in the solitude of the room she'd shared with the love of her life. And then the tears would flow. That was her nature.

Two young children stood by her side. Grandkids, maybe. Or fosters, though it stretched my imagination to think the Gallaghers were still taking in children after so many years. To my surprise, Ryan got down on his knee, looked the kids in the eyes, and said something I couldn't hear. But the kids dropped their gazes to the ground. Nodded. Seemed to appreciate whatever it was he'd said, in their small, innocent minds.

As if to move away from feelings she didn't know what to do with, the little girl looked up with a smile and offered Ryan the leaf she'd been twirling in her hand. Ryan accepted it, then cupped the back of her head and planted a kiss on her forehead.

The sight twisted a knife in my soul. I'd always joked Ryan would make a terrible dad, back in the days when we were trying—and failing—to have a baby. I'd been teasing him, but it had probably been true. Ryan had still been a footloose, carefree soul, pulling pranks at work and enjoying the freedom we still had as a childless couple. Starting a family had been my idea, not his. In hindsight, I'd grabbed his wrist and yanked him all the way down that road, barely asking him what he thought, simply assuming he wanted a family as much as I did. Maybe that was why he'd made himself an out. Maybe that was why he'd slipped home another woman when he thought I was away and blown up every bridge between us.

But we'd been apart ten years, and now here he was, listening to a pair of children ramble on, accepting priceless little tokens that were going to shrivel up later that afternoon. Looking as if he would have been so goddamn natural at the job of parenting. There was Bailey Johnson for proof, too. Ryan was married to the mission of getting her out of her abusive foster home. When she was around, wings practically sprouted from his back and wrapped around her like feathered shields.

What had happened to the Ryan I knew? It was as if he'd shed everything I hated, kept everything I loved, and added a few things I never dreamed of. The new Ryan was irresistible. He was perfect. His soul called to my soul, and my soul screamed to take him back.

But our relationship had been built on honesty. There was no way it could survive after everything we'd done to each other. How could he cheat on me? How could I have made this decision about our baby without so much as telling him? Without including him? My reasons at the time had been bulletproof. But now...

Nausea wrenched my stomach again and tears flooded my eyes. Neumiller and Lehman were comparing the virtues of various brands of car wax, barely noticing me anymore.

"I'll see you at the reception," I blurted and turned away. I made for the cars parked by the road.

They stopped talking and watched after me but didn't stop me. I just kept going, shoulders square, trying to hold it in as long as possible. They would think I was crying for Bill or Schultz or both, and that was fine.

But I wasn't. I was crying for the life Ryan and I used to have together. The new stage in life we'd almost had together. The life we hadn't actually been ready for.

Finding my own car, I planted one hand on the hood and fisted the other one to my mouth, trying to push back all the years of second-guessing and regrets.

Trying to accept the impossibility of ever getting together with Ryan again.

Because now, ten years later, he would be the best dad ever. And I couldn't imagine how to tell him he would have had a child of his own. There was no way he'd understand why I'd made my decision, without a single word to him. He'd be devastated. He'd never speak to me again.

And I couldn't blame him.

Chapter Three
ANGELICA

To cross the Wisconsin border in the middle of a rain shower felt appropriate. Angelica Read held the steering wheel in both hands, grounding herself with the feel of firm leather beneath her sweating palms, and followed the prompts from the screen on the dash. She'd told the map to take her to Lake Geneva without being more specific. There was no friend she'd come to visit. No hotel she wanted to check into. No restaurant to try. No attraction to take in.

She just wanted to find the place, hear the map tell her, "You have arrived," and breathe. Then she'd drive aimlessly for as long as she needed. Explore the streets. The neighborhoods. The outskirts. Wrap her mind around the idea that this place was in fact real.

This place where her husband, Will Read, had grown up. Where, three weeks ago, he had been murdered. Drowned. Left tied to a pier post somewhere in a lake she'd never heard of before. Because he had never told her.

While the rain was perfectly on cue, the corn was a surprise. There was just so much of it. And not a billboard in sight. No flashy signs advertising the numerous delights to be had if you only pulled off the highway for a moment. For a popular Chicago tourist destination, this town gave no hint it existed, beyond a few unassuming green signs along the road. Lake Geneva, twenty miles. Lake Geneva, ten miles...

As the distance shrank, her soul twisted into ever tighter knots. Should she be here? Should she be asking questions about her husband's past? Was it better to live with a beautiful lie—a shrine to a beautiful nothing—or to know the ugly truth?

Her hands tightened on the wheel as her resolution grew firm. Truth. It was always better to know the truth. That was what she and Will had always valued togeth—

The tears wrenched free. In a moment, she could barely see the road. She twisted her head, fighting the pain. Truth? What was truth anymore? How could she say she valued truth when her entire marriage had been a falsehood? A flimsy stage prop? A cheap roadside attraction? Light and mirrors and illusions? *A lie?*

But still, ten thousand questions screamed for answers. The desire to feel something firm under her feet demanded her attention. All of it. She could no longer sit at home in LA pretending to grieve like a normal widow. She hadn't merely lost a husband. She had lost every precious moment with a man she only *thought* she knew. A man who had played her, and played her well.

She would seek the truth, even if the word itself was now tainted in her mind.

She turned onto another country highway, one of a million that seemed to spiderweb northern Illinois and southern Wisconsin. An iron fence appeared on her right, and instead of green stalks, stone monoliths cropped up from the ground. There was a black canopy. A crowd. A white casket on a scaffold. A funeral. Like the rain, this, too, felt appropriate.

Filled with morbid curiosity, she scanned the crowd. A military funeral? Half the people were dressed in uniform. But then she saw the dozens of police cars.

Returning her eyes to the road, she pressed her lips together and remembered to breathe. She was naturalized now. Her parents were, too, and her aunt and uncle and cousins. It had taken twenty years, but it had happened. For all of them. Still, she often had to remind herself she was no longer an undocumented immigrant. There was nothing to fear.

But when she had married Will, and especially when the boys had been born, she would sometimes lie awake at night. What if they arrested her? What if they sent her back to a country she barely knew anymore? What if she never saw her boys again? What if she lost everything they had gained together?

Will's job as a bank executive had allowed them every luxury they wanted. He'd encouraged her to follow her passion of becoming a realtor. She loved beautiful homes. They'd had their two sons. Lived in a house in Malibu with a view of the ocean. They'd created a life together beyond her wildest dreams. And in the back of her mind, she feared losing it all because she didn't have paperwork. No one could hand her a form to fill without her heart rate going up. What if it asked...?

On nights when the fears were too real, she would cling to Will and cry into his shoulder. Even in his sleep, he would wrap an arm around her. Mutter that everything would be okay. That he loved her. And somehow, she had believed that love as real as theirs was equal to anything the world could throw at them. It was all that got her through.

But when it turned out a man had told you nothing about himself—nothing that was true—could such a love have been real at all?

Three weeks ago, Will had flown to a conference in Las Vegas. That was what he told her. Then he quit calling and texting. Then there had been a ring at her bell. Two police officers. They told her that her husband was dead. Murdered. He had never been in Vegas. He was killed in a small town in Wisconsin. They told her they had no answers. They left her blank. Hanging. Confused. Disoriented. She told herself they had identified the wrong person. She didn't know why Will didn't call, but they *had* to have the wrong person. He'd never been to Wisconsin in his life.

Then a detective from Lake Geneva, a woman named Monica Steele, had flown all the way to Los Angeles to tell her that her husband had been a fugitive. A bank burglar. A member of an infamous ring. A man named Fritz Geissler, not Will Read. And did Angelica know where his accomplice was?

Angelica flared her nostrils and wrung the steering wheel. No. No, she did not know where his "accomplice" was. What was the woman talking about? This was madness.

But the days had rolled on and Will had not come home. The papers and news stations reported that a long-lost member of the "infamous" Markham Ring was dead. Then they sent his body. They flew it home. They asked her to identify him. The police showed her a picture of Will's face. His face after death. Calm. Composed. Lifeless.

She broke in two.

It was true, then. Will was gone.

They had a funeral. It was small. Few friends showed up. No one knew what to say. Her family wept. Brought her food. Tried to comfort her.

There was no comfort for this.

She'd sent her boys to her parents' and come to Lake Geneva for answers. Answers about the man she'd loved. The man she'd devoted ten years of her life to. The man she'd never actually known.

How could he lie to her like this? How could he betray her? He was her heart. Her everything.

It turned out, she'd never even known his real name.

Chapter Four
RYAN

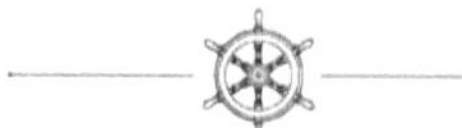

I paused outside the door to the chief's office, cupped my hand to my mouth, and breathed. Yep. I smelled like beer. Also, I'd changed out of my uniform ages ago and was now dressed in ratty jeans and a tee shirt. Well, Wade had known I was going to Foley's. If he'd wanted me well-dressed and sober, he should have texted me earlier in the evening.

I knocked on his door.

"Come in."

I entered. He sat at his desk, leaning his jaw on his fist. He was still wearing his dress uniform from the funeral, but he'd pulled off his tie and loosened his collar. The windows behind his desk were black, the blinds forgotten open. The room was softly lit by the floor lamp behind his desk, easier to reach from his chair than the light switch by the door. Put together, the evidence suggested he'd been sitting here for hours.

"Burning the midnight oil, sir?" I asked, closing the door behind me.

He shuffled the stack of papers he'd been looking at. "No shortage of oil to burn."

"True," I agreed. "How's the task force getting along?" After three homicides, a shooting, and a bombing, all tied to a cold case with no end of leads to follow, Monica and her partners in the detective bureau had simply run out of manpower and daylight hours. They'd reached out to both neighboring and overarching departments, asking for aid, and those departments had swooped in to help the way you'd rush to a kid getting his ass pounded on the playground. That's about how our department felt. And that's about how the other departments felt, watching us.

"They're keeping plenty busy," Wade said. "But that's not what I called you in to talk about." With his pen, he pointed to a chair in front of his desk. "Have a seat."

I sat, half wondering if I'd done something wrong. Getting called into the chief's office was about as tense as being called into the principal's office.

Wade rotated his stack of paperwork so it faced me. The one on top said "W2."

"Fifty-one thousand a year," Wade said. "All the usual benefits and pension. And you can park the ten-speed. We'll get you a patrol car." He threw the pen down on top and leaned back in his chair.

I glanced between the paperwork and Wade. He was offering me a year-round job. He wanted me off the summer reserves. Off bike patrol. And I knew why. He was short an officer. Mike Schultz was dead.

The fan inside Wade's computer hummed to life, only emphasizing the silence. A few months ago, when I'd applied for a job in my hometown, I would have been thrilled to get a year-round. That was before I'd known Monica was working at our home department again, too. I'd known better than to kick the broken bee's nest of our relationship. But for some reason, Wade had never thought to warn me that I'd be working with my ex again when he hired me on.

I coughed into my fist. Shifted in my seat. "You, ah... You want me to stay?"

Wade nodded.

"Permanently?"

"Yeah."

"You'll lose Monica." I'd heard the rumors. She'd threatened to resign if I didn't leave by the end of the summer like I was supposed to.

Wade shook his head. "Monica's not going anywhere."

I raised an eyebrow. "What makes you so sure?"

"She'll never leave you."

Wade's words socked me like a brick to the chest, not least because he well knew I was the one who had left her ten years ago. Well, I had cheated on her, and she'd kicked me out. Same difference. I gaped at the chief, waiting for my lungs to function again. He simply punched me again.

"She's in love with you. Always has been, always will be."

I laughed, finally finding the air for such a thing. "Is that why she invites me to go down-range any time she's practicing?" In her eyes, I made a more appropriate shooting target than the paper posters.

Wade looked me pointedly in the eye. "That's why she's never dated anyone else."

That stopped me. He was right. In the ten years we'd been apart, I'd gone out with whole carousels of women. But Monica? I'd never so much as heard that she'd gone for drinks with anyone. Taken in a movie. So far as I knew, she'd never even let someone jog with her on her morning runs. The vast, sheer loneliness of the past decade of her life slammed into me full force.

Wade drummed a finger on his desk. "Ryan, I knew the day I accepted your app for bike patrol that there were going to be fireworks. I also knew it would be nothing but a show. Because that woman has loved you and no one else since high school." He twisted his head and lifted his hands. "She was going to demand her pound of flesh, absolutely. But that's only because she could never dream of being with anyone else."

And I screwed it up, I added silently. I toyed with a rip at the knee of my jeans. "I just thought you'd forgotten we had a history." I shrugged. "I mean, either that or you enjoy watching gladiatorial combat."

Wade chuckled. "I didn't get to be chief of police by not knowing my officers." He nodded his chin at the pen and the sheet of paper. "Go on. Sign it."

I hesitated, then tapped the page, eying Wade dubiously. "You're telling me that if I sign this, Monica won't pack up her desk tomorrow?"

Wade steepled his fingers and shook his head. "Not tomorrow or any other day. Especially not with a case like this on her hands."

He had a good point. Monica would never abandon her hometown right when it needed her.

I drew a deep breath. So this was it, then. The moment when I decided once and for all whether I was staying or going. If I was the drifter or the dreamer. If I was ready to take up the challenge of relentless love. For Monica. For Bailey. And let's face it—for me. For my own dreams. For my own future. For possibilities I could barely glimpse, even if I couldn't quite believe in them yet.

I swallowed down one last gulp of terrified insecurity. Then I grabbed the pen and firmly scrawled my name.

Wade smiled. "Welcome home, Ryan."

SATURDAY, JULY 12, 2014

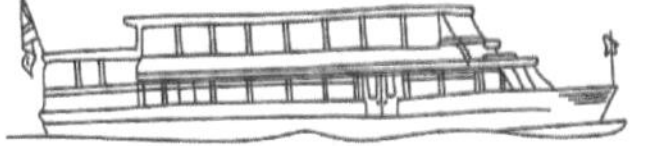

Chapter Five
TOMMY

Wade had me cushioned in so many pillows and blankets, I'd hardly need the airbags if they went off. He kept glancing between the road and me as if he were taking a newborn home from the hospital. Well then, why didn't he just put me in a car seat?

Worried as he was about *my* health, he looked positively terrible, like he hadn't slept in a week. He'd been at a funeral last night and another one the day before that. I wasn't sure he had any business picking me up from the hospital today. He'd lost an officer, Mike Schultz. Bill Gallagher, the chaplain, had died, too. Maybe that was why Wade was worried about me. There'd been a lot of death lately.

A lot of death. And somehow, I was still alive. I wasn't sure why I'd been the lucky one. If this was luck.

"You comfortable, Tommy?" Wade asked for the third time.

I sighed and turned to gaze at the grass and the trees flying past the passenger-side window. We'd barely gotten on the interstate ten minutes ago.

"I'm fine," I grumbled. "Quit treating me like I'm made of glass." I didn't tell him the half-healed bullet wound in my side ached with every vibration of the car.

Wade narrowed his eyes at me, upset that I'd taken offense to his concern. "You're a seventy-five-year-old man who took a bullet to the gut. I'm not even sure how you're alive right now."

Because I need to be, the answer flashed through my head. And maybe it was true. My son Jason was dead. I'd buried him alone, then waffled on whether or not to tell my mail jumper, Bailey, that she was my granddaughter—a fact I had only just learned. And then some renegade had pulled a gun on me. The reason was as blank to me as any memory of his face. I'd almost died before I had the chance to tell Bailey the truth. I'd dragged my carcass through drifting consciousness and crazy dreams for no other reason than that I *needed* to tell her. I'd never had the right to keep the truth from her.

I pictured vividly the day I'd finally woken up in the hospital after a thousand crazy dreams, fantasy and horror mixed with reality. And then the light was finally real, and there was Bailey sitting in a chair beside my bed. She smiled, as thrilled as the day she'd become a mail jumper. She smiled as if she were happy to see me. As if she were relieved. And then I finally—*finally*—told her the secret only I knew.

And I hadn't seen or heard from her since.

Not one word.

I still had no idea what she thought of having me as a grandfather. Maybe she recognized a flunky when she saw one. I hadn't done that great with her dad...

Wade broke into my thoughts. "Lindsey and Jon wanted to be at the house to greet you, but I told them we should wait. The kids can be pretty active, and I figured the drive might wear you out."

"Hm," was all I said. If I had my way, Wade would drop me off at my own house instead of holding me captive at his place for the foreseeable future. But the doctor had backed him one hundred percent, and not just so Nancy and Wade could assist with my recovery.

Whoever had put a bullet in me, he was still on the loose. My own home was the last place I should be. The fact I was going to Wade's house instead was known to only a select few, and I was under strict orders not to share that info.

I struggled to admit it was better this way.

"The grill-off is next Sunday," he rambled on. "You'll see everyone then. I have to defend my title against Jon. Lindsey had no business marrying a man who can grill a tenderloin as good as he can. The competition's stiff, but I still have the best steak for two years running. Oh, and the kids are at summer camp this week. Brace yourself; you'll be required to be amazed at a literal mountain of badges and crafts, all at the same time."

I sighed, anger simmering. Above all, this was why I didn't want to stay at Wade's. I didn't need to be constantly reminded that his life had turned out better than mine. That he still had a wife and children. That his son had a sparkling career in the Air Force. That his daughter was a beloved teacher and was happily married to a hard-working welder. That Wade had a pair of beautiful, vivacious grandchildren and a third on the way. That they were all happy and healthy.

My wife was dead. My son was a fugitive, and he had been murdered. His girlfriend, whom I thankfully never met, had been a drug addict who died of an overdose. And my granddaughter—the one I didn't even know I had until now—was stuck in foster care with a man who sent her to work with bruises on her face and arms.

I closed my eyes. What had she said when I told her? What did she think? Why couldn't I remember her reaction? I'd spent my remaining weeks in the hospital wracking my brain for the memory, but it was gone. My mind had chosen random information to delete. Like anything that could help Wade identify the person who had shot me.

Maybe Bailey hadn't answered at all. Or maybe I already had her reply: Three weeks of silence. Complete and total silence.

I leaned deeper into Wade's pillows and sighed, but shallowly so as not to trigger the pain in my side. The fact that Bailey had a grandfather didn't necessarily mean she needed one.

It didn't mean she even wanted one.

CHAPTER SIX
BAILEY

Standing at the counter at the front of the Mailboat, I prepped the mail for the day's run. I curled a newspaper around a stack of mail, then snapped a rubber band around the whole thing, securing it for the crazy thing that was Lake Geneva mail delivery—jumping from a moving boat to put the mail in the boxes on the piers.

That's when I saw that Brian, our stand-in captain, had misspelled the name written on the top corner of the newspaper. It was supposed to be *Olsen*, not *Olson*. Tommy never would have written a name wrong. I mean, he'd been delivering the Olsens' mail for, like, half a century.

But everything at the Mailboat was different now. We'd forget to stock the Doritos before heading out on the cruise, and of course there would be at least five tourists who really wanted a bag of Doritos. Or a cover would turn up dogeared on a magazine. Or the address would be smeared on an envelope because our hands were wet. We straight-up forgot to deliver to a house once. And my inner thighs were always sore, strained from jumping further than I was used to. Brian was afraid of getting too close to the wooden piers and knocking them down. I guess three weeks of driving the Mailboat didn't give you as much finesse as fifty.

Everything was a mess, barely bobbing along. And it was better this way. It would actually just be better if Tommy never came back. My brain still felt like it was exploding after what he'd told me.

That he was my grandpa.

I'd had a long time to think about it now. And crazy as it sounded, I didn't want him to be. I know, I know. His being my grandpa was *literally* the thing I used to daydream about. Thing is, dreams are great and all, but mostly because they aren't real. In my dreams, Tommy would love me, and we'd be super happy together, and we'd spend summer *and* winter together, and he would never, ever abandon me, like everyone else in my life literally. Foster care just sucks.

But now that he was really, truly, actually my grandpa... Something felt weird about it. Rotten. Like a peach that looks great on the outside but is all black and moldy on the inside, and the pit is just a fuzzy black ball of death. Something would happen to ruin everything. And I didn't want to be around when it did.

I looked up through the front window and my eyes crossed, blurring the bow of the boat and the beach and the Riviera Ballroom. For a moment, I kind of wasn't on the Mailboat anymore. I was crouched on the pavement in the middle of a blackened street and bullets were zinging over my head. And a perfect stranger—a man who had tipped me a hundred dollars at my other job as a waitress—was using his last breaths on this earth to fire back, trying to save my life.

I kind of wish he'd used his last breath to tell me he was my dad instead, and then I could have just died amazed and happy. He would have been everything I'd hoped and dreamed of. A superhero.

Instead, he died without telling me a thing. He left that job to Tommy, who also informed me that my dad had been a bank burglar, a cop killer, and a fugitive. Had he even known I existed before that night? Apparently not.

And with that information, I was now just as confused about my dad as I was about Tommy. How was I supposed to feel about either of them anymore? How come my life couldn't just turn out the way I wanted?

The sound of gulls screeching as they found something interesting on the beach helped bring me back. Uncrossing my eyes, I dropped my gaze to the rolled-up newspaper and the way Brian had misspelled Olsen. I could grab a pen. Scribble it out and write it over. Let the Olsens know somebody noticed and somebody cared.

Or I could pretend I never saw it. I could let it slip by like the dozens of little mistakes that had earmarked this entire summer—not to mention the category-five catastrophes.

I tossed the mail onto the shelf with the other deliveries. "Screw it," I mumbled. Nothing was the same anymore. Why not embrace the fact?

Tommy's being gone was a clean slate, in a way. A fresh start. I knew all about fresh starts. A new foster home full of new possibilities and an uncomfortable room full of strangers and a bed I got to share with a girl who didn't like me. Also, she wasn't about to let me use her hair dryer or her brushes, and I didn't have my own, so my hair was always a disaster.

But I'd finally figured it out. Change—this thing I'd always hated and hoped to banish from my life—was the only thing I'd actually been able to count on. Broken dreams were my oldest friend. Darkness was the foundation to my entire existence.

I could trust these things. At least they were honest with me. At least I knew they would never abandon me.

And where did a dad fit into all this? Or a grandpa, for that matter?

Nowhere.

Nowhere at all.

I snapped a rubber band around another newspaper and didn't even check to see if Brian had spelled *Alsbach* right.

CHAPTER SEVEN
ANGELICA

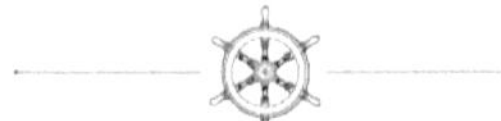

Head in her hand, elbow on a broad, round table, Angelica leaned over a newspaper, its spine protected by a wooden dowel. Light spilled across the yellowed page, pouring in from the picture windows that made up the southern wall of the Lake Geneva Public Library. The view of the lakefront was pristine, providing brief escapes when she thought her head and her heart could take no more. Shifting to rest her chin in her palm, she let her eyes rove for the hundredth time.

Down the shore to the left, a brick building with a pointed roof and stubby corner towers stood on the shore. A fleet of navy-and-white cruise boats sat at the piers below it, occasionally coming and going. She could hear their horns and whistles from anywhere downtown. Children played in the water at a little beach, their laughter drifting through the glass. The sound reminded her of her own boys back home, playing on much larger beaches, splashing through much larger waves, and she smiled. They were in good hands back home with her parents, but she missed them so much.

She'd been coming to the library every day for four days, hunting down articles from all the local and regional papers. Anything to do with the Markham Ring. Anything to do with the Geissler family of Chicago and Lake Geneva. Anything to do with Will. The articles all called him Fritz. But she had promised her hand and heart to Will Read, a man she was gradually accepting had never existed.

"Will" was from Grand Rapids, Michigan, or so he had told her. His father had been abusive and that was why Will had left for California, why he had never spoken of his past. Out of respect for this supposed pain, Angelica had rarely pushed him to talk about it, beyond the brief glimpses he offered, though reluctantly. And now she knew why.

They were all lies.

Fritz Geissler, on the other hand, had been born in Chicago in 1969. His parents owned real estate in the city and were considerably well-off. Well-off enough to own a mansion on the south shore of Geneva Lake. That's where Fritz had spent his summers as a child.

Angelica drank the information in like an alcoholic drank wine—knowing on some level that it was hurting her, but unable to stop. She would deal with the pain these articles provided by drinking in more of them. By crying alone in her hotel room at night. By staring at the ceiling, feeling hollowed out like a shell and asking a thousand more questions. Once she had drained the newspapers dry, and any other source she found, once she could soak in no more, perhaps her heart could finally heal.

Turning a page from 1986, she found a photo of Fritz. Thinking of him by his real name felt awkward, as if she were researching someone other than her husband. But it was easier that way. Fritz was the boy from Lake Geneva. Will was the man she had married. For now, the two weren't actually related.

In the photo, Fritz was seventeen years old, standing on a pier with two other boys, one of whom was holding a trophy. Behind them, a sailboat was tethered to the pier. The headline declared that they'd just taken first place in a regatta.

Angelica stroked the outline of the boy's face, fascinated by how similar he looked to her Will, by how much her older son Kaydon was destined to look like him in a few years. She studied the boat moored in the background. Fritz liked to sail? She and Will had lived so close to the ocean in Malibu. Why had they never bought a boat? Why had Will never felt drawn to the water, beyond taking his boys to swim on the weekends?

How could a man box up an entire past as if it had never existed? How could he not only lie to her, but also turn his back on everyone he had ever known—his friends, his family? How did a person do a thing like that? Why had he never told her *any* of this?

She studied the other two boys in the photograph. By now, she'd seen them so many times, she could recognize them by face: Jason Thomlin and Bobby Markham, her husband's childhood friends—and later, his companions in crime.

The articles covering the Markham Ring had dissected every aspect of their pasts. She now knew that these boys had grown up together. Gone to college together. Gotten jobs together at Bobby's father's bank. And together, they'd used what they knew of bank security to break into banks all over Chicago, Milwaukee, and Madison. The papers speculated they were responsible for the loss of millions of dollars. They also named Bobby the ringleader, thus the development of the name "Markham Ring," which was eventually applied after the ring was broken, right here in Lake Geneva. Their last job had been interrupted by the local police. There had been a shootout. Bobby had been killed. Jason and Fritz had fled.

That was the same summer that Will had moved to Los Angeles.

She couldn't begin to imagine how he had completely transformed his identity. How he had literally become another man.

Nor could she understand what would inspire Will—the Will she had known—to be involved in such a crazy thing. He and Bobby had both come from wealthy families while Jason was comfortably middle-class. All three boys were college-educated and had gotten good, lucrative jobs where they were promoted quickly. She knew little yet of Bobby and Jason and what may have motivated them. But Will?

She had shared a life with him. He was hard-working. He was kind. Above all, he was honest. To a fault. His most-valued ethic was to deal straight with every human being he met, whether a client, an employee, his sons, or his wife. He couldn't be five minutes late home from work without explaining to her the exact reason why. And she still remembered the soul-wrenching honesty with which he'd confessed about forgetting to take out the trash. She'd thought his nervous habit was habituated from fears of his father's abuse.

Now she wondered if Will was just overcompensating for the wreck of lies that trailed his wake. As if he feared that one day, Angelica would suddenly stop believing him.

Had their marriage in fact been that fragile? Had they always been a breath from failure? Had Will been the only one who'd even known it? Had he lived in fear of someday tipping his hand, giving up the game, and losing the picture-perfect life he'd gotten away with?

Tears welled in her eyes for the thousandth time since she'd gotten to Lake Geneva. She'd learned to keep a packet of tissues in her purse. But now she didn't care. She stretched her arms across the newspaper and flopped her head down. She let the tears run. Let them fall to the pages, where they would leave smeared ink and raised welts.

"Are you all right?"

The voice came in a whisper, appropriate for a library. She lifted her head and found an old man leaning over her, his sparse white hair combed over his scalp, one hand tucked into the pocket of a dusty-blue knitted cardigan. In his other hand, he held a heavy, hardback book. She glimpsed the title. *American Prometheus.* The cover showed the gaunt face of the man who had invented the atomic bomb.

She wiped the tears from her face. "Yes." She dug in her purse for the tissues, but before she could find them, the man handed her a crisp white handkerchief. The corner was embroidered in red thread with a coat of arms. Surprised by the offer, she took the handkerchief nonetheless and dabbed her eyes. "Thank you."

"Oh, don't mention it," the man said. "Is there anything I can do for you? Anything you need?"

She shook her head. "No, it's fine."

"You're new in town." He said it as an observation, not a question.

She furrowed her brow. "How do you know?" Who was this man? Was he stalking her? Fear rose in her throat. Why would someone want to stalk her?

"Oh, well—" He checked his watch. "It's late on a Saturday afternoon, and the tourists generally find more exciting distractions than the library and past editions of the *Lake Geneva Regional News.*" He motioned to the paper. "Did you just move here? Are you looking for work?"

"No." She folded the newspaper quickly and smoothed it down. She was beginning to wish he would go away. She didn't need friendly locals prying into her business—knowing who she was and why she was here.

But the man held up a hand to stay her. "I'm sorry. I really am being very clumsy. You see, I couldn't help but notice. You were looking at a photo of my son."

Angelica's ears perked. He... he knew one of the boys in the photo? Which one? Will? Adrenalin began to surge through her body. What was lies? What was truth? Could this be Will's father?

"Your son?" she asked, annoyance replaced with thrill and terror.

The man opened the page again and pointed to the young man in the middle, holding the sailing trophy. "That's him," he said. "Bobby. He was a very good sailor. All these boys were." He laughed. "Well, that's obvious. They won the regatta."

Not Will's father, but Bobby's. Angelica's heart pounded nonetheless, perhaps in relief. This was no time to finally meet her in-laws.

But it *was* the time to find answers, and Bobby's father might hold the ends of a thousand threads. This was the man who gave them all jobs at the First National Bank of Chicago. Until this moment, he had been a name in ink. Now here he was, living and breathing. She hadn't really had a mental image of what he should look like, but she had perhaps pictured someone with broad shoulders in a well-pressed suit, not a quiet old man in an oversized cardigan.

Her voice trembled as she asked, "Did you know the other boys, too?"

"Fritz and Jason?" The man looked through the window toward the lake and his eyes turned cloudy and distant, as if dwelling on long-ago memories. "They were like second sons to me. They practically grew up under my roof."

A lump rose in her throat, threatening to choke her. Tears watered her vision once again. Suddenly, the voices of the children on the beach became the long-ago voices of Bobby, Jason, and Fritz.

"Why?" the man asked. "Did you know them?"

She found herself nodding. "Fritz was my husband." Saying it with his real name felt strange. Like she was admitting to an affair.

But to her surprise, saying his name out loud—and tying herself to it—rolled a weight off her chest. No one in this town knew why she was here. She kept conversations short. Avoided eye contact. What would anyone think if the wife of one of their most infamous criminals showed up? Perhaps she shouldn't have told even Bobby's father.

But his face lit up. He dropped into the chair beside her, laying his book on the table, and took her hand in both of his. "My dear girl, I'm so delighted to meet you."

Angelica's uncertainty wavered into a smile. He welcomed her? Relief slowly trickled through her veins.

The old man's smile faded as he looked deeply into her eyes. "You never knew, did you? About... all this?" He waved his hand vaguely over the paper, the window, the lake, as if referring to a greater whole so vast, it defied brevity. "Lake Geneva. Your husband's life here. That's why you're here at the library, reading dusty old newspapers, isn't it?"

She nodded. Tears pricked her eyes. Embarrassed, she dipped her head and dried them with the handkerchief.

"Oh, my dear child." His crystal-blue eyes filled with sympathy.

His look, the tone of his voice—together they triggered that vulnerable place that continually threatened to erupt without warning. When she was cleaning the sheets and found a strand of Will's hair. When she was watching the sun set over the ocean, alone. When she was just trying to choose a bunch of tomatoes in the grocery store.

The newsprint in front of her blurred. Her throat constricted. Then the flood burst out, and she buried her sobs in the handkerchief.

The old man sat in silence, letting her cry. He didn't seem put off by her emotion. His quiet company was comforting, even. Her parents and her dear aunt and uncle, even her brothers and sisters and her cousins, would have been more boisterous, convinced the way to banish tears was to drown them in hugs and talk about what a bastard Will was and force quesadillas on her. But this man's wrinkled hand on hers was more than enough. She hadn't realized how badly she simply longed for a sympathetic face. Quiet company.

When she could breathe normally again, the old man spoke. "I can't begin to imagine what you've been through." He lifted his eyebrows and nodded. "You're very brave to come here and do this."

Angelica forced a smile and toyed with the edge of his handkerchief.

"I want you to know... Even after everything that happened, I never stopped thinking about Fritz and Jason. Wondering where they were. Hoping life was treating them kindly." He smiled at Angelica. "I see it did for Fritz."

She lowered her chin, offering a half-hearted grin in return for the compliment. Yes, perhaps life had treated Will kindly. But at her expense. Where she came from, *familia* was everything. You did not betray your family.

The man sat up abruptly. "Are you free tonight? I would be delighted if you joined me for dinner. You can ask me anything. I'm sure I knew Fritz as well as anyone around these parts. And I must admit, I'd be thrilled to get to know the woman he married."

She parted her lips, seeking an answer. Yes, she wanted this so much. But was she ready? If reading newspapers in the library had been like tippling drinks all day, going to dinner with Bobby's father would be like throwing back shots.

"We can go to Anthony's," he went on, then checked his watch. "The rush will have started, but they'll get me a table. They always do. The staff are superb. It'll all go on my tab, of course."

Angelica smiled, humored and enchanted by his eagerness. Would she be stupid to say no? What if she never saw this man again? The newspapers could only offer cold reality and harsh facts. Here was someone flesh-and-blood who had known her husband as a person.

She made up her mind. "Yes. Yes, I will have dinner with you. It would be my pleasure."

The man smiled. "Excellent." He offered his hand. "My name is Roland. Roland Markham."

She accepted the shake. "Angelica Read." She smiled. "I'm very glad to meet you."

CHAPTER EIGHT
ANGELICA

Angelica laughed over her Merlot. Their waiter had cleared the plates two hours ago and filled their third round of drinks, and Roland had not yet run out of tales with which to regale her. Bobby, Jason, and Fritz had been inseparable, sunup to sundown all summer long, and the return to school and the city at the end of the year was considered a great tragedy. Jason alone stayed at the lake, since his father worked for the cruise line, and the other boys counted him lucky.

Angelica set down her wine and leaned back in the luxurious, leather-trimmed captain's chair. She let her eyes rove over the paneled wood, the dim wall sconces, and time-darkened mirrors. Like Roland himself, Anthony's exuded the feeling of old money and the kind of grace, luxury, and etiquette one would have expected in the days of Audrey Hepburn and Cary Grant. What better place for time travel than a place like this, frozen in time?

Her eyes were finally out of tears—this time from laughing. She'd never thought she'd be able to laugh about her husband's past. But Roland had managed to keep the evening light, every memory a treasure. His love for these boys and this lake was palpable. Overwhelming.

Bobby had been the gregarious one, often leading the children on their wildest of adventures. Jason had been a capable first mate and Fritz their loyal crew. She could see it so clearly now, how the quiet but loyal boy Fritz had later developed into the calm, considerate man Will.

But what had happened in between? How had the metamorphosis happened? All night, Roland had carefully avoided any mention of the ring. His son's death. The night Fritz and Jason had run away.

Angelica breathed deeply. She had come here for hard truths. She couldn't put them off forever. The time was now.

"Roland," she said, meeting his clear blue eyes, letting him know she was taking the conversation down a notch. She dipped her chin. "It was your pier, wasn't it?"

He stared at her, jaw loose, hands fidgeting with his wine glass, eyes darting away almost imperceptibly, as if seeking to avoid this part of the story. They had spoken all night of youth and vigor. Of course, he didn't want to speak of her husband's murder, just three weeks ago.

Angelica shook her head. "You don't need to deny it. I already saw it in the papers. Will's body was left at the end of your pier."

Roland released his breath and nodded. "Yes. That's true."

"Were you the one who found him?"

He shook his head. "No. It was one of the mail jumpers." He had already explained how Jason's father, Tommy Thomlin, drove the locally-famous Lake Geneva Mailboat. "She fell in, and..." He turned up his hands. "There he was."

Angelica didn't blink. Didn't waiver. There was time for tears, and there was time for truth. This was a time for truth. She forced her breath to remain steady. "Why? Why would he be left at your pier?"

Roland laid his linen napkin on the table and stroked the hem. "Until we know who killed him, I doubt we'll know why he was left where he was."

"Are there no theories? Do *you* have no theories?"

"Well, there *was* a theory, but it now has some rather obvious holes in it. And now there's a new one." Roland grinned, acknowledging the amorphous nature of the case.

"What was the first theory?" She didn't care if it had been disproved. She needed to know everything. She didn't just need to know who her husband was and how he could have betrayed her. She needed to know who had killed him and why. Who had shattered the bubble of her perfect life. Who had slapped her awake and plunged her into cold water.

"The first theory is that Fritz was killed by my neighbor, Charles Hart."

Angelica frowned, searching her memory. "I've read his name. Where do I know his name?"

"He murdered Jason Thomlin, days after your husband was killed. Charles kidnapped Jason and then shot him. But Jason fought back. Charles died that night, as well."

Angelica nodded, the facts resurfacing from the many articles she had digested over the past four days.

She had placed more emphasis on learning anything related to her husband and hadn't yet addressed the murder of his accomplice Jason. "And why would your neighbor want Jason and Will dead?"

Perhaps her eyes were tricked by the dim lighting, but she thought Roland blushed. "Well… Charles and I… We knew each other for years. Decades. He, ah…" Roland hesitated. "Well, he was married, but they were never precisely…"

Angelica narrowed her eyes. "You had an affair with his wife?" She didn't mean to be unfeeling. She just wanted the truth.

Roland blinked, genuinely surprised. "Wh—? No."

"He had an affair with yours?"

Roland stirred in his seat, frowning. "No, no, not at all."

Angelica mentally flipped through the remaining possibilities. Landing on one, she smiled knowingly. "He was gay."

Roland slouched and looked down, curling up inside himself. "Yes." He drummed his thumbs on the base of his wine glass.

Angelica raised an eyebrow and grinned. "He liked you?"

"Yes."

"But you didn't like him?"

He sat up a little straighter, a flustered bird ruffling its feathers. "Well, no."

Angelica thought she believed him. His neighbor's sexual orientation genuinely seemed to trouble him. She shook her head. Roland was from such another era. "So, why would he kill Jason and Will?"

Roland shifted in his seat, continuing to appear uncomfortable. "Perhaps I railed against Jason and Fritz one too many times..."

She frowned. "What do you mean?" Despite what they had done, Roland claimed to be full of nothing but love toward the boys. After listening to dozens of his tales, she truly believed it.

He couldn't seem to meet her eyes. "At one time, I may have felt that they... er... had some hand in turning Bobby astray."

Her frown only deepened. "You said Bobby led the shenanigans."

"Burgling banks isn't exactly shenanigans."

"They named the ring after *him.* The Markham Ring." She wasn't sure why she was defending her husband. The man had lied to her. Maybe she was only clinging tenaciously to truth. There was no way, knowing what she knew, that Jason and Will had been the ring leaders.

Roland leaned back, raising his palms. "I only mean to say..." He drew in his breath and clenched his hands helplessly, then tilted his head and tried again. "You have children, Angelica."

She pictured her boys, Kaydon and Mason. If anyone accused them of a crime, wouldn't she defend them to her last breath? Hadn't she defended Will, until it was obvious she couldn't?

"I lost Bobby seventeen years ago and was as blindsided by the truth as you. I had dinner with them the night before they tried to rob the Grand Bank of Geneva. The next morning, the police told me they had shot him." He shrugged. "Anger needs an out, and Jason and Fritz had made themselves convenient scapegoats. They had fled. They would never even know how much blame I laid at their feet."

Angelica nodded. Perhaps she could understand. "And what do you believe now?"

He sighed and collapsed his hands on the table in front of him. "I believe it becomes harder to fight the truth. Which means I'm not sure how I..." He lifted his eyes to stare across the room, and to Angelica's surprise, they glistened. "I *thought* I raised him well." The hopelessness hung in every word.

She let it soak in and again thought of her boys. How would she feel if, after the countless hours of love and devotion she'd poured into them, they turned their backs on everything she had taught them? Would it be easier to blame someone else than to face the fear that you had failed your own child?

She didn't want Roland to spin off into despair. Questions like these—did they ever have answers? "Charles clearly believed Fritz and Jason were more culpable than Bobby."

Roland laughed softly and stared at his hands. "Yes, I suppose he must have."

"And that's why he avenged your son's death?"

Roland shrugged. "So the theory goes. Now that he's gone, we can never really know. But why else would he have killed Jason?" He lifted a finger. "Keep in mind—while he has been officially accused of Jason's murder, he's not been accused of Fritz's." He shrugged. "Granted, I'm sure the police have more information than gets into the press, but if he were guilty, wouldn't they have said? Rather, by all accounts, they appear to still be looking."

Angelica nodded. It seemed cosmically unfair that Jason's murder should be solved while her husband's was left a blank page. Was anyone even investigating? It had been so long since she'd heard anything from the police...

She pushed on. "You said this theory has holes in it. That there's a second theory. What is it?"

"That there was a fourth member of the Markham Ring."

Angelica frowned. "A fourth member?"

Roland nodded. "Charles wasn't alone the night he murdered Jason. There was a witness to the crime, and according to her, there was an accomplice. A man who took part in Jason's murder. A man who got away."

"They haven't caught him yet?"

"No. I'm not sure they so much as have a clue as to his identity."

"But he was working with Charles."

"Clearly."

"Then there were five members. Charles was in on it."

"At the very least, Charles had to have been aware of what he was doing and who he was dealing with."

"Why do they believe there were more members of the ring? Why didn't Charles maybe have a friend helping him with his revenge pact? A hired gun, even?"

"Because the violence didn't end with Charles' death. A week later, Jason's father was shot."

Angelica sat up straighter. "Tommy Thomlin, the boat captain?"

"He survived," Roland assured her. "But I haven't heard he was able to identify the villain."

Angelica shook her head. "But why go after Jason's father?"

Roland shrugged. "Because he thought Tommy knew something? You must admit, it's the best theory available so far."

Angelica narrowed her eyes. "And why would this fourth member leave my husband's body at the end of your pier?" A thought clicked into place and her eyes widened. "As a warning? Roland, you aren't in danger, are you?"

Roland looked away, rolling his head as if annoyed. "Oh, the police insist I am."

"And?"

"And it's been three weeks. Yet here I am."

It was a fair point. Still, Angelica wasn't sure if Roland was being brazen or just naive. After all, Tommy Thomlin had been shot.

Roland lifted his glass. "Angelica, this conversation has grown too morbid. You'll never be able to sleep tonight. Let's change the subject. Come, now. What else do you want to know about Lake Geneva?"

Reluctantly, Angelica picked up her glass and sipped her wine. She'd let Roland ramble about days gone by. She would smile. She would laugh. She would treasure every memory. But in the back of her mind, she would turn over everything Roland had told her about her husband's death. She couldn't tolerate the vacuum of answers. She wouldn't let Will's murder go unsolved.

Chapter Nine
SKULL

In a corner booth, a man dined alone. He'd combed the usual care-free spikes out of his hair, styling it into something more suave and sophisticated. The full tattoo sleeves down his arms were concealed by the white button-down shirt. Some jobs required him to put his ink under wraps. Images such as the cracked skull with the rose adorning its forehead didn't exactly fit in at Anthony's.

He was known for that tattoo. His buddies called him Skull.

The Man paid good money for him to blend in—and good enough money for Skull to order a forty-dollar steak. The job was beyond easy—for now. All he was supposed to do was sit and watch for a woman named Angelica Read. He would recognize her as a petite Hispanic woman with long black hair, fashionable style sense, and a light Mexican accent.

And just like The Man had said, there she was, sitting with none other than Roland Markham, wining and dining the night away. The bug he had dropped in her purse in passing fed every word of their conversation into an invisible piece in his left ear. When she left, it would track her location.

Regardless, he was to never let her out of his sight.

It was worth getting in a good meal now. Running surveillance without backup was a demanding job. But Skull was used to it. Discreet information was his business. And the only other person in on the contract, Bud Weber, was both an idiot and out of The Man's graces. That's what you got for insubordination. In a game like this, you didn't run around following personal vendettas, shooting targets that weren't included in The Plan. Bud had taken offense to Jason's father, Tommy Thomlin, for being a decent human being. The boat captain had reported that Weber beat his foster child, and that raised Weber's ire. Well, Bud shouldn't have touched the girl in the first place. Getting arrested on an unrelated charge could ruin everything. And The Man would be none too pleased.

At one time, Skull wondered why The Man kept Weber around at all, but eventually the answers came clear. Bud was a good gun. He could keep a crime scene pristine. He had a sixth sense that kept him both alive and beyond the reach of the law. Once you understood how many murders Bud had committed—and gotten away with—you understood why he had been on the contract.

But most importantly, The Man thrived on people he could manipulate. And Bud was nothing if not manipulable, just as Charles Hart had been. When working with The Man, you couldn't show emotion. Not without exposing yourself to him. He would use you every bit as much as he did his victims. The Man always got what he wanted.

There was only one other person on the team, a brilliant teenage boy named Baron Hackett. He was currently serving time, however—a move that had been carefully planned and executed. The boy would be out soon; his impeccable behavior behind bars was also carefully planned. There was an accomplice Skull would have trusted. But that didn't help Skull tonight. He'd have to do everything solo. So long as Angelica didn't become suspicious of him, it shouldn't be a problem.

And the subjects of his inquiries never became suspicious.

Roland Markham and Angelica Read finally rose from their table. Skull gave them a few minutes, then casually followed. He stopped outside the door to light a cigarette, noting that Roland and Angelica were still talking next to their cars. Their conversation buzzed in his ear, but it was meaningless. He would smoke and enjoy the evening, and if they talked long, he would pull out his phone and pretend to make a call.

But the two hugged goodnight and got into their own vehicles.

Skull dropped his cigarette and ground it under his toe. He made his way casually to his car. It was late, and in all likelihood, Angelica would go straight to her hotel. If she did, he'd learn what room she was in, then try to get one nearby. In the morning, he would be up early, ready to follow her wherever she went.

The Man couldn't manipulate his victims without knowing every last detail about them. Luckily, being nosy was Skull's specialty.

MONDAY, JULY 14, 2014

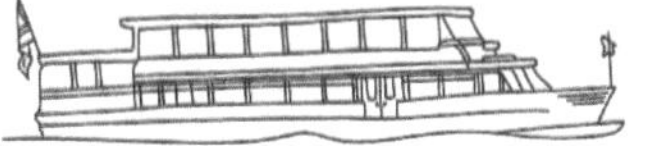

Chapter Ten
MONICA

My pen flew across my legal pad, disjointed thoughts racing out of my mind. I wrote names. I wrote dates. I wrote theoretic connections between people. I asked questions. I suggested leads to follow up on. I ground my forehead into the hand supporting it, wracking my brain for answers.

Who was The Man Upstairs?

The second-floor meeting room at the LGPD buzzed with half-sleepy, nine-in-the-morning conversation. The air smelled of fresh-brewed coffee, donuts, various brands of shampoo and aftershave, paper and ink, and the electricity from the projector. People were dressed in suits and ties, or in slacks and polo shirts like me. They all carried a service weapon on their hip. I could identify the badges of half a dozen departments—Walworth County Sheriff's Office, as a matter of course; a humbling array of nearby city and county principalities which had volunteered their personnel and resources; and one agent each from the Wisconsin Department of Criminal Investigations, the FBI, and the ATF.

After three homicides, a shooting, and a bombing—all in the course of two weeks—the workload was simply more than Lehman, Neumiller, and I could handle on our own. So we'd formed an investigative task force and invited the entire cavalry. For the most part, we weren't even sure yet what we were investigating. Why had the surviving members of the Markham Ring been murdered? Why were near family apparently being targeted, as well? Jason's father, Tommy Thomlin, had been shot, while Bobby's father, Roland Markham had been warned.

And then a boy named Jimmy Beacon had detonated a bomb in the middle of downtown on the Fourth of July. The incident wouldn't have been related at all, except for that anonymous phone call I'd gotten afterwards. Someone calling himself The Man Upstairs. Someone claiming to be behind it all, the bombing included. Someone saying he knew the town's deepest secrets.

Including mine.

I frowned at my tangled swamp of notes. Finding The Man himself wasn't *supposed* to be my part of the investigation. I was assigned to follow up on Fritz Geissler, the first murder victim.

I snorted. Like hell I was going to leave it alone. I wasn't going to let someone get under my skin like that.

My partner, Stan Lehman, stepped behind the desk at the front of the room. "Good morning, good morning," he said, tapping a stack of papers together loudly.

Members of the task force grabbed last-minute muffins and cups of coffee, then migrated toward their seats. Metal chair legs clanged against tables. People flowed around me like a herd of cows, while I was a rock in the middle, already at my desk. I frowned down at my black leather portfolio and the yellow legal pad inside. The page looked like the ravings of a madwoman. Maybe they were.

Mark Neumiller, my other partner in the LGPD Detective Bureau, pulled up a chair beside me and set down a notebook and a paper cup full of water from the cooler. I flipped the cover of my portfolio to conceal what I'd been working on and turned my attention to the front of the room.

Leadership of the task force had fallen to Lehman, as Detective Sergeant of the department where the case had originated. To colleagues who only knew us marginally, it had apparently come as a surprise that Lehman held rank over me. Based on their expressions, it was even more stunning that I could sit amongst the rank and file and take orders from someone else. Even in passing, I tended to form a reputation as a strong woman. (Read that "bitch.") But I didn't like people well enough to lead them. Lehman could have that job. Besides, in our bureau, we knew who really wore the pants.

Lehman picked up a marker from the whiteboard tray and glanced over his notes, scrawled in a first-grader's handwriting. While we all had access to a database containing every detail of the case, Lehman still insisted on his color-coded note system. No one else bothered to reference it, especially as new notes in unestablished colors were squeezed in at odd angles. So far as I could tell, Lehman just wanted to play with markers while looking important.

"Okay," he said, popping the marker cap on and off. "Neumiller, Thompson, how are we doing on Amelia Beacon's case?"

Mark Neumiller had partnered up with Detective Al Thompson from Racine PD to investigate that angle. Before detonating his bomb, Jimmy Beacon had accused his boss, Bud Weber, of murdering his little sister years ago when his family lived in Racine. Weber had been interrogated twenty ways to Sunday that night. He'd admitted to living in the same city at that time, but maintained his innocence, even refusing a lawyer. But it didn't help his case that he'd been recently under investigation for allegedly abusing his foster child, Bailey Johnson. We were merely looking for the chink in the story that would blow it all apart.

Neumiller sipped his water and glanced over his notes. "We've been to the apartment complex where Weber lived. It's literally ten minutes from the playground where Amelia was kidnapped."

"Weber declined a voluntary DNA swab?"

"That's right."

"Can we court order him yet?"

Neumiller shook his head. "I've hashed that over with the DA. He doesn't think the judge will go for it without more evidence."

I tapped my foot impatiently. Suspicions and proof were two different things, and the gray zone in between was where scum like Bud Weber thrived and did their dirty work.

"We're talking to the landlord and the neighbors," Neumiller went on, "trying to dig up Bud's friends and figure out if we can confirm a location for Weber that day. His reference swore Bud was at work. Bud's employer said he might be able to produce records of who was on shift that day and when. He's just got some digging to do."

"That's a good lead. Do we know where Jimmy got the pink bow?"

Witnesses on the day of the bombing claimed Jimmy had confronted Bud with a pink bow, which he claimed his sister had been wearing the day she disappeared. Later, we found remnants of pink polyester satin in the blast zone.

Neumiller shook his head again. "No one ever saw him with it until he displayed it to Weber."

"Who, of course, never saw it in his life..." Lehman's sarcastic comment trailed off as he added new notes to his marker board. "Anything else?"

"Nope. We'll keep you posted."

Footwork. Rock-turning. Haystack-poking. Paper pushing. Those words described the nature of the entire investigation. It wasn't that we had a lack of leads; it was that we had too many, and yet not enough. Every tiny fact could prove pointless, or it could be the clue we so desperately needed to unravel the entire case.

There was a subdued vibration in the air that was palpable. Our focus was controlled, intense. I'd once seen a bloodhound track a scent for thirty miles on winding county highways, never giving up, never forgetting what he was after, never being distracted by irrelevant scents. That was us. At the end of the trail, there *would* be arrests, at least two of them—Bud Weber and The Man Upstairs.

Lehman twiddled his marker. "All right. Let's talk about God. I mean, The Man Upstairs."

People snickered. But I leaned on my hand to shield my face from the room. I didn't need my cheeks to flush. Every time The Man came up in discussion, I felt exposed. Vulnerable. Afraid of what my unknown nemesis knew. Equally afraid of what my colleagues might find out. The men and women of the Lake Geneva Police were something like family to me. But to this day, not one of them knew about my baby or my abortion. It was a side of me I'd never shown. A side I was still hopeful never to reveal. No one belonged in that sanctuary of pain and confusion but me.

So how had The Man Upstairs gotten in? I had questions. And I had ideas on how to find the answer.

Lehman was still talking. "Hayworth, you were cleaning up that audio file. Did you get anything?"

Detective Adam Hayworth from Walworth County tapped the touchpad on his laptop. "I don't know what he did to conceal his voice. I haven't been able to strip it out yet." He frowned at his screen. "But I managed to pick out some noises in the background. Listen to this."

He clicked his mouse again. Sound came from a USB speaker plugged into his laptop.

"I even know how to exploit your children," the rasping voice said—the one I couldn't get out of my dreams at night. "*Yes, Monica. YOUR children.*"

Hayworth had clearly rebalanced the sound to emphasize the background. But all I heard was the voice. Taunting me. Challenging me. Whispering to me. *I know you were going to have a child. And I know you ended the pregnancy without even telling your husband. And I know how badly you want to protect that information...*

The first time Lehman had played the recording for the task force, half the room had turned to look at me. They knew I didn't have kids.

"There's, ah... There's nothing personal to that, right?" Lehman had asked uncomfortably.

"No," I snapped back. And since that was my usual tone of voice, no one had questioned me further.

Maybe even *I* was paranoid. Children? There had only been one pregnancy, one fetus. Had The Man really been suggesting he had information on me personally? If so, it was bad information.

Or had he used the plural on purpose? To keep me guessing? Doubting? Underestimating my opponent? Was he inviting me to assume he was stupid? He claimed to know the deepest secrets of the entire town. Did he *want* me to think he didn't?

I shot breath through my nose. This was why I couldn't sleep at night. Why the bullet journal in my ledger was more like the chalk on the walls drawn by an inmate at an asylum for the insane.

As Hayworth played the audio again now, I bit my lip and forced myself to concentrate. I had to catch this guy. I had to catch him...

A rhythmic ticking sounded quietly in the background noises that Hayworth had isolated.

"That's a clock," Lehman observed.

"So he made the call indoors in a room with a clock," Neumiller concluded. Pens scribbled around the room and keyboards clicked.

"An old clock," Hayworth added. "I haven't fully isolated this sound yet, but you can just hear the gears turning, and then—there. That was the clock striking the quarter hour."

"The Man Upstairs hangs out with Father Time," quipped a young detective from Janesville. The room laughed.

"So, is this a grandfather clock? A wall clock? A mantle clock?" asked Lehman.

Hayworth shook his head. "Sounds old. Mechanical, obviously. I have an appointment with a clockmaker this afternoon. I'll run it past him and see what he knows."

It would have been far more helpful to pick out a Harley Davidson idling in the driveway, or better yet, a recorded voice for the blind saying that it was safe to cross name-of-street now. Something that could help us identify the location from *outside*. With the audio of the clock, all we could do was verify we had the right place *after* we'd found it and physically been *inside*. Good stuff if this all came to trial—but the slow boat to China while we were still trying to find the place.

But if the clockmaker was good—and if clocks could, in fact, be identified merely by their sound—we could turn more stones. If it was a rare antique, we could possibly create a list of those clocks still in existence. From there, it would be a matter of tracking down every single one until we found an owner and a location that might fit the case.

This was the nature of the evidence we had to work with. It was going to be a long, long road. Normally, this was the kind of tedious, OCD work I thrived on.

But it was hard to focus on the details when I heard The Man's voice screaming in the back of my head day and night. I wanted him behind bars *now*.

Lehman's marker squeaked across the board, leaving a trail of orange. "Were you able to pick out anything else? Traffic? Other voices?"

Hayworth shook his head. "Just the clock."

Lehman nodded. "All right. Well. Let us know if you make any more progress on the disguised voice."

"Will do."

Lehman capped his orange marker. "Okay. What else? Oh, right. Brandt. You turned up something on the abuse case. Bailey Johnson. Why don't you fill us in?"

People shifted in their seats to face Ryan. He sat near the door, dressed in a patrolman's uniform—navy blue, almost dark enough to be black. The lack of reflective striping, royal blue yoke, and cargo shorts meant he wasn't on bike patrol today. Still, this was the first I'd ever heard of a seasonal bike patrol officer getting a seat in an investigative task force. But in the earliest days of the case, Lehman, Neumiller, and I had been strapped with the murder investigations. So Ryan had ended up spearheading the investigation into Bud Weber, Jimmy's boss and Bailey's foster dad. Ryan had a rapport with Bailey, plus plenty of past experience as a detective, and that had landed him the project. Even after the case had grown, the task force had seen no reason not to let him continue his investigation on Weber. The chief had promised to allow for room in his schedule.

Before Ryan could speak, Lehman added, "Oh, and congrats on the promotion."

Neumiller leaned back in his chair to address the room. "He's permanent now," he announced.

The room applauded politely and a few hands thumped Ryan on the back. He grinned appreciatively.

So it had happened, then. Ryan was year-round. Dammit. I gripped my pen so tightly, I felt plastic crackle. I'd sworn I'd leave if he stayed. Would I? With a case like this on my hands? With a madman toying with the intimate details of my life?

Ryan stood, staring at a printout in his hand. "Okay. I don't have a lot. I mean—" he lifted the paper. "I found this half an hour before the meeting started."

Maybe Wade "making room" in Ryan's schedule was a little too generous an expression.

Ryan scratched his head, scanning the writing. "Anyway, Bud Weber is listed as a witness in regard to a murder that took place in downtown Chicago on October 29, 1994."

"Who was the victim?" asked Lehman.

"Zayne Mars," Ryan read. "Male, twenty-one years of age. He was Bud's roommate."

Lehman paused, purple marker hovering. "And you say Bud was a witness? Not a suspect?"

Ryan scanned the report again. "Yeah." He shrugged. "Go figure."

A few detectives smothered laughter. There was no love lost around here on Bud Weber.

"Anything else?" Lehman asked.

"No, just that." Ryan shrugged as he sat down. "I'm heading to his bar after the meeting to see what I can learn."

"Okay. Interesting lead. Keep us posted." Lehman twiddled the marker. "Who's next? Tolsky, you were piecing together a timeline for Jason Thomlin. What've you got?"

I sat through another hour of reports, jotting the occasional note, bouncing my foot, itching to get out of this meeting room and back on the street. Lehman and I planned to speak with the staff at the Abbey Resort in Fontana. We now had all of Fritz Geissler's phone and Internet data as well as his bank records. With that, we'd pieced together a timeline of exactly where he'd been and when, from the day he flew out of Los Angeles to the day he was murdered in Lake Geneva. He'd spent his last night on earth at the Abbey Resort. We wanted to talk with the staff to see what they knew and if he met anyone while he was there.

Anyone like The Man Upstairs.

The sooner we caught the bastard behind all this, the sooner I could sit him in a chair and demand an answer out of him.

How did you know?

"All right," Lehman said. "Good work, everybody. You all have your assignments. We meet again tomorrow, same time, same place. Good luck."

Chairs bumped over carpeted floor. Conversations resumed. Notes were compared in more detail. Empty coffee cups were thrown into the trash can by the door, Styrofoam gliding down the filmy trash can liner.

I closed my portfolio and made for the escape, avoiding eye contact with anyone in the room. I didn't need questions. I'd recorded my conversation with The Man Upstairs and I'd shared it with the task force. I'd been a very good girl, sharing it at all. I didn't need to be taken off the case because I was suddenly too close to it. Worse, I didn't need prying eyes and ears inside my personal business. I didn't need a whole crowd inside my confused and ravished heart. It had already been invaded. It had already been ransacked. I didn't...

I bit my lips so I wouldn't cry and sucked in air through my nose. I didn't need to fall apart in front of all my colleagues. Because fall apart was all I knew how to do when it came to the questions that clandestinely defined my life—the questions of what exactly I'd done ten years ago and why and if I should have waited until I was less furious with Ryan and if I should have told him.

Ryan. Against my bidding, my eyes flickered to him as I passed. He was looking at me, too. Of course he would be. I moved faster so he couldn't stop me. No, I didn't want to go out for drinks. No, I didn't want to talk about the case or his promotion or anything else on the face of the earth.

I just wanted to disappear. I wanted to feel safe again, all my secrets hidden where only I could find them, hold them, comfort them.

No one was supposed to be allowed in there.

Chapter Eleven
RYAN

Pretending I was still invested in my conversation with Al Thompson from Racine, I watched out of the corner of my eye as Monica bolted from the room. She was avoiding me—nothing strange. But I wanted to know how she felt about me staying on. Was she upset? Was she going to resign? Unfortunately, I couldn't interpret her current level of snark any different from the usual.

I wished Lehman hadn't said anything. I'd wanted to tell her myself. Not necessarily to get her response; just to show her I was being up-front. Now I'd lost that chance. And with her bolting through the door, I'd lost the chance to apologize afterwards.

Regardless of her reaction, I was worried about her. I'd been watching her over the past week of these task force meetings, and I was beginning to see a pattern. Every time we got around to The Man Upstairs, she looked down. Got very busy with her notes. Looked uncomfortable. Why?

Granted, I'd be pretty pissed, too, if the unknown mastermind behind a string of murders had my cell number. I wanted to ask her if she'd changed it but didn't know how to do that without coming off creepy—you know, her ex making sure he was up-to-date on her phone number.

But knowing her, she wouldn't change it. She would tempt The Man Upstairs to bite again. She wanted to hear from him. She wanted to catch him. There was no criminal she feared to face.

But was she taking other precautions? Was her home secured? Did she park in well-lit areas? Did she keep her gun within reach at all times?

I could keep myself from following her around the room like a love-sick puppy. But keeping myself from worrying about her was a lost cause.

Chapter Twelve
MONICA

From the meeting room, I breezed toward the stairwell, portfolio pressed to my chest, and unlocked the door with the key card in my hip pocket.

Lehman dashed out of the meeting room on my heels, fumbling a folder, his phone, and a set of car keys. He caught the door just before I let it swing shut on him. "Hey, all good?"

"Yeah, fine," I lied. "Ready for The Abbey?" I headed down the stairs, my shoes pounding every step as if to punish them.

"Yes, ma'am." I heard his fingers paging through the folder and pictured the sheets and colored sticky notes protruding in every direction. "Knowing how you're allergic to moss on your rear, I thought to grab everything I needed ahead of the meeting."

"Finally, some efficiency around here!" I spat back. The vitriol, of course, was not intended for him. But he was a convenient target.

I threw myself against the door at the bottom of the stairs and spilled out into the light of the July day.

Two men and one woman dressed in business casual were waiting, one with a TV camera on his shoulder, the others with digital cameras around their necks and notepads in their hands. Their swag was from three different media outlets. "Detective, a word!" They crowded toward me, starved dogs to an already-picked carcass.

"Jesus Christ," I muttered.

I felt Lehman behind me and heard him whisper in my ear. "Meet you at the car."

I took his offer of escape and pushed through the reporters, stiffening my back to warn them against messing with me.

"I'll take your questions," Lehman said, drawing their attention. Communicating with the media was his job anyway. But still, I owed him a solid for getting them off my back. While the media storm had died down in the week since the bombing, some hangers-on stuck like leeches, positive we were concealing information the public desperately needed to know. Turns out, setting off a bomb in a popular tourist town is a juicy story.

Over my shoulder, I heard them launch questions in rapid fire.

"Is there any connection between the bombing and the recent spate of murders?"

"What's the condition of the five individuals injured during the explosion?"

"Is there any evidence yet that Bud Weber murdered the bomber's sister?"

I huffed a sigh—then nearly walked head-first into a large woman stepping out from a park bench under a tree.

"Detective Steele," she cried in a ragged voice tarred by cigarettes, "I've been calling you all week."

I know, I almost replied, but bit my tongue.

Delilah Beacon's greasy hair hung in gray tatters around the shoulders of her drooping tee shirt. Her eyes were red with tears, and she reached for me with a crumpled tissue in her palm.

"Detective Steele, I buried my son yesterday," she went on. "I buried my Jimmy. I couldn't even have an open casket. They wouldn't even let me see my baby."

She wouldn't have deserved one anyway. When we asked her who her son spent time with, hoping to find a connection to The Man Upstairs, she couldn't give us a single name. She literally didn't know who her son's friends were. Turned out, he barely had friends at all. And she hadn't known that, either.

"Please, detective, why didn't you stop him? He was a good boy, really." Even as she spoke, her eyes flickered to the media and their cameras, a hungry look in her expression.

I bit back my rage. *You never cared a wit about your son, you attention whore.* Her son had been a child genius—isolated by his brilliance. But Delilah Beacon was incapable of being a mother long enough to notice. When we'd come to search her house, she'd told us we were welcome to take him. She couldn't wait for him to be off her hands. How did such a woman deserve the name of mother?

The familiar pain stabbed through my belly again. The long years of waiting. Of wanting. The soul-sucking thief—infertility. The child that was finally, beautifully mine, but whom I turned against on the same day I learned of her, for the sole sin of being her father's daughter.

I never would have hesitated to support another woman pursuing an abortion after her husband cheated on her. But never in a million years had I seen *me* making that choice. It was for other women with other problems. Not me. My marriage was beautiful. My life was promising. My family was finally going to be complete... And then I was slapped in the face with reality. Suddenly, I *was* "other women."

A woman who was hurt in the deepest way possible by the love of her life.

A woman who grabbed her choice feverishly and wielded it like a club.

But I was the one who took the blows.

Self-loathing pointed a gnarled finger in my face. *You're no better than Delilah Beacon.* The pain shot up my core into my face, twisting my mouth and brow.

One of the reporters glanced our way. Delilah didn't miss it. She grabbed my shirt and fell to her knees, like a saint from a Renaissance painting. Like she had a halo over her head and rivers of light pouring around her.

The feel of her body glued to mine shot terror up my back. What was wrong with me? How had I allowed her into my personal space? Every training video I'd ever watched of cops being grappled and killed flashed through my mind. I put one hand to my gun to head off the chance of her disarming me and tried to break away.

She wouldn't let go. My shirt tugged on my shoulders. "He didn't mean to," she wailed. "He was my son." I could almost feel her throwing an inviting wink to the reporters.

"Back off!" I said in a commanding tone, still trying to step away. I didn't dare touch her. The last thing I needed was a picture of me in the papers attacking the bomber's mother.

A manila envelope appeared out of nowhere, bristling with a rainbow of sticky notes. It slipped between me and Delilah Beacon.

"Hey, hey, hey," said Lehman. He firmly removed her hands from my shirt. "This is called assaulting an officer of the law. You can't do that."

Mrs. Beacon looked up at him with tearful eyes, hands clasped in prayerful innocence. "Are you going to arrest me, officer?"

Why did I think she would be delighted? Lehman clearly saw it, too, and wasn't about to give her the satisfaction.

"You harass Detective Steele one more time, and you will give me no other option. Now go about your business." He put a hand on my back and steered me toward the car. "Let's go."

I didn't waste time arguing. But I couldn't help looking over my shoulder. Mrs. Beacon was making a show of struggling weakly to her feet, wiping tears from her eyes. Meanwhile, the reporters were closing in on her, slow but eager, no one wishing to break propriety, no one wanting to be the last to a juicy source. In the end, they all arrived at the same time.

"Are you James Beacon's mother?" one of them asked.

She blinked tearfully, looking them up and down as if she hadn't noticed them until now. "I am," she said, twisting her tissue in her fingers.

"May we ask you some questions?"

"You have to understand, I'm still grieving." She dabbed her eyes.

The man with the video camera pushed to the front. "My channel will pay for an exclusive interview."

The other man shot him a dirty look. The woman reporter simply dug in her pocket. "My paper will pay, too! We'll give you a thousand dollars!"

And with that, the bidding war began. Delilah Beacon smiled. I knew in my gut she would take the highest bidder—then call the others later, claiming the deal had fallen through. She would collect her fee from them all and make bank off her son's story. And behind the reporters' backs, she would boast that Jimmy's death was the best thing that had ever happened to her.

"My God," I swore.

Lehman took my arm and forced my attention forward. "Just walk away," he said. "There's nothing you can do."

I clenched my fists and pushed a guttural scream through my teeth. Lehman was right, but that wasn't going to stop me from venting. Women like her didn't deserve to be mothers.

But neither did I. Given a second chance at motherhood? I would walk away. I had proved I wasn't deserving. Children didn't exist to be used by adults.

Lehman moved to the driver's side of our SUV, pulling keys out of his pocket. I crossed to the passenger side, scanning my surroundings as I reached for the door handle. I'd let my guard down, allowing myself to be surprised twice in a row, first by the press, then by Mrs. Beacon. I wasn't going to give Lehman the opportunity to rub my nose in that fact. Neither was I going to let it happen again.

That's when my gaze landed on a woman standing on the sidewalk across the street. Her eyes were hidden behind large sunglasses, but her whole face was centered on mine. Her skin was brown, her hair long and black. She wore a breezy white top and pale pink shorts. Her wide straw hat matched her straw handbag, which matched her beaded sandals.

I know you, my brain said. I squinted. *Where do I know you?* I met hundreds of people in my line of business, and it was vital I remember them all. Any one of them could prove an ally or an enemy at the drop of a pin. It disturbed me when I couldn't remember if I'd returned a person's stolen purse or called them because their kid was purse-snatching.

Moments passed, and she didn't look away. Her mouth remained a concrete line. Definitely an enemy, then. That made it all the more imperative I remember her name. And soon.

The engine turned. Lehman rolled down the window beside me. "Monica? You coming?"

I glanced at him. Hot air rolled through the window, hurried along by the AC Lehman had cranked up. "Yeah, coming."

I looked again, but the woman was walking down the street as if nothing had happened. I climbed into the passenger seat. I had the drive between here and The Abbey to try to remember who she was.

CHAPTER THIRTEEN
ANGELICA

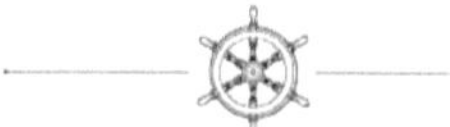

Angelica Read clutched the strap of her straw handbag and pounded down the sidewalk. That woman... So much for avoiding Monica Steele. At least she didn't seem to recognize her. Angelica would never forget her.

Only three weeks ago, Detective Steele had shown up in Malibu, on her doorstep, and sat in her living room. In one breath, she'd offered her condolences for Will's passing. In the next, she'd demanded information on his criminal past—a past Angelica knew nothing about. Detective Steele had ripped off the blindfold and the Band-Aid, both at once, leaving Angelica reeling. Who did a thing like that? Angelica had just lost her husband. Her sons had lost their father. The woman was cold. Heartless.

Angelica bit her lip and fought back angry tears. No, she would not let this ruin her day. She would go on. She would keep searching for truth.

But if there was anyone she wished to avoid in this town, it was Monica Steele.

Chapter Fourteen
SKULL

Leaning against a tree across the street from the police station, Skull dragged on his cigarette and exhaled a cloud of smoke. Today, he was dressed as a tourist. Tee shirt. Shorts. Baseball hat. Sunglasses. The rose skull could get some daylight this time. He'd sun-screened carefully to save the ink.

The vignette across the street was very interesting. Monica Steele and Angelica Read had crossed paths—and the tension was so thick, he could have sketched an idea for a new tattoo on it.

The Man would want to hear about this.

Of course, there was no love lost between Steele and Jimmy Beacon's mother, either. Skull would include that in the report, as well. Maybe The Man would bite; maybe he'd let that bait go without so much as a nibble. He was a wise old trout, hard to predict. Maybe he was tired of the Beacon family. Maybe he felt he'd already wrung every last drop of blood he could from them.

But Angelica Read? She was new. She was exciting. Or perhaps, despite appearances, the smooth socialite Angelica was the woman more capable of destruction. After all, what The Man wanted was blood, plain and simple.

The Beacon woman was a glass of nitroglycerin, ready to explode at the trembling of a hand. So what was Read? Maybe a slow, steady boil. Maybe a jet of steam The Man could concentrate and direct wherever he wanted.

Maybe she was just more of a challenge. Yes. The Man would be drawn to a challenge.

Skull pulled his phone out of his pocket. He'd report what he saw to The Man and let him choose his own victim.

CHAPTER FIFTEEN
RYAN

The neon OPEN sign was dark, but when I tugged on the front door of the Geneva Bar and Grill, it swung open. I let myself in.

"Hello! Weber?" My voice echoed off the concrete of the empty lobby. The red and green lanterns on either side of the counter sat cold and lifeless. I peeked through the wide doorway into the dining room. Chairs sat on top of tables, their legs sticking in the air. I couldn't help thinking of last week, when this place was packed during a Fourth-of-July rush. Thank God Jimmy's bomb hadn't gone off here, like he'd originally planned.

"Oh, hey!"

I turned at the voice. A large, round face appeared in the pickup window behind the front counter. Bud

Weber held a metal spatula in one hand. The sounds of grilling wafted from the kitchen.

"How's it goin', Ryan?" he asked in his thick, Chicago accent.

It disgusted me that we were on a first-name basis. Given a dark alley and a lack of witnesses, there was no telling what we'd actually do to each other. "You got a minute?" I asked. "Just wanted to go over some details again."

"Hell, yeah, I got a minute. Sure. Anything."

Weber's overly helpful manner disgusted me more than the grease on his spatula. I knew he was abusing Bailey. It wasn't a stretch for me to believe that he'd kidnapped, raped, and murdered Jimmy Beacon's sister, Amelia. We just couldn't prove any of it yet—beyond the fact that at the time of Amelia's disappearance from Racine, Weber had lived only ten minutes from her home. Yet all records pointed to his having a glittering past—all except the one I'd found this morning.

"Hey, you want somethun to eat?" Weber went on, his head still craned through the window. "It's on the house. Burgers? Soup? I've got beef Stroganoff ready in about ten minutes."

I held up a hand. "I'm good, thanks."

Weber stepped away from the window long enough to slot the spatula into a holder on his grill and wipe his hands on the dirty apron that covered his bulging middle. "How about a drink, then? Soda? Lemonade? Coffee? You want a beer? I'll never tell."

"No, thanks," I insisted again. "This shouldn't take long."

Weber wiped his hands some more. "Oh. Well, you wanna come back to the kitchen? I should keep an eye on my stove."

"Sure."

"Great." He flapped a hand through the pickup window. "Just help yourself to the soda fountain. Glasses are right there."

Ignoring his insistent hospitality, I made my way through the dining room and the dish room into the long, narrow kitchen. Over a glowing blue flame, Weber stirred a steaming pot of beef chunks and creamy gravy that smelled frustratingly good. Still, I wouldn't have been shocked if his kitchen was as full of roaches as his tongue was full of lies.

"Smells good," I commented. I had to be civil if I wanted any information out of him.

"Hey, thanks. Shit, grab yourself a plate." He motioned to the shelves above the grill, stacked with cream-colored ceramic ware.

I nodded at the stove. "You learned how to cook when you worked at Mama Neelah's?" I'd been doing my research on Weber. A lot more research. Mama Neelah's had been a hole-in-the-wall diner on the north side of Chicago, apparently a favorite in its own neighborhood.

Weber chuckled. "Shit, you been doing some homework. Yeah, I worked there. God, way back in high school. Started as a busboy. Made my way to waiter eventually. Then Mama Neelah figured I got a knack for cookin'. She put me in charge of baking the buns at first, and eventually I got to grill the steaks."

"And you dreamed of owning your own place ever since?"

"Sure, off and on. Never had the dough for it until, you know, five-six years ago when I opened up this place. Finally got a loan." He turned to me with a huge grin. "All bought and paid for now." He tossed down his spoon, laughing heartily.

I couldn't help thinking he paid that off fast.

Weber grabbed a massive kettle of noodles off another burner, hefted it to a nearby sink, and dumped the contents into a strainer. The rippled noodles steamed.

"Why Lake Geneva?" I asked. "Did you have ties here?"

He shrugged and shook the strainer, which rained water from the bottom. "Nah. Visited once or twice when I was a kid. But it's a tourist town, you know? If you can't make money here, you can't make money anywhere. Seemed like a smart place. And whatdya know? I was right. Business has been good." He poured noodles into a pair of stainless steel warming pans.

I glanced at the floor and scratched the back of my neck, dropping the next question casually. "Did Zayne Mars work at Mama Neelah's, too?"

I watched Weber's face like a hawk, though it was turned half away from me, shrouded in steam as noodles tumbled from his strainer into the pans. I thought a muscle twitched in his neck. That was all.

"Zayne? Hell, no. *I* didn't even work at Mama Neelah's anymore when I knew Zayne. Him and me had a little bitty apartment just off downtown. Roommates, you know? Drafty old place. Shit, we stuffed socks and underwear into the cracks in the brickwork. But the location was good. I was workin' at a fancy-ass restaurant, working my way up from the bottom all over again. And Zayne, he was into fashion and hair and makeup and God knows what. He was a strange bird, you know? Shit, he painted his fingernails. But hey, he forked over his rent on time. Anyway, he was saving up for his own place, too. Like a hair salon or somethun. Can't say I got any of it."

"Where were you when he was murdered?" I asked.

Bud didn't flinch. "Up in the apartment. Zayne went across the street to grab noodles for dinner. There was this little Thai place we kinda liked. Anyway, I hear *pop, pop, pop.*" He shrugged. "But it's Chicago, you know? Guns going off every night. Anyway, I have a peek out the window, and whatdya know? There's my roommate lyin' in the street, dead."

Bud's story matched perfectly with the reports I'd read that morning. Much as I wanted to peg him for a murder, I had no way of making this one stick. Not yet, at least.

"Why was Zayne killed?" I asked.

Bud shrugged. "What do they call it—a hate crime? He was off a bit, ya know what I'm sayin'? He liked guys. And some days, he didn't know if he was a dude or a chick." He humphed a laugh. "Queer bird. Still, I dunno why people gotta stick themselves in other people's business. He paid his rent."

In the silence that followed, I struggled to wrap my mind around Bud's morals, but it hurt too much. He hurt girls—murdered them, maybe—but was upset that someone killed his queer roommate?

"That's when you moved to Racine," I observed. "After Mars died."

"Hell, yeah. I was sick of Chicago. Can't even eat noodles without somebody waving a gun in your face."

"I find it interesting you didn't mention any of this when we talked before," I said. We'd grilled Bud for hours after the bombing.

Bud lifted a spoonful of Stroganoff to his mouth and gave it a taste. "Why should I have?" He grabbed pepper off the counter and shook it generously over the kettle.

I shrugged. "We were talking about murder. Your roommate was murdered."

"We were talking about Jimmy and Amelia Beacon. It's not like they knew Zayne. I never thought of them in the same breath until you brought it up just now. Jesus Christ, you were askin' so many questions, how was I supposed to bring it up, anyway?" He gave the kettle a stir, then tapped the spoon on the side, flinging gravy back into the dish. "Look, hey, I'm sorry. Maybe I shoulda mentioned it. It was just such a long time ago, you know? And maybe it shook me up a bit, having a roommate killed, right out in my own street. Maybe I've tried not to think about it much. So yeah, sorry it didn't cross my mind to say somethin'." He shrugged and thrust his hands into oven mitts. "Well, you figured it out on your own anyway, so no loss in the long run." He hefted the Stroganoff onto a metal countertop and began ladling it into a new set of warming pans.

"Yeah," I agreed. "No loss in the long run." I still didn't get his morals.

Weber's nostrils flared as he concentrated on the dish he was preparing. "Look, hey, I'm all upset about Jimmy. He was a decent kid in his own way. Pretty good dishwasher. Showed up on time. He just had problems, you know? I've been thinkin' about him a lot, ever since he chased me all around with that bomb of his. I don't know how he got it into his head that I had anything to do with his little sis. He must have been crazy with grief, and it was just a pressure cooker, you know? It had to blow sometime." He glanced up quickly. "Oh, shit, sorry. Bad choice of words."

I waved it off, even though he was right for once. He was talking, and that's what I wanted.

"Anyhow, I'm just glad it wasn't worse. I'm real proud of Bailey for giving you folks a ring and warning you ahead of time. No telling how bad it could have been without you all on the scene—and shit, that police chaplain fellow. God, he was a real hero, throwin' himself over that bomb." He held up a hand. "I mean, sorry for your loss and all."

I didn't want his condolences for Bill Gallagher. Besides, my mind stuck on the words "proud of Bailey." No doubt he was proud of her every time she kept her mouth shut about the welts on her arms, the bruises around her eyes.

"We appreciate the sentiment," I lied. There was nothing I appreciated from Bud Weber, unless it were a confession. "Sorry to bring up bad memories. We just had to check into it."

"Yeah, sure, I get it." He held up a ladle full of stew. "Seriously, no Stroganoff?"

I raised a palm. "I'm good. Thanks anyway."

"Well, yeah. Any time. I mean it, too. I wanna help you guys. You know that, right?"

I merely nodded. "Thanks for your time, Bud."

I turned and walked out of the kitchen. That man made me want to barf. There were too many shady events swirling around both his past and his present. I just couldn't get any of them to turn into something resembling probable cause.

But I swore he wouldn't escape me forever.

For Bailey's sake. I wasn't giving up on her.

Chapter Sixteen
BUD

As soon as the bell dinged over the door, Bud put a lid on his last warming pan, stuck it in the steam table, and made for his office. He closed the door behind him. Locked it. Reached up high on a shelf above his desk—the one where he kept his collection of beer steins. From the back, he pulled down one with a lid covered in dust. He hadn't touched it in years. But someone else had.

He plopped down into his desk chair and turned the stein over in his hands, examining the fingerprints that were too small to be his. This was, of course, where Jimmy Beacon had found the little pink bow with the butterfly on it. The one Amelia had been wearing the day she died. Finding that bow was what had started Jimmy on his rampage, convinced Bud had kidnapped and murdered little Amelia.

Bud had practically forgotten her name. But he'd never forget the way she cried that day he carried her off from the park in Racine. He'd put his hand over her mouth so no one would hear. Especially the scrawny half-wit of a kid that had been with her. Huh. Jimmy. Never thought their paths would cross again. He should be more careful about the people he hired.

No doubt, Ryan Brandt would have been interested to see this stein. But Bud had no intention of ever telling him about it or the things inside. Memories. Mementos. Bud lifted the lid. Jimmy had pawed through them all—the faux pearl necklace and earrings. The pocket knife.

While he was on the topic, there were other murders Bud Weber had never told the cops about.

Bud lifted the crusted tube of lipstick and the onyx locket with the silver spider on the lid. Zayne's.

His nostrils flared. This stein was private. Jimmy'd had no business digging around inside it like it meant nothing to anybody.

With a corner of his gravy-stained apron, Bud wiped the dust from the stein, and with it Jimmy's fingerprints. He'd stick the stein in his safe, along with the black leather vest he liked to wear when he was in a mood to kill. The cops never needed to find this.

Question was, what set Jimmy on to Bud in the first place? What led him to poke around in Bud's office and ultimately find his secret stash?

It didn't take no genius to figure it out. The Man was to blame for this. There were no two ways about it. He was still sore about that time Bud went rogue on his precious plan and shot Tommy Thomlin, the boat captain. Well, what was Bud supposed to do? Thomlin had been getting nosy, threatening to take Bailey away from him. He'd needed to teach Thomlin a lesson.

But in payment for messing up the plan, The Man Upstairs had sicced Jimmy and his bomb on Bud. Bud's spider senses and quick reflexes were the only things that had saved his bacon. The upshot? Jimmy was dead. Bud was alive. Jimmy's big plan had totally failed—and with it, The Man's.

Well, Bud had plans of his own now.

The Man was gonna pay for this.

Chapter Seventeen
ANGELICA

Roland Markham turned a page in the leather-bound photo album that rested on his lap. Angelica gasped, laying her finger on a faded picture. "He looks just like Kaydon!" Her older son took strongly after his father, with blond hair and blue eyes, leaving all his mother's Latina genes to his younger brother Mason.

Angelica and Roland sat knee-to-knee in a deep leather sofa in his study. Floor-to-ceiling bookshelves flanked the walls, an oceanic mahogany desk dominated the center of the room, and towering French doors gave a breathtaking view of the lake. This was the kind of house she loved to sell back in Malibu. The expensive ones. The dream homes. The castles. This place didn't look like it had been redecorated since its original design in the late nineteenth century, but it didn't need a thing changed. Every panel of wood and every converted gas lamp spoke of stately elegance and history.

Luxury like this hadn't existed in Angelica's tiny village in rural Mexico, where she butchered chickens in her own backyard and scrubbed the family laundry on a washboard. It had never so much as entered her wildest dreams until her family had left their village, crossed half of Mexico, and come to the States. She'd seen glorious architecture and stately buildings in Guadalajara, and on the other side of the border, she'd discovered the mansions overlooking the ocean. And now, as a realtor, these kinds of houses were literally her bread and butter. Historic, modern, rustic, tropic, she didn't care, so long as it had walk-in closets and a Jacuzzi. Once she had learned what luxury was, she had wanted it in every part of her life. Maybe it had even been part of her attraction to Will; he had money. Eventually, they had bought a gorgeous Spanish-style villa together in a gated community in Malibu.

Only now did she realize that mansions had been the staple of Will's life from birth, not something he had worked towards, like her. What on earth had led him to the disastrous decisions he made?

She tapped the photo. "How old is Will here?"

Roland leaned forward and placed his iced tea on a coaster on the coffee table. "Oh, eleven or twelve, I'd say."

Angelica smiled, bittersweet emotions mixing. "Kaydon is twelve."

This was the first she'd ever seen pictures of Will as a boy. It was a completely different story from the one he had fabricated about an abusive father and unhappy childhood. She could see now that the story had been a cover, a convenient way to never talk about his past. According to Roland, Paul and Kathleen Geissler had been loving parents, crushed by their son's betrayal, shunned by the community when the tale began to be told. They had sold their lake estate and returned to Chicago, where Roland still had occasional contact with them until their passing several years ago. Angelica was sad she would never meet her mother- and father-in-law. But there were still far too many emotions crashing through her system to fully dwell on that.

But between Roland's stories and these photos, the truth was slowly coming to light. Will's boyhood had been full of smiles and sunshine, sand and water and fireworks. The kind of privileged, carefree, innocent childhood she'd worked so hard to provide her own boys was the childhood her husband had lived.

Her boys. Carefree no longer. Not after losing their father. Not after beginning to glimpse the truth of who he was and what he had done. She couldn't shield them from it all, and she didn't want to. But she couldn't describe yet how they felt. What this had done to them. She was still a deer staring into the headlights herself. She should be more present for them. She would be, as soon as she got home. She would start over. She would have her answers—as many as she could find. If possible, she would leave knowing who had killed her husband and why. Then she could mourn properly. She would bury what needed to be buried, and she and her boys would find a way to move on.

Angelica stroked the photo of the pre-teen Will. "It must have killed him to leave this place," she said softly. "The memories. The magic."

There was no other word for it. The *magic* of this place. She looked through the French doors toward the lake itself, glittering, tranquil, eternal. She had come here expecting grit and blood, determined to find the reason behind it all. Instead, she had found a place that, until now, had known little but peace and goodwill. It hadn't taken long for the lake's quiet beauty to seep into her system. To whisper to her, suggesting that it, too, felt the pain of these recent days and the destruction that had come with them. It watched her, all-knowing, all-loving, a sentient, caring being as old as the earth. It wasn't quite real. The rain itself sparkled with sunshine.

She looked at Roland through vision gone blurry. "He was happy here, wasn't he?"

Roland nodded. "The happiest."

"Then..." Angelica blinked back tears. "How could he pretend it never happened?"

"He must have loved you and your sons very much to never speak of his past—to protect you from the man once known as Fritz Geissler. I've told you how his crimes destroyed his parents' reputation, as Bobby's nearly did mine. He was a man on the run. There was no way he could tell you the truth *and* have a life with you." He laid a hand on hers. "I hope you can believe that, Angelica. He did it to protect you."

She scowled and shook her head angrily. "You don't betray family," she said firmly.

"But for your own good. For your sons—"

She locked eyes with him. "Roland, there are many things I left behind in Mexico. Many friends and places and a thousand memories. When I crossed that border, I came with only one thing. *My family.* And that is the only thing I will ever have." She began to count items off on her fingers. "If my car breaks down, my papá will be there to fix it. If the furniture doesn't show up for a house staging, my mamá and my aunt will show up with furniture they got from God knows where. If I lose my husband—" her throat caught here. "My entire family will be there. Because that's what family is. They are *there* for you. You might be mad at them, you might shout at them, you might annoy each other to the moon and back. But at the end of the day, family is all you have. You *do not* betray your own family."

Roland regarded her carefully and nodded somberly. "That's why it's so very hard for you to accept how Will treated you."

Angry tears pricked her eyes. She tilted her head back, trying to keep them from falling, and breathed heavily. Studying the crown molding on the ceiling, she asked, "Were we even married at all?"

Roland reached for her hand and squeezed it tightly. "Nothing can negate the love you had for each other."

A single tear streamed down. "But who did I love?" She turned to face Roland again. "Was I in love with a dream? A made-up story? Someone who never existed?"

"He gave you his heart." He dipped his head, meeting her eye. "And I know—as well as you do—that his heart was gold."

His heart was gold... and yet he burglarized banks? He took other people's hard-earned money? Roland didn't understand. She brushed her tears away. There was no point dragging the conversation on when it was stuck in a dead end.

She turned again to the album and flipped a page. A black-and-white photo in the middle of the right-hand leaf caught her eye, clearly older than the rest. Yet like so many of the others, Geneva Lake was prominent in the background, easily identifiable by the white piers along the shore. Three young men, possibly in their twenties, smiled into the camera—but they were not Bobby, Fritz, and Jason.

Angelica squinted. "Roland, is that you?"

He slid the photo from the album, examining it through his readers, then turned it over. A date in a fine scrawl read 1959. He laughed. "Evidence of my terrible organizational skills. This belongs in a different album." He flipped it forward again and pointed. "An older set of musketeers. That's me, and that's Tommy Thomlin."

"Jason's father?"

"That's right."

She pointed to the third man, straight-backed and taller than Roland by a full head. "And who's this?"

Roland paused, lips slightly parted. His face seemed to sink. "That's Wade Erickson."

The name clashed through her head like a bell falling from a bell tower, hitting every stair on the way down. From her research, she knew this name well. "Wade Erickson?" she said, looking Roland in the eye. She squinted, unbelieving. "The man who killed your son?"

Roland nodded, still staring at the picture. He seemed to be lost in memory.

But for Angelica, the idea still didn't connect. It was unfathomable. "He was your friend?"

"The three of us were as close as Bobby, Fritz, and Jason ever were."

Angelica sank back into the sofa cushions, jaw slack. "One of your best friends... killed your son?"

Roland tossed the photo onto the coffee table as if casting it away from him. Groaning under his breath, he leaned back into the cushions. "We had fallen out long before that."

Angelica shook her head. "How?"

Roland stirred uncomfortably, hesitated, then heaved a rueful laugh. "As a teenager, Bobby developed a—well, a knack for trouble. Shoplifting. Breaking into candy machines." He shrugged. "Just little things. But after a while, I lost count how many times Wade drove him home in the back of his patrol car. Eventually, Wade became very firm with me." Roland sat up and scowled, as if imitating an angry Wade. "He told me if I didn't straighten my boy out, things would only grow worse." He shrugged. "Well, I didn't listen. I told Wade that Bobby was only sowing his wild oats and he'd grow out of it soon enough. It was practically a Markham family gene. I myself was a bit of a wild card when I was young."

Roland stared out the French doors overlooking the stone patio and the lake beyond. He twirled his thumbs. "But the next time it happened, Wade didn't drive Bobby home. He drove him to the police station and booked him. Put him in a cell. He had to appear before a juvenile court." Roland's brow went heavy as if confused. Betrayed. "The boy was only fourteen. I couldn't believe Wade did that." He sighed and turned up his palms. "Granted, I suppose Wade did the right thing. Bobby didn't get into any more trouble after that. Well, not until..."

His voice trailed off, leaving Angelica to fill in the rest. Not until he grew up and moved onto targets infinitely more sophisticated than candy machines.

Angelica frowned. Something didn't make sense to her. The other night, Roland had admitted that he blamed Will and Jason for leading Bobby astray. But how could he, when Bobby already had a history of petty criminal behavior at such an early age? Was Roland that blinded by fatherly devotion? Her own sons would be grounded for years if she ever caught them stealing.

On top of this, she couldn't help but wonder. Had Bobby truly quit his misbehavior after Wade taught him a lesson? Or had he simply gotten better? How did someone go from shoplifting candy bars as a boy to planning elaborate and wildly successful bank heists as an adult? Did he have help? If so, from whom?

Angelica rose from the sofa and paced between the sitting area and the desk, arms folded, chin in her hand, a lush Persian rug cushioning her steps. "Roland, who was there the night Bobby died?"

"Well… Fritz, Jason, Wade, and Wade's partner, Sidney Kruse. They were both detectives."

Angelica nodded. "Tell me what happened. Tell me the story the way you heard it. The way you were told."

Roland sighed and cast his eyes downward. Angelica had not given him a pleasant task, and she knew it. But she needed to know. He folded his hands around his knee and launched into the tale without further prompting.

"The boys had apparently been at it a few years and never were caught. Eventually, they got pretty brazen. For their next target—their last—they chose a bank right here in Lake Geneva, their hometown. They broke in, they loaded the contents of the vault into their getaway vehicle, they were about to leave, and—" Roland sighed heavily. "And that's when Wade and Sidney Kruse caught them in the alley behind the bank. Wade was a detective then. As I understand it, he'd taken an interest in the spate of bank burglaries that had taken place over several years across Chicago,

Milwaukee, and Madison. They credit him as the first one to suppose they could all be connected." Roland shrugged. "I can't begin to imagine how he thought Bobby was behind them. A grudge he couldn't let go? It's beyond me."

Angelica moved to the French doors, framed by lush velvet drapes that piled on the floor. She stared across the lake. "Go on."

"Well, once again Wade was right. Who should come out of the bank, literally carrying the money bags, but Bobby, Jason, and Fritz?"

Here, Roland halted. Angelica knew why. She knew what had happened next. But this was the important part. The part she needed to know. "Please tell me," she muttered to the glass. "How did Bobby die?"

Silence lingered before Roland found his words. "Bobby was startled. He fired his gun." Roland stared at his hands again. "I can't imagine how frightened he must have been."

Angelica tuned out the excuses. They were inconsequential, if what she suspected was true. "So, Bobby shot first," she repeated. "According to whom?"

"Well... Wade, I suppose. Anyway, it was the conclusion of the grand jury. They ruled that Wade had fired in self-defense, and so there was no trial."

"Was there security footage?"

"No. If I remember, the boys disabled all the cameras."

Angelica nodded. How convenient. "Police dash cams?"

"I believe their unmarked car wasn't outfitted with a camera."

She smirked. Also convenient. "What happened to Wade's partner? Sidney Kruse?"

"He caught a bullet. Died at the scene."

"Whose bullet? Who killed him?"

"Jason."

"Based on Wade's testimony?"

"Yes, I suppose so. I imagine there was some forensic evidence backing that up, as well. The location of shell casings, or however that works."

Angelica chewed on her lip. Jason killed the only other witness? That didn't fit her developing theory. But she could think of explanations. Maybe Jason was in on it. Maybe the police lied about the evidence. "And Jason and Will vanished," she concluded the story. "Disappeared without a trace. Were never heard from again until now."

"That's right."

Angelica turned and met his gaze. "In other words, five men entered the alley that night. And only *one* remained to tell the tale?"

"Well, yes. But as I said, the forensics—"

Angelica blew through her lips and waved her hand. "Evidence can be staged. At the end of the day, Wade Erickson got to tell his story *his* way, and there was no one else to say otherwise, not even his partner."

Roland frowned and tilted his head suspiciously. "What are you suggesting?"

"The fourth member of the Markham Ring. What if we knew who he was all along?"

Roland tilted his head. *"Wade?"*

"Yes."

Roland fell back into the cushions, frowning, turning over the idea, not looking particularly convinced.

Angelica held up a finger. "Listen. Bobby gets himself arrested when he's fourteen, and then he never breaks the law again. But did he have a change of heart, or did he have *help?* Maybe Wade found a reason to turn a blind eye. Maybe he taught Bobby how to hit bigger and bigger targets. Maybe he cleaned up after Bobby—for a price. For a cut of the profits."

Roland opened his mouth, but no words came out.

It didn't matter. Angelica was on a roll. She began to pace. "It's years later. Bobby's all grown up, and he's playing in the big leagues. He's taking down banks. But he needs help, and that's why he recruited Will and Jason—however he talked them into it." She rolled her eyes dramatically. "And the newspapers say, 'Oh, Wade Erickson, he was the first one to link all these burglary cases.'" She threw up her hands. "Really? Chicago's not his jurisdiction. Milwaukee's not his jurisdiction. *Lake Geneva* is—this tiny little town that has nothing to do with them. He wasn't linking cases; he was *in* on them."

She tapped her chin with the nail of her manicured thumb. Was she a lunatic, or had she hit on something? "Are we supposed to believe the Markham Ring just *happened* to choose Lake Geneva next, the town where this one little detective was piecing things together, linking these intricate heists to the boy who used to help himself to candy bars? Do you realize how crazy that even sounds? How much money could they even expect to take from a bank in a town this small? And the next thing you know, Bobby and Sidney Kruse are both dead, Jason and Will have vanished, and Wade Erickson is free to sing whatever song he wants. And here's the only thing we need to know." She pointed a finger across the room at Roland. "Did Bobby shoot first—or was it Wade?"

Her words hung in the air. Roland didn't so much as blink, much less offer a rebuttal. At last, he stirred. "But... why? If Wade was in fact benefiting from Bobby's activities, why would he kill him? That's turning off the faucet, don't you think?"

Angelica shrugged. "Relationships go sour. People get greedy. Maybe Bobby was short-changing Wade. Or getting careless and becoming too much of a liability. There could be dozens of reasons."

Roland leaned back, silent, and Angelica knew she was making her case. "But... he's always lived simply, not like a man of means..."

She tilted her head. "If you were chief of police over a small department, would you live like you had millions? Maybe he's got a bank overseas. Or he's going to retire in style abroad. Maybe he's got a second wife somewhere. Maybe he's just a hoarder."

Roland shook his head. "I just can't believe..."

Angelica planted a hand on her hip. "Why not?"

"Well, I've known him since he was this tall." Roland held his hand two and a half feet off the floor. "We called him 'Shorty' because he didn't hit his growth spurt until he was fifteen. I played baseball with him when we were kids." He shook his head, turning his hands palms-up. "He was a brother to us, Tommy and me. We looked out for him."

Angelica folded her arms and couldn't help looking at him pityingly. Bobby couldn't be a bad boy, because he was Roland's son—even though Roland admitted Bobby had committed petty crimes as a teen. And Wade Erickson couldn't be guilty, because he had been Roland's friend—even though the two of them had fallen out years ago.

"Roland, you are the blindest man I have ever met."

He dropped his gaze without arguing and twirled his thumbs, looking more humbled than affronted.

Angelica sighed and fell into the sofa beside him, lacing her fingers around her own knee, imitating his stance. For several moments, they gazed across the room and the lake and said nothing.

Roland was the one to break the silence. "Do you think he killed your husband?"

Angelica let the question soak in. Let it seep in through her pores, enter her bloodstream, and become part of every fiber of her being. Of all the questions she had come here to answer, this one was at the center of it all. Who had killed her husband? Why now, after all these years? Where was the culprit? Why was he still free? Why was someone allowed to devastate her life like this—stealing not only the love of her life, but every precious memory she had of him? She reviewed everything she now knew—the facts of the case. And everything she now suspected. And then she closed her eyes and tuned in to her heart.

"I don't know," she said. "I need evidence."

Roland nodded. In the distance, power boats cut the lake. "I'll help you, if I can."

Angelica smiled and took his hand. She wasn't sure where she'd be if she hadn't met Roland.

The stately grandfather clock against the wall groaned to life and struck the hour.

Chapter Eighteen
ANGELICA

Angelica peered through a glassed-in service window toward the collection of desks and office chairs beyond, two of which were currently staffed. She'd never requested trial transcripts at a courthouse before, so she wasn't sure what to expect. Hopefully, this wouldn't take long.

A woman glanced up, noticed Angelica, and rose from her desk. She approached the window.

"Can I help you?" Her voice emanated from a circular speaker mounted in the glass. Her short, wavy blond hair had gone gray at the roots, and she apparently hadn't learned how to let her makeup enhance her features instead of painting them over. Still, her eyes were kindly, and Angelica wasn't here to give style tutorials.

"Hello," she said. "I'd like to request the records on a court proceeding?"

The woman nodded. "Let me get you a request form."

A request form? Forms took time to process. Angelica had the sinking feeling she might not receive her documents this afternoon, as she'd hoped. Still, she would go through with it. It would be worth the wait. "Thank you."

The clerk walked to a file cabinet.

Angelica toyed with her clutch. She knew from the newspapers that a jury had declared Wade not guilty of murder. The transcript would contain every iota of evidence that had been collected that night. She needed to review it. To search for a flaw. Roland had told her to ask at the county courthouse in Elkhorn, only a ten-minute drive from the lake. And so here she was.

The clerk pulled a slip of paper from the file cabinet, then returned to the window. Laying it on the desk on her side of the glass, she pointed out two separate sections.

"Just fill out this part here, and leave this one blank."

Angelica nodded. The woman slid the paper through the tray under the glass, along with a pen. Angelica thanked her, then found a nearby chair to sit and write.

The form requested the date, time, and location of the incident in question, and the name of an involved person. For the name, she put in Wade Erickson, feeling a little nervous about leaving a paper trail indicating she was investigating the case. For the type of proceeding, she wrote "grand jury transcript, reports, etc."

At the bottom, she noted a charge of fifty cents per page, which was no problem. But there was also a note explaining that a records request would require ten business days for a response. She sighed, but checked the box asking to have the documents mailed to her at her address in Malibu. She'd be home again by that time.

She stood and approached the window again. The clerk met her on the other side, and Angelica slid her paper through. The woman scanned it.

"Oh, honey, I'm sorry. We can't release these records."

Angelica's heart skipped a beat. "I'm sorry?"

The woman turned the page so Angelica could see it and pointed out the line where she had written, "grand jury."

"Grand jury proceedings are secret."

Angelica frowned. "Secret? I thought all court proceedings were public record."

"Not grand juries, dear. A grand jury convenes to determine whether to indict a person of felony offenses—whether to bring them to trial. The proceedings are secret to protect the witnesses and the jury against retribution."

Angelica felt as if something had been stolen away from her. Hope. Facts. *Truth.* "And if the grand jury did not indict someone, there would be no trial—and thus no trial records and transcripts?"

"That's correct."

Angelica's heart sank. The grand jury had indeed failed to indict Wade Erickson. He had never been accused of murder, and never stood trial. Without the records from the grand jury, where else could she find details?

"Is there nothing that would be public record?" she asked, desperate. "Surely they at least published their findings? Their conclusions? A report of some sort?"

“I can look,” the woman offered, giving a kind smile.

“That would be very meaningful to me.”

The woman took a pen and added a note. “If nothing was released to the public, I’ll send you a note anyway.”

Angelica’s heart filled with gratitude. “Thank you so much. I appreciate the extra work you’ll go through.”

“It’s no problem, dear. Is there anything else I can help you with?”

“No. Thank you.”

They said their good-byes and Angelica headed back to her car, her high hopes a wreck. But she squared her shoulders. There had to be other options. Other records and documentation detailing what happened that night.

She would go to the source, if she had to.

Chapter Nineteen
MONICA

The light had long since faded outside the windows of the detective bureau. My partners and I were working overtime again. I was finally typing up the report from our visit to the Abbey Resort.

Lehman and I had been lucky enough to talk with the clerk who had served Fritz Geissler at the front desk. Geissler hadn't had a reservation. He'd walked in around one in the morning on June sixteenth. He'd been polite, but his demeanor was forced. The clerk felt as if Geissler had really been tired and stressed, as if he were pissed off about something. He only stayed the one night. He never asked for room service. He had no visitors. In fact, he only stayed at the hotel a few hours. He checked out at 4:45 a.m.

According to the medical examiner, Geissler had been murdered no later than 7:00 a.m. that same morning.

Lucky for us, Geissler's hotel room was empty today. Unfortunately, it had been cleaned—more than once, in fact. We searched anyway. And of course, we found nothing.

We knew that Geissler's plane from LA to Chicago had landed at 9:05 p.m. on the fifteenth. Which meant, if he'd driven straight to Geneva Lake, a ninety-minute commute, he'd spent a grand total of, at most, eight and a half hours in the area before he died. Subtracting the four hours he spent at the Abbey, we had to account for just four and a half hours of his life, maybe less. Four and a half hours that led to his murder.

Meanwhile, our evidence files now contained a copy of the death certificate for someone named William Michael Read from Grand Rapids, Michigan—in other words, Fritz's alias. The real Will Read had died in 1997—the same year Fritz disappeared. I wondered if Fritz had been skilled in forging IDs as well, or if he'd had help stealing Mr. Read's identity.

Tonight, there were still far more questions than answers.

Lehman sighed and clicked his mouse loudly—the sign that he was finally putting his computer to sleep. I heard his voice beyond the gray cubicle wall. "Whatdya think, Neumiller? Call it a day?"

Mark Neumiller groaned appreciatively. "Don't have to ask me twice."

Lehman's chair squeaked as he stood, his head and shoulders appearing above the divider. He gripped his hands together overhead and arched his back. "Anybody down for a beer? My ex has the kids, and the cat isn't talking to me 'cause I forgot the canned food."

"You're on," Neumiller agreed, tossing files into a cabinet and turning the key in the lock.

Lehman leaned over the top of the cubicle, staring down at me. "Steele?"

"Another time," I replied. "I have a few things to finish up."

"It's okay to breathe for a minute." He nodded, as if berating himself for saying something asinine. "Oh, I forgot. You *don't* know that." He tried a new tactic. "What if I buy?"

"Rain check," I said, still typing. All I wanted was for him and Neumiller to go away.

Neumiller slung his jacket over his shoulder and shrugged. "You tried, Lehman. She has a date with her job."

Lehman cocked an eyebrow at me. "Well, I expect a wedding invitation when you two finally tie the knot."

I shifted an eyebrow at him. "Noted."

The guys turned and left, chatting on their way out. Their demeanor was subdued, not like they were about to hit the bars. This case had us all exhausted and constantly on our toes. What if, while we finally took a rest at the end of the day, The Man Upstairs made another move? What if, while we sifted through details, he moved mountains, ruining more lives? We never felt safe.

Still, Lehman had a point. Working myself to exhaustion ran the risk of dulling my mind.

Especially if I was secretly working two cases at once.

For the next half hour, above the clack of my own keys, I listened to the sounds outside my door, waiting until the station felt sleepy—or at least as sleepy as a police station ever gets.

When I was convinced the last of the day-shifters were gone, I picked up my cell phone and searched my contacts. Tara Slater. We hadn't talked in years.

I took a deep breath and hit send. The phone rang. Tara's voice came over the line.

"Well, hey, stranger! Long time, no chat."

I smiled. She was the kind of friend you could pick up with right where you left off. I leaned back in my desk chair and swiveled lazily, letting the movement dissipate my anxiety. "Hey, Tara. What up in Madtown?"

"Oh, the yoozh. We added a new position in homicide. You looking for a job? We miss you up here."

I grinned, a touch of nostalgia creeping in. Tara and I had shared an office in the Madison PD Detective Bureau. Lunch breaks usually found us at any one of the small ethnic restaurants on State Street—Thai, Greek, Russian, Indian, take your pick—or at a coffee shop that served beet sandwiches and offered water in upcycled glass jars. On weekends, we jogged together on the shore of Lake Mendota, winding our way past the stately, historic buildings of the University of Wisconsin-Madison. And like any self-respecting Madisonian, we proudly wore tee shirts sporting pink plastic flamingos.

But for all the fond memories, you'd have to threaten me at gunpoint to get me to go back. Madison was the city where my marriage had fallen apart. Where Ryan had had a fling with another woman. Madison was where I'd finally gotten pregnant. And where I'd had my abortion.

I diverted the conversation away from the notion of returning. "I'll wager Lake Geneva is more exciting than Madison right now."

"No shit, lady. I get the news from Luke." Luke Foreman from Madison PD Homicide had volunteered to join the investigative task force. He made the ninety-minute drive three times a week to attend our morning meetings. "What the hell's going on over there?" Tara demanded.

"Well, that's the question, I guess."

Tara's voice turned serious and sincere. "What do you need from me, girl?"

I twirled a pen on my desk, my stomach cramping. Tara Slater was deeply intuitive. It didn't shock me that she already knew this wasn't a social call.

"I just need to know..." My mouth went dry. Aside from the staff at the clinic that performed my abortion, Tara was the only person who knew about my pregnancy. I'd had to tell *someone.* And with her whole heart, Tara had offered me a shoulder to cry on. She helped me think through all the options—even though I'd been in no thinking mood. As always, I'd wanted swift and sudden action. But when I chose, she didn't judge. She offered to go to my appointment with me. In the end, I took that journey alone. But I had never forgotten her willingness and support.

And then we never spoke of it again. She knew it was off limits. But sometimes a spark of knowing passed between our eyes. And hers always seemed to say, *I'm here for you. I'm ready to talk when you are.*

But I'd brushed that offer off as well, telling myself I was fine.

Now, ten years later, how did I bring it up again? How did I ask her... whether she had really kept my secret?

"I just need to know..." I tried again. "Tara, did you ever tell anyone about...?"

She seemed to know immediately what I was trying to get at. "No. Never. Not even Max." Her husband.

The fear released my heart, one piercing claw withdrawing at a time. I found myself sniffing back a tear. "Thanks," I said in a husky voice. "That means a lot to me." And it did. But if Tara had never told, how did The Man Upstairs seem to know about my pregnancy? Or was I interpreting his words incorrectly? But if he wasn't talking about my baby, what *was* he talking about? *Yes, Monica, YOUR children...*

"Why do you ask?" Tara inquired. She gave a little gasp. "Ryan hasn't found out, has he?"

"No, no, he hasn't."

"Oh, thank God. That would be... awkward." The word itself fell short, and she knew it.

I leaned forward to place an elbow on my desk, cupping my whole upper body around my phone. "It's... it's related to the case we're working on."

"What do you mean?"

I closed my eyes for a moment, the voice of The Man Upstairs circling through my head. "We're trying to locate a suspect. A suspect who..." His words stabbed into my heart again. "Tara, I think he knows."

"What?"

Forcing my emotions to remain at bay, I told her about the phone call I'd received moments after the bombing. The challenge to play The Man's game. The boast that he knew everything about everyone in town—even me. The hint that maybe—maybe—he knew about my child.

"Holy shit," Tara breathed. "Monica, I promise, I never said a word."

"I know. I believe you."

"That leaves only one option."

"The clinic."

"Someone who worked there?"

"It has to be."

"Do you want me to look into it?"

I thought about that. "No." I was already out of bounds, sharing details of the case with someone who wasn't assigned to it. Right now, the only person outside of the task force who knew about that phone call was The Man Upstairs. If we caught a suspect and he let on that he knew about the call, we'd know we had our man. It was bad enough that I'd shared this detail with Tara. It could only make things worse if I let her involve herself in my investigation. "I'll look into it myself," I said.

"Okay." She seemed to think for a moment. "Have you told the task force?"

I drew circles on my desk with the back end of a pen. "No."

She didn't answer. Her way of not judging, but silently forcing me to consider what I was doing.

"Ryan's on the task force." It was all I needed to say.

"Ah."

Silence stretched uncomfortably. I knew what she was going to say before she said it.

"Have you considered telling him?"

I bit my lips together. Under different circumstances, maybe I would have. Or rather, I would have let him find out. I pictured Ryan walking into the meeting room just as Lehman added a note to the marker board in bright red ink: *Monica's baby.* Ryan's reaction would be the same as if someone had put a slug between his eyes. To hold a secret this long, only to dish it up semi-publicly for the sake of an investigation, would be the ultimate way to let him know how much I hated him.

Except that I didn't hate him anymore.

Quite possibly I was in love with him.

I was nowhere near being able to explain any of that to Tara. I hadn't squared with it myself yet. Nor had I figured out how I could possibly tell Ryan about our child more privately. Not without losing him all together. My only excuse was that I couldn't bear to raise our child alone—to see a miniature version of Ryan's face every day, reminding me both of him and of what he had done to me. To us. All three of us.

Had I considered telling Ryan? Yes. A thousand times, in a thousand different ways. None of them seemed right—or even like the right thing to do.

"That's not an option," I said, and left it at that.

"You sure?"

I thought again of the shock that would pass through his eyes, followed by the anger. I wasn't able to face that yet. "Yes."

"Okay." She was quiet for a moment. "You're investigating this on your own?"

"Yes."

I waited, maybe hoping she'd shrive my soul. God knew, I should have told the task force. I was playing with fire, not sharing everything I knew. What if I hamstrung the investigation? What if running an independent inquiry put me or my colleagues in danger? I was a cop who played by the strictest interpretation of the rules. Always. No exceptions.

Until now.

I guess we each have our own breaking point. I had clearly reached mine. My psyche was a mess.

But once again, Tara neither condoned nor condemned my actions. Perhaps it was merely a way of shriving her own soul of my questionable decisions. "You're walking a wire," was all she said. An observation, and nothing more.

I dipped my head, as if I had to hide my shame over the phone. "I know."

"What are you going to do if you turn up anything?"

"I'm not sure. I'll find a way to get the relevant details to the task force."

"But not your pregnancy?"

"I'll cross that bridge when I come to it."

Tara sighed. "Okay. Well... you know I'm here for you."

I smiled "Thanks. I appreciate that."

We said good-bye and hung up. I folded my arms on my desk and dropped my head on top of them. Damn The Man Upstairs. Who was he? How did he know? I had to find him. And I had to find him first—before the task force did. The truth would be out as soon as he was caught. And every word he said would be hashed over a thousand times.

I even know how to exploit your children. Yes, Monica—YOUR children.

What did you mean by those words? some interrogator would ask.

And he would tell them. And my life as I knew it, both good and bad, would be over.

The Man Upstairs had invited me to play his game. But maybe he had already won. He'd told me his goals: Control. Manipulation. Clearly, he already had perfect control over me. In some dark room hidden from my sight, he was chuckling to himself. Reveling in my mental turmoil. If he really knew everything, then he knew that I was a crumpled wreck. Fighting to protect my secrets. Fighting to find him. And shedding fresh tears for the baby I'd wanted desperately, then didn't keep because I didn't know how to be anything short of an asshole.

With the whisper of a few words in my ear, The Man Upstairs completely owned me.

Chapter Twenty
RYAN

Once the elevator doors had parted, I stepped out onto the second floor of the police station and looked down the hall toward the detective bureau. It was late, and I had a hunch that Monica, never sensible about little pleasantries like sleeping and eating, would still be there. I hoped she was. I needed to apologize for not being the one to tell her that I was staying with the LGPD.

A door clicked behind me. I turned to see who it was and found Chief Wade Erickson leaving the executive suite, where he and the lieutenant had their offices.

I paused as he made his way toward the elevator and hooked a thumb on my duty belt. "Calling it a day, chief?" I asked.

"Yep. Nancy told me she'd throw the rest of the lasagna in the trash if I didn't get home soon."

I laughed. Then remembered Wade and Nancy had special company at their house. "Hey, how's Tommy?" I hadn't seen him in weeks.

Wade shrugged. "Grumpy. Impatient. Basically back to normal, in other words." He laughed.

I smiled. "Glad to hear that. Hey, I don't suppose Bailey Johnson's dropped in to visit, has she?" The last time I'd spoken to her was the day of the bombing, when she'd called to tip me off to Jimmy Beacon's intentions. For a while before that, I'd brought her to the hospital every day. It had seemed to mean a lot to her to be near Tommy, even if his speech was incoherent for days. I had held out hope that, between me and the captain, we could finally unlock her soul—maybe get her to admit that Bud Weber was abusing her. But as soon as Tommy woke up, she had abruptly terminated the visits. All my calls and texts after that had gone unanswered. I still had no idea what had gone wrong.

Wade shook his head. "I haven't seen her."

I chewed my cheek. "I'll check on her." She'd only broken the silence that once to warn me about Jimmy. I wasn't the one who interviewed her afterwards. I was busy getting stitches for a ball bearing that nearly took out my noggin.

"While you're at it," said the Chief, "see if she knows anything about Weber's previous lives." He leaned in closer and lowered his voice, as if to prevent Weber himself from hearing. "Maybe talk to social services. See if there's any way to get her into a different home. The longer she's with Weber, the less I like it."

I nodded somberly. I couldn't agree more. In fact, I'd already done some research—and it wasn't promising. According to state law, Weber could only be denied his foster home license if he were *convicted* of a crime. Still, I couldn't help but think that social services would try to pull some strings for us, once they understood the kinds of offenses for which he was under investigation.

Wade checked his watch. "I'd better run before that lasagna hits the trash."

I nodded. "Have a good night, Chief."

The elevator bell dinged, and Wade stepped through the doors. A moment later, he was gone.

I puffed my cheeks, then turned my attention once again to the door to the Detective Bureau. Time to face the tiger. I continued down the hall and stopped to peek through the narrow glass pane. The lights were on, but the desks were empty—except for one. Monica stared into her monitor as if her scowl could force it to relinquish the answers she sought.

I couldn't help but smile. No other woman had ever been that beautiful in my eyes. The tidy ribbon of her mahogany hair trailed down her back. Her brown eyes, almost black, were intense as storm clouds. Every feature of her face remained sharp and focused like an icebreaker, forcing immovable objects to shatter before her path.

There was much she kept close to her vest. I wanted to know it all. But if there was anything I had learned from Bill Gallagher, it was to respect her space—to simply stand by to support her. If she so chose, maybe one day she would trust me with the burdens of her heart.

And that trust started with my coming clean. Apologizing for not telling her right away that she was stuck with me—unless she decided to keep her promise and dump all our asses.

Butterflies in my chest, I pushed open the door.

CHAPTER TWENTY-ONE
MONICA

Mesmerized, I listened to the voice as it hissed over my speakers.

"I know your strengths. I know your weaknesses..."

My ears were on The Man; my eyes were on my phone. *Call me, I dare you. Give me another clue. I WILL find you.*

I should have been researching names related to the clinic where I had my abortion. Instead, I'd been drawn back to the recording like a moth to flame. The chilling message rasped to the end. I dragged the slider bar back to the beginning and listened over. Who was he? Did I know him? Even if he'd disguised his voice, was there anything I could recognize?

Call me...

"A frown like that might crack your screen."

I started and looked up. "Ryan." He stood just inside the doorway, arms folded, a teasing smile on his lips. I fumbled with my mouse, trying to hit the pause button. *"Yes, Monica—YOUR chil—"* I finally connected with the button and stopped the unearthly voice, my heart pounding.

Ryan's smile turned into a concerned frown. He stepped further into the room and motioned toward my computer. "What the hell was he talking about, anyway?"

"Nothing," I said, then realized I'd said it too quickly. Ryan quirked his head, lifting an eyebrow. "He's psycho," I added. "I mean..." I shrugged and snorted, waving a dismissive hand at the screen. "He thinks he's God."

Ryan laughed through his nose. "Yeah." He leaned against a table opposite my desk. I'd gotten used to him in cargo shorts and a shirt with a royal blue blaze across the shoulders—the bike patrol uniform. Tonight, he was dressed head-to-toe in the navy blue of a regular patrolman. He jabbed his chin at my computer. "I thought County was working on the audio?"

I shrugged and minimized the file. "Yeah, well, you know me. Gotta do my own work plus everybody else's."

He nodded, smiling again. "Oh yeah, that's right." He looked at me sincerely. "I hope you're not letting him get to you."

I dropped my gaze and twiddled a pen. Let an edge creep into my voice. "You know me," I repeated.

Ryan nodded. He understood. And he wouldn't get in my way. "I dropped in because..." He jabbed his head in the general direction of the conference room. "I didn't mean for you to find out that way. I meant to tell you myself. Wade asked me to fill Schultz's position. I said yes. But you should have heard that from me."

I quirked a snarky smile. "You didn't tell me you were seeing another woman, either." I meant his affair in Madison. But why was I always looking to shoot him down? To keep him at arm's length?

"I will apologize for that as many times as you need."

I lifted an eyebrow. His response was kind of... chivalrous. And yet his back was straight, his head held tall. He wasn't demeaning himself. He was a man who had come to terms with the suckiness of his past self—but no longer living with it. At the very least, he had its back against the wall.

He bowed his head and scratched his neck. "I, uh... I'm not trying to crowd you out. I hope you know that."

My jaw clenched. Truth be told... I was really confused right now. I had been ever since the bomb went off and Ryan threw himself over me, offering his own body to shield mine.

No, before that. When we both jumped up on that park bench, drawing our sidearms in sync, like two bodies with one mind. Together, we tried to take down Jimmy Beacon before he could pull the detonator cord and devastate our town. Knowing that if we succeeded, we would devastate our own minds—because who could live with killing a sixteen-year-old boy? Believing, like we did once upon a time, that maybe we'd be there for each other to clean up the mental mess. To cry. To scream. To pound the wall. To hold each other close and let the tremors pass. Had we? No. Would we?

I didn't know.

For weeks, we'd circled each other, me growling, him cowering. But at first opportunity, our rhythms had fallen into sync. One soul. One mind. One purpose. We once had believed that there was nothing we couldn't overcome together.

I leaned back in my chair, mulling his unspoken question of whether I was leaving. "I mean, I'd have to be some kind of asshole to peace out in the middle of an investigation like this."

A smile turned up the corner of his mouth. His eyes twinkled. My staying made him happy.

It made *me* happy. I should have hated myself for that. Instead, I worried that the conversation was over. That Ryan would leave. I didn't want him to leave.

I wanted to bury my face in his chest and cry. I wanted to feel him comfort me the way he used to. I wanted to stop being the only one carrying my mental mess.

Ryan waved at my computer. "Anything I can help you with? Get you out of here a little faster tonight?"

I eyed the icon representing the media file player. I didn't want his comfort so much that I would risk letting him get near my investigation of The Man Upstairs. I tried to wrap my mind around telling Ryan about my abortion—and once again, my brain took a hard left. He was a different man. His fathering instinct had finally kicked in. He was sorry for ruining our marriage. There was no way he could love me, knowing what I'd done without his knowledge or consent.

I shook my head. "I'm leaving soon anyway."

He nodded. "Okay." Then he took in a breath and clapped his hands on his thighs. "Well. Now that I'm staying, I guess I should finally unpack."

I raised an eyebrow. "You haven't unpacked?"

He shrugged again. "I mean, the boxes make such a great dining table."

A laugh snorted its way past my defenses.

He smiled. A smile I hadn't seen in more than ten years. There was light in his eyes. Life. Heat. Interest.

He was absolutely in love with me. He proved it with his next words.

He gestured towards my desk again. "If you ever need a break from all this..." He fumbled towards what he was trying to say. "I can nuke a really good frozen dinner."

Against my better judgment, I laughed again. So I turned away and swiveled my chair. What was I doing? I shouldn't encourage him. But the concrete wall between me and the world was fissuring. The warmth was creeping in. Calling to me. Begging me to give it a chance. Taking a breath, I mentally cracked the door open. I didn't know why. Just to flirt with the dangers that lived outside. Possibilities slipped in like a stray cat. So bruised and unloved. But with so much potential.

But when I tried to open that door any wider, all I felt was emptiness inside. A jumble of ugly secrets cluttered the path. Twisted my soul. Stole the words away. My eye drifted to the media file.

Yes, Monica, YOUR children...

"I'll keep it in mind," I said, my smile crashing. The fear building.

Ryan nodded. "No worries." The excitement faded from his eyes, but he looked neither crushed nor surprised. He pushed off from the table. "Need anything, give me a call."

I nodded but couldn't draw out another word, or so much as look at him. He walked out, closing the door softly. Silence settled in behind him. The very walls seemed to watch me, silent, sad, disappointed. Like a thousand nights, I was alone in the office, nothing to keep me company but a glowing screen and the profiles of a hundred criminals.

Tonight, my companion was The Man Upstairs.

I was lousy at choosing who I hung out with.

TUESDAY, JULY 15, 2014

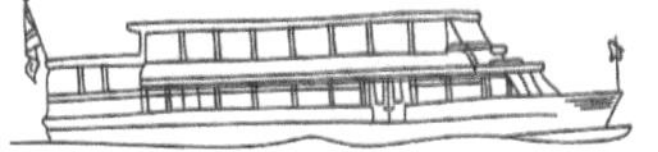

CHAPTER TWENTY-TWO
RYAN

I leaned against a brick half-wall, enjoying the shade of the Riviera breezeways, the view of the lake, and a ham sandwich from Potbelly's down the street. I figured I may as well take my lunch here and catch Bailey as she came off work.

Meanwhile, my thoughts constantly returned to last night. My stomach filled with butterflies, which made no sense. Monica had declined my lousy idea of date night—as well she should. But she had smiled. She had laughed. I felt as giddy as I had in high school when I first realized we were more than "just friends."

A whistle blew. Moments later, the Mailboat eased around the end of the pier and nosed toward its berth. I smiled when I saw Bailey standing on the rub board at the bow of the boat, a coiled rope in her hand. She looked up and spotted me. I lifted my sandwich in a wave. She gave me a little wave back. The boat slid parallel to the pier, and she hopped off to tie her line. When she was done, she turned to me and lifted a finger.

I nodded. I was in no rush, unless my radio squawked. I remembered her routine from my own days as a mail jumper: Moor the boat, drop the gangway in place, disembark the passengers (probably pose for a few photos), then tidy the boat quick for the next round of tourists.

I watched her chat with the happy excursionists. One of them, an elderly lady, pinched Bailey's cheek, and from my post ten yards away, I heard her call Bailey "so gosh-darn cute." Bailey smiled. If she was offended, she didn't show it. But she was good at looking cheerful, regardless of whatever emotions were going on inside. So, I felt offended for her. That woman had no idea that, for Bailey, human touch meant bruises more often than not. Much as I wanted to wrap that girl in a protective hug, I knew it was off the table until Bailey herself allowed it.

The passengers gone, Bailey exchanged a word with the second mail jumper, motioning to me. The other jumper, a blond-haired boy, nodded and entered the boat, where I saw him sort boxes of mail.

Bailey walked up the pier toward me. The lake breeze played with her ponytail, and she brushed fly-aways out of her face. Dressed in white shorts and a navy-blue tee shirt, she was the embodiment of summer in Lake Geneva. It was hard to think of the shadows that dogged her.

She pulled herself up onto the half-wall beside me. I held out my open bag of sour cream and onion potato chips, and when she cupped her palms, I poured some in. She popped one into her mouth and joined me in staring over the lake, as if our sharing a lunch were the most natural thing in the world. I guess you could say we knew each other by now.

"This is where we exchange the secret info, right?" she quipped.

"Yup." I tried to keep a straight face and failed. I wanted to forget that I actually *had* come here to gather some info. "Sorry I haven't seen you. They put me on a task force on top of my patrol duties. I've been busy."

She shrugged. It was no biggie to her. But I couldn't forget the challenge that Bill Gallagher had dumped at my feet before he died: Relentless love. A love that never abandoned someone, especially when they'd already been abandoned so many times. Bailey was in her fourteenth foster placement.

It suddenly dawned on me that the change in my job status might actually be meaningful to her.

"By the way, I don't know if you even knew this," I started, "but until last week I was just a reserve officer."

She crinkled her nose. "Reserve officer?" She ate another chip.

"Yeah. A temporary officer. I was only supposed to be here for the summer."

She popped her eyebrows. "Oh." The information was new to her, but not earth-shattering. "'Was'?"

"Yeah. They took me on permanent."

She stared across the lake, her eyes distant, as if her mind were turning. "Because that other cop died."

For a moment, I was knocked speechless. I'd forgotten how perceptive she could be. Her silence hid much. "Yes. Because the other cop died."

She nodded, turning a chip in her fingers. "So... you're staying?"

I nodded. "I'm staying."

Her brow flinched in thought. "Cool." And that was all she said. If my words meant anything at all to her, it was unreadable.

"How are you doing with Jimmy's death?"

She looked down and shrugged. "It's weird. His not being around. He had a crush on me, you know?"

I nodded, letting her go on.

"And sometimes I think… I don't know. Maybe if I wasn't so hard on him…?"

I saw the lost look on her face. The hopelessness. The second-guessing. I caught her eye. "Hey, Jimmy's death is not your fault, okay? There were a lot of issues he was dealing with. Most of them had nothing to do with you."

She dropped her head and nodded. I could only hope some part of what I said would stick. I couldn't stand to think she blamed herself for what Jimmy had done.

"Did you ever hear him talk about his sister Amelia? I mean, besides that day?"

She shook her head. "No."

"How about Bud? Did he ever talk about her?"

She looked at me sharply. "He doesn't exactly talk about his past."

"Even after a few drinks?"

"When is he *not* drinking?"

I tilted my head. "Touché. Has he ever done anything to make you think he'd be capable of such an act?"

Her eyes turned narrow. Angry. She plunged into silence. I should have known she was too smart to step into any trap I'd lay for her. She still hadn't confessed that Bud was abusing her—and come to think of it, trying to trick her into saying something probably hadn't been the right move. The warning look was her only retribution.

Since dishonesty had failed, there was nothing left but the truth. "Bailey, I'm worried about you. I don't want you to end up like Amelia, okay? We're investigating Bud for some very serious crimes. I'm going to talk to social services and see if I can get you a new placement." When she was silent, I tried to find her eyes. "Do you understand what I'm saying?"

She nodded, emotionless.

"Are you okay with that?" I didn't really care if she was or wasn't. She wasn't staying with Bud anymore.

Her only response was a shrug. Ironically, it felt like progress. Previously, she had been against leaving Bud. My best guess was that she feared punishment. That was usually the reason people protected their abusers.

"Bailey. I'm not going to leave you."

That one seemed to take a moment to sink in, as if the concept were a little foreign.

"I'm seeing this thing through, and I'm not giving up until I see you in a beautiful, loving family, do you hear me? I'm going to be there on your adoption day, when the judge signs the paperwork. I'm going to be there the day you realize what love looks like and what it means to be precious to someone, okay?" I wasn't sure what led me to choose the word, but my voice caught as I said it. "I'm making you a promise."

A tear glittered in her eye, and I was afraid I'd said too much. But maybe tears were a good thing. Shedding a chrysalis that didn't fit anymore couldn't be pain-free.

And now I'd made a promise. A very thorough, specific one. To my shock, this one didn't scare me spitless, as they usually did. I somehow knew, in the pit of my stomach, that this was a promise I would finally keep.

I gave her several moments, and when she said nothing, I balled the empty chip bag. "You working the next tour?"

She nodded, her expression vacant.

"Good." Any time not spent with Bud Weber was good time. "I want you to stay safe, okay?"

Another nod.

"Okay." I bounced my heel, but there seemed to be nothing more to discuss. I stood up. "I'll be in touch."

She offered half a smile—a friendly gesture. A plea for me to go and leave her to her own thoughts.

So, I left, praying to God that something I'd said had finally broken through to her dark, hollow world.

Chapter Twenty-Three
TOMMY

Propped up by frilly, embroidered pillows, I stared at the opposite wall, pale peach with sconces that held trailing vines. A Thomas Kinkade painting stared back at me, depicting a cottage that glowed beside a gently rippling river.

Lying around wasn't my idea of a good time. My mind was on the Mailboat. At every minute of the morning, I knew where it was. Mentally, I reminded Brian that the Wilsons asked for packages to be left inside their boat; the wind on that part of the lake blew them right off the pier. And he needed to be careful in the subdivision run where the water was only five feet deep. Did he remember to reverse the screws regularly to clear the lake weed from the propeller blades? The other boats rarely had to worry about that; they didn't spend as much time so close to shore. I shuddered to think of the repair list he was leaving for me, when the boats moved to the docks in Willams Bay for the winter. I pictured everything from scratched paint to a broken rudder to—

Cracked glass. The bullet had barely missed my head. Shards like ice rained down on the back of my neck. The gun spit again. Lead hit wood with a hollow thud, as if the wounded slab of pine had pulled in a sharp gasp. The boat took a third round with a brittle crack of plastic, the snap of tiny electric arcs.

The next slug hammered me below the rib.

I dropped.

No. No. The walls were pale peach. I could see them. Vaguely. I could smell the raspberry air freshener plugged into the outlet. Yes, but not as strongly as—

The smell of lemon floor cleaner. It filled my nostrils. The pain was hot. White hot. The boat was suddenly silent except for the sound of my own breathing. Ragged. Agonized.

A shadow leaned over me. "Want any more, Tommy?"

I grit my teeth against the pain. "Please..." My vision swam. The light was in my eyes. I couldn't make out his face. Only a black leather vest with silver studs.

He laughed. "You'll bleed out before she gets here."

My heart pounded. He knew Bailey was coming. "Don't hurt her," I gasped.

He chuckled again. "Don't worry, Tommy. I won't."

A shout left my lips. "Bailey!"

The sound of my own voice snapped me back into the pale peach room. It had three dimensions again. Substance. Weight. I could feel the bed sheets and the down pillows. My heart was pounding. Sweat drenched my shirt. My breath raced.

Thank God Nancy and Wade were at work. Their burying me under mountains of helpful concern was the last thing I needed. And I didn't care to explain why I had yelled. What had I even said? I wasn't sure. I had an uncomfortable feeling it was Bailey's name. Well. Even more reason to be glad I was alone.

The therapist at Froedtert Hospital looked up from my chart after peppering me with a dozen questions. "Tommy, you're at pretty high risk for PTSD. Have you had any nightmares? Flashbacks?"

I'd lied to him. No. None. Well, it wasn't like they were so bad. I figured they'd go away soon enough.

They hadn't.

I should call him.

But I was already exhausted by the three days a week I was taking PT. I just wanted this nightmare behind me so I could get on with life. Get back to the Mailboat. Get back to Bailey.

Was she okay? Why had I heard nothing from her since that day at the hospital? Was Bud Weber beating her up again? Wade assured me there were no new reports. Well, of course there weren't. *I* was the one reporting her bruises.

I eyed my phone, charging on the end table. There was barely room for it amidst the flurry of cards, bouquets, and stuffed animals from well-wishers. I'd avoided texting Bailey or even calling her. The things we had to talk about deserved to be said face-to-face, not over a phone. And besides, I had no idea why she was avoiding me, unless she objected that strongly to being a blood relative of mine.

I chewed my lip, then picked up my cell. I couldn't stand the silence and inaction any longer.

CHAPTER TWENTY-FOUR
BAILEY

I was glad I was working concessions for the next tour. So far, the passengers were happy in their little plastic chairs, every head turned toward the shoreline while they listened to Captain Brian's narration. They wouldn't want chips and soda until Williams Bay or even Fontana. So, I sat on my bench behind the counter on the aft deck, elbows on knees, and twirled my phone mid-air. In my brain, I replayed the things Ryan had said.

He wasn't going to leave me.

He was going to take me away from Bud.

He was going to be there someday when I got adopted.

He almost made it sound like he took the permanent position at the police department specifically so he could be around for me. But that was a ridiculous notion, straight out of that part of my brain that used to daydream that my dad was going to rescue me someday. My dad was just shipwrecked in the Antarctic or something, fighting his way through shifting sea ice and yawning crevasses. Looking forward to warmer weather and a hot meal and holding his little girl tight.

But I knew now that my dad was Jason Thomlin and that he'd been a bank burglar. And he hadn't even known I existed. Not until the night he was murdered in front of me. And when he was dying right there on the street beside me, he didn't even tell me who he was.

I got to spend one night with my dad. Just one night. When knowing my dad was all I ever wanted.

Was I supposed to be mad at him? And if so, for what? For not telling me? Or should I back up even further and be mad at him for not even knowing I was a thing? For making me by accident, then abandoning me to a life of misery and pointlessness? Was he even sorry?

And if I *should* be mad at him... Why wasn't I? Why was God the only person I was mad at, for not even letting me have five minutes with my dad and know that it was him?

And then I realized my phone was ringing. I quit spinning it and looked at the screen. It said CAPTAIN TOMMY. The profile pic was from a screenshot of a news article. He and I were standing next to each other on the rub board after tryouts this spring. We both looked so happy. So clueless about everything that would happen this summer. Why had I chosen such a dumb picture? That was back when I daydreamed he could be like a grandpa to me—never imagining he actually was.

I stared at the picture and the little ringing bell icon. Why was he calling me? We hadn't spoken since that day at the hospital. Did I want to talk to him now? Did I want to start thinking of him as my for-actual grandpa? Did I want to accept that Jason Thomlin was my dad and that I'd lost the chance to know him forever?

No.

That was a lot to ask of a girl.

I just wanted to think.

To find my feelings in this whole mess—if they even existed anymore.

I set my phone on the counter and stared at the picture of me and Tommy until the phone stopped ringing and the picture disappeared.

Chapter Twenty-Five
TOMMY

The line rang half a dozen times before she picked up.

"Hey, this is Bailey."

Heart pounding, I opened my mouth to respond, but she spoke over me.

"Sorry I can't pick up right now, but if you leave me a message, I'll get back to you as soon as possible." There was a pause. "All right, 'bye." And then the tone sounded.

My first instinct was to hang up, my mind reverting to the notion that what we needed was a good, long talk—in person. But then I cast up how many weeks had gone by since we last spoke, and how many weeks were likely to go by before I could return to the Mailboat. Would I even make it back before the end of the summer? If not, was I willing to let all winter pass without speaking to her?

"Hey, Bailey," I said, my voice feeling scratchy and uncertain. "How ya doin'? Haven't heard from you in a while." I paused. Was I rambling? What was I supposed to say? "I hope you're okay. I think we've got some things to talk about. Call me.... Okay, I'll talk to you later."

I hung up. Laid my phone in my lap and stared at it. *Would* she call me later? Or would she go on ignoring me? I guess I'd forced the question at this point. If she never returned my call, then she was, in fact, ignoring me on purpose.

From the kitchen came the sound of the door opening and closing. Keys jangling. "Yoo-hoo! Tommy, you ready for PT?" It was Nancy.

Physical therapy. The current bane of my existence. I'd met my cheerful young therapist at the local clinic for the first time yesterday, and I wasn't sure how we were supposed to get along—not when she celebrated all my gains in mobility as if I were a toddler again. At my age, I didn't appreciate getting sent back to square one.

I glanced at the calendar on the opposite wall. July fifteenth. School started in a month and a half, and

Bailey's hours would be drastically cut back. In eight weeks, marine mail delivery would end, and she'd be more likely to be scheduled on other boats besides mine, her specialized skill set no longer a determining factor. We'd have fewer chances to talk.

Setting my jaw, I threw back the covers and eased my legs out of the bed. The ache in my side was still there, despite the meds.

Nancy appeared in the doorway. Her name tag from Blackpoint Estate, the historic house where she was a tour guide, was still pinned to her blouse. Seeing me upright, she stopped and folded her arms. "Well, look at you!" She smiled with pleasure.

I waved to the hallway, where she had parked the walker the hospital had saddled me with. "Well, grab my contraption."

"Aye, aye, Captain." She turned to shuffle it into my room.

I wasn't going to lie here the whole rest of the summer. One way or another, I was making it back to the Mailboat. I was not letting Bailey drift away from me.

Chapter Twenty-Six
BAILEY

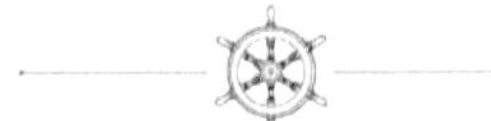

My phone blinked at me, and a notification popped up, saying I had a new voicemail. Feeling a detached curiosity—just my grandpa calling, no big deal—I tapped the notification and typed in my PIN.

"Hey, Bailey." Tommy's warm voice filled the aft deck. It sort of counted as the first time he'd been on the Mailboat in weeks. He asked how I was doing. He told me to call him. He sounded like he missed me.

I snorted and put my phone to sleep. That was the kind of thing old me would have believed in: That someone cared about me. That I was special for once in my life.

But seriously, I'd been smacked awake too many times to fall for that crap anymore. Family were people who left you. If I were special, my dad would have told me who he was, and then he would have survived instead of dying in front of me. Or at the very least, he would have told me he loved me.

But no.

He died.

He left me.

Maybe I *was* a little mad at him.

Anyway, it was going to be a good, long time before I believed Tommy was really going to be there for me.

Maybe forever.

Until then, he could talk to my voicemail.

CHAPTER TWENTY-SEVEN
RYAN

Elkhorn. The county seat. I wended my way through hallways that felt familiar. I'd followed the same wall-mounted directories eleven years ago, the night I'd dropped off a tiny little girl with big, brown eyes.

It was easy to remember the showdown between the arguing couple, each of them high as a kite. It was impossible to forget the wide-eyed five-year-old I'd found hiding in a closet. I would always recall that she shed no tears, even as I carried her down this hallway on my hip.

Eleven years ago, I turned Bailey Johnson over to the system, not exactly hoping her mother would figure her life out; naively believing Bailey would be adopted quickly into a loving family.

How had it gone so wrong?

I quickly silenced the voice insisting her situation was my fault. I was getting better at turning down the burden of blame. Bill Gallagher had ruthlessly pointed out that my self-pity was helping no one. The only thing that would help was taking action.

Today, I was more than ready for action. I wasn't leaving until I had assurances Bailey would be placed in a new home. *Today.*

I imagined she might be shuffled anywhere in the county, depending where social services had an available foster home. And she didn't have a car, so that probably meant she'd have to quit her job at the Mailboat. By extension then, she'd see less of Tommy—and that was a problem to iron out. I wasn't sure what had fallen out between them, but I still believed in my gut that he was a key connection somehow.

One thing at a time. First, I just needed to get her away from Bud Weber.

I found the door I was looking for. It pulled me strongly back to that night. I stared at it. Told myself I was finally making restitution. That Bailey's torment ended today. I pushed it open.

"Can I help you, officer?"

A large, comfortable woman sat behind the desk, wearing a flouncy polka-dot dress. She smiled warmly behind horn-rimmed glasses. Something about her reminded me of my favorite teacher from grade school. The nameplate on the edge of her desk said *Betty Evans.*

"Yes, I need to speak with the case worker for one of your fosters, Bailey Johnson."

"Certainly. One moment." She clacked on her keyboard with bright red manicured nails, her fingers blinged out with oversized rings. After a moment of searching, her face fell. "Oh." She chewed her lip, looking uncomfortable, as if she'd opened the door to the craft closet, only to find every piece of paper stuck to the wall with glue sticks. "I'm afraid Bailey's case worker isn't available. Would you like to speak with our director?"

"All the better."

The woman rose with a relieved smile. "I'll see if she's available. May I ask the purpose of your visit today?"

"Bailey's foster dad is currently under investigation for some very serious allegations. I'm here to see about getting Bailey rehomed."

The smile withered, but the woman concealed it with a quick nod. "Wait here, please."

She vanished down a hall, leaving me to stand, hands on my duty belt, staring at literature about how to become a foster parent. A man, a woman, and a child, bathed in sunlight, laughed joyously from the front of the brochure. I couldn't help thinking the advertising was off.

And for some reason, I couldn't help grabbing a copy and tucking it into my pocket.

I went on to study the furniture, the carpet, the adorable ceramic pig on the receptionist's desk—all while wondering if she was ever coming back. Was it me, or was she taking a long time?

At last, she reappeared, smiling warmly again—maybe because I was happily no longer her problem.

"The director will see you now."

I fell into step behind the woman, who led me down the hall. The receptionist stopped at a door and knocked brightly, then pushed it open and waved me in.

A tall woman stood from behind her desk, her brown hair piled artfully in carefree waves, her efficient form clad in a blazer and pencil skirt. She reached across the desk to shake my hand. "Good afternoon, Officer. I'm Michelle Stafford." Her handshake was firm and her manner of speech efficient.

"Thanks for seeing me. I'm Officer Brandt."

"Have a seat." She waved me to a chair, then sat and folded her hands on her desk. "I understand you have some concerns about one of our foster homes."

I settled into the seat offered to me. "Yes. Bud Weber."

"Would you please elaborate?"

"His foster ward, Bailey Johnson, has had some bruises no one can explain."

Ms. Stafford turned to her computer and clicked her mouse. "How old is the child?"

"Sixteen."

"Have you asked her how she came by her bruises?"

I shrugged. "She says she ran into stuff."

She looked at me over her glasses, her gaze pointed. "You don't believe her?"

I stopped, jaw slack. Surely she knew that "running into stuff" was the go-to explanation from every victim of domestic violence ever. In a heartbeat, what I'd taken to be a professional conversation had turned antagonistic—and I was the bad guy, or at least the bumbling cop.

She reached into a drawer and pulled out a sheet of paper, then laid it on the desk in front of me. "If you'd like to file a formal complaint, we'll look into it."

I wondered what "looking into it" entailed. I'd already interviewed Bud and Bailey—multiple times—and run a background check on Bud and was currently making him the focus of a full-scale investigation.

And I *still* had no concrete evidence. In light of that, what would this woman who didn't believe me accomplish?

I took the sheet, meeting Ms. Stafford's eye. "I *will* file a complaint. But the things I'm here to talk about go way past paperwork. Weber is currently under investigation for very serious allegations. We consider Bailey's safety at risk. I'm here to request she be removed to a new foster home—today."

"I'm afraid that would be very difficult."

"Difficult? We suspect Bud Weber of the rape and murder of a female minor."

She adjusted her glasses, her motion precise and practiced. "Has Mr. Weber been convicted of a felony?"

"No. The investigation is ongoing."

"Then I'm afraid we don't have sufficient grounds to revoke his foster care license."

"Are you kidding me?"

"No. We take the rights of our foster care providers very seriously."

"And in the process, you sacrifice the child. How is that right?"

"I'm not paid to decide what's right, Officer Brandt. I'm paid to provide child protective services within the legal framework as it stands."

"Ms. Stafford, I am an officer of the law. You won't even take *my* word that this home is unsafe?"

"It's not a matter of whether or not I believe you. It's a matter of what can be proved."

I leaned forward and tapped my fingers on the desk. "Technically, it's your job to determine whether a foster home is safe."

She smiled coldly and nodded at the document she'd handed me. "If you file the complaint, I promise I'll look into it."

"Fine. Yes. I'm submitting the paperwork. But I'm also going to continue my investigation on Weber. And I recommend you let me know what kind of coffee you like, because I'm going to be in this room *every day* presenting my findings until you have no choice but to care."

Her eyes turned to ice, her professional demeanor vanishing, the real woman suddenly and violently showing through. "*Don't* suggest I don't care."

Her outburst left me speechless—not only because of her passion but because I still couldn't reconcile her statement with the evidence to the contrary.

She composed herself, smoothing down her skirt, then added, "As someone who works at the intersection of the law and human nature, I should think you'd understand. I receive complaints every single day—from biological parents and family members, from adoptive parents, from the children themselves. Most are unfounded. The minute you take a child from their birth family, absolutely no one is happy about it and absolutely no one is civil. The worst kind of accusations ensue from all parties involved. I spend all day trying to sort these out."

Her position began to run clear. "I'm assuming it would be impractical to move a child temporarily until the investigation was resolved."

"Yes. For two reasons. One, every time you rehome a child, you only add to their trauma. Two, where am

I going to put her? To be frank, there is nowhere for Bailey to go."

"You don't have a home waiting for a child? Maybe even some nice couple looking to adopt?" Somehow in my mind, I had pictured dozens of families eager to fall in love with a new kid, especially one as sweet as Bailey.

The director folded her hands patiently. "Officer Brandt, on an average day in Wisconsin, the number of kids in need of a home outnumber foster homes four to one. We are maxed out. As for adoptive parents—not to be a pessimist, but Bailey's too old. People want babies and toddlers—kids too young to be 'tainted' by the system. Teens in foster care have usually been here half their lives. They're scarred, and they're working through a lot of trauma. And so, there are rumors. As far as adopters are concerned, Bailey Johnson is more likely to murder them in their sleep than become a natural fit for their family."

My jaw went slack. "Bailey's the victim in all this. She's just a kid—a *really good* kid." I tried to forget that one time she looked like she was ready to deck me.

"I'm merely explaining the facts to you as they stand."

I slumped in my chair and released a heavy sigh. I'd had no idea just how steeply the odds were stacked against Bailey's favor. No wonder she was still trapped in the system. No wonder she was stuck with Bud Weber. The entire foster care system, in its current desperate state, was a more perfect environment for child predators than for children.

I sighed and rubbed my forehead, trying to wrangle my thoughts. "Okay. All right. I'll, uh... I'll file the complaint, and I'll continue my investigation." I met her eyes, changing my tone. "And I'll share with you whatever I find."

"I can't revoke a license without good cause," she said firmly.

"I understand. I'll do my best." Meekly, I rose and made for the door.

"Officer."

Hand on the knob, I turned.

She twisted a pen in her hands, elbows on her desk, her eyes studying me as if she were trying to make up her mind. At last, she sighed and flipped up a palm. "I take tea, not coffee."

I smiled. That was as much as an invitation as I was going to get, and you better believe I was going to take it. In fact, I was going to try every variety of the best-brewed tea in the county until I figured out which one she liked best.

I left her office, wandered back to the lobby, and scowled at the document I was to fill out. Paperwork. This wasn't what I'd come here for. Bailey deserved more.

I sat down and poured my soul into that document, stacking every fact I knew and most of what I suspected—everything I could without compromising the investigation. When I was done, I sighed, rose, and approached the receptionist, Betty.

Her smile was genuine but demure, as if she knew what kind of conversation had happened behind the closed door. "Thank you, officer. I'll pass this back to Ms. Stafford right away."

"I appreciate that." I turned to leave.

"Um…"

I paused. Betty was biting the end of a pencil, staring at her desk as if trying to make up her mind. She lifted her eyes, looked at me, then pulled a sheet of paper from the corner of her desk.

"I'm not sure I should do this, but… I made you a list of Bailey's past case workers."

I took it eagerly. There were at least a dozen names. "So many?"

"It's hard to keep them. The work is very... Well, it's stressful. Most places have a fairly high turnover rate."

I nodded. It fit the picture that was coming together for me. The train wreck that I was just discovering was the environment these people worked in every day. And this list of names was one more reason why Bailey continued to flounder in foster care. No one knew her story from beginning to end except what they each read in impersonal documentation. It wasn't the same as walking her journey alongside her, knowing what she needed intuitively.

"Who's her current case worker?" I asked.

Betty chewed her lip, as she had the first time I asked. "Anna Clapton was the most recent. She left us about a month ago."

"So who's her worker now?"

"Technically she's with Chloe White, just until we fill Anna's position. But Chloe hasn't had a chance to meet with Bailey yet, so..." She trailed off.

So Bailey didn't even have a proper case worker right now. And she hadn't since I'd crossed paths with her this summer. I decided not to comment. Offloading my frustrations on the receptionist wasn't going to solve the problems she already seemed well aware of.

I carefully folded the list of names she'd given me. "Thank you. I appreciate this."

She nodded meekly. She didn't seem to have the heart to apply more words to the situation.

I left. I was sure I was going to see a lot more of that office. I was sure I was going to feel this same sick, twisted feeling in my gut every time I was there.

I just hoped I could save Bailey in time before anything happened to her. I'd made a promise to her today—a promise to be there when she was adopted into a real family.

But now I understood what she'd known all along: I had promised her something utterly impossible.

WEDNESDAY, JULY 16, 2014

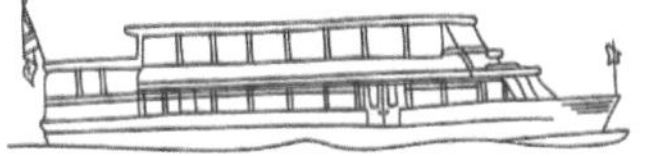

Chapter Twenty-Eight
ANGELICA

Angelica's heart pounded with every step from her hotel to the Lake Geneva Police Station. Was this the right move? What if she ran into Wade Erickson himself? Did he know who she was? What if he demanded to know what she was doing at the police station? What she was doing in Lake Geneva?

But where else could she find information on what had happened the night Bobby Markham was killed? Every original record was housed in this very building. There was no way around this.

Trembling, she pulled open the front door and stepped into the atrium. To her left was a glassed-in window like the one at the county courthouse. But this one had a phone mounted to the wall with a sign instructing her to pick it up for service.

She peered through the glass. Rows of desks were piled with computer monitors. Only one was currently manned, the one at the very back. The woman wore a headset and typed at a furious pace while staring at her screens and speaking into her microphone.

Slightly afraid of interrupting, Angelica lifted the phone from its cradle and pressed it to her ear. It rang. The woman on the opposite side of the room pressed a button and her voice came through the line. Her eyes met Angelica's across the room and through the glass. "How can I help you?"

"I would like to make an open records request?" Angelica said, her voice scratchy.

"Of course. I'll be with you in a moment."

Angelica nodded and hung up the phone. She folded her hands on the counter, one on top of the other. But her heart pounded in her chest. She just wanted to fill out whatever request form they handed her and be done with it.

The main door opened behind her, and a man stepped through. Seeing her waiting at the counter, he simply took his place behind her in line. Angelica would have preferred he weren't there, even though she told herself it shouldn't matter. Still, she felt as if the fewer people who saw her here, the better.

She studied his reflection in the glass. Tall, narrow, his dark brown hair highlighted blond. He wore pressed slacks with a belt and a plaid, button-down shirt. His style was sharp, and Angelica approved. With one hand in his pocket, he waited his turn, scrolling his phone. His lack of attention on her helped calm her nerves. It would be fine. It didn't matter he was there.

The dispatcher finally rose from her desk, approached the glass, and pulled a sheet of paper from an organizer mounted to the wall. Angelica's heart rate went right back up. This was a small department. Would Wade Erickson hear that someone was asking questions about Bobby Markham's death?

The woman laid the paper down, ready to point sections out and explain. But to Angelica, the general layout of the document already looked familiar. So did the sense of fear that, like last time, she would somehow be thwarted, nothing coming of her efforts. After all, would Wade Erickson still be walking free if the documents related to his case were this easy to access?

She held up a hand to stop the woman. "I'm looking for information on the Markham Ring—specifically on Bobby Markham's shooting." She was careful not to mention Erickson by name. "*Are* those records open to the public?"

The woman narrowed her eyes. Was it just Angelica, or did she detect a hint of caution? Did the dispatcher know more than she was willing to say? In all likelihood, this small department was abuzz with the words "Markham Ring," thanks to the murders so recently associated with it. Had Angelica tipped her hand? Ruined her chance?

"I'm with the press," she blurted. She wasn't even sure how or why she thought of it.

The woman seemed to accept her statement—to Angelica's relief. Of course, if the dispatcher had asked, she would have been incapable of providing credentials proving she worked for any media outlet.

"I wouldn't know whether those records specifically are open to the public," the woman replied. "But if you fill out the form, we can check. Your publication won't be charged for anything but our time."

Angelica glanced at the sheet. Like the one at the county courthouse, it asked for her name, address, and phone number. It would likely take the staff several days to dig up the records. Angelica would need to have them mailed to her address in Malibu—either her home or her office. Would the dispatcher believe that a publication all the way on the west coast had taken an interest in this story? Worse, did Angelica dare leave her calling card—and instructions on where to find her—under Wade Erickson's very nose?

Movement within the dispatch center caught her eye, shifting her focus. Two men walked into the room bearing Styrofoam cups. They leaned against a set of cabinets and began to chat, as if the dispatch center were their unofficial break room. One of the men wore a black polo shirt and tan pants and had spiky gray hair. She recognized him as the man who had gotten into a car with Monica Steele the other day—her partner, perhaps?

The other was half a head taller and wore a navy-blue uniform with gold trim. His facial features were firmly chiseled. His eyes intense, even as he shot the breeze with his co-worker. Angelica's heart stopped.

Wade Erickson.

He had barely seemed to age from the photos she'd seen in the newspaper. His hair had grayed, his build was perhaps a shade heavier—that was all. There was no mistaking it was him.

He lifted his cup to his mouth. Raised his eyes toward the glass. Their gazes met. Like a deer caught in the headlights, Angelica couldn't look away. Erickson merely looked at her with detached curiosity. Maybe he didn't know who she was, and he was wondering why she was staring. Maybe he knew *exactly* who she was but could put on a brilliant act for the benefit of Steele's partner.

"Ma'am?" The dispatcher broke into her thoughts. "Would you still like to fill out the form?"

Angelica tore her eyes away from Erickson and stared at the sheet, the empty boxes swimming before her eyes. Did Erickson know who she was? What she looked like? Had he researched every detail of Will's life—including his wife? His children? At the thought of her husband's murderer knowing the faces of her boys, ice cracked its way up her spine, sending her mind into a panic. She felt long, thin hands closing around her throat...

"No," she told the dispatcher. "No. Never mind. Thank you."

She backed away from the window, almost stepping on the feet of the man behind her. She muttered a quick apology and pushed through the door. The outside air and the sunlight greeted her as if she had been suffocating. She rushed down the sidewalk, stealing backward glances, paranoid someone might be following her—but she saw no one besides an elderly couple strolling arm-in-arm.

Stupid, stupid, stupid! What had she been thinking, walking in there? Had Erickson recognized her? Would the dispatcher tell him what Angelica had asked for? Would he understand she suspected him? What would be the repercussions? Had she just painted a blazing target on her back? On the backs of her sons?

She broke into a run and didn't stop until she reached her hotel room. Once she was there, she double bolted the door, collapsed against it, and buried her face in her hands.

She needed to talk to Roland.

She pulled her phone out of her purse. Dialed his number. It rang. And rang. Finally, the line clicked.

"Hello," a refined voice said.

"Roland—"

He spoke over the top of her. "—you have reached the voicemail of Roland Markham. Please leave a message and I'll get back to you as soon as possible."

A tone beeped.

Angelica hung up and let her phone drop to her side, her head leaning against the door. She stared at the ceiling, her heart still pounding. What was she going to do?

Chapter Twenty-Nine
SKULL

Humored by Angelica Read nearly running him over on her way out of the police station, Skull took note of which direction she ran. Her hotel. He'd follow her in a moment. For now, he pocketed his phone and approached the service window.

"How can I help you?" the dispatcher asked.

Skull offered a warm, professional smile. "Hello, I'm new in town. I'll be teaching fourth grade at Central-Denison, and I was wondering about having one of your officers speak to my class this fall?"

The dispatcher smiled. "Oh, of course." She grabbed a flier and paused to write something on the cover. "You should talk to Sergeant Brown. He'll be happy to set you up. I'm writing his hours. Just call the front desk, and we'll put you through to him when he's on duty." She slid it through the glass.

Skull took it and used it to offer a friendly wave. "Thank you. I can't wait."

He walked out the door. His whole time in the lobby, he'd been careful to never make eye contact with Wade Erickson. The Man wouldn't approve.

He wouldn't have needed to follow Angelica inside in the first place, except that keeping a bug on her was practically impossible. He'd dropped one into her purse the first day of the tail—but it turned out Angelica Read changed handbags as often as her makeup. A fashionista was a damn hard target to follow.

Once outside, Skull scanned the street and noted that Angelica hadn't gotten far. She was just rounding the corner a few blocks away, straight for her hotel, as he had guessed. He followed at a more leisurely pace. He didn't need to be seen again. Still, the risk had paid off. Her stress over wanting case records so badly—then abandoning them altogether—was very telling. He could smell her fear. The Man could use fear.

Of course, Skull hadn't known Erickson would be there. The Man might berate him later. He hoped not. This was a good gig. He didn't want to lose it.

Or become The Man's next target.

He gave The Man good information. Details. Nuances. After The Man's interest had been piqued by the boy Jimmy Beacon, it was Skull who had brought to his attention the fact that Beacon and Bud Weber were unwittingly connected by the murder of Beacon's sister. Skull was a finder and knower of facts. And he could connect facts, putting them into the right hands at the right time—for the right price.

He had, of course, told The Man about the electric enmity between Delilah Beacon and Monica Steele. But The Man had merely appeared to file the information, plugging it into whatever puzzle, whatever grand plan, he was building in his mind.

And then he had instructed Skull to continue following Angelica Read.

So follow her he did. And now that he understood how obsessed she was with Wade Erickson—he knew why.

The Man was going to go to town.

Chapter Thirty
ANGELICA

Roland's tone was apologetic over the phone. "My dear, I'm so sorry. The president of the board called an emergency meeting—the CEO retired. Health complications. I had to run to the city. It was all very last minute."

Angelica nodded, the lake breeze playing with her hair as she sat on a bench overlooking the marina. "I understand. Don't think of it."

"I should be back tomorrow. I'll take you to lunch. We'll discuss everything then. In detail."

She smiled. "Thank you." There was so much she wanted to go over with Roland.

She heard a voice in the background on his end. Then Roland spoke through the line again. "I'm so sorry, my dear. I have to get back to the board room. I'll see you at lunch tomorrow."

"See you then."

They hung up. Angelica sighed and gazed across the lake. Her investigation already felt as if it were at a dead end. She hoped Roland could help her find the trail. In the meanwhile, she had a full day to herself—and no idea what she was going to do with it.

She should call her mamá. Talk to her boys. See how they were doing. Lifting her phone, she speed-dialed her mother.

The line picked up. The voice of her nine-year-old son Mason came through. "Hi, Mom!"

Joy filled her chest. "Hello, Mason! How are you?"

"Good. I miss you, Mom. Are you coming home soon?"

Sadness tweaked her heartstrings. She'd been gone almost a week. "Soon, honey. You and Abuela are picking me up from the airport this weekend, remember?"

He sighed dramatically. "That's a really long time."

"Aren't you having fun with Abuela and Abuelo?"

"Yeeeaaah." He dragged the word out like a tire losing air.

"What's the matter, honey?"

He sighed again. His voice was tiny when he replied. "Kyle said my dad was a bad man, and it was okay he died."

Fury built in Angelica's chest. "Kyle Watson?"

"Yeah."

Angelica ground her teeth and bounced her crossed legs. This wasn't the first time the Watsons, her parents' neighbors, had dropped unfeeling remarks in front of her children, and the parents were just as guilty as the kids. "Well, you know what? You don't have to play with Kyle anymore. Okay?"

"Okay," Mason mumbled.

Her mamá's voice called from the background in Spanish. *"Mijo,* is that your mamá?"

Mason hesitated before muttering, *"Sí..."*

"Did you tell her what happened?"

He hesitated even longer. "Sí..."

"Did you tell her *everything?"*

"...No..."

Angelica frowned. "Mason, what happened?"

The silence lingered so long, Angelica knew her son was in trouble, and merely trying to stave off the inevitable.

"I kneed Kyle in the balls."

Angelica's jaw dropped. "You *what?*" She'd never imagined her son doing such a thing.

The phone clattered as if changing hands. "Go outside. Go." Abuela spoke to Angelica next. "*Mija.* Where are you? When are you coming home?"

Somehow, Angelica felt as if she were the one in the hot seat now. "I'm coming home this weekend. Like we discussed."

"Make it tomorrow."

"Mamá?" After raising Angelica's two brothers, she couldn't imagine there was anything her mother couldn't handle.

"Angelica. Your sons need you. Kaydon? He sits and stares out the window. Mason? He gets into fights. They lost their papá. They don't need to lose their mamá, too."

Her words hit home deeply, tearing open her already-devastated heart. The last thing she needed was her mother telling her what a horrible parent she was.

"I'm trying to find out what *happened* to their papá."

"Phbttt, he was murdered. Leave it to the police."

Tears stung Angelica's eyes. Her mamá hadn't hated Will, but mostly she had loved his money. Now that he was dead and a wanted criminal, she had no love for him at all.

"Mamá, how can you say that?"

"With my mouth," she said bluntly. "If you prefer, I'll send it in a letter. Now. Are you coming home, or do I have to put the boys on an airplane for Chicago?"

Angelica closed her eyes. Her mamá would do it, too. She never made a threat she wasn't willing to follow through on.

"All right, all right. I'll check the flights. I'll come home as soon as possible."

"Gracias."

Her mamá sounded both gratified and grateful. She never minced her words, nor did she spare anyone's feelings when she felt the truth needed a good airing. "Love you, *mijita."*

"Love you, too, Mamá." And she meant it—hard as it was to admit sometimes.

She hung up and tilted her face to the sky. Her mother was right. Kaydon and Mason needed her. But she felt torn. She would not be able to live her life without knowing why her Will had died.

Metal clanged gently. Angelica noticed a nautical flagpole. The US flag was on top, pennants running down the sides in the shape of a triangle. She kept staring as the breeze played with the colorful fabrics, not sure why she was so fascinated. The image was quintessential of Lake Geneva.

The breeze wisped a leaf across the path in front of her, drawing her eye. The paved trail seemed to run infinitely in either direction along the shore. Her feet felt compelled to move. To follow.

She got up and walked, choosing the right-hand side at random. The path led past the marina, then plunged into the trees. From there, it seemed to open straight into someone's yard, switching from pavement to gravel. She wondered if it was okay to keep going, then noticed other walkers on the trail. Despite being so cozy with the lakeside houses—coming between them and their own piers—it was apparently a public walkway. Fascinated, she kept going.

The houses were immaculate, well-appointed on open green lawns. Shingle, Cape Cod, farmhouse—they were each beautifully executed.

Some were clearly original to the late nineteenth and early twentieth centuries, flawlessly maintained or restored. Whether the main color was delft or beige or dove, white trim was a going theme, tying in with the white piers on the shore, adding to the air of light and leisure that embraced Lake Geneva.

The breeze caught Angelica's hair. Like a gentle hand, it caressed her face, pulling her attention toward the water. A bright yellow catamaran eased past, its sails full of the wind. She smiled. Roland had spoken of the catamaran that had been Bobby, Fritz, and Jason's pride and joy.

And then she noticed the young sailors out on the boat. Three pre-teen boys. She stared, feeling as if she were seeing a ghost from the past. The boys laughed and teased, but handled their craft expertly, tacking into the wind. She watched until they were a dot on the horizon.

The wind touched her face again, and with it, she thought she heard a voice.

Angelica.

The voice was Will's. It sounded not only like her husband, but like something that had sprung from the very ground she stood on, as if his voice and this lake vibrated to the same frequency. As if their souls were one and the same. As if this were the place he had always belonged.

I wanted so badly to bring you here.

She blinked and a tear rolled down her cheek. If Will had wanted to show her this place, why didn't he *say* something? Why did he lie to her? About everything? She whispered through gritted teeth. "You do not betray your family. You betrayed your own sons. You betrayed *me.*"

Some deep part of her mind continued to breathe the things she imagined Will would try to say to her.

I'm sorry. I never thought I'd have a family. Not after what I'd done. I tried so hard not to fall in love with you. I tried so hard...

It was true. The heat had been so strong, from the moment they met. And yet he'd taken an eternity to ask her out, after weeks of clumsily trying to avoid her.

Would it have been better if we'd never met? his voice seemed to ask, hesitating.

She thought of the moments they'd shared together, from the giddy highs of falling in love, to the lows of family emergencies, to the mundane tasks of doing dishes together. She thought of her two boys. How Will had treated her like both a queen and an invalid for the entirety of each pregnancy. How he had been there for each delivery. How his eyes had glowed when he held his sons. How he had cried with her and kissed her with passion and joy.

And then she thought how every moment of that journey had been a complete and utter lie.

She locked her jaw as the tears came hot and fast, blurring her view of the lake.

"Yes," she spat out. "It would have been better if we never met."

Chapter Thirty-One
BAILEY

Who would have thought there was a website called "Find a Grave dot com"? But there is, and that's how I figured out where my dad was buried.

Though what had possessed me to look it up, I don't even know. It wasn't like I was ever going there.

On Wednesday morning, my day off, I pushed my bike out of the weeds growing beside Bud's garage, strapped on my helmet, and started pedaling. The cemetery was five miles outside of town. I'd never biked beyond the city limits before. But in a matter of minutes, I found myself pedaling along the shoulder of the highway like some health enthusiast, jumping out of my skin every time a car zipped by.

This was dumb. I told myself I could turn back whenever I felt like it. But I never did. I kept going. I told myself it was because the farms were pretty, with their silos and big, red barns.

Before I knew it, I was staring at an iron fence along the highway and the headstones beyond. I got off my bike and walked until I found the gate. Then I leaned my bike against a tree and started looking for fresh graves.

The first one wasn't it, but I got all nervous-excited anyway, just to find a totally different name on the temporary plaque. I didn't let myself get so worked up the next time, even though the name on a nearby stone said MARTA THOMLIN.

My stomach twisted into knots. Nearby stones said HENRY THOMLIN. ELAINA THOMLIN. SEBASTIAN THOMLIN.

I made a double take on the last one, my mind scrambling. Sebastian was Tommy's real name. It took me forever to notice there wasn't any end date. It was a double headstone, like for a husband and wife. The name on the left... Elaina. She'd died ten years ago.

I sat in the grass in front of the graves and wrapped my arms around my knees. So. This was my family. This was where I came from. Elaina, my grandmother. Henry. Maybe a great-uncle or something. Based on the dates, he was two years younger than Tommy and died young. And Marta? My great-grandmother. That tombstone was really old.

Did I seriously belong to these people?

And why did they all have to be dead?

I finally pulled together my courage and turned to the new grave. The one on the right. The dirt was heaped on top of it with sod rolled over that. A little brass plate read JASON THOMLIN.

Jason.

My dad.

For the next eternity and a half, I just sat there and stared. This was the guy I'd been looking for all my life. My hero who was supposed to swoop down and rescue me. He was supposed to explain that communist spies had been holding him captive for the past sixteen years, and that was the only reason he never came for me. But he'd escaped—past concrete walls and razor wire and search dogs and flood lights—and he'd combed the world over until he found me. And then he was supposed to bring me to a cozy little cottage on the seashore with ivy growing up the chimney, and he was supposed to sit me down and hold me close and promise that he would never, never leave me again.

But he was dead.

Maybe replaying my fantasies was a bad idea. My eyes got all watery, and my nose started to run.

The newspapers said he was a bank burglar. A high-profile thief. A fugitive. A murderer. Even Tommy said so.

I didn't care what he was. I just wanted to know one thing.

I rubbed my nose on the back of my arm and tried to see anything past the curtains of tears now streaming from my eyes. My ears felt hot. My voice was in a noose. I croaked the words out anyway.

"Did you love me, Daddy?" That's all I'd ever wanted to know.

But of course, he'd never had the chance to love me or not.

THURSDAY, JULY 17, 2014

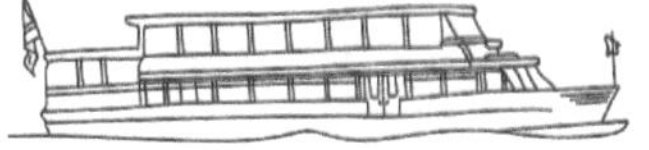

CHAPTER THIRTY-TWO
ANGELICA

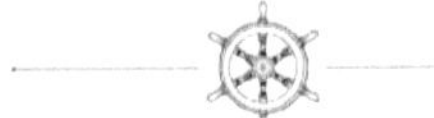

Raindrops plinked the window beside Angelica's booth. She clutched a warm mug of coffee between her hands, studying the emblem of a red rooster and the words Egg Harbor Cafe. Every time the door opened, she looked up. But it was never Roland. She tapped the mug impatiently. He'd agreed to change their appointment to a morning meal, but he'd only gotten back to Lake Geneva late last night. She felt guilty rolling him out of bed.

Glancing through the rain-streaked window, she saw her rental car, waiting in a nearby stall. She'd return it to O'Hare later this morning. And then she'd board her plane for LAX. She was leaving Lake Geneva in a matter of hours. Worried as she was about Kaydon and Mason, her heart twinged a little at the thought of leaving this place, and not just because of her unfinished investigation.

Thanks largely to Roland, she'd gotten to know Lake Geneva in a different light than she'd expected—the way Will had known it. Not as the place where he had died, but the place where he had lived. Where he had grown up. Where he had laughed and played and made friends and built an entire life and dreamed of a future.

Forgiveness was still a long way off. But at least she had solved one mystery: the identity of the man she had married. She had context now. A depth of personal and family history she'd never known, in all their years together. It was something.

The bell above the cafe door rang. Angelica's eyes flashed upward. The patron who entered was Roland. She smiled and sighed in relief. She would get to speak with him one last time before she left.

He paused to talk with the hostess, who pointed out Angelica's table. He nodded, then hurried over. In honor of the weather, he'd donned a thicker sweater, cream-colored with knitted cables and carved wooden buttons. He slid into the booth opposite Angelica and reached for both her hands.

"My dear, I'm so glad I caught you before you left."

She smiled weakly. "I need to get home to my boys."

"Of course you must. Are you all right? You sounded distressed when we spoke over the phone."

She took a deep breath, then told him in more detail of her failed quests at the county courthouse and the police station. She described her terror at practically coming face-to-face with Wade himself. But nothing had happened since, so surely she was overthinking the encounter. Regardless, her investigation had reached a dead end, unless the county clerk in Elkhorn actually managed to find some documents that weren't tied up by secrecy laws. Even then, she'd have to be lucky enough for such a record to provide proof that Wade was, in fact, guilty of murder. Or that there had been a mistrial. Or a flaw in the investigation. And what were the odds of finding anything so obvious?

Deflated, Angelica leaned on her hand and stared across the table at her friend. "What do I do, Roland? I don't know where to go next."

He drummed his fingers together, a pensive look on his face. Then he cocked a smile. "For starters, we order breakfast. An investigation such as this really does call for a full stomach."

Angelica allowed an exhausted smile to slip across her face. He was probably right.

Roland ordered hash browns and fried eggs, sunny-side-up, while Angelica asked for toast and fruit. Once the waiter took the menus away, Roland folded his hands and looked Angelica squarely in the eye.

"First of all, I wouldn't discount a clue that isn't yet firmly in your hand. You don't know what your friend at the courthouse may turn up. Whatever she finds, it probably won't be a smoking gun in the hands of Wade Erickson." He tilted his head. "But it might point toward another door. A door you haven't tried yet. Don't give up too quickly."

Angelica nodded. Of course he was right. She wasn't known for her patience. She wanted the first door she opened to have all the answers.

"Second, we may not have to give up on those reports from the police station."

Angelica sat upright. "What do you mean? Is there still a chance?" She shrank into her seat again. "Roland, I don't think I can go back there."

He waved a finger. “Neither you nor I shall go anywhere near it. You forget, I have connections. Your media ruse wasn’t a bad idea, but what if an actual reporter requested the records?”

Angelica’s eyes widened. “Do you know someone?”

Roland grinned and twiddled his thumbs. “I believe I have an old favor I can call in. The man could get secrets from a marble statue. If those documents can be had, they will be had. Frankly, I don’t know why we didn’t try this in the first place.”

Tears nearly threatened to fall. “Roland, you’re wonderful.”

He waved a hand. “Don’t thank me yet. There’s still every chance that, despite all our efforts, we may come up empty-handed. Should that prove the case...” He spread his palms. “Where shall we turn next? We may as well plan our moves ahead of time.”

Angelica rested her chin on her hands, fingers laced, and searched the corners of the room for ideas. “The shootout, the end of the Markham Ring—this was a major case. Would other agencies have helped with the investigation?” Police departments did that sort of thing, didn’t they? Crime reports in the papers always ended with a list of agencies that were assisting.

"In fact, I believe other agencies *were* involved," said Roland. "The Walworth County Sheriff's Office, as a matter of course. Chicago, Milwaukee, Madison—their departments would have wanted their fingers in the pie; it was their banks that were broken into. Perhaps a smattering of other agencies, both local and state. I'll have my reporter friend inquire after them all."

"You're wonderful." Another idea leapt to Angelica's mind. "We should speak with Jason's father, Tommy."

Roland leaned back, an expression of warning on his face. "That may not get you where you think it will."

She frowned. "Why not?"

"Wade and I may have parted ways, but he and Tommy have always remained close."

"How close?"

"I have it from the grapevine that Tommy is spending his recovery at Wade's house."

Angelica stared at Roland, slack-jawed. "But Wade was the one who shot him!"

Roland twisted his head and spoke haltingly, as if the full horror of the situation were forming in his mind. "If Wade is the missing fourth member, then yes."

Angelica reached for his wrist. "You have to talk to him. To warn him. He has to get out of that house."

Roland leaned back, pressing his fingers to his chest. "But will he believe me? They've been best friends since they were boys. They're more than brothers to each other. And once again, we lack evidence. How am I to convince him?"

Angelica shrugged. "Maybe you don't need to. Ask him to find out for himself." She leaned forward and pressed her finger into the table. "He's in Wade's house. Maybe there's evidence. Ask him to look."

"Recruit him?" Roland's expression was dubious. "I'll do my best, but I make no promises."

Angelica shook her head. "You have to try. Tommy's in danger as long as he's in that house."

Roland nodded somberly.

Angelica leaned back in her booth, satisfied that she'd won that argument. "Who else can we talk to?"

Roland twirled his thumbs. "Monica Steele may prove an invaluable ally."

Angelica stiffened. "The detective?"

"That's right. Do you know her?"

"She flew out to California to interview me after Will's death."

"Did she?"

Angelica nodded, memories of the woman's coolness spinning icicles in her brain. "I don't like her."

"Whyever not?"

"She's a cold, heartless bitch—pardon my French."

Roland's mouth initially fell open, and then he quirked his head, conceding her point. "Well, I can't say you're wrong..."

Angelica nodded conclusively. "How do you know her?"

"Well, after your husband's remains were left on my property and a warning written in blood on my window, she's had occasion to come around."

Angelica nodded her head side-to-side. Fair. But the real question... "Do you trust her?"

"She is the most sensible, clear-sighted woman I know. She harbors no fools." He raised a finger. "Which is a vital point. She's Wade's protégé. Getting her to turn against him may prove no easier than Tommy."

Angelica raised her eyebrows in surprise, then shrugged, trying not to look too delighted. "Then we leave her out of it."

"Sooner or later, we may have no choice. Once we have evidence, who do we give it to?"

"Anyone. Another agency. The state police."

"And then what will happen to the evidence you paid your blood, sweat, and tears for? Will it be taken seriously—the findings of an untrained civilian? Will law enforcement prove reluctant to turn against its own? What if your evidence isn't conclusive? What if it's merely suggestive? What if it gets trapped in differences of opinion? Departmental politics? Bureaucratic nonsense? No. When you pass this baton, it needs to come to the hands of someone who will carry it over the finish line."

Angelica scowled. "And why is that Monica Steele? You said yourself, she's Wade's protégé."

Roland grinned. "You yourself described her as a 'cold, heartless bitch.' And that is what makes her the right woman for the job. She will never put a personal friendship, however close, above doing the right thing—of that, I'm sure. That woman has a moral code engraved in iron."

Angelica let the thought soak in. If Roland was right, then no doubt that was why Steele had been so heartless during their interview. Finding the truth was simply more important to her than catering to Angelica's raw emotions at the time. Still…

"I don't like her."

Roland dropped his chin and twirled his thumbs. "Fair. But when the time comes, I do hope you'll heed my advice."

"And until then, I hope you won't let her know we had this conversation—or any other. I don't like her, I don't trust her, and I don't want her anywhere near this investigation."

Roland sighed. "Agreed. I won't speak of it without consulting you first."

Angelica nodded, satisfied.

The waiter breezed to a stop at their table. "Sunny-side up?"

"Ah!" Roland smiled and raised a finger.

The young man set down their plates, and when he was assured that they had everything they needed, he left.

Roland unfurled a napkin and laid it on his lap. "Enough detective work. You have but an hour left in

Lake Geneva. Let it be a pleasant one." He raised his water glass.

Angelica smiled in acquiescence and tinked his glass with hers. She knew these last few moments would slip by far too quickly. She already knew she would be coming back—as soon as she felt the boys would be okay without her.

But she also knew, beyond the shadow of a doubt, that she would have to be desperate to work with Monica Steele.

Chapter Thirty-Three
ANGELICA

They stepped out of the cafe, under a bright red awning. Roland folded up a worn leather wallet and tucked it into his cardigan pocket; he'd insisted on paying.

"Well!" he said cheerily. "Are you ready for the road?"

Angelica tilted her head and watched the water run from the edge of the canopy. She had arrived in Lake Geneva in rain, and she was leaving in rain. And yet her feelings now were so vastly different from what they were then. In ways, no less confused. But somehow, Lake Geneva rain carried with it memories of sunshine. It splashed the sidewalks with echoes of laughter and washed the streets in hope. She had never seen rain like this. She had never been to a place like this.

She didn't want to leave. In the short week she had been here, the lake had somehow burrowed through her skin, become a part of her soul, filled her with its own peculiar light and promise and hope. The sensation was so subtle, it defied description or even notice. She imagined a lifelong resident like Roland never even saw the light peeking out through his own eyes, glowing in the wrinkles of his skin. But it was in him, just as it was now in her. As if the blood in her veins had been replaced with spring-fed lake water, clear as glass, glowing with sun.

The questions were still there. The pain. The betrayal. But she felt almost as if the lake itself promised the wounds would heal. The lake was glad she had come.

She tilted her head and smiled at Roland wanly. "How can I ever thank you?"

"Oh, my dear, don't even mention it." He turned up the collar of his cardigan. The damp air carried the smell of wool with the lanolin still in it, and Angelica noticed a raindrop roll off the sleeve instead of soaking in. "I'm so glad you came," Roland went on. "I can't tell you how deeply I appreciate getting to know you. I'm so glad Fritz found you."

Angelica nodded but could offer no smile.

Roland took her hand in his. "Remember him the way you always knew him. Remember him happy, as I do. There were very few moments in his life when he wasn't truly happy."

Maybe. One day. When she was ready. "You'll let me know as soon as you hear something from your reporter friend?" she asked.

"Of course. Immediately. And you must let me know when you have a reply from the courthouse."

"I will."

"Excellent." His eyebrows lifted. "Oh! I almost forgot. Wait here a moment."

Roland stepped off the sidewalk into the rain and unlocked his car, a black Cadillac SUV with silver trim. He opened the door, took something from the passenger seat, and tucked it under his sweater. Then he jogged back to the awning, shrugging his shoulders against the rain.

"Here," he said, removing a bulky, square item from under his cardigan.

Angelica gasped, recognizing the rich, dark red hue of the padded leather cover. "Your photo album."

He pushed it toward her. “Take it. It’s yours.”

“But there are so many pictures of Bobby in here.”

Roland waved his hand dismissively. “I have millions. My wife was a little camera happy. Please, it would honor me if you had this.”

Angelica folded the album to her chest with one arm, then leaned forward and wrapped Roland in a hug with the other. “Thank you,” she said, forcing herself to hold back tears.

Roland seemed surprised by her gesture, but quickly settled into the embrace. “You’re very welcome.” He pulled back. “If you need anything at all, don’t hesitate to pick up the phone. And bring those boys of yours to visit sometime. I don’t have the catamaran anymore, but we could fire up the old steam yacht. Take them on a grand tour of the lake, the old-fashioned way.”

Angelica nodded. “Yes, I will bring the boys. Definitely.” Maybe not on her next trip. Not if she was still investigating. But later. One day when she had more answers for her sons. Coming here might prove healing for them.

“Good. Well, then. Have a safe flight.”

“I will.”

Angelica smiled, then turned and got into her car. Once she'd turned both the ignition and the windshield wipers, she paused to wave, then pulled out into traffic. She drove towards the highway slowly, trying to soak in every last glimpse of the town, the trees, and the lake beyond. Trying to drink a few last drops of the mystic light that lived here. Trying to reconcile it with the darkness that still filled her soul.

Yes. She would be coming back. Soon.

CHAPTER THIRTY-FOUR
MONICA

Angelica Read. The name popped into my head as if it had been on the tip of my tongue since the day I first saw her in Lake Geneva, almost a week ago. My unmarked vehicle moved at a crawl down Main Street through traffic already growing thick for the upcoming weekend, never mind the rain. The petite Hispanic woman with the long, dark hair had embraced Roland Markham, then gotten into a black sedan with Illinois plates and driven away. I was too far away to read the numbers, but it was probably a rental.

What on earth was she doing here? Details of my interview with her in Los Angeles flashed through my mind. She'd sat on her fancy white sofa, looked me in the eye, and swore she'd never heard of Lake Geneva before. That she'd never met her husband's childhood friends, Bobby and Jason. In fact, she denied that Fritz Geissler was her husband at all. She insisted his rightful name was Will Read and that he had been born and raised in Grand Rapids, Michigan.

Then why was she here? Hugging Bobby Markham's father? When I interviewed her at her home, my conclusion was that she had been as deceived as anyone about her husband's identity and background. But was she?

I slipped into her parking spot and hopped out of the SUV. Roland was still standing under the awning outside Egg Harbor, hands in his cardigan pockets as he watched Angelica drive away.

"Hey, Roland." Rain tapped against my black weatherproof jacket with the embroidered badge on the left breast.

"Monica." Roland grinned, straightening as he saw me. "How are you this fine, wet day?"

I stepped next to him under the protection of the canopy and nodded at the retreating black sedan. "Wasn't that Angelica Read?" I pushed my hands into my pockets to keep them warm.

"Why, yes. She mentioned you two had met."

"How do you know her?"

"We bumped into each other at the library. Struck up a conversation and found out we had… well, that we had common connections."

I shifted an eyebrow. They'd just happened to meet… at the library? Then again, what were the alternatives? That she and Roland had known each other all along? If that were the case, how? She'd married Fritz years after he vanished. If Roland knew her, then he'd known where Fritz was—and never told me. The initial investigation had cleared him of any involvement in the Markham Ring—I'd double checked every detail personally.

The next possibility was that Angelica had sought Roland out on purpose. I remembered her tears and shouts during our interview. She'd been the inconsolable, terrified, disbelieving wife—not buying for a minute that her husband was a fugitive living under a false identity.

But did I buy that? How could a woman be married to a guy for fifteen years and have no idea who he really was?

"She's a long way from LA," I commented.

"Yes." Roland shrugged. "Well, you can understand, I'm sure. Her husband's death, the truth of his past—such a shock. She came to see the place where he grew up."

"Why?" I asked, perhaps too bluntly.

Roland looked at me, befuddled, offended even. "To get to know him. Granted, most people square that away during the dating phase, but not every couple is that traditional."

I couldn't help grinning acknowledgment of his witty and annoyed comeback. I nodded my chin in the direction Angelica had driven. "Looks like you two hit it off."

"Yes. We had many memories to exchange."

"What did you tell her?"

Roland's sky-blue eyes turned a little harder. "Everything I could," he said firmly. "She has a right to know, don't you agree?"

I decided to try to cool the conversation down. "Sure, yeah," I said with a generous shrug. But was it really a coincidence that she'd managed to find Roland Markham, one of the few people in Lake Geneva who had known all three members of the Markham Ring intimately? What did she want from him?

"You're upset with me, aren't you?" Roland went on. "You think I've told her too much."

"I didn't say that."

"But you thought it. Tell me, Monica, does solving crime mean we must all cease to be decent people? She lost her husband."

I sighed. I hadn't wanted this to turn into an argument. "I just want you to stay safe," I said. "I don't know much about Angelica Read—"

He pointed across the street. "You don't know much about that woman, either, I'll wager." He'd indicated a random shopper with paper boutique bags in her hand and an umbrella over her shoulder.

Heat rose to my face, despite the cold in the air. His point was irrelevant. "Angelica was directly connected to one of the members of the Markham Ring—a member whose murder is still unsolved." I motioned toward the lake. "We found his body at the end of *your* pier. Did you tell her that?"

Roland met my gaze and nodded soberly. "Yes, I did." In the tense silence that followed, the raindrops drummed on the awning. "You believe she's a suspect?"

"At the least, she's a witness who has proved very uncooperative."

"Well. I won't interfere with your job. Mistrust is the price you paid, I suppose, when you donned the badge." He lifted his thin white eyebrows. "Lucky for me, I never took any such oaths of office. Which means I can blithely go on treating her like any decent human being—one who just lost her husband violently and tragically."

I wasn't sure if his naivety made me love him or hate him. I sighed. "Promise me you'll be careful."

He grinned. "If I had a dollar for every time you told me to be careful, I'd be a rich man."

I scoffed. "You *are* a rich man. But you'll be a *dead* rich man if you don't start taking that promise more seriously."

"Well." Roland smiled. "I can think of a number of charities that will be delighted to finally receive my estate."

I groaned and turned away. My conversations with him made me feel as if I were running in a hamster wheel. I felt his hand on my arm and looked at him again.

"I don't mean to distress you, Monica. I'm sorry."

Well, that was something anyway. I sighed. "Will you let me know if Angelica does or says anything strange?"

He hesitated, mouth open as if he wanted to speak but thought better of it.

I frowned. "Roland, what do you know? What has she said to you?"

He groaned. "I really do think the two of you need to sit down and have a good talk sometime."

"We already had a talk."

"It wasn't a very good one."

"Well, don't worry. I have every intention of talking to her again."

"All she wants is to know who killed her husband and why."

"I'll notify her as soon as we have information."

Roland looked away and rocked on the balls of his feet. "Unless she notifies you first," he muttered absently.

"What's that?" His meaning clicked into place. "She's investigating her husband's death?"

Roland looked momentarily guilty, as if he'd said something he wasn't supposed to. But immediately afterwards, he turned defensive. "Well, can you blame her? It's been three weeks without a scrap of information. The girl is starving for answers."

"Has she found anything?"

"No. Of course not. You know best that clues to this case aren't exactly littering the ground."

I nodded, feeling justified. "But you'll tell me if she finds anything?"

"As I've already said, the two of you ought to sit down and have a good talk."

"Work with her?"

"Well, yes. Why not?"

"She's not law enforcement."

"And she wasn't born yesterday, either. I think you're missing an opportunity."

"Duly noted. In the meantime, you'll at least tell me if she says or does anything strange?"

He scoffed. "I hardly think—"

I hardened my gaze. "Roland, I'm about to investigate the very real possibility that Angelica Read knew exactly who her husband was and what he did. I don't know how deeply involved she could be or what her goals and motives are. And so I want to know why she came here and why she's talking to *you*, someone who knew Bobby, Fritz, and Jason closely. She could be playing you for information."

His brow went stormy—an expression I'd never seen on him before. "I've told you why she came."

"And I'll accept that—for now. In the meantime, please, *please* be careful."

"I promise," he said, underscoring his words with a lift of his shoulders. "If Angelica does or says anything strange, you will be the first to know."

"Good." I pulled the car keys out of my pocket and stepped back into the rain. "Stay safe," I said, pointing a finger at him.

"Duly noted," he said, throwing my own words back at me.

I wagged my head and got back into the SUV. There was no helping Roland Markham, and it annoyed the piss out of me.

Chapter Thirty-Five
ROLAND

Roland watched Monica drive away and sighed, squeezing his hands into fists inside his pockets. Well. He'd already gone back on his promise to Angelica not to mention her investigation. No doubt she'd be furious. Still, he had said nothing about her primary theory: that Wade Erickson was a member of the Markham Ring. And besides, he'd stood by his convictions; Monica and Angelica *should* speak to each other, and not in an interrogation. Then Angelica could air her beliefs herself.

Meanwhile, Angelica had given him work to do. He pulled his phone out of his pocket, stared at it, and sighed. May as well get the hardest task out of the way first.

He found Tommy Thomlin in his contacts and pressed his number.

Chapter Thirty-Six
TOMMY

My phone rang just as I was rolling up the TheraBands my physical therapist had given me. She'd taught me a number of exercises I could do while seated, and as such, I was taking up a well-cushioned recliner in the living room, listening to the radio while I worked on max reps. So far, I could do all of five without a break. Regardless of my prowess, Nancy was impressed by my self-motivation. They say all you need is the right reason—and Bailey was as strong a reason as they come.

I reached for my phone, half wondering if it could possibly be Bailey, finally returning my call.

It wasn't. The screen said Roland Markham.

I frowned. We barely talked these days unless it had to do with his mail. He generally preferred to call me directly, rather than the cruise line office. But he could read the barometer and knew where my loyalty lay. Much as I hated choosing between my two oldest friends, Wade had been right to take a firm stance with Bobby when Roland couldn't. Still, I'd always felt like a middle child, trapped between siblings and wishing there were a way to keep the peace.

I picked up. "Well, hello, Roland. How are you?"

"I'm fine, Tommy, fine. The better question is, how are you? You sound well."

"Oh, I'm staying pretty snug." I avoided mentioning that I was at Wade's house. In addition to being instructed against doing so, I felt no need to open old wounds between Roland and Wade.

"I was shocked when I heard the news. I'm so sorry."

I tried to formulate a response and realized I didn't know what to say. There was no etiquette surrounding how to talk about an attempt on your life.

No. He'd never meant to kill me. He'd said so himself. I frowned as fleeting memories teased at the edge of conscious thought. What he'd wanted was to *play* with my life.

My gaze slowly fixated on the radio. My mind tumbled down a long, black tunnel. At the other end was another place. Another voice. I found words that were seared into my memory without my even knowing.

"There's no fun in killin', did'ya know that? I kill you, it's over. But this way?" He smirked. "You'll never be the same man again, Tommy. I promise you that."

"Tommy? Hello? Are you there?"

Roland's voice chased me down the tunnel. Nagged at the corners of my awareness. Introduced discord into my reality. Shattered the images playing before me. It wasn't real. I was pulled back up the tunnel, moving faster and faster, until I emerged again in the recliner in Wade's living room, staring at the radio.

I shook my head, confused, trying to grasp what was real and suddenly realizing I was talking to Roland. "I'm sorry, what did you say?" How long had I checked out?

"I was just asking, is it true that you're staying at Wade's house?"

Well. The secret was out, then. My heart sank. How common was that knowledge? "Where'd you hear that?" I knew better than to outright admit it.

"Oh, I had it from Brian. He said that's where Robb Landis was forwarding all the cards and flowers that were showing up at the cruise line office."

Well, that was that. If Brian knew, then everyone knew. He was too affable and simple-minded to realize that he shouldn't spread that information. I'd have to tell Wade that my whereabouts were no longer a secret.

"I was just curious," Roland went on, "I don't suppose you've noticed anything... unusual while you've been at Wade's?"

"What do you mean?"

"Oh, I don't know. Everyone's behaving normally? I mean—they're treating you well?"

Behaving normally? What was that supposed to mean? The question was so odd, I asked myself again whether I was experiencing the real world or lost in some other daydream.

Still, it made the most sense to continue the conversation. I eyed the stack of books, glass of water, and plate of healthy snacks Nancy had left within arm's reach of the recliner. "I haven't been so coddled since I was six months old."

"Oh, really? And you're allowed to go out, of course?"

"I'm sure I would be, if I could cross a room on my own."

"Ah. I see." He sounded disappointed, like someone who hadn't gotten the answer he wanted.

Why was the conversation so bizarre? "Roland, what's this all about?"

He groaned under his breath. "It's nothing, Tommy. I'm sure of it. You see, a friend of mine—well, we were examining the facts at hand and there's a remote possibility…" He trailed off.

"Spit it out." We were both too old to dally around like this.

Roland sighed. "There's talk of a fourth member of Bobby's old ring. Our sons are gone, Tommy. Who else could be cleaning house?"

Cleaning house. The words left in blood on both my window and Roland's. My retribution had already come for me but failed.

No, that made no sense. *There's no fun in killin'.* If the man who shot me was some fourth member of the Markham Ring bent on cleaning house, why was I still alive? Why did he spare me?

To toy with me. That's what he'd said. Why did he want to toy with me?

I stared at the vivid memories, lost at the end of the black tunnel. Screwing up my courage, I stepped into the darkness. Reached out. Pushed against the memories, trying to touch them, to see them clearly. But the images resisted, like frosted glass. Now that I wanted them, they wouldn't come. But I knew there was a reason why my assailant had attacked me. He'd *told* me the reason. What was it...?

"Whoever this fourth member is, he's shown a keen interest in anyone even remotely connected to the old gang—even next of kin."

I stared at the blurred memories. A keen interest, yes, hence the warnings drawn in blood. But the fourth member hadn't acted on his threats. Roland was alive. I'd been attacked by someone else, so far as I could tell. Why hadn't the fourth member acted on his threats? Why had I instead been left to the mercy of some other lunatic with some other agenda? *What was that agenda?*

And then the frosted glass cracked. Vanished. But the scene I saw wasn't the assailant kneeling over me. I saw my son Jason. Alive. Our last conversation as we stood in darkness in my own backyard. I didn't know it then, but it was mere hours before he was murdered.

"I gotta tell you something. I don't have much time..."

The words played through my mind, but I glanced around me. The recliner was real. The side table was real. The phone still pressed to my ear was real. This wasn't a flashback. I was in control of this moment. I allowed myself to explore the memory. There were answers here. Answers I needed to know.

I remembered his pleading tone. But I'd been furious with him and his every life choice, from allowing himself to be dragged into Bobby's schemes, to murdering a cop to save his own skin. Worst of all, I was livid that he had gotten his girlfriend pregnant and then abandoned both of them without so much as knowing about the child. That child was my mail jumper, Bailey, and she was doing her best to survive in an abusive home.

"Please, you don't know what's coming," Jason pleaded.

But *he* had. Somehow, he had known everything—who the fourth member was and what he wanted—but in my pride and self-righteousness, I hadn't let him get a word in edgewise. The next thing I knew, he was dead.

And I knew who had killed him.

I turned to another pane of opaque glass. A memory I was hesitant to trigger. But there were answers. I needed them. I touched the glass, and it shattered.

I breathed. Fought against the pain. Struggled to keep my mind clear. "You killed my son." It wasn't a question.

The head bobbed, the sunlight from behind blurring all his features. "He went down blazin'," the man assured me.

"Why did you kill my son?"

He shrugged. "Money."

Squaring my jaw, I stroked the leather arms of the recliner. Felt the seams and the stitches. The cracked, supple edges, worn by use. I was still here. I was still in control. I kept asking questions.

Had the man who shot me simply lied to torture me more? Or was it true? Was he in fact related to the Markham Ring? Was he the fourth member? If so, who hired him to kill Jason? Why? And why did he shoot me? Shoot me, but not kill me?

"Tommy," Roland went on.

His voice didn't have as far to tug me this time. I had avoided drowning in the memories. They didn't dominate my mind, controlling me like a rogue sailor hauling lines he shouldn't. I was the captain now. Why wasn't I always? How did I have the bars stripped from my shoulders sometimes? The helm pried from my hands?

"Tommy," Roland went on, "have you ever considered that..." He sighed heavily. "Well, that Wade could be the fourth member of the ring?"

His words brought my swirling thoughts to a screeching halt. The entire ship crashed on rocks neither I nor the rogue sailor had known were there.

"Wade?" I repeated, incredulous.

"Well, yes. Consider it—"

But I couldn't. Not even for a moment. "Wade wouldn't kill my son."

Roland paused. What he said next, he said flatly but tinged with anger. "He killed mine."

The hull scraped harder against the rocks. What was happening? What was this conversation anymore? "It's not the same," I blurted. "That was self-defense, Roland. He had no choice." I knew immediately it was the wrong thing to say.

His voice was cold. "Yes. I've heard his story."

"Story? You think he lied?"

"I'm merely saying he had room to do so, if he chose."

I shook my head. This was insanity. Maybe I shouldn't have left Roland to himself for so long. I couldn't begrudge him his anger, nor for directing it at Wade. But was this what he was doing all alone in that big house? Concocting wild theories?

"I'm merely suggesting there are oddities," Roland went on. "For instance, what drew Wade's attention to those burglaries in the first place? They had nothing to do with Lake Geneva. And then what would induce the boys to target a bank *here,* of all places? Conveniently in *Wade's* jurisdiction?"

Did Roland really not know the answers? "The burglaries drew Wade's attention because they had Bobby's personality all over them. And Bobby chose a bank in Lake Geneva because he was cocky and wanted to pull one over on his own hometown. Wade caught him in the act because he knew Bobby was in town and he knew by then what to look for. Wade told me everything. Everything he was free to talk about, at least."

"I understand," said Roland. "You don't believe me. Frankly, I'm not sure I believe me, either. The only reason I mention it is because—well, I'm worried. You're there. In his house. And if there were a remote possibility the theory were true, I wouldn't count myself any kind of friend if I said nothing."

"If your theory is true, then Wade not only murdered my son; he had me shot, too. And now he's putting me up while I recover? What would be the point?"

"You don't have to believe me. I only want you to keep your eyes open. You should be careful."

"And you? I hear Monica Steele's got her hands full trying to get you to take your own security more seriously. Your bank balance isn't going to leap between you and a bullet, Roland."

He was silent, and I realized I'd utterly failed at stopping while I was ahead. In all the long years we'd known each other, the vast disparity in our financial situations had never been an issue. I had truly never cared that his checkbook could lap mine twenty times. If anything, I'd pitied him when we were boys. He was growing up alone and unloved in that vast mansion while his parents dallied in society and finance. So why was I rubbing his wealth in his face now? Was I that upset he suspected Wade?

"Should you ever find that I'm right," he said, "I recommend you say something to Monica. Nothing leapt between *you* and a bullet, either."

He hung up.

I sighed and slapped my phone down on the side table.

The kitchen door opened. Nancy's voice called from the kitchen. "Tommy! Ready for PT?"

PT? It couldn't be that time already.

But then the mantle clock, a stately antique that had been in Nancy's family for generations, groaned to life and struck the hour.

Chapter Thirty-Seven
ROLAND

Roland paced beneath the awning in front of Egg Harbor, fuming. What was wrong with this town? Monica was convinced a mourning widow could be a murder suspect, and Tommy couldn't fathom Wade killing his son.

Well, Roland could picture it just fine. As clearly as if he'd stood in that alley, watching as Wade pulled the trigger and the light left Bobby's eyes.

He had been surprised at just how vehemently he'd defended Angelica's argument. The theory was based on nothing but conjecture and suspicion, with literally nothing to back it up. Well, perhaps Tommy's naivety had pushed him beyond the point of resistance. After all, why was Tommy's son more special than his?

Chapter Thirty-Eight
BUD

Rain was lousy for business. The morning's mist had turned to a regular downpour, and no one was coming into the bar besides a handful of the boys. They sat on stools drinking beer, chewing the fat, and half-interestedly watching a replay of last Sunday's ball game. Bud polished his taps, running a soft chamois into every nook. There were few things more beautiful than a gleaming row of stainless steel taps. He'd cleaned the bar, too, rubbing in the polish until the wood glowed. The chips in the finish only added character, as did the stickers from various beer companies. He loved that bar. Just wished he were serving more drinks on it right now...

The bell above the door chimed, and Bud looked to the front room. Skull crossed the threshold, his

Guns N' Roses tee shirt speckled with rain and his spiked hair damp. He looked tired and sorely in need of a drink.

"Well, looky, looky!" said Tony, a wiry kid who could stride confidently in any direction with any number of feet stuffed into his mouth. "Where the hell you been, Skull?"

He slid onto a stool and rested his arms on the bar, the rose-and-skull tattoo he was known for in plain view on the back of his forearm. It was a gorgeous bit of work. Bud never let on he was jealous.

"My aunt was sick. Had to head out of town." Skull nodded to Bud by way of greeting. "The usual."

Bud pulled a pint glass from the shelf and filled it with Pilsner, eying Skull through slitted eyes. The guy didn't have an aunt...

Tony didn't know that. "Sorry to hear it, man. Hope she's doing better."

Skull nodded. "She is, she is. Thanks." He nodded to the TV screen. "I missed that game. Who won?"

"Oh, my God. We creamed 'em. It's almost painful to watch, man."

"That bad, huh?"

"Eleven to two, Brewers."

"Ouch."

"I dunno," said Steve, a slouchy kid with a dopey face who somehow reminded Bud of Kung Fu Panda. "Cardinals still have a shot at Central."

Tony scowled at him. "How you figure that?"

While Steve and Tony argued the fate of the season, Bud slid the beer across the bar to Skull. He nodded his thanks and took a thirsty pull. Sometimes when Skull was busy at work, he didn't even have the chance to stop for a drink.

Bud leaned on the bar, turning his shoulder to the others. "So, where were you really?" He spoke low so no one but Skull would hear. "You told me you had five uncles, and not a girl out of the whole lot."

Skull stared past him to the TV. "I could have been talking about my mother's side."

"But you weren't, were you?"

Skull took another drink, saying nothing.

"Where were you?" said Bud.

"I had a job."

"For who?" Skull only had one line of work, and the people who paid him paid dearly. Though to anyone who asked, he was a contractor who built agricultural sites—feedlots and the like. But he was never taking new clients. His schedule was full, but thanks for asking. That is, unless you needed the co-owner of the feedlot shadowed and his every secret revealed, business or personal. Then Skull had an opening. An opening that more often than not ended in the subject of his investigation turning up dead. But the dirty work was never Skull's job. Sometimes it was Bud's.

Skull remained silent, and that made Bud hot under the collar. Granted, in their line of work, you didn't drop names unless there was a reason. But if this was a simple case of client confidentiality, why didn't Skull just say so and tell Bud to buzz off? Why was he being so cagey?

"You're not working for The Man still, are you?"

Skull sipped his beer. His lack of response was admission enough for Bud.

Bud leaned back but kept his voice low. The rest of the guys were having an animated discussion about baseball, anyway. "Aw, c'mon, how could you do that? How can you sit there drinking *my* beer and tell me you're still working for him?"

"You and I were contracted independently. When you went outside the bounds of your agreement and closed down an entity The Man never specified, your contract was canceled."

Closed down? He meant shooting Tommy Thomlin. Well, the bastard deserved it. He'd told the cops that Bailey had a black eye. Tried to get her taken away from him. Bud spread his hands. "I'm a freelancer. I can work my own gigs."

"Not when it interferes with a contract. It's all about making the customer happy, remember Bud?" Skull tilted his head and lifted his glass in a toast.

Bud leaned in and tapped the counter. "He tried to have me..." He struggled to come up with the metaphors as gracefully as Skull did. "Terminated. Don't you know that? He sicced JB on me—" he jabbed his thumb to the dish room where Jimmy Beacon used to work "—with a freakin' bomb!" He was out of metaphors—and patience. This game was stupid, anyway. "Firing me is one thing. But tryin' to blow my ass to bits? What the hell?"

Tony looked back over his shoulder. He'd heard Bud's tense tone and had a look of curiosity on his face.

Skull set the mug down and stood abruptly. "Come 'ere."

"What?"

He beckoned vigorously, making his way toward the end of the bar. "Come 'ere, come 'ere, come 'ere. C'mon."

Bud glanced at Tony and Steve. They were both staring now. Bud followed Skull. Skull grabbed him by the elbow and steered him inside the walk-in liquor cabinet behind the bar. He closed the door behind them, then whirled on Bud. Bud braced. If Skull threw him a punch in here amongst all his best liquors...

But Skull merely braced his feet and squared up to Bud. His voice was low but tense. Bud could still hear the bar music above it. "These aren't games we're playing. You know too much. You're a liability to The Man now."

Bud jabbed a finger in Skull's face. "Well, too frickin' bad. He shoulda known better than to piss me off. Calling a hit on his hit man? No way. No one's ever put a tail on me, no one's ever got the drop on me, and no one's ever had a hit on me. You got that? The Man's in deep shit now, and he's gonna pay."

Skull glared at him. "What are you saying?"

"There are two things I'm good at—cookin' and killin'. And he ain't gettin' my cookin'. You can tell him I said that, Mister Info Man." He pushed past Skull and grabbed the door handle.

"You're playing with fire, Bud."

"I'm a chef. It's my job." He swung the door open and waved his hand. "Now get out of my liquor cabinet. In fact, you can get out of my bar."

Skull glared at him, then brushed past and didn't stop until he was out the front door.

Bud didn't even care if Skull warned The Man. Once Bud decided someone was going to die...

They died.

His mind was made up.

Chapter Thirty-Nine
TOMMY

The day's rain had built to a gale by the time Nancy put dinner on the table. Since I'd been here, she and I had eaten alone every night. Apparently Wade hadn't managed to keep regular hours since the day Fritz Geissler was murdered. Nancy simply kept his dinner warm until he was able to put in an appearance.

She was scrubbing the dishes and I was in my chair in the living room, feet up with a book in my lap, when the kitchen door opened. Nancy and Wade's hellos were followed by an embrace, their nightly ritual, no matter how late. I tried not to think of my Laina, gone these fifteen years. The empty ache was still there.

Instead, I thought of my conversation with Roland. When I considered how tender and affectionate Wade was with his wife, his children, his grandkids—I felt fully justified in believing that Roland was insane. He couldn't face the fact of what his son had become—not just a thief, but a man willing to draw a gun on an old friend. And yet I understood Roland's incredulity. I still couldn't believe my own son had aligned himself with Bobby's madness.

Nancy's voice carried from the kitchen, despite keeping her tone to barely a whisper. "I think you should talk to Tommy."

"Oh?"

"There's something on his mind. I can tell."

"Okay."

"I'll fix you a plate."

"Thanks."

They kissed. Wade moved into the living room. With a scratchy rip, he pulled apart the Velcro of his duty belt. His rank gave him the privilege of dressing in office attire, but he generally opted for the uniform. Showing solidarity for the rank and file of the department was important to him. He never wanted to forget the countless hours he'd put in behind the wheel of a cruiser or what it was like being out on the street.

"Good book, Tommy?" he asked. Like every night, he blocked my view of his sidearm with his body, then slipped into his office where he kept his gun safe. I tried not to shake my head at him. I liked to think I could handle the sight of a gun. He and Nancy were going to exhaust themselves with their never-ending coddling.

I eyed my place in the book—a collection of biographies of Wisconsinites who had fought in World War II—and found I'd read the entire book in a day. "Nancy might have to make another run to the library. I'm almost through the stack she brought me."

Wade returned to the living room, removing his tie and loosening the collar of his shirt. "You're going to run out of Wisconsin history. Might have to cross over to Illinois."

"Never."

He laughed. Wisconsin's opinion of being overrun by weekenders from Illinois was infamous. But I was only being obstinate for the sake of the joke. I'd read plenty of histories of Illinois. Lake Geneva's history was so closely linked with the Windy City, it couldn't exactly be avoided.

Wade hiked up his pant legs and dropped into a nearby easy chair. "Nancy thought you had something on your mind today."

"I did. I was only waiting for you to get home to tell you about it."

"Oh, good. I was afraid I'd have to bring out the thumb screws."

I ignored Wade's lousy humor. It was a thin cover. Clearly, he thought it was his duty to nourish my mental health as well as my physical health. I couldn't wait to get back to my own house and my own routines.

Though I'd prefer if the guy who shot me was captured, first.

I looked at Wade significantly. "It's not a secret anymore that I'm here."

The lighthearted humor faded from his eyes. His businesslike cop face pushed through, an expression I was familiar with. He needed to hear details.

"I had a call from Roland today. He knew where I was. He had it from Brian Meissner, my replacement driver. If Brian knows, the whole lake knows."

Wade's brow furrowed. If he wasn't already keeping a gun by his bed, he would now.

A moment later, he wiped away his concern, sat up straight, and rolled his shoulders. "All right. Good to know." And that was all. Again, he was trying to protect me from worrying. Anyway, it wasn't like there was a lot more he could do. He already had an alarm system. And unless I'd missed my guess, he already had extra patrols going past the house. I couldn't remember that many police cars slow-cruising down this street during a normal summer. I just hoped he wouldn't ask Nancy to stay home from work to guard me. I didn't think I could swallow that many bowls of chicken noodle soup in a day.

The microwave beeped in the kitchen. Nancy peeked around the corner, wiping a glass with a tea towel. "Sweetheart, your dinner's ready."

Wade rose and moved toward the kitchen. Should I say anything about the rest of my conversation with Roland? About his suspicions of Wade? It was such insanity...

Nancy looked at me. "Tommy, I made peach cobbler. Want any?"

I shook my head. But the more I thought about it, the more I felt I should tell Wade everything. This was no time to keep him in the dark.

"Wade?"

"Yes?" he stopped where the carpet turned to tile.

"There's something else Roland said."

"Yeah?" He rested his hands on his hips and shifted his weight to one foot.

I paused. Now that it came down to it, how did you even say such a thing out loud? *Our old friend is convinced you're a serial killer.*

"I think he's going a little batty in that old house of his," I said.

"How so?"

"He thinks…" I thumbed the book, struggling one more time with how to say it. I finally just let it spill. "He thinks you're some kind of fourth member of the Markham Ring." When Wade failed to react, as if my words hadn't registered, I made it more blatant. "He thinks you killed Fritz. He thinks you killed Jason."

Nancy's mouth dropped open. The glass fell from her hand and shattered on the floor.

Wade only continued to stare, his face unreadable. I wasn't sure if he was angry at Roland…

Or me.

CHAPTER FORTY

BUD

Bud poured more whiskey into his shot glass, his hand unsteady, some of the amber liquid sloshing over the side. Leaning over unsteadily, he slammed the half-empty bottle into a pile of magazines on his living room coffee table. Then he threw back the shot. The alcohol burned down his throat, setting every muscle fiber on fire.

He stared into the TV and the sitcom showing stupid people living stupid lives. When the audience laughed, he raged. What was so funny? *What was so funny?* Why were they laughing at him? The faces on the screen morphed into the faces of his past. Pointing. Laughing. Calling him names. He was too fat. Too ugly. Too dumb. Too klutzy. And that wasn't even the worst of it. Cold rage poured through his veins. He flexed his fingers. Instead of cold glass, he felt the cold skin of his first victim.

She was so tiny. So innocent. Amelia Beacon. What had possessed him? The need to make someone else feel the numb, cold hurt that he felt. The desire had been there for so long. He was done tamping the rage down. Keeping it bottled up.

He hadn't meant to kill her. But the girl's screams had turned to sobs, and then her sobs had gone cold quiet. He had the chance to stop, and he didn't. He just kept going. He remembered looking down at the cold, dead body and feeling the icy cold fear of knowing he was a murderer. He'd ditched her body. He'd run. He'd hid. He'd waited. And after months and months went by without a single tail put on him, he felt the confident, cold certainty that no one would ever catch him. That he was invincible.

That he could kill whenever he wanted.

And kill, he did. Again and again and again...

He wiped his mouth with the back of his hand. "No one kills a killer," he muttered to the idiots on the TV screen. "No one puts a hit on the hit man."

Chapter Forty-One
SKULL

Skull stepped into his bedroom, his shoes silent on the plush white carpet. The recessed lights were dimmed, and he left them that way. He set his phone on the black walnut vanity and pressed the home button.

"Siri, play strings."

Siri chirped pleasantly and began to play soft violins, piano, and guitar. Skull breathed deeply, allowing the stress to flow off him. Tonight was the first time he'd ever been kicked out of a bar. He wasn't shocked it was Bud's bar. Bud Weber was ruled by his emotions. In the dangerous game he played, he trusted his success—his life—to luck.

Skull wasn't sure why The Man had hired Weber in the first place. But then again, raw emotions were

The Man's plaything. He molded and twisted them however he saw fit. It was art. Skull had never seen his own clandestinely-acquired information fed into such a breathtaking symphony before. So many melodies. So many counterpoints. His other clients were cave men by comparison. It was a pleasure working for The Man. Watching him at his art.

Of course, Bud was too simple to appreciate something like that. And too dumb to value his own hide. Maybe he thought his services invaluable. How would The Man finish all his plans without a hit man?

But didn't Bud see? There was no need for a hit man. The Man Upstairs could manipulate the most ordinary of souls into doing the unthinkable. He'd pushed Jimmy Beacon, a lonely teenage boy, into killing innocent people in his thirst for revenge. Everyone had a breaking point. It was merely a matter of finding that wound and leaning into it until the subject snapped.

If Bud wasn't careful, he'd make himself The Man's next object of affection. Skull didn't even consider *himself* above The Man's notice. This was definitely a client to keep happy.

He pulled his tee shirt over his head and stared into the mirror. Thorny vines embraced the *roseschadel*, cradling the cracked skull like a lost loved one. From there, they twisted up his arm, transforming into flowing wind across his shoulder, turning into a stampede of horses across his chest. From there, the ink gathered into billowing thunderheads on his right bicep, slashing his arm with lightning and rain. Hidden in the clouds was the image of a weeping woman.

He'd already lived a long life. He already had a long story to tell—though he'd never told it. Instead, he'd gone under the needle and bought a lot of ink. His right forearm was still blank. He didn't know yet what would go there. He dreamed of a glorious sunset, breaking through the clouds of the thunderstorm.

Other times he saw knives. Daggers. Blood dripping off the points and running down his fingers.

Only a handful of women had ever seen his ink in its full glory. They asked him what it meant. But Skull wasn't in the business of giving up his own information. He diverted their questions with a warning look, followed by a tantalizing kiss and a night of ever-spiraling passion. After all, a man of secrets was alluring. He knew girls in many cities, wherever his jobs took him. But none of them provided what he had lost. He didn't ask them to. Only to help him forget.

When he thought about it, the daggers were far more likely than the sunset.

The violins stopped, interrupted by his phone vibrating softly. Skull glanced at the screen. It brought up a string of numbers he'd committed to memory. He picked up his phone. His business hours were whenever his clients needed him.

"Yes?"

The Man's voice crooned low, calm, in control, like it always was. "Are you available tonight?"

Angelica Read was back in Los Angeles, so she wasn't the subject, unless The Man wanted him to explore her digital life. But then why the late-night call? No, in all likelihood, there was a new target. But who? Skull was eager to find out. To see the next melody line in The Man's symphony come to the forefront.

"What do you need to know?"

"Things are maturing nicely," said The Man. There was satisfaction in his voice, and Skull took that as a personal compliment. "I think it's time to start Phase B."

Skull smiled. "I'll do it tonight."

"Excellent. I look forward to hearing from you."

"Yes, sir."

The Man hung up. The violins played again. Skull set his phone down. Studied the thunderhead and the weeping woman in the mirror.

Phase B. Things were about to get interesting. This town hadn't seen anything yet.

He opened a drawer, found a plain black hoodie, and pulled it on over his head. He dug deeper into the drawer, found his 9mm, and popped in a clip.

Killing wasn't his department. But for The Man, he might even consider it.

Chapter Forty-Two
TOMMY

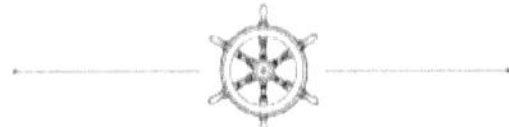

The mantle clock struck once.

My eyes fluttered open. I was still in the recliner in the living room. I must have fallen asleep during the ten o'clock news. A quilt lay over me, a fresh glass of water sat on the end table, and my phone was plugged in to charge—all Nancy's doing, no doubt.

After she'd dropped the glass earlier, she'd apologized and cleaned up, chattering about poor Roland and how terrible it must be to live alone in that vast house.

Wade had passed wordlessly into the kitchen to eat his dinner, and never commented. Well, the man was exhausted. I'm sure being accused of murder—when finding the murderer consumed his every waking moment—was the last thing he needed.

And so the rest of the evening had passed in awkward silence.

I looked to the mantle clock. Half past eleven. What had woken me up? I didn't think it was the clock itself. Granted, I hadn't been sleeping very deeply lately. My subconscious seemed determined to keep one eye open.

I scanned the room, my eyes traveling between the pools of darkness in the room and the windows overlooking the street. There were plenty of shadows for my imagination to play in. But nothing moved. My gaze shifted to the spindled oak railing, the hardwood stairs down to the split-level foyer, and the front door. It had no window, but the sidelights glowed softly, illuminated by the streetlights beyond. The swirled stained glass muted the view of the small front porch and the yard beyond.

I made out the shadow of a man crouching by the door.

My heart leapt into my throat. A voice rang through my ears.

"IF you live, I'll see you later. But I promise you this: YOU won't see ME."

A hand touched my shoulder. I startled so hard, I nearly shouted. Wade appeared from behind my recliner. My eyes went to the gun in his hand and my heart nearly stopped beating.

But his eyes were focused across the room. I followed his gaze to the door.

The shadow was gone. I frowned. Had I only imagined it?

"Stay here," Wade whispered. As if I were capable of going far on my own.

Without a sound, he moved to the door, turned the lock, and slipped outside. I was relieved to hear the lock snick shut behind him. His shadow passed the sidelight, then vanished.

I strained my ears, not sure what I was expecting—a shout, a scuffle, Wade's gun going off. But minutes dragged by, and all I heard was the beating of my own heart and the ticking of the mantle clock.

Chapter Forty-Three
ROLAND

Roland turned a yellowed page in *Anna Karénina,* the original 1887 translation. Gold light pooled on the page from the lamp behind his armchair. He never stayed up so late, but sleep eluded him. The day's drizzle had built to a storm, then broke. Billowing clouds scurried toward the far shore, carrying their wrath elsewhere but leaving behind erratic bursts of wind and flashes of lightning. Meanwhile, his mind still roiled over his conversation with Tommy earlier in the day. Even Angelica's text, reporting that she'd landed safely in Los Angeles, had failed to lift his spirits.

He hadn't spoken to his friend yet, the reporter. But he would. He felt a little more determined now to follow up on Angelica's suspicions.

Metal clinked on stone.

Roland looked up at the French doors but only saw the reflection of a floor lamp, a wingback chair, and an old man reading a book. Something must have been knocked loose by the gale and fallen, but for a moment he couldn't think what it may be. Then he remembered that he had been re-potting the flowers in the cornice pieces the other day. Had he remembered to put away the hand trowel, or was it still lying on the stone railing, the last place he could remember seeing it? The wind might have slid it toward the edge.

He considered getting up to put it away. But it was dark and unpleasant out, and he had arrived at one of his favorite chapters. He settled deeper into his armchair. The trowel could wait for the morning, provided he remembered.

Two pages later, an uncomfortable sensation crept up his back. That feeling that someone is looking at you.

Knowing he was being ridiculous—hoping he was—Roland looked again to the doors. Old as they were, the wood was softened, chipped in places despite countless layers of new paint, and the panes remained speckled with age, even with a maid coming 'round every week to clean. The grandfather clock ticked the seconds ponderously. Was it his imagination, or was that the shadowy outline of a man beyond the glass?

Roland closed his book and raised his voice, knowing it would carry. "Who's there?"

The silence that followed could have proved Roland a madman, talking to an empty room, accusing his grandfather clock of breaking and entering.

Roland laid *Anna* on the side table, rose, and faced the doors. The waves churned against the shore and thunder rolled in the distance. Through his own shadowy reflection, Roland caught a glimmer of light, as if streaming down the barrel of a gun held low.

Every muscle tensing, Roland stared boldly where he knew the eyes must be. "Come into the light."

As if by answer, lightning flashed, illuminating the silhouette of a tall man dressed in black, a gun in his hand.

The man raised his arm, then brought the butt of the gun down hard on the glass and the fragile wooden frames. They exploded. Roland threw up his hands as the shards flew toward him.

CHAPTER FORTY-FOUR
BUD

It hadn't gone right. Nothing had gone right. The Man was still alive. How was The Man still alive?

Bud ran through the woods, rain soaking his tee shirt and jeans, tears soaking his face. Branches ripped at his cheeks and arms. Flashes of his confrontation with The Man tore at his soul.

"I'll kill you." Bud had pressed the gun to The Man's temple, his own vision swimming from rage and whiskey. "I swear to God, I will make you eat these bullets one-by-one."

The Man was unmoved. He smiled, mouth closed, eyes bright as daggers. "Bud, Bud. You aren't going to kill me."

Bud dug the barrel in harder. "Oh, yeah? Watch me." Once he decided someone was going to die, they died.

So how had it all gone wrong...?

The Man's ugly smile only deepened, the grin of a soul that lived in an even lower circle of hell than Bud's own. The blood running down the side of his face only made him more sinister. "'Killing 'em all gets so boring.' Isn't that what you told me once? Didn't you tell me you were the cat that eats the legs off a spider, one-by-one? No, what you want is to torture me. Aren't I right?"

Bud cocked his head noncommittally. "Sure. I can torture you first. I'll leave you half a face if you like. You can have it for a whole hour. And then I'll kill you. No one puts a hit on me. You told Jimmy Beacon I killed his sister. You sicced him and his bomb on me."

"Jimmy who?" The folds of his smile diverted the trickle of blood. "I never heard of him."

"Why, you—" Bud grabbed a fistful of The Man's shirt.

"I'm not really the one you want to torture," The Man whispered. His eyes delved deep into Bud's, as if he were reading his soul like a book. "The person you want is beyond your reach. You can't get to him to give him

what he truly deserves—because he's behind bars. The world is safe from him, and he is safe from you."

Bud backed away, lowering his gun, jaw slack.

But why had he lowered his gun? Why had he let The Man get to him?

Bud stared in disbelief. "You didn't..." was all he managed to say. He tilted his head, anger and injury mixing in a poisonous cocktail. "You had Skull investigate me?"

Lightning flashed, illuminating The Man's face. "Of course I did."

Bud crashed through thick bushes, the twigs and leaves scratching his bare arms. Where had he hidden his car? He couldn't even remember. He was lost in the woods around The Man's neighborhood, running frantically as if someone were chasing him. But no one was. No one but the ghosts of his past—and the voice of The Man ringing in his ears.

Bud had shaken his head in disbelief. Still, even if Skull had dug around in Bud's past, there was no way he knew all of it. Even back in the day, there was hardly a soul who had known the truth. There was no way The Man knew—

But as The Man went on, sickening dread filled his entire soul. Dread that he didn't have a secret in the world.

"The man you want is protected by too many people, by too many laws that were far too lenient for what he did to you. For what he did... to your lover."

Bud began to shake.

"Maybe you simply never found the nerve to fight your way through to the bastard who murdered Zayne Mars. Maybe then, you didn't know your own power. But ever since, you've taken out your fury on others. Innocent bystanders. After all, that's what you and Zayne were. Just innocent bystanders, living your lives together in a world that hated you for being different."

Bud backed away. His gun hand shook. He needed more control than this. He needed control...

The Man stared him down furiously, his keen eyes turning to rage, the blood dripping from his jaw. "You've lived nothing but murder and lies ever since. Do not threaten me for telling you the truth."

Bud fell head-long in the mud, the tears streaming down his face. He grabbed fistfuls of muck, leaves, and roots. They squeezed through his fingers, escaping his grasp just as any hope of happiness had.

"Zayne," he whispered to the night. Years ago, he had screamed it in the walls of his apartment, after seeing his boyfriend dead on the pavement. How could anyone hate so much? How could anyone hate something so beautiful as two human beings in love? What did it matter to anyone else?

"You want to torture the innocent?" The Man had asked, watching Bud's tears fall as if every one were precious to him. "Then do so. You have my blessing. I understand." And like a loving father, a pontificate who cared for his flock, he had welcomed Bud into his arms, let him lay his head on his shoulder, let him weep. "Believe me, I understand." His voice shuddered with emotion as he said it.

"Zayne," Bud whispered again. In all the years since Zayne's death, the name had barely passed his lips. The only way to move on had been to forget. And to let the pain escape any way it could find a way. Once he decided someone was going to die...

He bowed his head and wept. Zayne would never recognize the animal he had become. Everything that had once been beautiful was gone.

Chapter Forty-Five
TOMMY

Nancy tiptoed into the living room, tying a thick, fuzzy bathrobe. She crept to my chair and leaned over to whisper in my ear. "Is Wade outside?"

I nodded.

She folded her arms, as if warding off a chill, and huffed a sigh, staring at the door. She shuffled to a nearby ottoman and sat down, still holding herself tight, bouncing her foot. The job of being a cop's wife wasn't an easy one—never knowing just where your husband was, how much danger he was in, or if he'd even make it home that night. Nancy bore the stress with grace and poise. This was as visibly anxious as I'd ever seen her.

A cordless phone weighed down the pocket of her robe, as if she were ready to dial the station at a moment's notice. The thought flitted across my mind—hadn't Wade alerted the station already? Was he out there with no backup? Or was I just overthinking this? Had I only imagined a man outside the door?

Lightning flickered and thunder rolled in the distance. There were no voices. No commands to put hands in the air. No fleeing footsteps. Nothing.

Still, I envisioned what it would be like if the man who shot me was put behind bars tonight. And I suddenly realized how vast was the sea of mental energy he had claimed. Below the surface, I was drowning in fear and vigilance. Even here at Nancy and Wade's house—even with Wade actively searching the yard—it felt as if I were alone; as if there was no one else to take the watch.

I closed my eyes, clenching my teeth. There was nothing to worry about... There was nothing to worry about...

The door latch clicked. My eyes flew open. Wade stepped into the foyer, a splash of moonlight illuminating his shoulders and the back of his head. He secured the door behind him, then turned to look up at us. Even though his face was hidden in shadow, I thought I could read his disappointment.

He shook his head.

My heart crashed. The watch wasn't over...

"Nothing?" Nancy asked.

"Nothing." Wade climbed the steps, one hand on the railing, the other behind his back. I assumed he was keeping his gun out of sight again. "Just a squirrel trying to make a nest. It chewed a hole in the siding."

"A *squirrel?*" Nancy's voice actually squeaked in surprise.

Wade stepped into the living room and looked down at me. "Sorry it woke you."

I searched the shadows of his face. Did I believe him? Was he trying to withhold information from me again in a misguided effort to protect me from the facts?

Nancy reached over and flicked on a lamp. When she looked at her husband again, she shouted. "You're bleeding!" A trickle of blood ran from his temple to his chin. "Oh, look at your face."

"My face?" Wade lifted his hand to his head—and then we saw where the blood actually came from. It welled from a cut in the skin between his first finger and thumb. He pulled his hand away and stared, as if seeing the cut for the first time.

Nancy rose and put a firm hand on her husband's chest. "Sit down. I'll get the first aid kit."

Wade caught her wrist with his bleeding hand and stopped her. Under his breath, he whispered, "I need a paper bag."

Nancy frowned. "A paper—?" Her eyes dropped to his other hand, which he'd taken from behind his back, but still concealed from me with his body and Nancy's. Her face illuminated. "Oh! Um... Here. I've got it."

I wasn't sure, but I thought she used a fold of her bathrobe to take something from Wade's hand. I strained to see. It looked like a piece of plastic cut from a disposable water bottle. I knew as well as Nancy why Wade wanted a paper bag—it was one of the best ways to store evidence without destroying delicate indicators like fingerprints. Still, I couldn't envision what was so vital about a square of plastic.

Wade sat down and elevated his injured hand, applying pressure. He seemed lost in his own thoughts. He looked pale. I couldn't imagine it was from blood loss; the cut really didn't look *that* bad.

"How'd you cut your hand?" I asked.

He took an extra second to respond. "Trying to flush out the squirrel. I must have cut it on the siding."

Why had he paused? To think up a lie? If I looked at that squirrel hole, would I find blood on the edge? Would I even find a squirrel hole? What was he trying to hide from me? Why did he insist on coddling me? What did a piece of plastic mean? I couldn't take this cloak and dagger anymore. I screwed up my nerve.

"You're lying."

Wade's eyes lifted. Met mine. His were dead inside. Exhausted. Angry.

I didn't care. "Wade. Quit acting like I'm made of glass."

He drew in a deep breath. "Fine. Okay. You're right. There was someone in the yard. I found a piece of plastic by the side door. It was dark, and I cut my hand on it."

"It's just a piece of trash," I said. "Thc storm could have blown it into the yard."

"You can also slip it into a door jamb to pop open a lock."

Lightning chose that moment to illuminate the room in eerie blue. Wade's gaze on me was unwavering.

"Does that make you feel better to know someone was trying to get in?" he asked.

The thought turned my stomach, so I opted not to dwell on it. Instead, I let my simmering temper build to a boil. "Being kept in the dark doesn't contribute to my sense of safety." Finding a soap box, I climbed right on up. "Wade, I'm aware someone shot me. I'm aware he's still out there somewhere." I waved vaguely toward the windows. "Let's quit pretending everything's fine. I need *more* information, not less."

Wade bowed his head and studied his hand. He let the blood soak into the cuff of his shirt, sacrificing that rather than Nancy's beige carpet. Part of me felt awful for chewing him out while he sat there bleeding.

At last he spoke. "I'm sorry. It's not always easy to know what to do." He tilted his head, as if studying a curiosity instead of his own hand. "Did you know that after I killed Bobby Markham, I had nightmares every night for three years?"

I had no words for that. I hadn't known. But his vulnerability, after all these years, deserved a response. I shook my head.

"You'd think I would have mentioned it. Maybe I thought talking about the nightmares would make them more real. Every night, I saw a kid I knew looking at me with absolute hatred in his eyes. And then he aims the gun at me. And then I pull the trigger and kill the only son of a man I grew up with. That night never really ended. Just went on and on..."

At Wade's words, my own frustrations crept away, ashamed. I'd been so absorbed in my own feelings, I hadn't stopped to ponder *why* Wade might be handling me with kid gloves. There had been a time when the shoe had been on the other foot—when Wade had faced down a gun and someone reckless enough to use it on another human being.

"I became a cop so everyday people like you would never have to endure something that horrific. I signed up to serve and protect. And I failed." He looked at me. "I failed my best friend. I'm failing my entire town. People are dying. I lost one of my own men. And I can't stop it."

I sighed, and then I found that I had been turning the wedding band that Laina had given me. I forced my hands to be still. I guess I'd never been good at heart-to-hearts. Wade was far better at them than I had ever been. Somehow he'd managed to change my fury to guilt that I'd ever brought the topic up.

"You're doing fine, Wade," I managed to croak out while staring at a set of curtains. "Whatever madman's on the loose, you'll catch him. You always do."

Wade nodded his appreciation. "I'm sorry, Tommy. I'll try to be more open."

I just nodded. This conversation could be done now. I was sorry I'd brought it up.

Nancy swept into the room, arms laden with bandages and bottles of antiseptic. "Now, show me that hand." She settled onto the ottoman again, took her husband's hand and slapped a sterile pad over the cut. "It's barely bleeding now. Good. Oh, your poor shirt. That'll never come out. I can't believe all this over a squirrel—"

Wade stopped her in the middle of wrapping his hand with gauze. "I told him."

She blinked. "Oh." She looked for a moment like she was shifting gears. A second later, she had adjusted as if we'd been talking about a criminal the entire time and not a rodent. "Well, anyway, they never got in, whoever they were. The alarm would have gone off." She finished off Wade's bandage with tape. "Is that too tight?"

Wade flexed his fingers. "It's perfect."

"Should you call your detectives?" I asked.

Wade nodded and rose. "Guess I'll roust Lehman out of bed." He motioned with his bandaged hand. "Thank you, Nancy."

She smiled and nodded. Wade passed into his office, closing the door behind him. A moment later, we heard his muffled voice through the wall.

Nancy clasped her hands, as if to calm her own tremors. If I wondered whether I was still welcome company, she settled the question with her next words. "Well. How about a cup of tea? Once the cavalry gets here, it'll be impossible to get any sleep."

I nodded absently. I didn't want the tea. I wanted space to think. Nancy left, and I was grateful.

Roland's words swirled in my mind. *"Tommy, have you ever considered that Wade could be the fourth member of the ring?"*

No. And I never would. If Wade was behind the murders, why would his home be the target of a break-in?

The only scenario in which that made any sense was if the hunter was being hunted.

Chapter Forty-Six
SKULL

Skull slid behind the wheel of his car and stowed his gun in the glove compartment. He hadn't really needed it in the end. That was good. In fact, the entire mission had gone quite well. Clean. Efficient. His handiwork would never be noticed. Time to report to The Man.

He dialed, then turned the key in his ignition and calmly pulled out of the neighborhood. The phone rang four times. Had The Man already gone to bed?

At last, he picked up. "Yes?"

"I'm not waking you, am I?" Skull asked.

"No. It's been a busy night."

The abrupt way he said it—almost angrily—left Skull wondering what he meant. But in this line of business, you didn't ask unnecessary questions. So why did he feel... concerned?

The Man must have sensed it. That didn't surprise Skull. What did was the fact that The Man deigned to elaborate. "Bud was here. He tried to kill me."

Skull's grip convulsed on the wheel. "What—? Are you all right, sir?" What an idiot. Did Bud understand who he was messing with? He would wind up dead.

"I'm fine. Don't think of it. Give me your report. Is the job done?"

"Yes. The house is fully bugged, inside and out."

"The, ah—the devices. They'll never be found?"

"Never."

"Good. Good. Thank you."

Skull thought The Man sounded either distracted or vaguely incoherent. How bad had the encounter been? Was he hurt? Or just planning Bud's demise?

"I'll be in touch," said The Man. "I have another call to make. Good night."

"Good night, sir."

Skull let The Man hang up—it was good customer service—then dropped the hand with the phone into his lap.

The Plan felt off the tracks somehow. Did this change things? Then again, The Man was good at adjusting to the circumstances.

Skull had no idea what might happen next. He didn't imagine it meant anything good for Bud Weber.

Chapter Forty-Seven
ROLAND

The phone line clicked alive. "Nine-one-one. What's your emergency?"

Emergency. Yes. The glass. The door exploding. He remembered that part clearly. And then he must have blacked out. He remembered coming to. And possibly blacking out again. What was left of his French door hung from one hinge, flopping in the wind.

"Yes, there was a break-in. I need an ambulance, please."

The handkerchief he pressed to his temple was no match for the blood streaming down his face.

"What's your address?"

"Nine Eighty South Lake Shore Drive."

"All right, sir, an ambulance is on the way."

The 911 operator went on to ask for more details—something about the nature of the break-in and his injuries. But the room was going topsy-turvy, and the woman's words made no sense. He tried to speak, but his voice failed him. In the end, he could latch onto only one thought.

Monica was going to kill him.

The room dimmed, then went black.

DON'T STOP READING!

You Could Be Reading My Next Book As I Write It!

Patreon is a website where top fans can support their favorite creatives in exchange for exclusive benefits. My Patrons get to read my chapters the minute they're out of my pen.

Beyond that, every chapter comes with Book Club Questions, which have prompted some amazing, uplifting conversations. (Good vibes only in my online spaces!) I also post Behind-the-Scenes info, revealing what went into the creation of the story, and the thoughts going through my heart and soul as I write.

My Patrons get a more intimate experience than any other fan. So, come aboard! This is a cruise unlike any you've experienced before.

Join Us Today!

BENEATH THE SURFACE

THE HUMANITY BENEATH

Mailboat IV: The Shift in the Wind was largely written in the red-letter year of 2020. Not only were normal activities slowed to a trickle by the Coronavirus pandemic, but new riots flared up in response to the death of George Floyd in police custody. It was a hard year for me; I couldn't get into my favorite coffee shops to write. And as someone with friends representative of both sides of the fray—people of color and people in law enforcement—I felt torn in two.

Coincidentally, one of my main characters in *Mailboat IV* (and coming back for *Mailboat V)* is a woman of color, Angelica Read. I allow my characters to be themselves, whatever that may mean. And Angelica let me know when I first met her back in *Mailboat I* that she was a Mexican-American immigrant.

Another one of my writing rules is to portray people as accurately as I can. For Angelica, that meant reading a stack of very good books about the Mexican-American experience, as well as enjoying some delightful exchanges with Alondra Gaspar, a friend of a friend and a first-generation Mexican-American. Her insights and reviews of my manuscripts were invaluable for bringing Angelica to life.

A *personal* rule is to avoid thoughts of either-or when it comes to how I view and treat people. Through the race riots of my lifetime, the plight of African-Americans and other minority groups has come to the forefront, as it should. Modern policing has come under question—and under fire. Solutions have been suggested, some of which I find innovative and relevant. Others I find dubious, and it's my opinion that the founders of some theories have no working knowledge of policing and the unique circumstances around it. In short, I'm suspicious some of these theorists have never actually known a cop.

But frankly, few people have. Sheriff Andy Taylor and his deputy Barney Fife were beloved members of their community. But today, police and the communities they work in live in different worlds. The thought of approaching a cop for anything but a truly serious dilemma is unheard of. They seem distant. Detached. Barely human. If you're a member of a minority community, odds are you'd never voluntarily approach a cop at all.

But just as I have always sought to look past skin color, language, accent, sexual orientation, gender identity, disability, religion, politics, social class, et cetera—I have sought to look past the uniform to find the humanity beneath. Thanks to an early interest in writing "cop stories," I've had ample opportunity and excuse to study American law enforcement.

Two of my long-running main characters in the Mailboat Suspense Series are Officer Ryan Brandt and Detective Monica Steele. The story carries us deeply into their personal and professional lives. Behind their pages lie countless hours that I've spent with men and women in uniform, whether on the streets, at their police stations, in their homes, or (in one case) on the trails of our national parks. (Girl, you know who you are.) And it dawns on me that I have a unique and valuable perspective. I know cops. I know the stereotypes we deal with in the real world; the stereotypes that have been handed down through literature, film, and television; *and*—importantly—I know the truth. I know what cops are really like.

Becoming more attuned with minority groups has become a more recent goal, and when I've finished listening for a good, long while, I'm sure I'll start speaking. I've always been the girl in the middle, the one who believes there's a way to solve any argument, if we only listen. I believe in the basic goodness of people, no matter what they look like. But I've already been listening to cops for years. And considering the experiences we've recently had here in the U.S., I thought it was time to show you what I know, with the veneer of fiction removed, and take at least one tiny step toward clearing up the dissonance.

When I began writing the Mailboat Suspense Series in 2014, I knew I needed to add new depths to my law enforcement research. Every department is different, based on the size and makeup of its staff, the size of its geographic and demographic area, the size of its budget, the resources at its disposal, the cooperative arrangements it has with neighboring departments—I could go on.

So to write about the Lake Geneva Police Department, I knew I had to get to know *the* Lake

Geneva Police Department. In the spring of 2014, ahead of my first research trip, I called their front desk.

To be frank, I hate making these cold calls. I knew before I picked up the phone that the person on the other end would expect questions about how to pay parking tickets and where to report a crime—not how to get a private tour of their police station for the purposes of writing a novel.

But I sucked it up and called the number. When the telecommunications officer picked up, I did my best to explain myself clearly. I was an author. I was setting a suspense series in Lake Geneva, and several of my main characters were police officers. I was planning to set several scenes at the Lake Geneva Police Department. So was there any way I could get a tour?

"Okay, how big is your group?" the telecommunicator asked, with the sound of a woman ready to take routine notes.

I sighed. This was why I hated these calls. I started over.

"Oh-h-h," she said, now grasping the unique nature of my request. "Hmm. Let me put you through to the lieutenant."

I ended up leaving a voice mail for Lieutenant Ed Gritzner. When he called back, I explained my project and told him when I'd be in town. To my delight, he agreed to arrange a private tour for me with one of his sergeants.

It was a humid August day when I walked through the front door of the Lake Geneva Police Department. At the glass-protected front desk, I explained to the telecommunicator that I was there to meet Sergeant Jason Hall for a tour, and she buzzed me through to a secured waiting room.

A few minutes later, Sergeant Hall walked in, dressed in a navy blue uniform. His silhouette was made bulky by a ballistic vest and a belt bristling with tools, black pouches, and, of course, his sidearm. His manner when he greeted me was professional, his handshake firm, his spine straight, his shoulders square. This was the front most people encountered when they placed a call for service. The stone wall. The nameless soldier. The soulless robot.

I wasn't intimidated. I already knew several law enforcement officers. I knew what I saw was a mannerism they wore when meeting any member of the public. I knew there was so much more to Sergeant Jason Hall. It was only a question of if and when he chose to let down the front. I entrusted that decision and its timing to him.

Once he understood a little about my project, he proceeded to lead me room-by-room through the police station, explaining what each was for, where things were stored, and what kind of technology they had at their disposal. As I asked questions about their resources, their policies, and the unique culture of the Lake Geneva Police Department—steering clear of both cultural and fictional stereotypes—I saw it dawn on him that I wasn't a total greenhorn. Where I was still uneducated, I endeavored to ask my questions in an open, assumption-free manner with genuine curiosity.

And gradually, the front came down. He wasn't a law enforcement officer giving a tour to a citizen anymore. We were two enthusiasts talking shop. With the gusto of a kid showing off his toys, he pulled open cupboards and drawers to reveal all the gear his department had on hand. And I glimpsed the real person behind the bullet-proof armor. I saw the guy who was once a little boy with a fascination for flashing lights and breaking-edge technology. I saw how that fascination had never abandoned him, even as the harsh realities of law enforcement set in during his training and after years of service behind the badge.

I saw what was true of most cops: that in his hands, these tools were the means to help people.

I make a habit of asking cops why they went into law enforcement. The most common answer?

"I just want to help people."

Then why do we so rarely see that side of our law enforcement officers? Why are we presented with a stone wall, a nameless soldier, a robot? There are many reasons. But for one, cool professionalism and command presence are trained into a cop at the police academy. It's literally their outermost layer of armor and can straight-up save their lives on the streets.

Hours later, our tour—and our by-now lively conversation—came full circle to the break room. As if someone had flipped a switch, we both ran out of things to talk about. Jason drummed his fingers on the back of a chair, the thrum filling the empty room. He cast about as if reluctant for the tour to end. As if hopeful he could make my research experience even fuller.

"Well," he said, then shrugged. "Wanna go for a ridealong while you're here?"

"Yes!" I said.

I signed a waiver and spent my afternoon with Officer Katie Tietz, one of their female officers—who, by the end of our time together, had also felt comfortable enough to let me see her real personality. Like every female cop, she was made of some combination of tom-boyishness and tungsten steel and was eager to prove her guts. Deep into our ridealong, she lit into a gruesome tale about a small accident at the shooting range. Ultimately, the story was funny, but she spared no details. Suddenly, she stopped herself, remembering she was talking to a citizen and not another cop.

"You okay with me telling this story?" she asked, a brow lifted.

I waved my hand palm-up, butler style. "Proceed."

"Good!" And she dove back into her tale. Cops are always trying to one-up each other with the strangest, most disgusting story. Frankly, I was honored that she forgot she wasn't talking to a sister cop.

But perhaps the most dramatic transformation from unknowable law enforcement officer to human happened a few years later on another trip to Lake Geneva. Lieutenant Gritzner and Sergeant Hall arranged for me to go on another ridealong, this time during Sergeant Hinzpeter's shift. Hinzpeter introduced me to Officer Kara Richards and explained that I was her ridealong. Her face went blank. She scanned me up and down, her eyes barely flicking, but I caught the movement. Then she threw a glance at Hinzpeter that said a thousand words. *Thanks a lot, Sergeant.*

The next moment, she forced her annoyance aside, donned her cool professionalism, and shook my hand. "Follow me," she said.

I fell into step behind her, trying not to laugh out loud. I already knew how this was going to play out. *Ma'am, you won't believe everything you'll end up sharing with me today.*

I was right. What was meant to be an hour or two ridealong stretched deep into the evening. By the end of it, Kara had told me her life story, stories about her family, the things that mattered to her, her hopes and dreams for the future. I watched. I listened. I didn't judge. All I wanted was to get to know her. She attacked everything she did with intensity. When responding to a medical emergency, she took the stairs two at a time as if she weren't weighed down at all by her vest and belt, while I, unencumbered, struggled to keep up with her. While walking through a darkened hallway at the high school, I noted aloud that she had literally vanished into the shadows, and the only way I was able to follow her was by sound.

"Good," she said. And I understood that the ability to hide—to not be a target, to come home to her family at night—was important to her.

We only cut the ridealong off when I had to leave for a book signing that night. She dropped me off at my car with a look of genuine regret that this was our good-bye.

I've had this happen to me so many times, and not just with law enforcement officers, but with people from every walk of life. My job is not to opine, but to listen—and maybe to amplify the voices I hear by writing about the things they tell me. A couple of weeks before writing this essay, I met a Mexican-American man at a book signing. Noticing that my books were crime fiction, he told me at length about the interactions he'd had with cops, few of them pleasant. He asked if I talked with cops, the way I was talking with him. I told him yes.

"Good," he said. "All we know is what we see on TV—cops busting down the door, cops hiding in your own house waiting for you. We see them being way too aggressive. And so we get scared, and we do something dumb and it only makes everything worse. But you know that's not what it's like. You know what they can and can't do. If you write about them the way they really are, maybe it'll help somebody."

I told him I'd never thought of it that way, and I thanked him for giving me that perspective.

When you greet people with openness and interest, all biases set aside, chances are they will feel secure enough to show you their true colors. My goal, as a person and an author, is to push past external differences to see the human underneath. It's never failed to make me friends from all walks of life. And the truth is that we really are the same at the most basic level. My belief is that if we could set aside fear and replace it with curiosity, relations between our police and minority communities could finally change for the better.

As the Mailboat Suspense Series has continued, so has my partnership with the Lake Geneva Police Department. In fact, the chief of police officially assigned Lieutenant Gritzner and Sergeant Hall as my liaisons. Not only do they field every wild research question I can come up with, they also play through scenarios with me and read every word I write to check for accuracy.

My readers have sometimes likened my relationship with the LGPD to a sort of real-life *Castle.*

Personally, I think it's even better. For one, I've never actually risked my life while hanging out with them. For another, their help means my novels are as real as they can be. But I also get to follow my passion for understanding people—all people—for whoever they are, exactly as they are, and sharing my explorations with my readers.

Did you enjoy this glimpse beneath the surface?

JOIN ME ON PATREON

ACKNOWLEDGMENTS

Twenty twenty was a terrible year for writing a book—at least for me. Unable to access my library and coffee shops, I was forced to write from home—something I already knew I was bad at. (That's why I *have* my library and coffee shops.)

So first and foremost, epic thanks to the two book coaches who saw me through, *Jacquelyn Scott* and *Tiffany Herron*. Thanks, ladies, for keeping my squirrel brain focused! Also, huge gratitude to *my patient fans,* who waited an extra year for this book to come out. Not only did you give me time and space to write, you continued to talk up my books while you were waiting, making this release the biggest one yet.

As always, my gratitude to the Lake Geneva Cruise Line (CruiseLakeGeneva.com), owners and operators of the real-life Mailboat. Special thanks to *General Managers Harold Friestad (ret.)* and *Jack Lothian,* to *the Mailboat Captain Neill Frame,* and to *Office Manager Ellen Burling.* Your combined contributions allowed my imagination to set sail.

I don't know why my characters decide to be what they are—I just know not to meddle with the process. So when Angelica Read informed me that she was Latina, I had my homework cut out for me. Prior to writing this book, I had had all of one conversation with someone of Mexican-American heritage (Sandra Cisneros' brother, ironically enough). Massive thanks to *Alondra Gaspar* for talking with me about her Mexican-American background, for reviewing my manuscripts, and for teaching me how to use both vulgarity and terms of endearment in Spanish. (At least on the page. My spoken Spanish will never sound as beautiful as hers.) Thanks also to our mutual friend *Michael O'Leary* for introducing us.

Much appreciation to *David Congdon,* Threat Assessment and Countermeasures Specialist. I always look forward to our conversations on my books from a psychological perspective.

Many thanks to my writer's club, *We Write Good,* and especially to *Elaine Montgomery* for telling me how good my manuscript was, and to *Rachel Surtshin* for telling me how bad it was. Seriously, Rachel, I appreciate your holding my feet to the fire. Thanks for questioning early attempts at Angelica's portrayal by speaking from your experiences with the Mexican-American community, and thanks for helping me clarify Monica's feelings by being a bad-ass feminist who couldn't understand anyone in Monica's circumstances regretting her choice. I wasn't satisfied until you were satisfied.

My thanks also to *Carrie Lynn Lewis,* my trusty brainstorming partner. Thanks for helping me find the path when I'm not sure where my characters have led me this time.

Before publication, this book was thoroughly examined by my sharp-eyed Early Reader Team. I promise, one day I'll know the difference between *suit* and *suite.* By name, thank you to *Susan Beatty, Stephanie Brancati, Kathy Collins, Brenda Dahlfors, Nancy Diestler, Lynda Fergus, Lisa McCann, Elaine Montgomery, Rebecca Paciorek, Linda Pautz, Pat Perkins, Sanda Putnam, JoAnn Schwartz Schutte, Kathy Skorstad, Suzette Titus, Judy Tucker, Lisa Vint, Kimberly Wade, Carol D. Westover,* and *Mary-Jane Woodward.*

Also, a huge shout-out to the members of my very first Street Team, especially *Paula OBrien-Slaasted* for being the first to jump on board. Thanks, all of you, for helping me promote the new book and create a bigger splash than ever.

For their unique contributions that resulted in my stunning cover art, thanks to *Matt Mason Photography* (MattMasonPhotography.com) for the imagery, *W. J. Goes* for helping my photographers chase down the Mailboat, and *Maryna Zhukova* (MaryDes.eu) for bringing the images to life.

Rebecca Paciorek, Susan Beatty, and *JoAnn Schwartz Schutte,* you are the most enthusiastic, tireless, and determined group of publicists an author could ask for. I wouldn't be where I am without you. Looking forward to seeing you in Lake Geneva this summer!

More than my thanks—my heart and soul to those I hold close. *Fergus,* you've turned into such a cuddler, I'm not sure you're the same unhappy cat I adopted four years ago. *Angel,* that little German Shepherd puppy who couldn't sit still for a photo with the Lake Geneva PD is long gone—and you're actually growing into your name. And *Charles William Maclay.* Congrats on your graduation from Western Colorado

University with a Master's of Fine Arts. Congrats on your first published short story. Congrats on placing in two separate screenwriting competitions. I'm so proud of you. Thanks for accomplishing all that while taking more than your fair share of duties so I could kick out another novel on time. Pretty soon, we won't be "the educated one" and "the successful one." We'll just be successful together.

Also, we survived a pandemic together without murdering each other. If that isn't winning at life, I don't know what is. I love you.

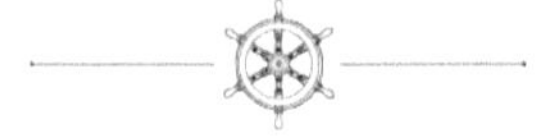

Books by Danielle Lincoln Hanna

The Mailboat Suspense Series

The Girl on the Boat: A Prequel Novella

Mailboat I: The End of the Pier

Mailboat II: The Silver Helm

Mailboat III: The Captain's Tale

Mailboat IV: The Shift in the Wind

Mailboat V: The End of Summer

Mailboat VI: *coming soon*

DanielleLincolnHanna.com/ShopNow

About the Author

Danielle Lincoln Hanna is the author of the Mailboat Suspense Series. While she now lives in the Rocky Mountains of Montana, her first love is still the Great Plains of North Dakota where she was born. When she's not writing, you can find her hiking with her boyfriend Charles, adventuring with her German

Shepherd Angel, and avoiding surprise attacks from her cat Fergus.

www.ingramcontent.com/pod-product-compliance
Lightning Source LLC
Chambersburg PA
CBHW020555310726
48979CB00008B/1228/J
* 9 7 8 1 7 3 7 6 0 8 9 4 3 *